O9-BUA-276

The White-Flower-Farm Garden Book

Amos Pettingill

The White-Flower-Farm Garden Book

Drawings by Nils Hogner

Little, Brown and Company Boston Toronto

A

Published by arrangement with Alfred A. Knopf, Inc.

LIBRARY OF CONGRESS CATALOGING IN PUBLICATION DATA

Pettingill, Amos, 1900–
The White-Flower-Farm garden book.

Reprint of the 1971 ed. published by Knopf, New York.
Includes index.
1. Plants, Ornamental—United States—Dictionaries.
2. Gardening—United States—Dictionaries. 3. Flower gardening—United States—Dictionaries. I. Title.
[SB405.P46 1977] 635.9'0973 76-52499
ISBN 0-316-70400-8

Published simultaneously in Canada
by Little, Brown & Company (Canada) Limited

PRINTED IN THE UNITED STATES OF AMERICA

to Jane Grant, my partner in everything

Acknowledgments

Harold Calverley and David Smith, White Flower Farm's Manager and Director of Horticulture, respectively, gave invaluable assistance in reading the proofs of this book and in keeping the horticulture on the track at points where I had obviously slipped off. Jane Grant, as editor, saw to it that clarity was observed.

Photograph Credits

Tom Yee: Pages 2, 5, 11, 14, 18, 20, 25, 27, 28, 29, 35
Robert Brandau: Pages 4, 7, 19, 30, 31, 32
William Harris: Pages 6, 8, 9, 10, 12, 13, 15, 16, 17, 21, 22, 23, 24, 26, 34

Contents

The White-Flower-Farm Garden Book

Foreword

In the late 1930s Jane Grant and I made a house out of a small barn in Litchfield, Connecticut. The idea was to have "a little place in the country" to which we could bring our work, and where we could vacation. We were writers, and it seemed reasonable that writing could be done as well in the country as in New York City. Other people did it. We did it. But for me, trying to write in Litchfield was torture, for nature beckoned so seductively that I spent far more time with her than with my work. This book, a record of my first-hand experiences as a gardener, starts properly from the day when

The fields at White Flower Farm are typical of New England—small, gently rolling, each neatly packaged between dry stone walls, some massive, which were laid (according to oldtimers in the neighborhood) by prison labor. The sugar maples, which line them at random, provide great, green accents. Facing page: The owners pose for Tom Yee, a House & Garden *photographer.*

I stopped pushing furniture from one place to another inside and went outside and found, with some amazement, that we needed a lawn.

To get the other principal character in this cast into the reader's mind at this point, I shall explain that Jane Grant and I are married. She is a professional woman who has always kept her maiden name on the grounds that it's the only thing she has so really her own it can't be taken away, and that as men don't lose their names on a marriage day she sees no logic in a woman losing hers in this unequal tradition. I subscribe to this and object just as much to being called Mr. Grant, which sometimes happens, as I do to hearing her addressed as Mrs. Harris, which happens frequently with new friends or acquaintances who sit in the front row of traditionalism. My habit of referring to her as "Grant" goes back to the 1920s, when I worked on a newspaper. In the city room we put a "Mr." in front of the names of all our immediate bosses, except for the assistant city editor, a fellow we did not hold in high regard—a former colleague of ours. He was a feckless reporter, we thought, just the type of fellow who could be put into the routine of that lowly job. We called him by his last name, as usual, just as we were called. Miss Grant, who had a long stint on *The New York Times,* was first called "Grant," then nicknamed "Fluff," largely because she worked out her assignments quickly and had time to give dancing lessons in the halls to reporters who had never bothered to learn to dance.

When we moved into our house in the Litchfield hills (the contractors-builders were no different from those today), Grant and a friend took over the inside of the house; my work, except for shoving heavy stuff around for them, was on the outside. The builder's litter came up quickly, and the useless bits made a fine fire. Heavier pieces were saved; I still have a few of them stored away for that day when they may become useful. Our lot consisted of one and one-third acres. It was knee high in hay, except where it had been battered down by the workmen. When I discovered that we needed a lawn, I decided that to get one we would have to plow up a bit of the meadow and seed it. But this idea met with no enthusiasm—Grant said that dust would blow into our nice new quarters during the rest of the summer. I certainly did not want to do the inside cleaning, including windows, that would be necessary, although I had been offered the job, not very politely, if. . . .

A neighbor, the woman who had sold us the barn and the land, and who was a gracious lender of tools offered me a scythe and a hayfork. I had used a scythe years before; it was a tool for which I had never developed any affection. But I got hers, and though I found it just as demanding as the one I had used years before, I hacked down the hay, carted it to a pile, and burned it. Today, of course, that grass would go straight to a compost heap, but at that time I had never heard of such a thing.

Straightaway, we purchased a lawn mower. It was a fine machine, the kind one pushes—a tool new generations may never see because today they are so hard to find. It cost $15 and lasted nearly 30 years, until 2 small parts couldn't be replaced because its maker had switched to power mowers. Before running this jewel over the hacked up meadow, it was necessary to "stone" the small area. Stoning is a ceaseless chore for all who work in what the glaciers left of New England's originally rich, thick topsoil. Some stones that peeked through the surface turned out to be large; a couple of them were so big that it took a tractor and 2 men to dig them out and cart them away. I was quite proud of the manicured look the mower gave the meadow grasses, and Grant and her friend were complimentary. I knew the grasses were mostly timothy and perennial rye—Jim

Bristol, who took care of Dr. Turkington's neat establishment across the lane, had told me.

At this point it seemed to be a good idea to buy some kind of a small book on gardening, which I did. It suggested spading as the proper way to prepare a seed bed for a lawn. I shuddered at the idea, for it would not eliminate the dust problem and spading even a small area is fierce work.

Whatever else I knew about grass I had learned from my mother, a strong-willed woman who really knew nothing about growing anything but who was an expert at getting maximum work out of her nearly 6-foot, chubby (oh well, fat), 13-year-old son and paying him, as was the habit of the times, starvation wages, or 25 cents every Friday night. Sometimes I was handed a dime because the week's work had been unsatisfactory. At that time we moved rather frequently, invariably into a house on a corner lot, which almost always had a larger lawn than the other houses on the block. My father, who had done this outside work by himself, well, I vaguely remember, but he never had asked me to work with him, because, I like to think, he wasn't going to raise *his* only child to be a handyman. He died when I was 12, and though Mother wanted to have her yard kept "like father used to keep it," her only instructions were to water the lawn and mow it regularly. My great aunt, however, was a remarkable old lady who seemed to know something about everything; she told me to plant grass seed in the fall, to sow it into the old lawn, scuffle it with a rake, then roll it lightly. This I did every year until I left for college, because my mother, who had heard these instructions, would buy the seed herself every August, and would announce, "William, the grass is here." It was always Kentucky Bluegrass seed. "Never buy anything else," my aunt had said. This exceptional aunt also knew about fertilizing the lawn heavily every spring.

When the bluegrass browned in August (its characteristic I discovered much later), Mother claimed that not enough fertilizer had been used. In our case this was probably true: I had observed that fertilizer stimulated grass into such rank growth that the lawn was always in need of cutting, so I used as little of the stuff as possible.

As I recalled these routines, I worried about the amount of water available from above—most of my experience had been in arid California and Colorado, where we irrigated with hoses because there was never rain when it was needed. In Litchfield our water source was a bell-bottomed dug well. According to local legend, which we foolishly believed, it had not gone dry in 200 years. But about a month after we moved in, on the day of our house-warming, it did go dry—so any lawn we attempted would have no help from a faucet. Then I met George Luca. George was a strapping, handsome lad, about 22 years old, who lived down the Turnpike. He needed work, we needed him, and these needs worked out until he died, tragically, in the middle of his life a few years ago. George had worked at the Litchfield country club for a spell and had learned a lot about grass. George Luca assured me that the country club never irrigated its fairways and that they always looked well. He also told me that the club seeded its fairways in the fall and that the dairy farmers seeded hay meadows as soon as they had cut corn for ensilage, which was just before the first frost. This certainly confirmed my aunt's fall-not-spring seeding ideas. The turf, if it can be called that, of hay grasses is thin and reedy and when first cut the ground shows through plainly and is downright dusty in a hard wind. But after several mowings these field grasses start to spread a bit and seen from the distance they look well.

Grant came out one day and said, "What are you playing?" I said that I was playing digging dandelions out of the lawn, a weed that

"The Cub," smallest of the nursery's four tractors, is the busiest. Facing page: Perennials planted in six-foot beds, six rows to a bed, are weeded once every two weeks. The weed seedlings, then less than one-quarter-inch high, are easily destroyed. The perennials soon spread; they provide so much shade that few weeds germinate. Bed planting produces up to 150,000 perennials an acre.

Misting frames. Prepare a cutting, dip in hormone, plunge into damp sand, then provide a fine mist at intervals of 30 seconds for about 6 seconds: instead of withering at once in dazzling sunlight, the cutting roots. Facing page: Cold frames are covered with black plastic after deep frost to keep young plants from heaving during winter thaws and to protect them from cold, killing winds.

had plagued me in Colorado, and plantain, another broadleaf weed whose name Jim Bristol had told me. She said she would play, too, and from that moment on she became one of the world's most competent weeders. I guess a good gardener always starts as a good weeder. Weeding is always hard at first if the things have been allowed to grow big enough to be noticed. Later she learned to attack them when they could just be seen; their destruction then is so easy that weeding might even be called a pleasure. Anyway, killing them when they are that small is not much work.

In September, George Luca and I seeded the lawn. We scraped the surface lightly with iron rakes, sowed the seed, and then, with a makeshift drag made of a gunny sack, worked the seed lightly into the surface. Afterward, we pushed the mower over it, making believe it was a light roller. The fall rains came, the nights cooled and the new grass shot up, some of it almost immediately. It turned out that the seed which germinated so quickly was annual rye, which I later learned was called "real estate" grass, because speculative builders, who want their houses to look like homes quickly, use it for its rapid growth and deep green color. The only trouble is that it doesn't last over the winter. The cheap mixture I had bought contained 30 percent of the stuff, but there was enough Kentucky Bluegrass in it so that we at least had the start of what was to become, after a while, a fairly respectable lawn.

Meanwhile, Grant had the inside of the house in such good order that she started to give parties for friends. This required flowers. She discovered that dandelions with stems cut short and massed and floated in a bowl made sprightly, short-lasting bouquets. She also saw many different kinds of wild flowers in bloom in the surrounding hay meadows. She picked these largely from the edge of the meadow bordering my so-called lawn.

"There is a big patch of blue ones out there," I said, pointing to a slight rise about 200 feet from the house.

"Come on and help me get them," she said. At the moment I was busy trying to get 15 coats of paint off an old pine table we had picked up at an antique shop.

"I play weeding dandelions with you—you should play picking pretty flowers with me. It's only fair," she added.

That seemed logical. In a few moments the flowers were harvested and I went back to taking paint off with sandpaper, decidedly the hardest way to remove anything.

In about an hour I heard her in the living room talking sternly to the wild flowers. That's the nice way to describe her remarks. Never have flowers been cussed out so expertly. There are no swear words Grant doesn't know. Her education in them, which is *magna cum laude,* came from sitting in the society department when she first joined *The Times* and hearing, through the thin partition that separated the two departments, the sports writers and the various fighters who visited them discuss ordinary matters in extraordinary language, known in these gentler days as filthy—words anyone can see now chalked on walls or on display advertising signs in the city subways. "You're a bunch of —— —— ingrates," she said at the end of a blacker sentence, "and to think I risked my life to pick you."

"Such language, Grant," I said.

"Look at them," she said. "Dead in 15 minutes!"

There was no doubt that the flowers had collapsed, and I commiserated with her. But the business of her risking her "very life" stumped me. It was then I learned that Grant, whom I thought feared nothing, feared snakes. I don't think she saw any snakes on our little walk to get the blue flowers, but she said she did. Such fear may not be rational, but it is real and therefore entitled to respect.

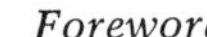

So after that I picked the wild flowers she found, and later, when we had gardens, walked before her through the ones she wanted to work—and I still do—to startle any wriggling or other living thing that might startle her.

To console her on the afternoon of the great wild flower collapse, I said, "Next summer I'll grow some flowers for you that will be better and prettier in a bowl than any wild flower." This was sheer imagination, for I had never grown any flower, except sweet peas. Mother had had rose gardens, but she only picked the blooms; the bushes were planted and cared for by a Russian woman who worked for us for years. The sweet pea period of my life came after World War I, when I attempted to run the family's ranch east of Boulder, Colorado. Mother insisted that I grow sweet peas for her. Dutifully, every year on St. Patrick's Day, I planted sweet peas, because that was the traditional day to plant peas of any kind. It was simple. I ran a furrow about 100 feet long, distributed seed, covered them with about a half inch of soil, cut some branches from the willows at the creek, and stuck them into the furrow for the peas to climb on. The furrow, only partially filled with soil, served as a ditch into which irrigation water could be turned. When the flowers started to bloom, Mother and a friend would appear daily in her aged Hupp-Yeats electric brougham, which she had learned to drive forward but had never learned to back, and they would pick the blooms. One can readily see that a slight knowledge about growing alfalfa, sugar beets, and sweet peas from seed, the first 2 planted and harvested with machinery, was poor preparation for making good my promise.

Late that fall I turned over a small bed close to a stone wall near the house. It was about 30 feet long and 3 feet wide. Until then I'd never seen so many rocks outside a gravel pit. It was a very large garden for a beginner, particularly for a fellow with a completely inadequate water supply. My garden book told me to make a *p*H test, without being specific about how to do it, in order to determine how much lime the soil needed. It didn't take long to dig the details of *p*H out of an encyclopedia, so I discussed the problem with our Litchfield druggist, who offered to make the test. He did this with litmus paper and distilled water, and charged $1.50 for it. (I later bought a small roll of graded litmus for 25 cents, got a pint of distilled water from the local filling station and did it myself.) The druggist's test showed the soil to be slightly acid, which the garden book said it should be. However, I had already bought a bag of hydrated lime, so I put on a little, anyway, and raked it in.

"Putting on a little, anyway," of anything handy, particularly fertilizer, I found to be a habit that was hard to break, for like most people starting to garden it seemed to me that if a little was good, more of the same would be better. It isn't. That fall I planted a fine little flowering peach tree on the lawn and added far more fertilizer than was called for. Its buds all bloomed the next spring, but it shrivelled up and died soon after. I can still remember how pleased I was with the blossoms, how sad when it died, and how guilty I felt when Jim Bristol said that he guessed it got too much fertilizer when it was planted. He was careful not to say that I was the one who put on the fertilizer. It was nice of him to save my face.

Right after Christmas that first year it obviously became time to do some studying about annuals, so I bought a little book devoted exclusively to them, and discovered it said no more than my slightly larger general garden book. The fact is that in comparing them I found that even the language seemed similar. Both told me a lot that I didn't really want to know and neither book got down to the

The Exbury Azalea "mother" garden, so called because it provides cuttings and is arranged as a deciduous shrub border, instead of being planted in long rows. It is extravagantly beautiful in late spring. The large Terra Rosa *pot is strictly ornamental; when empty, it takes two men to move it to winter quarters. Facing page: A block of perennial Aster, the common Michaelmas Daisy that the British have developed so well, in full bloom in September.*

real nuts and bolts—the simple "how-to's" that I needed. It seemed to make the growing of annuals a complicated business. So I visited a store on Madison Avenue that I had always marvelled at. It was Max Schling, Seedsman, owned by the Max Schling who was also the famous Fifth Avenue florist. There I was greeted by a huge man, a Mr. Platt, who managed the store. It was a no-nonsense garden store, large, its walls covered with small drawers in which countless varieties of seeds were stored in small, neatly arranged envelopes. Various garden tools, all hand-held kinds, were displayed on tables. There were a few bulbs. I told Mr. Platt my problem and the amount of space I had. Mr. Platt said it would be easy. Even though I might get better results by starting some of the annual seeds indoors or in a greenhouse, he said that under the circumstances I should plant the seeds directly in the ground—I'd get a somewhat shorter blooming period, but excellent results nonetheless. He told me to plant the seeds as soon as the soil dried and was easily worked into a bed with a smooth surface. The very fine seeds should be planted a bit later, and instead of covering them with soil they should be pressed into it by using a piece of two-by-four about 5 inches long. He drew a small plan and suggested kinds to plant in each space. The bill came to $5.55. He escorted me to the door and said, "Good luck. Let me know how you come out."

It is impressive to be escorted to the door of an upper-class establishment when you have bought practically nothing and have taken up at least a half-hour of time. I asked Platt about this long afterward, when we had become friends. He said, "Well, it's a polite thing to do. I try to do this with all customers, but I always do it with new ones who say they have just started to garden. They think gardening is hard. It isn't. I contend that anyone can grow anything by following a few rules, such as plant it, water it, weed it. People just start-

This four-foot Gypsophila Bristol Fairy *was corseted (19th C. tight) with stakes and twine in early spring. Side growth soon hid the stakes. The head now stands well instead of sprawling under the powerful sprinkler. Facing page, top:* Chamaecyparis p. s. minima *being shaped in the form of a poodle scratching its chin; bottom, hundred-year-old* Tree Lantana Semantha.

ing probably should not read garden books. At that early point in a gardener's life, books make gardening seem too hard. Garden books become important after a man decides he wants to know more. They are essential then." When I got home I showed Grant the small package of seeds. "It's next summer's garden," I said. She looked at the seed packets. "My," she said, "it will all be so nice and brown." The venerable house of Max Schling, Seedsman, had no truck with pretty color pictures of flowers on their packets. Quality stores in those days were frighteningly austere. I recall that Bonwit-Teller, a fancy specialty shop for women at the corner of 56th Street and Fifth Avenue, didn't even have its name on the door. They were just around the corner from Mr. Platt's place.

That spring I had a fearful time deciding when to plant the seeds. Of course, many springs had come and gone in my adult life, but never before had they seemed so fickle. Since then they have not improved a whit. There seems to be no sure signal when spring will definitely arrive. It is not spring when Crocus or Forsythia bloom. Nor has it come on those 3 or 4 red-hot days in April or May when you can practically hear things growing. Whatever it is that is human in humans demands at such a time that something be done about planting something. But as soon as I set out plants a spell of 20° weather invariably blows out of the northwest, and the things collapse in the cold, along with some tender young shoots that have been taken out from under the winter cover because it seemed that the little fellows would smother to death in the heat if left there another minute. Once I successfully timed spring to the minute, because I had been ill during its false starts. This, obviously, is a way of beating this fickle thing, but timing an illness is tricky. Now I pick up the dead twigs that ice and snow have felled during the winter, thatch the lawn, roll it lightly, fertilize it heavily, patch win-

ter holes in it by seeding or by moving a bit of turf, edge the borders, and prune the shrubs that should be shaped in the spring. By this time a late ice storm usually knocks down some more twigs, so these have to be picked up. Then I cut the lawn. Meanwhile, I have looked (more often than necessary) to see how the plants are sprouting in the perennial borders by lifting a bit of the cover of evergreen boughs. Peonies are particularly frightening. Their shoots always seem to be so long that when the cover is finally removed they will get entwined with it and broken. It is consoling now to know that a few Peony stalks are of little moment, for they should be thinned a bit anyway. This procedure has been advocated in recent years for their culture and for several other perennials, such as Phlox, that grow from a compact crown.

"Harris," Grant said that first spring, "if you don't stop worrying about those damned seeds, I shall go nuts." This period of the year is now known as the time of Harris's spring-planting syndrome.

Obviously, one could just sit back and put seeds and plants in the ground a week after the time of the probable "last frost," but in northern climates with short growing seasons such a gardener would get a short season of bloom, and, if the weather got hot early, there is a good chance that some of his precious new plants would not root in sufficiently to save them from the summer sun. When plants should be set out in the spring is about the only gardening problem I can think of that has no pat answer.

Nevertheless, I got Mr Platt's seeds in the ground, successfully in most instances, and they grew well. He had warned me to plant not more than half of the seeds in each packet, in order to have a reserve if anything happened to the first planting. After seeing how few seeds there were in each tiny packet, I cheated a bit, as do all new gardeners, and as a result had much thinning to do. Mr Platt had thoughtfully written thinning distances on each packet, and had told me that if the bed was rich more thinning would be needed as the plants developed. There was no doubt about the bed being rich—I had seen to that. At first I didn't have the heart to pull out enough seedlings so that good ones would be left to develop on 4- to 6-inch centers—they all looked like good plants. It's remarkable how much top one silly little seedling can throw in a short time, particularly if the shoots are pinched out to make it thick and sturdy.

"What a pretty bed of flowers," a visitor remarked that year in late July.

"Yes, it is nice, and I planted it myself from seed," I remember saying, fatuously.

It cut me to the quick each time Grant would decimate a part of it for flowers for the house, and I complained. "You said you were growing those flowers for me," she said. Coldly. When she gets that cold tone in her voice I invariably find something to do out of her sight; but I still insist that when flowers are cut for the house a carefully nurtured border looks like hell for a while, and sometimes it never looks right again during the summer—to the fellow who plants it, I mean.

About the third summer in Litchfield Mr. Platt introduced me to Shady Lawn Seed. This mixture, according to Platt, contained the Fescue race of grasses, along with Bluegrass. Fescue grew well under the shade of trees, he said, but I discovered that this claim was only partly true. It grew well in light shade; but in heavy shade it did no better than any other grass—it didn't grow at all. These were facts I discovered by planting it. But a lightly shaded area under a single large maple, where the grass had been ragged, now was green.

This shrub is Weigela middendorfiana, *a species. Its trumpet-like flower is intensely yellow with a slight brush of red on the lip, a most unusual combination. It bloomed in the spring of 1970, the first time since it was imported from England in 1956. The plant itself is winter-hardy in Zone 4, but the flower buds are not. It will be tested in less rigorous zones before being offered. Facing page: Bedder Dahlias, although not hardy, bloom early, require little staking, and keep blooming until frost.*

However, the Kentucky Bluegrass browned in a neat circle around it. To a man watering annuals with a sprinkling can this was a fine fact. Furthermore, Fescue was finer textured than Bluegrass, and the stuff seemed to creep instead of growing in a tuft, like Blue. Logic also indicated that if Fescue did that well in shade it should be great in full sun. Platt failed me. He admitted that my deductions seemed right, but he knew of no all-Fescue mixture, which I had asked for, and allowed that this was because of expense. Shady Lawn Seed cost far more than regular mixtures, and only a fraction was Fescue.

So I went over Platt's head and wrote to several agricultural colleges and to the Department of Agriculture in Washington. Thus I discovered the Kentucky Bluegrass lobby, a power then and a power today, for every letter I received said that my ideas about Fescue were unsound. In a nutshell, every writer—and all had professorial initials appended to their signatures—said that Blue was the only grass for northern U.S.A., and each asked if I had heard of Merion, an improvement on Kentucky Bluegrass recommended by all golf clubs in the North. I had heard of Merion. Just as I was ready to retreat, a second letter arrived from a young scientist in the Department of Agriculture. He said, "I guess your letter was passed on, finally, to me, because I agree with you." He said that several varieties of Fescues were superb lawn grasses, and that worn out lawns did not have to be dug up, treated with lime and reseeded, as with Bluegrass, if Fescues were used. He had one warning: If I lived in a climate where nights stayed hot over a considerable time, the Fescues would fail. He also said to feed the lawn heavily in early spring (when Crocus bloom) and again in late June or early July, and that a time would come when there would be little or no seeding to do in the fall, that if it were irrigated regularly the lawn would stay so thick that crabgrass, which roots well only in bare spots, would disappear. He gave me the name of a wholesale seed house to which I promptly dispatched a letter. The price of the mixture I ordered specially then was $4.50 a pound—in 100-pound lots. I drew a deep breath, wrote a check, said nothing to Grant about the cost, borrowed my friend's scythe, and cut back into the meadow a bit. I've learned other things about lawns since then, but the routine worked out then is the basis of what White Flower Farm calls its lawn rehabilitation program (see Lawns), which has been used successfully by many gardeners over the last 20 years. In this time Kentucky Bluegrasses have been vastly improved, and most modern varieties do not go completely dormant in mid-summer, but one still can't rehabilitate a lawn with them as successfully as with Fescue. The Blues require a deep, carefully prepared seed bed to be fully effective.

After 3 summers with annuals I tired of them and asked Mr. Platt what else he had that might be used in a garden. He wondered if I had heard of perennials. Of course I had heard of perennials. Every Sunday the news in the papers waited until I had finished the garden sections; I subscribed to 4 garden magazines; I now owned 6 garden books—how could I have kept from hearing about perennials? But that I knew nothing about growing perennials was obvious to Mr. Platt. He tried to sell me plants. They seemed expensive. The seeds, which he picked out, were perennials of different heights and colors and bloomed at different seasons, facts that he noted on each packet. They added up to about $40, and it turned out to be a surprising amount of seed. Seeds of perennials, he said, should not be sown where they were to grow. They had to be started in flats, then transplanted to 2¼-inch thumb pots, and only when they had developed

This contorted, attractive thing is Fagus sylvatica pendula, *the weeping form of the European Beech. It started life with a strong leader, lost it in an accident, and is now doing very well indeed as a small patio plant. Facing page: Homemade Bonsai from the Dwarf Evergreen collection. Above,* Chamaecyparis obtusa gracilis. *The one below is* Pinus strobus nana. *Both are six years old, respectable young Bonsai.*

Fuchsias in hanging baskets just before being moved to the sales yard after frost in late May. Facing page: Pettingill explains the culture of named-variety Blackmore & Langdon tuberous Begonia, a rarity he grows from cuttings. These mother plants put on a spectacular show and are visited by hundreds of people annually from June through October.

into sturdy little plants were they ready for the border. We had built a small garden house on the northwest corner of the property, and had run a pipe to it from our precious water supply to take care of spot watering, by hand from a can, of a small garden plowed up in front of it. Because a friend had given us a few plants of Cymbidium orchids, we had built a miniature lathhouse at the end of the little garden house to house them during the summer. This left barely enough room to protect about 35 small flats of seedlings, which I made by cutting down tomato crates. Looking back, I feel sure that no other gardening project I have since attempted was grander than this first go at growing perennials from seed. Also, it was at this point that my garden books became indispensable.

As soon as the weather warmed up, in mid-May, George Luca, Grant and I spent from Friday until Monday planting the seeds in flats—some 30 different varieties of about 20 genera. We covered them with glass to keep them from drying out, shaded them from light, and protected them from wind and rain as well as we could. George was charged with inspecting them daily. I had a fair idea of when they would sprout, for I had looked up their germination periods. By the second weekend there still was no germination, for the weather had been in the 40's. Then they started to pop. I told Platt we would soon need those clay thumb pots. I ordered 1000 at 3 cents each. When they arrived no one was around to instruct the driver, so he dumped them in the driveway, about 50 yards from the garden house and up a rather steep grade. One thousand 2¼-inch clay pots turned out to be far too heavy for George and me to handle. We had a wheelbarrow, bought at a country auction and painted a fine shade of green, but it had an idiosyncracy—whenever it was loaded, even lightly, the wheel dropped off. So I broke open the crate and carried the pots to the garden house as they were needed.

"Why don't you use a coolie pole?" Grant asked. She was the smarty who had been to China.

By this time many of the seedlings had produced pairs of true leaves. When this happened, the books said, they should be "pricked" off. Seedlings at this stage are small and frail compared to fingers, and during the first 2 dozen attempts my fingers turned out to be all thumbs—the gossamer roots broke and the little leaves pulled off. However, the knack of handling them came quickly, and when the first flat (of Delphinium) had been transplanted the 40-odd little plants looked great. I could imagine them in flower, although I must admit that at the time I had only the vaguest idea of their shapes or colors. I went ahead, doggedly, with the second variety. Now a few over 100 plants were finished, but it was apparent I would not come out even—there would not be enough pots. There also were not enough flats to grow all of them and certainly not enough garden to plant them in if they grew. So I began transplanting only 18 seedlings per variety. By the time I was finished I had had my fill of them—and so had my managing editor. I had explained to him that I needed a week off as sick leave because my presence was needed to perform the duties of a mid-wife to a lot of plants I was bearing.

Platt had said that as I didn't have a greenhouse it would be wise to transplant more seedlings than I could use. He was right. Casualties were high. Storms took some off, and once George let the watering go too long "because it was going to rain" that night. By the time they were planted in our new perennial border, there were about 180 plants, representing a few of all the varieties that had germinated. We planted all of them. Then the things just sat, growing tops, but never showing a flower. I complained to Platt. He said, "Oh, none of them will bloom until next year." It was a point the

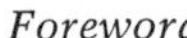

The author and Grant prune back a prickly spreading Juniper in the Dwarf Evergreen border. Facing page: The white perennial border, from which the nursery gets its name, puts on a last big display when the Phlox take over, then settles back to pleasant greens. In the right foreground is Veronica Icicle. *It will bloom until frost; spikes last ten days in water.*

books had neglected to mention. Grant said she would rather have had annuals—at least they bloomed and were not so much work. The next spring this simple perennial garden of ours threw bloom the likes of which have never been seen, and when 19 surviving Delphinium plants reached to a regal 6 or 7 feet in July—well, I was hooked, as the saying goes, as a gardener. The winds were kind and did not blow and I did not have to stake the stately things.

One evening as the shadows lengthened in the dusk, Grant came over to where I stood looking at the lovely sight. "I thought I'd come out with you and watch them grow," she said.

When World War II came along we switched to vegetables. The small plot of ground at the garden house was enlarged. It didn't seem large then, but a piece of land 45 feet by 100 feet is a sizable piece, and produces a surprising amount of food—even when a third of its rows are planted with annual and perennial plants. Grant and I took care of it with minimum help from George, who by then spent most of his time caring for our now sizable lawn. At this time we were in Litchfield only on weekends and holidays. A gardener can usually let a weed-free garden go 2 weeks before it requires weeding again, but hardly a minute longer. Weeds then are visible quarter- to half-inch seedlings. Knocking them over with a hoe is no problem, although hand-hoeing is slow. A wheel hoe, which I bought, is the fastest hand cultivating tool extant, an almost perfect piece of machinery, for by using it correctly nearly all weeds in the row, even those very close to the plant itself, can be downed with minimum effort. It beats any power hoe I have ever seen for weeding a small garden. Also, it can be guided so that it just scuffles the surface. A hand hoe, unless properly adjusted for the height of the user, tends to dig too deeply, which destroys the myriads of fine feeding roots that annuals, perennial plants and many shrubs grow just below the surface. (Incidentally, the metal crook that attaches the blade of a hand hoe to its handle was made so the user can bend the angle of the blade to his height. As few people know this, few do it. Also, a sharp hoe is a lot easier to use than a dull one. Gardeners out for a long spell with a hoe in these rocky parts carry a small steel file with them.) Once when we were cultivating every 2 weeks, it rained steadily when I should have been hoeing. The seeds had shot up when we got back and were nasty to get out. After that we went to weekly hoeing. Also, the old saw about not cultivating before a rain, because it will replant the weeds, must have been thought up by some sage who never did it. I find that few weeds get replanted, and those which do are mighty sickly things after a going-over with a tool. (Except purselane, a species of the *Portulaca* family, creeping fleshy things, the starfish of plants. Dismember one and each nasty piece roots and grows. Purselane waits for the heat of summer, then whooshes. It seems to thrive on herbicides. The first frost, fortunately, shrivels the repulsive things. "As ornery as purselane" is the worst thing unemotional New Englanders can think of to call a man.

Just before the war ended iron pipe came off priority, so we dug a deep well—550 feet of it, the deepest well in Litchfield County—which produced one and one-half gallons of water a minute. This was a disappointment. It couldn't possibly be enough for a lawn. But it produced about 2,000 gallons in 24 hours, and with a 1000-gallon tank there was sufficient water for the perennial garden we planned. The border of deciduous shrubs that had been started would not need it.

In 1946 we built an underground garage on the north side of the house, then terraced back the sharp hill. This gave us a large roll-

A strawberry jar is very hard to irrigate evenly unless centered with a 1½-inch pipe drilled with a dozen or more ⅜-inch holes. The climber covering the garage wall, Euonymus radicans vegetus Sarcoxie, *is an extremely versatile evergreen. Clip it to any form. Facing page:* Lantana Spreading Sunset *thrives only in full sun;* Spathiphyllum hybridum Mona Loa *gets only fifteen minutes of late sun (and hates it).*

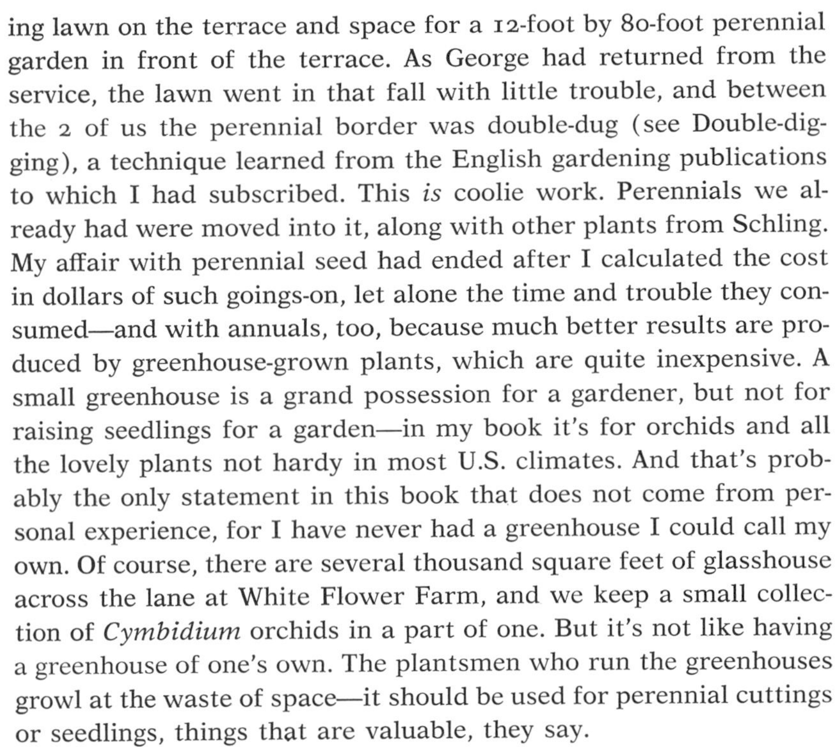

ing lawn on the terrace and space for a 12-foot by 80-foot perennial garden in front of the terrace. As George had returned from the service, the lawn went in that fall with little trouble, and between the 2 of us the perennial border was double-dug (see Double-digging), a technique learned from the English gardening publications to which I had subscribed. This *is* coolie work. Perennials we already had were moved into it, along with other plants from Schling. My affair with perennial seed had ended after I calculated the cost in dollars of such goings-on, let alone the time and trouble they consumed—and with annuals, too, because much better results are produced by greenhouse-grown plants, which are quite inexpensive. A small greenhouse is a grand possession for a gardener, but not for raising seedlings for a garden—in my book it's for orchids and all the lovely plants not hardy in most U.S. climates. And that's probably the only statement in this book that does not come from personal experience, for I have never had a greenhouse I could call my own. Of course, there are several thousand square feet of glasshouse across the lane at White Flower Farm, and we keep a small collection of *Cymbidium* orchids in a part of one. But it's not like having a greenhouse of one's own. The plantsmen who run the greenhouses growl at the waste of space—it should be used for perennial cuttings or seedlings, things that are valuable, they say.

The nice lady who had sold us the barn died the following year, and in her will let us have first refusal on the 18 acres that surrounded our small property. We bought it for protection. Shortly after, Dr. Turkington trudged up the hill from the Turnpike, and instead of turning into his place, he entered ours. He looked distressed. "Turk," the nickname we did not use to his face, had not much liked the idea of our moving in close to him, but when he discovered that we ran a neat place he became friendly. He told us he had just had his 2 horses shot and buried on the hill across the Turnpike, that he was not well enough to ride anymore, and that he was going to sell his farm. He offered us first refusal. He is not the kind of man one attempts to trade with. We shook hands on the deal on the spot.

"Gees!" Grant said that night as we had cocktails, "there's nothing like owning a house and one acre and protecting it with 90 acres, 2 houses, a 3-car garage, a hay barn, a horse barn, and a dog kennel. What are we going to do with them?"

We had better than a year to think about it, because Dr. Turkington did not want to give immediate possession. Our Litchfield friends, many with larger farms than ours, were becoming gentlemen farmers. Some established fancy herds of purebred dairy cattle, others started to raise purebred sheep. I wanted no part of 4-legged animals—I'd had enough of them in Colorado. Also, a gentleman farmer quickly turns into a roustabout when his herdsman quits or becomes ill. One evening, obviously after one more drink of bourbon than necessary, we said, "Let's start a nursery."

By that time we had become rather sophisticated gardeners, so sophisticated that we had turned the perennial border from mixed colors to pure white—what the English call a moon garden. The first idea, which lasted about a minute, was to produce only white-flowering perennials and shrubs, an obviously impossible idea commercially, because there are few gardeners who want to restrict their gardens to that extent, and because white flowers—in many instances albino forms or sports of species—have less stamina and are more subject to the strange ills of chlorophyll. But there was another reason for starting a nursery: we had found only a few

Several hundred yards of potting mixtures are made annually from builder's sand, peat moss, and humus, into which exact amounts of fertilizer are incorporated—no soil. Facing page: Students and housewives provide the hands needed during peak periods in the potting and packing sheds and the fields. Finished stock is graded by a handful of excellent gardeners. "Discard any plant you wouldn't buy" is their only guide.

mail-order nurseries in the country which produced quality plants true to variety. This is due to careless rogueing in the growing process (see Rogue), to avarice, or to petty fraud—substituting without permission when the ordered variety is sold out. Experienced gardeners complain when this happens; inexperienced ones (if they even know) are so pleased to see any plant flower that they don't complain. The not-strictly-ethical mail-order house or garden center will take the chance and substitute, feeling rather sure they will have to make good on less than 10 percent of their performance failures. Also, there is nothing more irritating to me as a gardener than getting a great clump of a plant that was obviously left over from a previous crop. If planted as it comes, the thing will collapse. Divisions can be taken from it and pampered into growth in a shaded coldframe, but the hole it was to fill remains in the border for a year. Anyway, nursing plants isn't a customer's job—that's the work nurserymen do. Today, the service industries, which include nurseries, are so dominant, many of them so downright arrogant, that many times the poor customer fears that complaints will cut him off from a service he needs. In the late 1940s, a seller's market was developing, and we felt that by establishing a nursery with complete integrity we could attract experienced home gardeners, many of them with horticultural knowledge professionals could envy—the top of the market, in other words.

We had another reason for starting a nursery. We had found that fine English nurseries were offering many new strains that were not catalogued in this country. Symons-Jeune Phlox, Exbury Azaleas, and Blackmore and Langdon Tuberous Begonias, to name a few. Also, the English offered exceptionally good species of genera that were impossible to find in the United States. So our nursery would bring in as much new plant material that we could find hardy in the colder zones. Shortly after buying the Turkington property we went to England to see, for the first time, the Chelsea Flower Show, and we introduced ourselves to several of England's prominent nurserymen. (Chelsea, it should be noted, makes American flower shows seem grubby and over-commercialized, which, indeed, most of them are. At Chelsea exhibitors are *invited* to show by the Royal Horticultural Society; they pay no rent for space, and are not invited back if they fail to produce good exhibits.) They welcomed us with more enthusiasm than our project at that time seemed to deserve. The reason: few U.S. nurseries seemed serious about importing plants that were not highly promotable.

J. J. Grullemans, co-founder of Wayside Gardens of Mentor, Ohio, a great plantsman with whom we had become well acquainted, was an exception, but he admitted that he no longer was as interested in innovation as he had been, largely because so few of his competitors were. He was also so far ahead of the field that he could afford to loaf a bit. Furthermore, although he did not say so, he already had a large investment in four-color printing plates, and new plants, no matter how desirable, had to be brought into his great catalogue slowly because of the cost of new plates. This is a reason we decided never to use color in our catalogue. Color is pretty, it certainly sells, but it also freezes one in. Anyway, few English catalogues had much truck with color and they did all right. Innovation is successful, as we have discovered, only when the rest of the trade starts to copy the innovator. Jack Grullemans lived to see us bring in *Abeliophyllum distichum* (commonly known as White Forsythia) just a year before he did, and *Exbury Azaleas* some four years before he was stocked. He more than anyone else revived our spirits when they were low, but I wonder now if he would relish the competition we have provided in the years since he died, years in which we came

to modest prominence nationally by nibbling away at the quality market, a satisfactory but not a particularly large one in this country. I am sure he would have applauded it.

A section of the Dwarf Evergreen border planted in 1953. Its growth has now slowed. Facing page: Tulips planted in mass make spectacular spring gardens; they are practical in beds removed from walls or other places where mice forage. But a lone hill can be as arresting as five hundred of them. Lily-flowered Tulipa Alaska *at the corner of a deciduous border make this point.*

To get started we needed a man to do the work, one who would graduate into the job of manager and part owner as the establishment grew. To find a knowledgeable fellow who was however young enough not to be influenced by the nursery practices we did not approve of, we wrote the deans of various Eastern horticultural schools and asked for candidates. We hired one from Rutgers. He turned out to be an exceptionally good grower, but for various reasons, including probably impatience on my part, it did not work out. After 2 years he left, and it was then that I became a split personality, if that's the proper term to use, for I took a pseudonym.

This came about because in the advertising copy we wrote for various Connecticut newspapers we had used our bright young man's name, as manager. Now we decided, far more realistically than when we had begun, that starting a nursery from scratch was not going to be in the least easy, and that we'd have so many changes in personnel in the future that featuring the "manager" (of the moment) would get us nowhere. We thought a pseudonym would both create continuity and permit us to style the establishment to appeal to enough like-minded gardeners to make a viable business.

The name Pettingill was chosen rather deviously, to keep some individual from claiming that we were using his name for advertising purposes. Admiral George Pettengill, a friend, said it would be satisfactory to him if we used his last name. It was his suggestion that we change an "e" to an "i," because, he said, he had never seen it spelled that way and it might be unique. We hit upon "Amos" for this spurious Pettingill's first name—a good Down East name. Once or twice a year we get letters inquiring about our relationship with this or that Pettengill, and my stock answer is to point out the difference in spelling. Once we got a letter from a fellow who spelled his name like ours. There seemed to be no point in answering the letter.

It was, however, inevitable that our cover would be broken someday. The first to suspect was Katherine White, who writes "Onwards and Upwards in the Garden" for *The New Yorker.* When reviewing an early catalogue, she observed that she "suspected Amos Pettingill" wasn't born with that name. Later, as White Flower Farm attracted publicity in more national publications (*Reader's Digest, House & Garden,* and *The National Observer*), the reporters, who were not in the habit of keeping talk about identity off the record, blew our cover entirely. But a surprising number of people do not read carefully these days—probably due to the influence of radio and television—and 9 out of 10 people who know of the nursery think of it as Amos Pettingill's place, if they bother to personalize it at all.

After *House & Garden* revealed that I was a former *Fortune* editor, a banker and a gourmet cook, a nice but plaintive letter came from a lady in Michigan. She said, "All my ideals are shattered! Now I find you a city slicker and a cook, instead of a man of the soil. Why don't you give us some tips on the market and print some of your recipes?" Maybe the letter did not require it, but I answered, for it brought up points I had been thinking about for some time. I told her that there was a Pettingill *and* a Harris, and that I was in a position to know both of them intimately. Harris, not Pettingill, is the city slicker, I said. Harris clothes himself

meticulously and expensively, something Pettingill wouldn't even think of doing. Pettingill isn't exactly a slob, but his clothes look terrible, and there are days, sometimes 3, when he doesn't get around to shaving. As for Harris's gourmet cooking—well, it's a laugh. He once took a dozen lessons at Joe Hyde's cooking school at Sneeden's Landing and learned a few basics about cooking vegetables and meats, but he never turned out a one of the fancy dishes demonstrated. The only reason he finished the course was that he liked being the only man in a class that included the most comely young matrons he had seen in some time. After he let drop a bit of conversation about "going to cooking school" his friends took it up and made his reputation, such as it is. On the other hand, every once in a while Pettingill bakes fine old-fashioned white bread—but he says nothing about it. It is Pettingill, not Harris, who has the deep interest in horticulture. All this, I pointed out to the lady from Michigan, made the case for 2 individuals, not one, as the *House & Garden* story had implied. There seemed to be no logical signature to use on such a letter, so it was sent unsigned.

Our next attempt to get a manager for this absentee-owner operation proved to be no more successful than the first, although it lasted about twice as long. The couple who took over were diligent, but their experience had been entirely in evergreens, trees, and shrubs, and they knew little or nothing about perennials. Also, their outlook on the business was conventional and our unconventional approach didn't make sense to them. A year before they left, we went to England to try to find an English plantsman, preferably one already working for a fine nursery, who had the professionalism for which British gardeners are so famed. The title "gardener" as applied in England has nothing to do with the lawn-mowing-weeder-hedgeclipper-hand-me-down man who is called a gardener here. A well-rounded English gardener is expert with nearly all kinds of plant material, and he gets along with a new and strange plant by working with it, gingerly, until he finds the combinations of soil, moisture, temperature, and location which are congenial to it. His father and grandfather were gardeners, and like him started to learn about plants even before entering school. Such men are sought after as judges of the many fine flower shows that are such a deeply-rooted part of British life; many write well and learnedly; some become radio personalities. Imagine the status of a concertmaster in an orchestra here, and you can get some idea of how the British feel about them. The good ones are perfectionists; it would never occur to them to substitute a variety. They know the optimum size for transplanting, an art which has been almost lost here because the first-generation European gardeners who owned or operated the fine American nurseries of the 1920's have either sold out because of high land values, or dropped out because of age. Today such men, true plantsmen, are difficult to find in England and almost impossible to find here. Most of the good ones own their own businesses.

But in 1954 we had luck. Grant said it was coming to us. At Baker's, one of England's fine nurseries, we encountered David Smith, 29 years old, whose only experience outside of horticulture was a turn with the Royal Air Force as a Spitfire pilot, late in World War II, just before hostilities in Europe ended. David, son of Roland Smith, head gardener for the Earl of Bradford and a B.B.C. garden commentator, was waiting for "a post," he said, "somewhere in the colonies" as head gardener for some municipality. As America was obviously still an English colony insofar as

Spathiphyllum hybridum Mona Loa, *a jungle floor plant, wants only minimum light, 70° heat (leaves yellow at 60°), and soaking wet roots. It is ideal for dark city apartments; is a boon to over-waterers. Facing page: Jane Grant arranging flowers in an eighteenth-century Waterford epergne.*

Symons-Jeune Strain Phlox was first imported by White Flower Farm from England in the early 1950's. It has a very long season of bloom; stems are strong, pips and heads huge—and there are dwarf forms. Colors are strong. All are sweetly scented and fungus-resistant. Facing page: Harris masquerading as Pettingill. "You can't understand a word he utters," Grant says. "It's that damn pipe."

gardening was concerned, we suggested that he come over and help us. He introduced his fiancée, Diana, an attractive girl with flaming red hair. They were married at once, and arrived in the late fall of 1954. If David had not been present in the spring of the following year when our managing couple returned to the Midwest, the chances are that Grant and I would have folded Amos Pettingill's tent and crept away. At Smith's suggestion we asked Harold Calverley, another Baker's alumnus, if he would come over to handle sales. He picked up his four children and his wife, Mavis, and arrived practically at once. The British are an adventurous people.

These Englishmen quickly adjusted their thinking to American ways, and, even more important, they found out how plants they had known so well in England respond in American climate. Smith is White Flower Farms' director of horticulture, and in my opinion one of the best in the field. Calverley, with a keen sense of selling and blessed with a high regard for detail, is the nursery's resident manager. They have proved to be a great team. Ian Waters, the son of a fine Scotch gardener, has also been with the organization for about 15 years; he heads production. These 3 are the horticultural core, so to speak, of the organization. Getting this nucleus of professionals together did not solve all our problems, but it helped.

As a business the nursery business is a hard one. The stuff you produce has very little shelf life. Hands, the finest of all tools, do most of the work, but they are expensive to train and difficult even to find these days. With a broad line of plants a manager has no really good idea of demand, and when he is out of stock he can't mix parts and come up with product—and if he does not substitute the waste is appalling. If a rogue is shipped the aggrieved buyer is heard from at once. And if a block of cuttings that will produce expensive plants fails to root, stocks of that variety won't be available next year or the year after. The weather and growth in volume of business are frightening things to an owner. Increased volume does not immediately result in increased profit, but it does require immediate addition to capital. It is un-American to say that you are against growth, but we have no intention of letting White Flower Farm reach more than a half-million dollars in sales, a point we are dangerously close to at this time. The reason is clear. This is the kind of service business where size does not produce economies, as in manufacturing. Size produces confusion and a deterioration in service. I look forward to the time, which, as noted, is not far off, when we can print a little notice to send to gardeners who order in May and want plants in April—ahead, in other words, of those who have placed orders in March. It might read: "Sorry, we can accept no new orders for shipment this season. Unlike an airline, which may have another plane in a hangar, we cannot over-book. We are holding this order for shipment at the proper time next season."

Obviously, that's no way to run a business.

WILLIAM B. HARRIS

Introduction

The following plants are those I know. The vast majority, say 95 percent, are very friendly things. Stick them in the ground and they grow. This, of course, is the reason that gardening is not the least difficult and why a great deal of horticultural knowledge can be acquired quickly and easily—it's the dirty thumb, not the green one, that makes plants grow. Some other plants are diffident and friendship with them is slow to ripen. Giant Hybrid Delphinium, the Queen of Flowers, is an example. The reader will recall that the first time I produced perennials the 6- to 7-foot Delphinium stalks

were so sensational that I gave up golf for gardening. Then it took me 10 years to reproduce that first crop. Why? Because I had done everything right the first time—without knowing it. The garden books say, "Feed Delphinium heavily," and they obviously don't define "heavily" because their cautious authors have no idea how well fertilized borders already are or the strength of available fertilizers. My first border was loaded with plant food. I was a rank beginner. Enthusiastic. Not only had the border been double-dug but I had laced it with twice as much manure and humus as the instructions required and then top-dressed it with commercial organic fertilizer, reasoning that if a little fertilizer would be good, twice as much would be better. I had also fertilized each Delphinium liberally a couple of times before it flowered. In a nutshell, that's the way Giant Hybrid Delphinium like to be fed; it took me all those years to reproduce the conditions of my first spectacular success. During that time I also learned that 1-year-old field-grown Delphinium, still the standard in the trade, is a fraud. If we can't transplant the things successfully in the nursery, and we never can, one needs little imagination to realize what a problem such plants are to the home gardener. The successful transplant is one started from seed in a 3-inch peat pot in a greenhouse in January. If planted early in a rich border it will hit 6 feet by the end of July. Also, few garden writers or nurserymen admit that Giant Hybrid Delphinium are so far from being true perennials that they must be planted like annuals to get consistent results, but that's God's truth about the lovely things. Of course there are a few Giant Hybrids that last for 5 years, but they are sensational only because they have lived so long—their flower spikes are just average.

The Tree Peony, King of Flowers, on the other hand, is not an intimate friend of mine. To me it is the most desirable plant in horticulture and I have admired the few well-grown ones I have seen in this country; but it hasn't responded to my care. If reading made a gardener an expert, I would be at the head of the class in Tree Peonies. A trip to Japan in 1968 helped. It also helped in importing stock so strong that it passed U.S. Plant Quarantine without loss, compared to total loss in years past. So it just may be that we shall learn what this aristocrat likes, for the literature obscures rather than clarifies culture, which isn't too surprising.

A last point to be made is that except for a very few genera in this book (such as Fuchsia, Gloxinia, Clivia), all are hardy in Litchfield, which is situated in the foothills of the Berkshires, where winter temperature normally drops to −20° F. and in a few abnormal years dips to −35° F. for a night or two. We get tropical weather during periods of the summer, but nights, mostly, are cool. This kind of weather (zones 4 and 5—lowest temperature −10° F. —on the end-paper maps) is typical of a great and heavily populated area of the United States.

Blooms of Tree Peonies open hugely, showing no centers—then shatter completely, usually at night. "Kissed by a moonbeam," an ancient Chinese poet said of them. This Tree Peony has been in the herbaceous border for 11 years, has been cut to the ground 8 times. It is a shrub, not a herbaceous perennial. Facing page: Herbaceous Peonies take over the garden's 250-foot traditional perennial border in May and June.

A Note on the Use of This Book

Plants are arranged alphabetically. Their common names are cross-indexed to the botanical genus of which they are members. Varieties follow the genus. Nomenclature and classification of plants generally follow that of the Royal Horticultural Society's Dictionary of Gardening. Phonetic pronunciation of general and botanical terms is provided. An asterisk (*) is used to refer to plants that can be used for the rockery; the superior character † refers to plants that can be used for forcing. Short essays on gardening practice are also alphabetized. These include Bulb Food, Cold Frames, Compost, Double-digging, Feeding, Sun, Shade, Insecticides, etc. For a full list see Cultural Instructions in the alphabetical section. The index is designed to supplement the alphabetical arrangement of the text rather than to repeat it.

Linaria Cymbalaria

Abeliophyllum

A-bee-leo-fill'um

White Forsythia. A genus having only one species, found in Korea in 1924, and first imported to the United States in 1955. It is a distant member of the Forsythia family (*Oleaceae*), generally hard to find but not expensive when you find it. It can be planted spring or fall.

A. distichum (dis-tick'um). Hardy zone 5, southward. This is a slow-growing and slightly spreading deciduous shrub that is twiggy rather than willowy, like, say, the spreading branches of old-fashioned varieties of yellow Forsythia. At maturity it reaches 5 to 7 feet in height, spreads slightly less, so for the shrub it is dwarf, a desirable characteristic. Leaves are a cool-looking bluish green.

The flowers cover the light brown stems about 2 weeks before yellow Forsythia comes into bloom; they are pink in bud but rapidly change to white upon opening, and are delightfully fragrant. Kew Gardens warned that very cold spring winds might blast the buds. However, it has withstood extremely cold weather in Litchfield for years with no bud damage. We can only conclude that it is so hardy it would survive, and even bloom, in Minnesota, if planted in a protected location. Branches cut in late winter can be forced into bloom.

Acer

A'sir

The Maple family. Hardy zone 4, southward. The 100-odd species of this great group of shade trees native in many of the northern temperate countries are mostly hardy. They seem to have few natural enemies. Living as we do in New England, we know Sugar Maples and the Norway varieties well and, as we guess early New Englanders did, we occassionally go to the woods in the spring and dig out sturdy Maple whips and plant a few here and there along fence lines. However, it's also a good guess that many a lovely New England lane owes its beauty to Maple seedlings that volunteered at the edge of old thrown stonewalls. Be that as it may, before one can turn around newly planted Maple whips shoot to 30 feet—in 15 years, to be exact. So it turns out that we turn slow, but that's the way one must turn to look at a recently transplanted tree—otherwise they don't grow.

A Norway Maple offered in the trade, *A. platanoides Schwedleri nigra,* generally called Crimson King, is a fine red-leaved tree that has been over-promoted as a novelty. Except for its red leaves there isn't anything very novel about it. I don't see what kick people get out of saying, "My Maple has red leaves," but they surely do or there wouldn't be so many sold. I've seen as many as 3 of them on one 50- by 100-foot lot and I tense up every time I pass the place. This maple should be used as an accent tree on estates or in parks. It's

Achillea The Pearl

probably camp to think that the leaves of trees should be green, but it's hard for me to get over that idea.

Other Maples are far less common, but obtainable in most nurseries. We like the small-leaved Japanese varieties, particularly the ones over here, which in New England are really more like bushes than trees. Their leaves color joyously and they make far better planting material for small grounds than the big fellows. The rarest, the Japanese Cutleaf forms, are delightful, but are devilish hard to find. They grow very slowly. A 15- to 18-inch plant costs up to $20; a 4-foot specimen, which would be about 5 to 6 feet in width, can be purchased for $250 or more (mostly more), if it can be found. They can be put in place spring or fall. There follow descriptions of 2 of the finest:

A. palmatun dissectum. This is the lovely green form of the Japanese Cutleaf Maple. To get fast growth from this dwarf it is best to plant it in a sheltered location, for fewer of the small branches will winter-kill at the ends. *A. palmatum* is quite successful when in tubs or large pottery, but such plantings must be protected in the winter. Height at maturity is about 8 feet; spread is always greater than height.

A. p. d. atropurpureum. This is the spectacular dark red form of the Japanese Cutleaf Maple. It is more popular because it is red, but it isn't the least more beautiful.

Achillea

Ack-ill-lee'a

Yarrow. These valuable garden plants from the North Temperate Zone are widely grown for the masses of flowers they bear throughout most of the summer. The foliage is attractive and fern-like. Plants grow well in dry, exposed places. They are not fussy about soil, but do best in a good garden loam. Plant them spring or fall.

Achillea Coronation Gold

***A. ageratifolia.** A very compact, free-growing carpet plant for rockery or front-of-the-border planting. Flowers are single, white, daisy-like, and appear on 4- to

6-inch stems from June to September. This carpeter does best in a well-drained alkaline (sweet) soil in full sun.
A. Coronation Gold. A showy, middle-of-the-border perennial. Its large heads of bright golden yellow flowers are excellent for cutting. The long blooming period, June to August, is also desirable. Coronation Gold also makes one of the best dried flowers. Fact is many think it is more valuable dried than fresh. It grows about 3 feet high.
***A. Millefolium Fire King.** The flower heads of this variety are rosy-red in color and are on 18-inch stems. It grows from a dense mat of silvery gray-green foliage and is best used in the rockery or for edging the perennial border.
A. Moonshine. Foliage is silver gray; it blooms in a profusion of sulphur-yellow flat umbels which appear on 18- to 24-inch stems from June until the end of September. Excellent for cutting. Put it in a dry and sunny position.
A. taggeta. Here is a sturdy plant in pale yellow that is 18 inches high. The blooming period is from June to September.
A. The Pearl. Pure white, powder-puff flowers in bloom from late June to September. It grows to about 15 inches, and is an excellent cut flower.

Aconitum Barker's Variety

Aconitum

Ack-ko-knee'tum

Monkshood. This genus of 100 species has many excellent fall-flowering varieties that help keep the perennial border in bloom before Chrysanthemums come into flower. Almost all varieties are extremely hardy. They thrive in good soils, and where shade is not too heavy they do as well as in a sunny location. They like moisture, but refuse to grow where the ground floods for periods or is too wet. Varieties can be planted in the spring or fall.

A. Barker's Variety. A robust perennial, 4 feet high, for the back of the border. It seems to do well in sun or light shade. Blooms are a delightful amethyst blue. It likes regular irrigation.
A. Fisheri. Flowers are a deep blue and typically shaped like monks' hoods. Flower stems are strong. Height, depending on culture and location, is from 2 to 3 feet.
A. Spark's Variety. A rich Oxford-blue flower. Its blooms on 3- to 4-foot stems come somewhat later than other Aconitum and last into September.

acrostichioides (a-cross-tich-oi'dees) forked-tip leaflet

Adenophora

A-den-off'ora

Adenophora. About 20 species of perennials from eastern Asia make up this genus, which, unless one is a botanist, is not easy to tell from Campanula. The flowers, however, are drooping and in racemes. The varieties are hardy and generally do well in rich soils that are not too dry. Warm and sunny describes the best location. Most Adenophora varieties are difficult to move, so plant them where they should stay. Increase stock by cuttings; dividing the plant is nearly impossible. They may be planted spring or fall. The following variety is an old friend, decidedly the best in the genus.

A. Farreri. Spikes of large, deep blue flowers appear in July and August on stems that are about 30 inches high. This is an excellent blue flower for gardeners who try to grow all-blue borders, not an easy thing to do.

Adenophora Farreri

Adiantum (*ay-dee-an'tum*) *Maidenhair fern*

Aesculus

Es'kew-lus

Horse chestnut. Zone 2. This genus, native to North America and Eurasia, has about 25 species of trees and shrubs, but the standout is *A. E. Hippocastanum,* as common as if it were called *vulgaris.* It's huge, grows to 100 feet, and produces probably the densest shade of any tree, which makes it ideal as a shade tree for streets. Certainly the French think so, for Parisian streets are lined with them. There are many of them in this country, but they are seldom used as in France. They are probably too messy for American taste. Thousands of lovely flowers cover the walks when they fall. They can be bought in white or pink forms, but only a few nurserymen carry them. It seems odd that so few people are willing to tidy up after a tree.

AFRICAN LILY—*see* Agapanthus

Agapanthus
Ag-a-pan'thus

African Lily or Lily-of-the-Nile. Not hardy. A showy South African genus of not more than 3 species widely grown for their showy flowers. The plants are tuberous rooted and of easy culture. Soil should consist of equal parts of rich loam, leaf-mold, well-rooted cow manure and sharp sand. In zones 8 and 9 they can be grown outside; elsewhere they grow well in large pots or tubs, which should be put inside before hard frost and kept moderately dry in a frost-free place—under a greenhouse bench, if one has a greenhouse, or wintered on a window sill. During the summer they can hardly be given too much water. Heavy feeding during the blooming period, a long one, is also in order, but food should be withdrawn as the season lengthens and they are stowed away for the winter. As they increase very rapidly by offsets, old plants may be divided in the spring; if not separated they require heavy feeding. Because the plants remain in bloom all summer, they are highly prized by gardeners. They are ideal patio plants. Get them in the spring for best results.

Ajuga

A. africanus. Showy deep blue clusters of flowers on 30-inch stems which rise well above the numerous long and narrow leaves. It makes an excellent cut flower.
A. africanus albus. Same as *A. africanus* but the blooms are white.
A. a. Peter Pan. This dwarf throws profuse deep blue flower clusters on stems that are up to 20 inches high. It's a delightful little fellow.

ageratifolia (a-jur-a-ti-foe'lia) leaves like Ageratum

AGERATUM HARDY—*see* Eupatorium

*Ajuga
A-joo'gah

Bugle. There are many splendid rockery plants in this European genus. It is also one of the best ground covers for locations in sun or light shade. It spreads quickly, mats so heavily when established that weeds rarely grow. For quick covers place plants 6 inches apart. It is evergreen in mild climates, and practically indestructible. It may be planted spring or fall.

A. genevensis. Dense, spreading mats of light green leaves with masses of dark blue flowers on 6- to 8-inch spikes in May and June.
A. g. rubra. This pink-flowering variety of *A. genevensis* is just as vigorous as the blue form.
A. pyramidalis. This variety is listed as an herb by herbalists, and we suspect that its dried leaves do produce a brew wondrously beneficial, but we like *A. pyramidalis* because it does not spread. It grows into a neat, small plant and produces perky spikes of blue flowers. Foliage is waxy green.
A. reptans rubra. The pleasant bronze foliage of this variety mats. The deep purple flowers bloom on 8-inch stems in May and June.

alba (*al'ba*) *white*

Albertiana (*al-ber-tee-ay'na*) *after Prince Albert*

ALKANET—*see* Anchusa

Allium

Al'lee-um

Allium (it is the Latin word for garlic) is a very large genus of about 280 species, many of them garden or house plants. The latter generally are not hardy. They grow from bulbs or bulb-like rhizomes, some of which creep rapidly and become weeds. Allium flowers are dense balls of color at the top of strong stems, and they make excellent displays in the garden or in bowls. Blooms also may be dried. (Chives—*see* Herbs—are a member of this family.) A well-drained, light soil that is not too rich suits all members of the genus. Plant the bulbs in the fall.

Allium senescens

A. giganteum. Its bright lilac-colored flowers on 4-foot stems appear in June or early July and grow to literally colossal size—and do it in a most intriguing way. The flowers start green, coloring first on top of the ball, then slowly change from green to lilac. As they mature they reverse to green again, as before—neatly, from the top down. Stake this Himalayan. When cut early the bloom lasts 2 weeks in water. Depending on size, bulbs cost from $3 to $5 each and are generally available from quality mail-order nurseries.

A. luteum. This species has sweet-scented blooms which are golden yellow. They show in June on 12-inch stems. Although from the Mediterranean region, *A. luteum* is hardy. It multiplies rapidly in light, well-drained soil. Plant it in low-growing ground cover in full sun.

A. neapolitanum. A very sweet-scented white species which also makes a good pot plant. Blooms appear on 16-inch stems.

*__A. Ostrowskianum.__ This native of Turkestan has carmine-red blooms on 8- to 12-inch stems. Use it in front-of-the-border or in the rockery.

*__A. roseum.__ Rose-pink blooms appear on stems of irregular height ranging from 6 to 15 inches. It is of Mediterranean origin.

A. senescens. The bloom is rose pink, very dense and quite large. It appears on an erect fleshy stem that grows to 30 inches and is very strong. It blooms in June.

Allwoodii (all-wood-eye) after Montague Allwood, English Dianthus expert

alpinum (al-pie'num) of the mountains

Althaea Rosea

Al-thee'a

Hollyhocks. The common Hollyhock is one of the most desirable garden plants nature ever invented. These stately beauties, thought by many to be native here, are Chinese. They should be planted in clumps close to every New England house. Those who live in today's glass houses find that a clump or two of them close by make spectacular foils. If placed in a protected location, they need not be staked. The plants reproduce in profusion from seeds. Plant them only in the spring for best results. The soil should be rich.

A. r. Double. This group of Hollyhocks is generally sold in shades of scarlet, yellow, pink and pure white. Although the selected seed strains run rather accurately by shades, some colors may disappoint you, but nurserymen grow them as biennials so plants can't be rogued. You have to trust to luck—but why not? Who cares about the color of this divinely formed plant? It blooms in July and can reach a height of 8 feet.

A. r. Powderpuff. The flowers of these charmers look almost like tennis balls cut in half; they are fluffy like a powderpuff. Really good cultivation (rich soil and adequate water) produces blooms up to 5 inches in diameter. Colors are subdued, but mixed; they are grown from seed without, as yet, color ranges. They grow from 6 to 8 feet high and bloom in July.

Alyssum

Al-iss'sum

Basket of Gold. Europe and Asia have given us the gorgeous and useful species that make up this genus. Plant them in ordinary, well-drained soil and they will be most rewarding. We suggest using them in groups in the perennial border, the rock garden, or as edging plants. They are also striking in baskets or patio containers. The flowers show in profusion in early spring. They are on stems 12 to 15 inches high. Plant them only in the spring.

***A. saxatile citrinum.** Showers and showers and showers of pale yellow flowers.
***A. saxatile compactum.** Ditto, but the flowers are bright yellow and the plant is more dwarf than other varieties.
***A. saxatile flora pleno.** An excellent double form of *A. s. compactum*, with, obviously, bright yellow flowers.

Amaryllis

Amaryllis

Am-a-rill'iss

Amaryllis. Not hardy except in zone 9 and southward. The finest strain we have ever seen is that produced and developed over many generations by the Warmenhoven family of Lisse, Holland. Colors are solid and iridescent; few scapes (the flowering stalks) produce fewer than 4 huge blossoms, many of which measure 8 inches in diameter. Other Dutch strains do not measure up, and the native American types have stripes in oddly ugly colors. Other strains are far more inexpensive, and one from South Africa, said to be based on Dutch breeding, is less than half the price, but it is just another Amaryllis to me. To be successful with Amaryllis one should purchase the biggest possible bulbs—as large as a big man's fist, say 12 inches in circumference or more—so that it will produce 2 or more scapes. It is best to pot the bulbs in rich soil in pottery that isn't more than an inch larger, all around, than the bulb, for roots should be pot bound. Incidentally, return any bulb to the supplier if it doesn't have a good supply of fleshy roots. Use bottom heat to get the bulb started—the top of a radiator with a thick copy of *Time* as an insulator. Its spectacular flowers appear in January or February and keep a week or more in a cool location.

After the flowers are gone, cut off the scapes. You'll note that the bulb is smaller after this massive flowering effort. Six to 10 huge leaves will then grow, and they should be kept growing until mid-October to rebuild the bulb. Then withdraw water. The leaves will wither. Then cut them off and put the pot in a warm (70°), dry place for a month to 6 weeks. This rest period sets the bud. Then bring it out again, apply water, bottom-heat, and you should have another excellent display—year after year, in fact. You need a modest amount of heat and full sun to make Amaryllis grow well—neither of which are too hard to find. The Warmenhoven strain can be bought in white, and in shades of dark red, scarlet, pink, salmon, and rose and white, the last quite lovely, for the rose seems to flow like water color on the white background. They cost about $7 each, bare root. Named varieties in this strain are hard to find, but worth the trouble. About $10 to $12 takes these home.

ambigua (*am-big'you-a*) *doubtful*

amethystinum (*am-e-this'tin-um*) *violet blue*

Amsonia
Am-sown'ee-uh

Amsonia. There are only 7 species in this genus—2 American, the rest Japanese. They are especially hardy, but few are grown for ornament. The following variety does best in ordinary soil in part shade. It likes moisture and makes an excellent plant for the edge of woodland, in a wild garden, or for a similar spot in a shrub border. It can be propagated easily by division in very early spring, which is the only time to plant or move them.

A. Tabernaemontana. This species has very dense clusters of soft blue flowers in May and June on stems about 18 inches high.

Anchusa
An-choo'sa

Alkanet. These charming early bloomers from the Old World belong to the Forget-me-not order and are grown widely for their showy flowers. They like a deep, well-drained soil, not too heavy, and do best in full sun. Plant them only in the spring.

A. Dropmore. Blue flowers all summer on 4- to 5-feet spikes. Use single specimens in the border or in groups of 3 about 18 inches apart.

***A. myosotidiflora.** Clusters of flowers resembling Forget-me-nots in May and June. This species does well in semi-shade or full sun. Height is 12 inches, which lets this plant fit neatly in front of the border.

A. Pride of Dover. This fine imported hybrid is darkish sky blue in color. As blooms are on 4-foot stems it is a back-of-the-border plant and probably should be staked no matter where located.

A. Royal Blue. Growth and habit are quite different from most Anchusa. It is pyramidal in shape and grows to 3 feet. The royal-blue color is just as intense as one can imagine. *A. Loddon Royalist* is so similar to *A. Royal Blue* that experts can't tell one from the other. Both appeared in England the same year. Actually, they are identical. We suspect *A. Loddon Royalist* was a name made up to make it different. It was seen at shows a bit earlier but *Royal Blue* had already been announced. To reach for that "something different" many plantsmen behave like golfers who, when reaching for a better score, have been known to nudge a ball to a slightly better lie.

Anchusa Dropmore

Anemone

A-nem'owe-nee

Windflower. This most charming group of perennials is widely distributed over the temperate regions in many forms. The genus is a member of the buttercup family. They generally do well in any ordinary garden soil, but rich sandy loam suits them well and woodland soil is even better. Varieties, herbaceous and bulbous, are hardy and grow from 6 to 9 inches tall. Spring planting is best.

A. magellanica. Because it is a native of southern Chile, West Patagonia and neighboring frigid islands, this species is exceptionally hardy. The creamy white flowers (up to 1 inch across) bloom on 6-inch stems in early spring.

***A. Pulsatilla alba.** A white form of the *A. Pulsatilla* group which some authorities say is not a true Anemone. Others say it is, still others argue that the family resemblance is so close that there's no difference. It looks like an Anemone, smells like one, grows like one—so in this book, *A. Pulsatilla*, with its finely cut gray-green leaves and woolly buds, is listed as an Anemone. This sounds arbitrary, but when authorities disagree ordinary plantsmen just have to take matters like this in their own hands. Stems are 6 to 10 inches; all *A. Pulsatilla* do best in part shade.

***A. Pulsatilla Selected Reds.** The range of red tones is broad in this series. Stems are 6 to 10 inches high.

***A. P. vulgaris.** Woolly buds open purple and then turn to violet in early May. Stems are the usual 6 to 10 inches high.

***Anemones, Bulbous.** Culture of these gay and floriferous bulbous forms is so simple that anyone can grow them. All they ask is a moist but well-drained, cool location in good soil and light shade. Bulbous Anemones are effective only when planted in large clumps —6 to 12 bulbs in a clump. Varieties listed are 6 to 9 inches tall. Plant them only in the fall.

***A. blanda Blue Star.** Large, deep blue, single star-like blooms show in early spring, usually following Snowdrops. The blue is best described as intense.

A. b. Pink Star. This variety has the usual star-like blooms of the species; its color is Cyclamen pink, the center yellow. Inside the color is slightly paler.

A. b. White Splendour. The bloom is composed of 2 rows of slender, pure white petals which are golden yellow in the center.
***fA. DeCaen.** Large single blooms during May and June on tall stems in all colors. It makes an ideal cut flower.
***A. fulgens.** Vivid red or scarlet blooms about 2 inches across appear in mid-spring.
***fA. St. Brigid.** Large double flowers of every color bloom from May to July.

ANNUALS. One definition of annuals is that they are herbaceous plants which, started from seed in the spring, flower and fruit (throw seed) before they are killed in the fall by frost. So they live through only one summer. The best definition is that annuals are a group of plants that provide such masses of flowers so vivid and so varied in color and form in the heat of summer (a time few perennials bloom) that it's hard to believe. I never appreciated annuals, except for Sweet Peas, Stock, Snapdragons, and Salpiglosis (Painted tongue or Tapestry Flower), until I saw them in Canada, about 150 miles above the United States border in a Quebec mining town. The climate there is ideal for them—pleasantly warm, long days and cool nights, the season short. Frost, which comes shortly after mid-August, seems to kill them in their prime, but the truth is that they have been sharply stimulated by the days—which shorten rapidly in that far northern location as summer quickly moves to winter, practically skipping fall—and are ready to die, for they have already produced an amazing amount of seed and an astonishing number of flowers. They don't have time before frost to look straggly and unattractive as annuals do in the warmer parts of the United States. All plants respond in varying degree to the length of days; annuals most dramatically, because they have such a short time to live. A perennial that creeps or multiplies from bulblets also flowers and produces seed, but it probably doesn't give a hoot if the seed crop happens to fail occasionally—it knows it has another chance.

In the past annuals have been a little trouble. They had to be started indoors from seed, transferred to small pots, hardened off (which means getting them acclimated to outdoor temperatures), and then planted. If the gardener does all this himself, it's a passel of work. In the 1930's I grew annuals and perennials for several years from seed without a greenhouse, and, looking back, it's a great wonder I didn't chuck the whole business and go back to golf. In those days, of course, it was not easy to get well-grown annuals and decently produced perennials. In our neighborhood a pleasant spinster and an accommodating Italian, both owners of small greenhouses, produced annuals of fair quality but offered few varieties, and to buy any of them we had to place orders in the fall. Although quality perennials are still a scarce commodity in most local markets—largely because they take at least a year to grow and are therefore not quick cash crops—since World War II there have been remarkable changes in the growing and distribution of annuals. This has been due to the development of first generation hybrids (F_1).

Before the F_1 hybrids, annual seed production was only a moderately specialized form of farming—if a seed company produced an unusual variety, all had it within a year or 2. A new inbred variety reproduced faithfully and all a competitor needed to do was to buy the other fellow's seed and grow it for his own seed. There was, in other words, little product competition. Plant patents were costly and very difficult to police. The first generation hybrid changed the industry to aggressive product competition in a very short time. The reason lies in the way F_1 hybrids are produced—from 2 uniform inbred parents by hand pollinization. As each parent is established from innumerable crosses and selections known only to the hybridizer, the seed of the F_1 variety from the two inbred parents won't reproduce truly. Also, the F_1 varieties have the great vigor usually found only in hybrids, which makes them far more desirable plants than varieties produced traditionally. They were eagerly bought by gardeners, and I suspect that the "seed-savers" among them must have been considerably perplexed that seed from the F_1s produced innumerable zany colors and forms. In any event, F_1 hybrid seeds are fine proprietary properties, for they require no patents and can be sold without price competition as long as newer F_1s don't replace them in their class. This revolution in seed production happily coincided with the development of the modern local garden center, with the result that gardeners no longer must produce their annuals in the laborious old-fashioned way—the gay things are available already grown at prices that seem quite reasonable.

F_1 development now covers a broad range of annuals—Petunias (which account for half of all annuals grown in the country), Snapdragons, Marigolds, Ageratum, fibrous-rooted Begonias, Zinnias, and Impatiens. There are others. New Geraniums (the originator calls his "Carefree") are also F_1s. They are fine bushy plants that bloom heavily from July on, don't go leggy, and stay in bloom after other annuals and conventional Geraniums have stopped blooming in late August. Impatiens have been in tremendous demand in recent years, because the new gardening public has discovered that it is the only plant, annual or perennial, that will provide bright color in deep shade. It also is wonderful in full light without direct sun—one small sunbeam causes it acute distress, the affected leaves curl so quickly you just know they are in pain.

As you must have gathered, I have high regard for annual varieties that are F_1 hybrids. The plants are covered so heavily with bloom that one can scarcely see the greenery. This is particularly true of

Petunias and other bushy annuals. The gardener gets a carpet of solid color. Double and semi-double Petunias, F_1s or not, don't send me, but this could very well be a minority opinion. The blooms themselves are huge, shaggy things, lovely by the bloom, but overpowering on the plant. They seem gross to me—moreover, the flowers are so large that they tend to flop quickly unless culture is superb. Use of a few in the cutting garden is a good idea—they make excellent bouquets. Most annuals, it should be noted again, are bedding plants to be planted in mass; paint broadly with them, make believe you have a big, wide brush and smash the color around your grounds like a Motherwell. It is rewarding and you'll get better at it year after year.

In a work of this kind it makes little sense to put down the names of the so-called best of the F_1 varieties of annuals, because they are (1) all good and (2) every season new varieties are competing for favor. Go to the country's many seed catalogues for this information. There are many of them, all are free for the asking, and few have any varieties exclusively, for most seedsmen buy from the world's outstanding growers and catalogue honestly. They don't, for example, put their names on new F_1 hybrids. The more prominent U.S. seedsmen are: Burpee Seeds, 6300 Burpee Bldg., Philadelphia, Pa. 19132; Park Seeds, Greenwood, South Carolina 29646; Henry Field Seed & Nursery Co., 106 Oak St., Shenandoah, Iowa 51601; and Olds Seed Company, Box 1069, Madison, Wisconsin 53701. There are also good smaller seed houses. (See Nurseries, Mail Order.) And in the spring, if you decide you must produce your own annuals, it is hard to find a grocery or hardware store, a supermarket, or drugstore without packets of seed for sale.

This brings me to the business of explaining, in detail, the various steps that add up to pure drudgery when a gardener without a greenhouse attempts to propagate his own annuals from seed. Readers could have been referred to the seed catalogues, all of which go through this drill with precision. I toyed with the idea, but haven't because some of the things I learned about growing seeds aren't in the catalogues or other garden books. Not many. Some.

Let's put this down in cookbook form. Ingredients and equipment needed to grow annuals from seed are: as many 6- or 7-inch pots or pans (short pots) as you have varieties of seed; pea stone, coarse gravel, or broken pottery; good garden loam; sharp builder's sand; peat; handful of fine, slightly damp sand; 1 coarse ¼-inch screen; 1 fine screen; 1 bottle with a perfectly flat base; 2¼-inch peat pots —quantity equal to the number of plants wanted; 1 pencil, the point blunted; 2 dozen 4-inch plant stakes (more if you have more than 24 varieties); 1 mist spray; 1 large tub; sheets of glass (7 by 7 inches); 1 newspaper; 1 deepfat fry thermometer; several tomato boxes or flats.

Fill large tub with water and plunge clay pots into it, removing only when thoroughly soaked. Take 2 parts of good garden loam, 1 part sharp builder's sand and 1 part peat, mix, then drive it through the coarse screen. Mix again. Add enough water so that the mixture is just slightly damp, mixing while dampening. Then steam the mixture until the deepfat fry thermometer reaches 210° in the center of the mixture. You will need enough of this mixture to fill the clay pots in which you will plant the seed, and the 2¼-inch peat pots, into which you will transplant the seedlings grown in the clay pots. You can eliminate preparing a soil mixture—a tedious and scruffy business no matter where it is done—by buying a sack of *Redi-Earth, Jiffy-Mix,* or any other prepared mixture from your local nurseryman or garden center. But follow directions—all of them require moistening 12 hours before use, and, as none of them contains soil, they have only enough fertilization to support plants for a month. Thereafter plants grown in them will require small applications of liquid fertilizer every three weeks. Besides being clean, they have many other advantages, not the least of which is that they hold water far longer than loam-sand-peat mixes. Of course, it will be far easier to exterminate plants in them by over-watering, but that is nothing to be concerned about until we come to seedlings.

Now take the well-soaked clay pots and fill the bottoms with 1½ inches of pea stone, coarse gravel, or broken pottery (called crock), being sure the hole at the bottom of the pot is not plugged. Put the damp mixture in next, firming it down with the fingers as you are filling. Pound the pot on the bench lightly to firm it further and level the mixture about an inch below the rim. Now take the bottle with the perfectly flat base and press the mixture down evenly about ¼ inch—the surface should be smooth and level. With a pencil mark a 4-inch label with the name of the seed selected and push it down below the top of the pot. You are ready to sow the seed.

Seeds of many annuals are very fine. Almost all packets seem to contain so little seed that one's reaction on opening an envelope is that the seed business must be a nice one to be in. But don't be misled, for if you are not sowing for an estate with 10 gardeners, that packet will have twice as much seed as an individual can use. Because some of the stuff is only a little coarser than dust, it is hard to sow evenly. Use only half of it; save the remainder in case the first sowing fails. You can tap half of the seed out of the envelope over the surface of the soil evenly, but only if you have superb tweezer-and-finger dexterity and there isn't the slightest breath of wind. What one tries for are seedlings, evenly distributed, about ¼ inch apart. The easiest way to get this result is to take a teaspoon of slightly damp fine sand on a piece of paper and put half of the seed on it. Using the blade of a pocket knife, turn this over 7 or 8 times until it is thoroughly mixed. Take a small pinch of this mixture and sprinkle it evenly on a part of the surface; continue until the surface appears evenly coated, which is easily determined because the sand will be a slightly different color from the growing mixture. Throw away any sand and seed you have left over, although this will be hard to do, for one's tendency is to use it all because there was so little seed to begin with. Wipe off the bottom of the flat bottle (it should be dry) and press the sand–seed mix lightly into the surface of the growing medium. Water with a mist spray, but don't flood or the seed will wash to the sides of the pot. Put a sheet of glass over the pot, cover with a sheet of newspaper, and place it in 70° night-and-day temperature. If you err on the high side, think little of it—low temperatures are actually more dangerous than higher ones.

We now have time to backtrack a little to report on how larger annual seeds are handled in pots. One obviously doesn't have to incorporate them with sand, they are big enough to see how thinly they are being sowed. After sowing, cover them with the potting mix by shaking it through the fine sieve. A rule of thumb is to cover them about 3 times their diameter with the potting mix, but never over ¼ inch. Then press the mix with the flat bottle, irrigate with a mist spray, cover with glass and newspaper, and place in 65° to 70° constant temperature.

The foregoing discussion of propagating annuals under controlled conditions (indoors) should be used by gardeners living in the medium-cold and colder locations of zone 5 or northward in order to get the longest possible blooming period. In the warm parts of zone 5 and southward all annuals can be sown directly in the ground where they are to grow, then thinned as the seeds germinate. However, pot propagation for varieties having extremely small seeds is a more successful culture since even moderate rainfall will wash such seed away. It seems sensible to sow the following group of annuals, even though some have seeds of respectable size under controlled conditions no matter where they are grown: Ageratum, African Daisy, Marigold, Coleopsis, Cosmos, Globe Amaranth, Summer Cypress, Lobelia, Four-O'clock, Nemesia, Tobacco Plant (Nicotiana), Petunia, Tapestry Flower (Salpiglossis), Salvia, Snapdragon, Verbena, and Zinnia. These are the annuals which need constant warmth. Also, they can be brought along in succession to get the most out of the crop in a growing season, and this can only be done by control during the entire propagating period. They are called the "tender" annuals. This tender group probably accounts for better than 90 percent of all annuals grown in the country.

It may seem odd, but annuals are divided into hardy, half-hardy, and tender categories in nearly all garden books. However, hardiness in annuals has nothing to do with hardiness as we think of it in terms of plants which live over winter. The breakdown is a convention one accepts; they are English terms taken over from our Anglo-Saxon cousins, who are so experienced in the art of gardening and from whom we have learned so much. I find it less confusing to group annuals as being either hardy or tender (throwing the half-hardy ones in with the tender) than to define hardy annuals as those whose seed may be sown where it is to grow as soon as soil conditions permit—after the thaw when the soil mellows and is not the least sticky. This is well before the last frost. The hardies will sprout, tentatively poke out a couple of leaves, and sit, hardly growing, as they wait patiently for true spring, knowing full well that they can take a couple of degrees of late frost if that is the way Nature wants to play the game. In this period of making haste slowly above ground they are developing fine, deep and broad root systems. However, if the plants are permitted to crowd during this period, subsequent growth will not be vigorous. If a gardener has for the first time put seeds in the ground and watched them grow, it is hard to ask him to rip out half or more at this early point. To him this is pure murder, and I have no intention of even suggesting it. He should learn from experience, as I did.

Now back to those pots we planted earlier, which are in neat array in the greenhouse or all over an establishment without one. Check them every day for dryness and germination. The most common cause of poor germination is dryness, and the most common form of failure after germination is too much water, so one has a narrow path to follow. The best way to irrigate during this critical period is to plunge the pots in a tub of water and allow capillary action to bring the water to the surface. Use of a fine mist spray is satisfactory, but second best for the gardener who has never before grown plants from seed. If you use prepared soil mixes and have them damp enough in the beginning, the pots may not have to be watered until they germinate. Upon germination remove the glass immediately and expose the seedlings to lots of light, but not direct sunlight. Don't wait for little stalks to appear—uncover them when you see tiny irregularities on the surface. It is unmistakable; overnight the soil's surface will have changed. This is seen much easier if instead of looking down on the surface one carefully looks across it.

As soon as the seedlings have developed 2 leaves they are ready for transplanting into peat pots. Fill them with soil, firming it in with the fingers but not tamping it in hard. Bounce each on the bench and leave ½ inch of space for watering. Now you are ready to transplant by "pricking" the seedlings out of their first home and planting them in the peat pots. You will be amazed at how small they are. To dislodge them, take the pencil with the blunted point and loosen a few. Try to save all the roots of each of them, and, if possible, lift them so that a bit of potting soil clings to the root. Now use the pencil to drive a hole deep enough to accommodate the root system in the center of the peat pot. With the thumb and forefinger of your left hand pick up a seedling by one of its leaves and settle it carefully into the hole—but don't let it sink out of sight. Still holding the seedling, use the pencil to firm it—be careful now!—then press it gently into place. The first dozen seedlings will not be easy. You'll feel all thumbs, not to mention feeling immensely silly pushing these infinitesimal things around. On some of them you will undoubtedly break off that leaf you think you are holding so gently, but pay no attention—grab the other leaf and continue. Seedlings, you'll be happy to know, can take a terrific beating and live despite it. When you have a tomato box or flat full of planted peat pots, mark them by variety with a plant stake, water with a mist spray (keeping the force of the spray well away from the little plants helps) and if you're lucky none of the seedlings will flop over on their side and play dead. They are not, and as soon as the flooded ones dry out a bit they can easily be straightened.

Place the box of new transplants in good light, but keep them covered for several days to keep them out of the direct rays of the sun. Grow them at 60°. In a short time you'll see them shake themselves and get along with the business of growing. Seedlings, of course, must not be permitted to dry out. Keep using your mist nozzle for watering. On the hot days of spring they may need water twice, but remember that more plants are killed in greenhouses by over-watering than in any other way. "Damping off," a term you are sure to see occasionally, describes the effect of a fungus that kills seedlings. This is usually experienced before they are transplanted and is caused principally by sowing too thickly and not providing air circulation. Air circulation, I hasten to add, doesn't mean drafts —young plants hate them. Steamed home-made mixes and purchased mixes help prevent damping off. But when it hits, you'll know: every little plant lies on its side, dead. The fungus sweeps through a stand of seedlings quickly. It can be arrested with a fungicide, but affected plants never recover.

Before you can transplant to the growing location, bring the boxes outside so they get used to the lower temperatures. You'll have to cover them the first couple of nights—and any night the temperature threatens to drop to 33°. Hardening off takes about 3 weeks. I recall, grimly, bringing a whole crop inside about 6 times, for I didn't have decent protection for seedlings outside until I built a couple of cold frames.

If plants are grown well in the peat pots the roots will strike right through them. When you are sure danger of frost is over, plant them outdoors. Plant the pot—but break it on one side with your fingers; it doesn't disintegrate quickly.

Of course, when frost has passed and spring is here I put on a jacket and go to my favorite garden center to find out what they have in the way of annuals. That's the best way to propagate them. But every gardener should work from seed—once.

Anthemis

An'them-is

Golden Marguerite. Few species in this large Eurasian genus have ornamental value, except *A. tinctoria,* and it is about as well known and as widely grown as can be. It is not the least fussy about anything. It can be planted in spring or fall.

A. tinctoria Kelwayi. Flowers of this hybrid are single, a full 2 inches or more across, and a delightful dark lemon yellow in color. The plant grows to 3 feet under good culture and looks almost like a sunburst. It apparently has no pests. When cut the flowers last a long time.

Armeria maritima Laucheana

Aquilegia

Ack-wi-lee'jee-a

Columbine. Lacey greens and dancing blooms characterizes this lovely border plant found in high mountains over a broad range of the earth. Varieties listed are mostly long-spurred hybrids. They make excellent cut flowers and bloom over a period of 4 to 6 weeks, beginning in early June. Use ordinary cultural procedures. Most varieties grow 24 to 30 inches high and should be planted toward the middle of the perennial border. They have an exceptionally long season of bloom. Mark the fact that they seed prodigiously and that the seedlings, although they can be used, seem more bother than they are worth. Crowns of old plants sometimes get too high and if left may winterkill—to fix, dig up and plant the crown at the surface, where it first started.

A. chrysantha. The *chrysanthas* are favorites of Aquilegia fanciers, for they are bushy and very floriferous plants; they do not require staking, and the flowers are lovely dancing things. This one is a golden yellow and grows from 24 to 30 inches high.

A. c. Silver Queen. Pure white and probably one of the most useful white flowers that can be grown; it has an unusually long blooming season. Height of the stems is 24 to 30 inches.

A. caerulea Mrs. Nichols. Blue and long-spurred. Except for its 30-inch height, the plant is a dead ringer for the lovely Columbine native in the high Rockies.

A. Crimson Star. It has long crimson spurs, the center white, tinted red. Height: 18 to 30 inches.

A. Langdon's Rainbow Hybrids. A fine strain developed by Blackmore & Langdon of Bath, England. The flowers are very long-spurred and come in bright mixed colors. They grow 30 inches.

A. McKana Hybrids. A recent strain, also in bold colors. They grow to 30 inches; colors are mixed.

A. Rose Queen. This lovely Columbine has flowers in shades of rose. The corolla is white. It flowers profusely over a long period.

aquilegifolium (ack-wi-lee-ji-foe'lee-um) leaves resembling Aquilegia

arborea (ah-bore'ee-a) tree-like

ARBOR-VITAE—*see* Evergreens, Dwarf Needle

Arenaria

Ar-e-nay'ree-uh

Sandwort. This genus of about 150 species grows in sand over the Northern Hemisphere, but very few are good garden plants. They like well-drained gritty soil. Arenaria can be propagated easily by division. They are basically rock-garden plants. Plant them spring or fall. The best species follows.

***A. verna caespitosa.** A very prostrate grower. Its foliage forms a dense green carpet which is starred in May with tiny white flowers rising an inch or so above the green. It is ideal for rockeries, or between paving stones or cracks in the terrace.

arenarium (ar-e-nay'ree-um) growing in sandy places

*Armeria

Ah-me'ree-a

Sea Thrift. A family of dwarf perennials with grassy leaves having a tufted habit of growth which are evergreen in most climates. Flowers are borne on globular heads. Armeria is useful as an edging plant and is excellent for the rockery. It grows best in a dry, sandy soil in full sun. Use 1-foot spacing, and plant it spring or fall.

***A. maritima Laucheana.** This variety is a 6-inch dwarf. Flowers are a deep pink in dense heads.

Artemisia

Are-ti-miz'ee-a

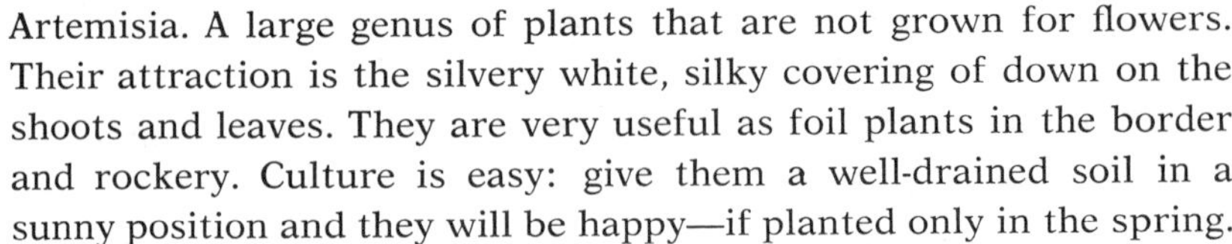

Artemisia. A large genus of plants that are not grown for flowers. Their attraction is the silvery white, silky covering of down on the shoots and leaves. They are very useful as foil plants in the border and rockery. Culture is easy: give them a well-drained soil in a sunny position and they will be happy—if planted only in the spring.

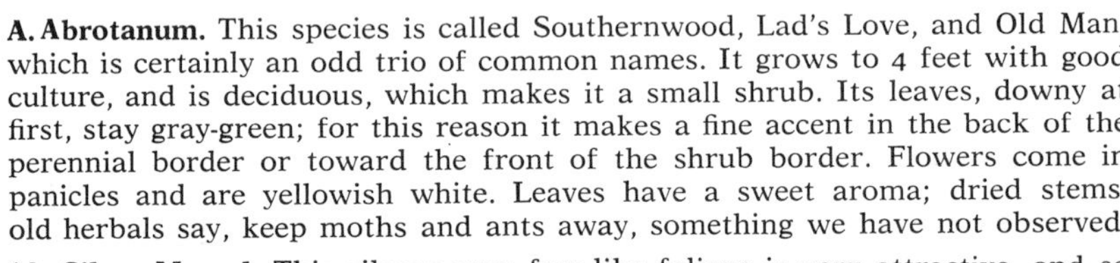

A. Abrotanum. This species is called Southernwood, Lad's Love, and Old Man, which is certainly an odd trio of common names. It grows to 4 feet with good culture, and is deciduous, which makes it a small shrub. Its leaves, downy at first, stay gray-green; for this reason it makes a fine accent in the back of the perennial border or toward the front of the shrub border. Flowers come in panicles and are yellowish white. Leaves have a sweet aroma; dried stems, old herbals say, keep moths and ants away, something we have not observed.

***A. Silver Mound.** This silvery gray fern-like foliage is very attractive, and so is the plant's form, which makes a perfect mound about 6 or more inches high and 12 or more inches across. It is an excellent edging plant, and we use it as a base for arrangements—it wilts at first, but is erect in a few hours.

***A. Stelleriana.** The deep-toothed, silvery white foliage makes this variety a showy plant for border or rockery. It spreads rapidly and grows only 6 inches tall.

Artemisia Silver Mound

Asarum

A-sar'um

Wild Ginger. Woodland perennials whose rootstocks have an aromatic odor. There are about 30 species, but few have garden value. Spring is the best time to plant.

A. europaeum. Shiny-leaf Ginger. This is a shade-loving plant that likes a good garden loam heavy with peat or leafmold and plenty of moisture. Although most Asarum are from the North Temperate Zone, few are hardy in very cold climates. *A. europaeum* should do well in protected southern exposures where temperatures do not go below minus 10°. Stems are long and fleshy, the leaves deep green, kidney-shaped, and slightly waved. Flowers are bell-shaped, brownish, and drooping. The rhizomes spread rapidly; plantings can be increased easily in the spring by division. Use it as a ground cover in a well-shaded area.

Asclepias
As-klee'pe-as

Butterfly Weed. There are over 150 species in this large group from the Western Hemisphere and Africa. Few are of interest in the garden and many are not hardy. The following species seems the best for most gardeners. It can be planted spring or fall.

A. tuberosa. This native American throws bright orange flowers in 2-inch umbels on 24-inch stems from July to September. It likes any good, well-drained garden soil in full sun. Plant it in bold groups for best effect.

Asperula
As-per'a-la

Sweet Woodruff. A genus of about 80 species of herbs (sometimes small shrubs) that are native to Europe, Asia and Australia. Flowers appear in terminal clusters, and although individual blooms are small the clusters produce an excellent show. They grow well in almost any garden soil, and may be planted spring or fall.

***A. odorata.** This herb can be used for flavoring wine (homemade wine), but its principal value is as a ground cover for shaded areas or in the rockery. It also does well in the crevices of walks or terraces or as an edging plant. The dried foliage is fragrant. What more can be asked of a plant?

asplenifolia (as-pleen-i-foe'li-a) having leaves much pinnately cut

Asplenium (as-plee'nee-um) ferns with foliage of leathery texture

Aster
As'tur

Michaelmas Daisies. We find it strange that American gardeners show so little interest in this lovely flower. Perhaps this is because the wild form is a weed in much of the country. The new hybrids, nearly all developed in England, are very popular in Europe. They grow in any soil and stand up under the toughest treatment. All they require is full sun and lots of water. There are scores of varieties, but we have found these to have the best colors and habits of

Asclepias tuberosa

Asperula odorata

growth. Remember, Asters bloom in August and September, so for this reason alone they are important plants in any herbaceous border. They should be planted in the spring.

Culture is very similar to the culture of Chrysanthemum insofar as separation and replanting is concerned. Dig them in earliest spring, divide and replant the vigorous outside growth, discard the old center. Asters may be pinched back to keep them from growing too tall, otherwise many varieties will have to be staked.

A. Ada Ballard. A lovely lavender-blue shade; each semi-double flower measures 2 inches across. Stems are about 36 inches high.

A. Alexander Wallace. The blossoms are pink with a yellow center, semi-double in form, and about 2½ inches in diameter when culture is good. It is a rather compact plant even though it reaches a height of about 36 inches.

A. Autumn Glory. Here is a variety that is ideal for the back of the perennial border, for it grows to 48 inches. Wise gardeners stake it. Blooms are large, double, and dark red.

A. Blandie. Ivory white and very floriferous, the form semi-double. Although this variety is exceptionally sturdy it will need staking, for it grows to 48 inches.

A. Blue Radiance. An import. For those who like light blue in Asters. Flowers are over 2 inches in diameter, petals finely cut. It has an exceptionally long blooming season, so use it for that reason, if no other. It grows to 36 inches.

A. Chequers. The blooms are dainty and single, ½ inch across, and light purple in color. They show a yellow eye. It grows mid-border to 36 inches, where it shows well. Best of all, it is a honey of a cut flower. It is also about the first variety to bloom.

A. Coombe Violet. The intense violet-purple variety grows into a strong 48-inch plant and its good looks won it an RHS Award of Merit.

A. Crimson Brocade. This is the finest crimson-red Aster we have seen. The bushy plants are covered with medium-sized semi-double flowers. It grows to 36 inches.

A. Davey's True Blue. Here is a color that is the nearest to Delphinium blue. It grows vigorously to a height of 42 inches.

A. Erica. It is Scottish heather in color, and produces masses of smallish semi-double flower on 30-inch stems.

A. Ernest Ballard. This variety carries the name of the man most responsible for the development of the modern Aster. Call these 2-inch, semi-double flowers, which are produced profusely, a rose carmine or a crimson pink, and you'll get some idea of how vivid they are. The plant itself grows to about 36 inches.

A. Eventide. The color to us is gentian blue, but some see it as purple—no matter, it's an excellent variety. Blooms are large and semi-double. The plant grows to 36 inches.

A. Farreri Berggarten. This large single Aster flowers from June until late summer. The profusion of Lilac-blue blooms, each with a large golden center, makes a great show in the border. Moreover, it's fine for cutting. It is a native of West China and Tibet and is not fussy about soils.

A. Fellowship. Flowers are a clear, light pink, of exceptional size and fully double. Furthermore, it is bushy, and rarely grows over 36 inches high.

A. F. M. Simpson. This variety produces an abundance of large single blooms on 36- to 48-inch stems. Color is purplish blue, which may add up to magenta to some, but not to us—it's really blue.

A. Frikarti. An old but fine summer-flowering Aster which blooms from late June until frost. This characteristic alone makes *Frikarti* highly desirable. The color is a delightful lavender blue. Its single flowers are from 2 to 2½ inches across and are excellent for cutting. It is a compact 24 to 30 inches high when grown well.

A. Harrington's Pink. This is an old favorite we cannot resist. It has pure pink blossoms in profusion on 48-inch stems. The variety should not be divided each year, but left until it crowds. It's a very satisfactory plant.

A. Julia. This big girl will grow strongly in the back of the border to 48 inches. Flowers are large and semi-double. The color is a pale Lilac pink. It is, as we say when words fail, a beaut.

A. Lassie. Flowers are large and double, and the color is the kind of lovely soft pink one generally associates with lassies. She grows to 3 feet.

A. Marie Ballard. This 36-inch variety is powdery blue in color, and the flowers are fully double when they first open. Later the eye develops, showing gold.

A. Mistress Quickly. This 36- to 40-inch variety is smothered with deep purplish-blue flowers. No, the color is not magenta.

A. Napsbury. This one produces large rich blue flowers with orange centers on 12- to 18-inch stems. It blooms from May until July and is an excellent cut flower.

A. Patricia Ballard. This lovely pink has a wine overcast which makes it unusual. Flowers are fully double in the young stage, with yellow eyes appearing as they age. It grows to 36 inches.

Aster Blue Radiance

Aster Napsbury

A. Peerless. The color of the semi-double blooms is a most satisfactory light silvery lavender. Put it in the back of the border, for it grows to 48 inches.

A. Picture. This one is very late flowering. The semi-double flowers are large, the color brilliant carmine with golden centers. It grows to 48 inches and makes a fine cut flower.

A. Prunella. Another ideal cut flower that blooms in September. It grows strongly to 36 inches, is covered with large, single, 2-inch rosy-purple blooms having yellow eyes.

A. Sailor Boy. Named because it is as robust as can be. But it is 36 to 48 inches high and we advise staking. Each stem has up to 40 violet-blue flowers with yellow eyes. It is a sensational cut flower.

A. Winston Churchill. Here is a variety that is very compact—it grows only to 2 feet. Blossoms, about 1½ inches across, are a deep violet red with pleasant yellow centers and they smother the plant.

Dwarf Asters. These varieties grow up to 15 inches high, and are segregated here for convenience.

***A. Audrey.** Compact as Asters come—well, more compact. It is 1 foot high and 1 foot wide, a lovely mound covered with lavender-blue flowers, and makes a fine edging plant.

***A. Prof. Kippenberg.** A compact, globe-shaped variety with dark green foliage and flowers of pale blue which completely cover the plant in August and September.

***A. Romany.** This is a spreading variety, 6 to 8 inches high, that is covered with single, rosy violet flowers.

***A. Snowball.** It grows into a big snowball 8 to 10 inches high and spreads 12 to 15 inches. The small white blooms have golden centers and literally cover the plant in early September.

Astilbe

As-til'bee

Spiraea. The best of these hardworking plants (beautiful for the border) come from China and Japan. They throw pleasant flowers in long panicles or spikes in June and July, then bush out with decorative foliage. Astilbe grows practically anywhere in full sun, but does far better with some shade, for the color doesn't burn out and the blooms last longer. It also likes a damp location but is not the least fussy about soils. Use the varieties in groups of three in the perennial border or mass them in shady locations for ground cover. They're tough and can be planted spring or fall.

A. Avalanche. Pure white flowers on 18-inch stems with deeply cut dark green foliage.

A. Betsey Cuperus. This pink variety is a very tall one—the flowering spikes grow to 40 inches and arch elegantly. It is old but one of the best.

A. Deutschland. The best white we have yet seen. It is very compact and vigorous. Flower spikes grow to 2 feet.

A. Europa. The spikes are of clearest pink and grow 18 to 24 inches high. The foliage is a very dark green.

A. Fanal. This variety has brilliant carmen-red flowers on 18-inch stems; the foliage is a dark reddish green.

A. Ostrich Plume. It is aptly named, for it reminds one of a plume of ostrich feathers. The color is a brilliant salmon pink. Height is about 40 inches when grown well.

A. Peach Blossom. A clear, light rose color, as you would expect, and the spikes are densely covered with flowers and grow to 18 to 24 inches.

A. Red Sentinel. The richest and brightest red variety. The plant itself has finely cut, distinctly reddish-green foliage. It grows to about 24 inches.

A. Rheinland. A vigorous and exceptionally bushy variety about 2 feet tall that is carmine pink in color.

***A. simplicifolia alba.** Its white sprays arch gracefully and are about 15 to 18 inches high. It will take lots of shade, and likes lots of moisture. It is a species of Astilbe from Japan and is generally hard to find.

***A. simplicifolia rosea.** The bright pink form of the foregoing, but somewhat taller. Like *A. s. alba* it is an airy, feathery thing.

A. sinensis hybrid Finale. Pink and also slightly arching; around 15 inches high. Its great value is that it is the last variety to bloom, the reason, of course, for its name.

athyrium (a-thee'ri-um) to sport leaf spores

atropurpurea (a-trow-pur-pure'ee-a) very dark red-to-purple

auratum (or-ray'tum) golden

aurea (or'ree'a) golden yellow

Astilbe

Aubertii (*awe-bert'eye*) *in honor of Pére George Aubert, French missionary to China*

Avellana (*ay-vel-lay'na*) *old generic name of Hazel*

AVENS—*see* Geum

Azalea

A-zay'lee-a

Azaka Exbury. Hardy zone 4, southward, zone 3 protected. Hardy Azaleas with very big blooms and brilliant colors were not available until the famed Azalea Exbury strain was developed in England by the late Lord Lionel Rothschild. They were developed from *Azalea Mollis* and *A. Ghent* types, and are as hardy. Unlike *Mollis* and *Ghent,* Exbury colors are vivid, blooms are large, many are attractively and brilliantly blotched with gold. Although offered by many nurseries today, *A. Mollis* and *Ghent* are inferior deciduous Azaleas, a bit cheaper in price but not worth the planting, for who wants to live a generation with a plant because it cost 2 or 3 dollars less at the beginning?

This strain of Azaleas was introduced to American gardeners about 20 years ago by what were then two small nurseries: one, in the Northwest, is known as Comerfords; the other, White Flower Farm, in which the author is a partner, is in New England. At the beginning neither organization had much luck with these exceptional plants. But that is the way it goes with plants other nurserymen don't know and don't sell. It seems to take the force of the whole industry to move the American gardener from his conventional ways. But about 10 years ago Exbury Azaleas began to be promoted by some of the larger nurseries, led by Wayside Gardens of Mentor, Ohio, which was being directed by its founder, J. J. Gruellemans, a great plantsman, now deceased. Almost without exception these powerful newcomers developed names that appeared a little different, certainly to the unknowledgeable, in an obvious attempt to make their strain seem unique; but all coupled Exbury with the Rothschild name in various forms—de Rothschild, Lionel de Rothschild, or just plain Rothschild. Some indicated broad exclusive agreements with the Exbury Estate, but these agreements cover only some of the varieties they offer. However, this jockeying for position should make no difference to the gardener. These new Azaleas are all Exbury Strain, a group of plants so remarkable that we have never seen a bad one.

The history of A. Exbury's development is interesting. Lord Rothschild, a member of the famous banking clan and extremely rich in the days before the Great Depression and World War II, was not only a great banker but a great gardener. He was no dilettante; Lord Rothschild not only worked over every detail in the development at his lovely estate in Exbury, but he also worked diligently on breeding Rhododendron—and Azalea, really a part of the Rhododendron family. He spared no money in his huge breeding program, for he had started it somewhat late in life and knew it could be successful quickly only through massive expenditures. He once employed 225 men—75 of them professional gardeners—to care for his 250-acre estate. By working with tens of thousands of crosses, instead of thousands, Lord Rothschild used his wealth to telescope time.

Lord Rothschild may have looked with a jealous eye on the work being done on Azaleas by Anthony Waterer, son of the founder of Knaphill Nurseries in Woking. In any event the Knaphill breeding was necessary to his work and so he bought control of it. This is why so many experts in the field tend to refer to the strain as Knaphill-Exbury, carefully putting the Knaphill name first. But we see no conflict and give each his due—certainly the strain would

Exbury Azalea

have moved slower into gardens all over the world without Lord Rothschild's prodigious energy and limitless money. Money, people are inclined to forget, is very useful stuff—whether we go to the moon or piggy-back a fine strain of plants with it.

Culture: In preparing the soil for Azaleas (or Rhododendron) one must be sure to load it with peat and humus, so that the roots will develop rapidly. For each plant use a bushel of ¾ damp peat and ¼ humus in the form of compost or leafmold, all thoroughly mixed with half a handful of an organic fertilizer—any that can be bought locally. After the peat and humus have been thoroughly mixed with the soil, dampen and let it settle for a few days. Then place the Exbury in a hole so that the branches are no deeper or higher than when the plant grew in the nursery. Do not place plants too close together, certainly not closer than 5 feet, for they grow higher than a tall man and spread like a fat one. Feed lightly in the spring every other year with organic fertilizer, and mulch the planting immediately with grass clippings, finely shredded year-old wood chip, decomposed leaves, or pine or redwood bark. Exburys do not resent slightly alkaline soils; they do well in them, in fact, but grow better in slightly acid ones. As many named variety Exburys are grafted on *A. Mollis* or *Ghent,* be sure to cut away suckers growing from below the graft when they appear, or one will soon have a plant showing two colors, one being the inferior understock. It won't be long before almost all Exburys will be produced from cuttings on their own roots. We suggest finding out what the root-stock is, and where possible, buy the plants that are not grafted. If the bushes become leggy and weak, or if they interfere with other Exburys, prune them back after flowering; new growth will appear about a month later, even on wood an inch in diameter.

Exbury Azaleas. Named Varieties. The following descriptions are sparse. The infinite parameters of beauty go sour when Exburys are heaped with adjectives. When you grow these things you will produce your own exclamations. There are, as noted earlier, many varieties of Exburys for sale in this country, and not all of them are English originations. This is the result of using outstanding seedlings as cultivars and propagating from them vegetatively. (Cultivar, an unfortunate term that has crept into horticultural language, means that the plant used for propagation is not a natural variety of the species, a difference so obvious that it makes no sense, but you'll see it used in most horticultural writing—it's horticulture's word of the year.) Also, in the quest for new-new varieties, hybridizers in New Zealand and Oregon, using Exbury as a base, are now introducing new strains "better-than-Exbury," they say. More power to them, I say, if they are successful. Their early work appears to be good. But those we've seen so far do not appear to be so much better than the Exburys as to be worth more than a remark now. It is inevitable that someday this great strain will be improved upon, but my guess is that it won't be until the present hybridizers collectively spend as much in time and money as Lord Rothschild did.

The following varieties are excellent, as good as the best in the field, even though some date back to Lord R.'s time. These and others in 15- to 18-inch sizes can be bought for about $10 each, but the price will probably creep up in the next year or so. Heights differ under best culture. As a guide we have called those that grow from 4 to 6 feet "short," "medium" indicates 6 to 8 feet, and "tall" applies to those that reach more than 8 feet. Rain or consistent irrigation from early spring to July, the growing season, is the principal factor that determines growth.

Aurora. Pale salmon pink with an orange blotch. Medium height.

Balzac. Red with flame markings on the upper petals; the flowers are fragrant. Medium height.

Berryrose. Rose pink with golden blotch. Short and spreading.

Brazil. Tangerine in color. Medium height.

Cecile. Salmon pink with yellow blotch. Tall.

Fireball. Deepest red. Medium to tall. Rarely puts on more than 6 inches growth a year.

Fireglow. Here is a vivid orange-vermilion color, as clear as a glowing fire. It is late flowering and has a spreading habit of growth. Short and spreading.

Gibraltar. Brightest orange red—a smashing orange with cherry, if you will. Tall.

Ginger. Brilliant orange overlaid with a pinkish flush, deeper orange lines down each petal. The upper petal is deep orange yellow. Medium height.

Golden Eagle. Bright, deep orange yellow. Medium height.

Harvest Moon. Lightest of yellows with a chrome blotch. Short.

Hotspur. Award of Merit. Flame colored. Tall.

Klondyke. Solid golden orange. Its dark reddish foliage enhances the golden bloom and the whole planting after flowers are finished.

Persil. Clear white with yellow blotch in the throat. Medium height.

Royal Lodge. Deep vermilion red becoming crimson; slight vermilion blotch on upper petal. It flowers late. Medium height.

Satan. A deep satanic red. This is a tall rather than a spreading plant. Annual growth is strong.

Saturnus. An orange-red as the delicately tinted rings of Saturn. Tall. Growth is strong.

Seville. As intense an orange as you will see. Blooms late. Medium height.

Toucan. Light creamy yellow, the margins of the petals tinged pink. There is a golden blotch inside. Tall and a very strong grower.

Tunis. Cardinal red changing to carmine, with golden flare. Another tall grower. It will produce up to 18 inches of growth a season.

Westminster. Clear almond pink. Medium height.

Whitethroat. This variety takes its name from an English warbler; it is purest white, and double. Very bushy. Short.

Seedling Exburys. Today, and probably indefinitely, the largest numbers of Exburys being grown in this country are seedlings. Hand-pollinated seed produce the best result, but little hand-pollinating is done here because of the cost. Most seedlings are satisfactory, but if one buys them there is a chance of getting plants that grow rapidly to almost giant sizes (10 feet or more) with few flowers. If a seedling sets lots of buds when it is 3 years old, the chances are better that the form and flower intensity will be more like the named Exburys. There is always the chance that the seedling will turn out to be worthy of propagation, but probably only a nurseryman will know this for sure. Seedlings are sold by color in 15- to 18-inch sizes for $6 to $7; those the nurseryman has not seen in bloom sell for a bit less.

BABY'S BREATH—*see* Gypsophila

BALLOON FLOWER—*see* Platycodon

baltica (*ball'tick-a*) *of the Baltic Area*

Baptisia
Bap-tees'ee-a

False Indigo. This very useful North American perennial adapts itself to most soil conditions, and, although it tolerates full sunlight, it appreciates a bit of shade during the day. Its root system is extremely tight and spreading. Fact is, once established, Baptisia can hardly be pried out of the ground and their vigorous spreading habit makes them weedy. The pea-like blooms are on 10- to 12-inch racemes; seed pods are valuable to birds that stay around all winter. It's a rugged plant that may be moved in spring or fall.

B. australis. This variety is dark blue, grows 4 to 5 feet high, making it an excellent back-of-the-border plant. Blooms show in June on 10- to 12-inch terminal racemes.

BARBERRY—*see* Berberis

BASKET OF GOLD—*see* Alyssum

Preparing and Planting Wire Baskets

Soak sphagnum overnight; squeeze out handfuls and mat it (left), as thin as possible, to the wires, so it will hold soil, which is added as mat is rounded over top wire. Put in plants, finish filling with soil, leaving 1½-inch dish at top. When irrigating, flood

BASKETS. Good hanging baskets are not too easy to find. The best made in this country are of redwood. The wire baskets fabricated here are dreadful—light in weight, the wires too far apart, and badly tinned. They have a short life.

Redwood Basket: In this type the redwood takes the form of long-lasting slats wired together with aluminum wire. The hangers go to each of the four corners. The basket is 12 inches square at the top, about 8 inches at the bottom. Larger ones are made but are hard to find.

Imported Wire Basket: This is the traditional planter used for trailing plants. The wire is heavily galvinized and will last 10 years or more; generally 12 inches in diameter.

Instructions for planting baskets: Cover the bottom of a redwood basket with large pebbles or broken pottery, add good potting soil, place plants, then fill with soil to within 1½ inches of the top, irrigate. Building up a wire basket with dry sphagnum moss and soil is a bit tricky, but following the adjacent drawing should produce satisfactory results. If preparing such a basket seems beyond you, ask a local florist to do it. (Note: You may live near swamps that grow mosses. If so, have it gathered fresh. Its use provides a fine, living green exterior.) Hanging baskets require attention when the weather is hot. Be sure the basket is thoroughly soaked each time. Frequent fertilization (every 2 weeks) is also necessary because constant watering leaches out plant food.

BEARD TONGUE—*see* Pentstemon

BEAUTY BUSH—*see* Kolkwitzia

BEE BALM—*see* Monarda

BEECH—*see* Fagus

Begonia

Bi-go'nee-a

Begonia. Tuberous-rooted. Not hardy. These lovely flowers of many tropical species have increased enormously in popularity over the years due to the work of hybridizers. Except for the culture of named varieties from cuttings by a very few fine nurseries (principally in England and Germany), all Tuberous Begonia bulbs are raised from seed, so the range is great, as no two bulbs can ever be exactly alike. Moreover, bulbs from seed vary in size from huge things 4 or more inches in diameter to an inch or smaller. Mere size constitutes the bottom of the market in quality, for blooms from very large tubers are generally small. The tuber which produces spectacular blooms is between 2 and 2½ inches in diameter, and thick. But more is required than correct size. They must be grown from hand-pollinated seed and then carefully selected for color. Most of this work is done carefully and well by a few large wholesale nurseries in California, which supply by far the largest part of the retail market. Other bulbs, mostly from Belgium, are cheaper but less satisfactory.

Culture: After pink buds start to grow on dormant tubers—generally when they are shipped, or in February when last year's tubers begin to show such buds—start them in flats or large pottery. The starting medium should be coarse leafmold or coarse compost, which will not pack and thus will not exclude air. Peat moss, which holds up to 90 percent of its weight in water, is not recommended. Space tubers evenly about 4 inches apart in the flat. Bury them with ½ inch of leafmold or compost. This is essential. We cannot point out too strongly that root development from the tuber's bottom, sides, and top is the way nature grows these things. The top of the tuber is the point where pink buds develop, and it should be placed up. Water carefully; maintain moisture, not soggy wetness. Place the

Rose-form Tuberous Begonia

Begonia Tubers from Cuttings

(1 & 4). Side shoot above leaf stem becomes cutting; (2) cut part of main stem and leaf stem, continuing into heartwood to get the necessary "eye" of heartwood (3), or cutting fails; (5 & 6) cut will quickly callus. Now prop cutting against side of 2½-inch pot (opposite) and fill with soil containing equal parts of loam, peat, and sand; water; put in box with glass top, expose to light—not sun. Rooting takes about a month, the tiny tuber forms later; first bloom following year

flat in strong light, but not direct sunlight—bottom heat of 65° to 70° will hasten growth. When the first two leaves are equally developed and after the danger of frost has passed, transplant to an outdoor bed or to a 4- to 5-inch pot.

Be sure to lift the tubers carefully, with their roots fully entangled in the starting compost. Remember, one is trying to grow close, compact plants. Lots of light, no direct sunlight, and dampness—not wetness—plus heat, give this result. If one pots tubers in small pottery (4- to 5-inch) repot them to 7- to 10-inch pottery when the root system fills the smaller pots. Both beds and potting soil should be ¼ sand, ½ leafmold or compost, ¼ garden soil.

When active growth is observed after transplanting, fertilize once a month with ½ tablespoon of water-soluble fertilizer (20-20-20) to a gallon of water (if you have 10-10-10 use a tablespoon). Proper fertilization maintains a deep green color and keeps the leaf "meaty" and thick. A slight turning under of the mature leaf is of no concern; a leaf that definitely "rolls" indicates over-feeding. The only disease Tuberous Begonias are subject to is powdery mildew, which can be controlled with *Mildont* or green sulphur (spray or dust with either). Don't let powdery mildew spread or it will destroy the planting for the season.

Allow plants to grow through November or until frost, for late growth stores up energy for the next season. Force potted plants into dormancy by gradually withdrawing water; dig bedded plants with an earth ball and let them dry out in a shed. When foliage drops and all growth breaks free of the tuber, clean it of soil (wash it), and cure it in hot sun for about four days until it is hard and dry. Be sure to remove every bit of old stem from the tuber or it will rot at that point. Store the tubers in open flats in a cool dry place until red buds again indicate growth—usually in February or

March. I do not advise using the same bulb over and over again. After the second year the tubers get larger and the flowers are smaller. New stock is required.

The technique of taking cuttings from named-variety Tuberous Begonias and developing tubers from them is clearly shown in the drawings. These are far too precious to use as bedding plants: use pot culture for terrace display.

Pendula Culture: Same as upright forms except that *Pendula* types are more sensitive to moisture. Use shallow baskets. Tubers which do not produce more than two runners at the beginning of the season should have the tips pinched out when first buds appear. This will make them bushy. Water carefully—never so much that they become soggy, never so little they become dry. Baskets, as noted, must be hung in locations free of wind. Like other Begonias they like lots of light.

Following are the various forms grown from seed; good stock can be bought for about $1 a bulb.

T. Begonia. Rose form from seed. The blooms look like great roses and the colors offered are wonderfully delicate. They come in white and in shades of dark red, scarlet, pink, salmon, yellow, and apricot.

T. Begonia. Picotee coloring in Rose form. This is the newest strain of Tuberous Begonias and it is great. The base color of the delicate Picotee form blends to a much darker tone on the edge of the petals. Flowers are huge. Colors are in shades of red, pink, rose, salmon, and apricot.

T. Begonia. Ruffled Camellia form. The flower is Camellia-shaped and large; petals are heavily frilled, ruffled, or scalloped. This type makes the best cut flower. Colors generally are white, shades of pink, red, scarlet, yellow, apricot, and flame.

T. Begonia. Hanging Basket form. Flowers, shaped like Rose or Camellia types but smaller, come in clusters and in great profusion. Nothing is as beautiful as a finely grown basket of the hanging form of Tuberous Begonias, and all anyone need do to be successful is to give these charmers the location they

Tuberous Begonias must be planted in shade; protect from wind. Start Begonias in damp compost in a warm place. Put tuber on side for drainage. Plant out in pots or ground after frost

Blackmore & Langdon Hanging Basket Begonia Roberta

require—a place free from wind and with lots of light, no direct sunlight. Patios are ideal. If you can't accommodate a hanging basket, plant a pot with three tubers, put it up high, and the lovely flowers will cascade to the ground. Do anything you can to grow them, for they are tremendously rewarding. White, shades of pink, crimson, salmon, and yellow are the usual colors.

Blackmore and Langdon Begonias. These hybrids come from the world-famous English nursery, Blackmore & Langdon, and are of a quality we have never seen equaled. Each tuber is produced from cuttings. There is no sense in talking about the form, color or the size of these flowers; they have to be seen—at the Blackmore nursery in Bath, England, or at White Flower Farm, Litchfield, Conn. Prices per bulb range from $3 to $25 each. Outstanding B & L varieties follow:

T. B. Crimson Velvet. A very large, bright crimson bloom. It flowers freely.

T. B. Crown Prince. A rich royal crimson. Blooms are unusually large.

T. B. Diana Wynyard. This variety produces about the largest pure white double blooms you will ever see.

T. B. Everest. It is obviously white and fully double. It differs from Wynyard in that blooms are ruffled like a carnation's.

T. B. Guardsman. A brilliant orange scarlet of unusual quality.

T. B. Harlequin. Snow white with a lovely pink picotee edge.

T. B. Lionel Richardson. Huge blooms that are a delicate salmon orange.

T. B. Ninette. Outstanding. It's a palest salmon apricot with very large blooms.

T. B. Rhapsody. This is one of the best of the salmon pinks and it is also easy to propagate.

T. B. Rose Princess. The color of the large bloom is between rose pink and salmon.

T. B. Royal Duke. A superb crimson. Blooms are not large but the color is deep and iridescent.

T. B. Sam Phillips. This is the best yellow in the B & L series. It's a little darker than lemon yellow. It can be propagated readily.

T. B. Symphony. A fine pink of medium size, which means it is not as large as a 10-inch dinner plate.

B & L Hanging Basket Begonias. Most of these hanging basket varieties are fully double and very floriferous.

T. B. Bettina. Pink; very free flowering.

T. B. Dawn. Buff yellow.

T. B. Lou Anne. Pale rose pink with larger flowers than are generally found in hanging varieties.

T. B. Red Cascade. A superb deep scarlet with a profusion of very large blooms. The stems are thick and handle the weight of the blooms to perfection.
T. B. Roberta. Deep scarlet. Small blooms.
T. B. Rose Cascade. Rose pink with very large blooms; it is the pink form of Red Cascade and just as good.
T. B. Yellow Sweetie. This variety with the awful name is pale yellow and is delicately scented, which makes it the first Tuberous Begonia variety we know of ever to have a perfume. The very pendulous large blooms literally cover the plant.

Belamcanda

Bell-am-can'da

Blackberry Lily or Leopard Flower. A genus with a single species which is grown practically everywhere. It is native to China and Japan. Plant spring only.

B. chinensis. This unusual tuberous-rooted plant looks like ordinary Iris when the leaves first appear. But when it flowers in July and August, the long sprays of orange blooms, spotted with crimson, bear no resemblance to Iris. Later the seed pods split and the seeds look like large blackberries. The plant grows best in rich sandy loam in full sun. Give it moderate protection in the winter.

BELLFLOWER—*see* Campanula

Berberis

Burr'burr-iss

The Barberry Family. This genus is widely used as hedging material because of its good fall color and berries. However, it is a major host of black stem rust, a dreadful disease of wheat, and some of the garden varieties have gotten out of hand by naturalizing. The U.S. Department of Agriculture is carrying out an extensive and expensive eradication campaign, and some wheat-growing states will not admit the stuff. Black rust has other hosts, none more accommodating than Berberis, but in my opinion the genus should not be grown in states that produce wheat. Also, there is always the danger of gardeners, who don't know of the peril, carrying it in. Some varieties of Berberis are less accommodating to the rust than others, but that's like having a typhoid carrier around who isn't a carrier all of the time. I also don't think gardeners are missing much; the Barberries are thorny things, not really outstanding enough to deserve the space many catalogues and nurseries give them. This is obviously a minority opinion.

BERGAMOT—*see* Monarda

Bergenia cordifolia

Bergenia

Ber-gen'ee-uh

Bergenia. An Asiatic native having 3 perennial species cultivated in gardens for their ornamental foliage. They need lime, gritty or sandy soils, and protection from the noonday sun. They grow in thick rosettes of fleshy leaves; the flower stems pop up from the base and provide panicules of bloom. Unlike many other Alpines they do not overrun other plants, another highly desirable characteristic. Plant spring only.

B. cordifolia. An excellent border or rockery perennial. This variety has large, thick, heart-shaped glossy green leaves. Large clusters of pink flowers about 12 inches high appear from May onward. The foliage is very useful for flower arrangements. It is hardy in Zones 4 and 5 if protected.

BERKSHIRE GARDEN CENTER. This is not a commercial establishment. It is a delightful, relatively small place to which one goes in Stockbridge, Mass., to see a wide variety of gradens in sizes that appeal to home-owners whose grounds are limited. Its curator seeks new varieties from sources all over the country and tests them for growth and hardiness in the rigorous climate of the neighborhood. He has discovered, for example, a variety of Holly that grows well in a protected location without special cover. Its growth is so slow it is practically dwarf. The center is endowed and managed by representatives chosen from a consortium of New England and New York garden clubs. No admission is charged, but most visitors, impressed by the quality and the low-key presentation of these delightful gardens, become non-resident members for a nominal fee, and thereafter receive its publications.

BETONY—*see* Stachys

BLACKBERRY LILY—*see* Belamcanda

blanda (*blan'da*) *pleasing*

BLANKET FLOWER—*see* Gaillardia

BLEEDING HEART—*see* Dicentra

BLUE COWSLIP—*see* Pulmonaria

BLUE SPIRES—*see* Caryopteris

BLUE QUILL—*see* *Scilla sibirica*

BONEMEAL—*see* Bulb Food

BONSAI (booun-sigh). Bonsai is the name of the highly specialized pot or dish culture Japanese and Chinese gardeners have used for centuries for growing very small trees in dishes. The trees are forced to grow into lovely shapes by tying their branches to heavy wires—and by judicious pruning. It is a culture that takes patience as well as skill. This is no place for a detailed discussion of this advanced gardening form. We refer you to the top U.S. authority of this culture. Write for *BONSAI—The Dwarfed Potted Trees of Japan*, published by Brooklyn Botanic Garden, Brooklyn, New York 11225.

The price is $1. Many plants in this book are useful for Bonsai work (*see* Evergreens, Dwarf Needle).

BOSTON IVY (small leaved)—*see* Parthenocissus

BOTANICAL TULIPS—*see* Tulipa

botryoides (*bot-ree-oy'deez*) *resembling grapes*

BOXWOOD—*see* Buxus

BROOM—*see* Cytisus

Buddleia

Bud'lee-uh

Butterfly Bush. This is a widely distributed genus of shrubby plants. Most of the 70 species are tropical. Six of them are cultivated in the U.S., but only 2 are hardy as far north as zone 5. One, *B. Davidi*, is in practically every nursery catalogue, and while the pictures of the many commercial hybrids are impressive, the plant in growth is not. However, it does attract butterflies, for it blooms from July onward, the time that butterflies are also in bloom. The species does not make much of a border plant—it's a tallish, flopping thing and in most cold climates it kills back to the ground each winter and should be covered to protect the crown. I suspect that its great popularity is due to the fact that its flowerheads take fine pictures and that it is so easily propagated that nurserymen can get a crop mature enough to sell in one season. Knowledgeable gardeners generally avoid them.

On the other hand, *B. alternifolia* and *B. alternifolia argentea*—both of which are hardy in zone 4 if planted in protected locations—are true shrubs with character. Both are shaped like fountains. Standing alone with their gray-green leaves they are beautiful, and when the branches are covered with dense clusters of dark, lilac-

Bulb Planting Table—Northern States

Arranged in Order of Flowering Period

Kind of Bulb	*Approximate Date Flowers Start*	*Height of Flowering Stalk*	*Inches to Plant Deep*	*Apart*
Galanthus	*Mar. 1-15*	*4″*	*3*	*3*
Eranthis	*Mar. 1-15*	*4″*	*2*	*3*
Crocus	*Mar. 15-30*	*5″*	*4*	*4*
Scilla sibirica	*Mar. 15-30*	*4″-6″*	*3*	*3*
Iris reticulata	*Mar. 15-30*	*4″-6″*	*4*	*4*
Chionodoxa	*Mar. 15-Apr. 10*	*3″-6″*	*3*	*1*
Erythronium	*Apr. 1-30*	*7″*	*3*	*3*

colored flowers in spring they are sensational. They do not attract butterflies because there are none around that early. Both species can only be bought in small pot- or can-grown sizes, because they are tap-rooted plants. They are almost impossible to move bareroot, and extremely difficult to ball-and-burlap. *B. alternifolia* is offered by several nurseries; *B. a. argentea,* with a tighter shape and more floriferous, is more desirable but harder to find.

BUFFALO GRASS—*see* Russian Buffalo Grass

BUGLE—*see* Ajuga

bulbocodium (bul-bow-kow'dee-um) Crocus-like

BULB FOOD. A recent cultural discovery in Holland indicates that as more and more gardeners hear about it, bulb food of the traditional kind, i.e., bonemeal regardless of how it is packaged, will gradually go out of demand. The Dutch bulb growers have found that by using sewage sludge they produce far heavier bulbs than ever before—bulbs that not only produce larger flowers but more of them. When planting bulbs in prepared beds the Hollanders mix 4 to 6 ounces of sludge per square yard, plus an equal amount of bonemeal; when planting in holes about a heaping teaspoon of sludge and one of bonemeal per bulb, mixed with the soil in the bottom of the hole, gives the same fine results. Milorganite is the only sewage sludge sold nationally in the United States. The Dutch say that this is the most important cultural development in the growing of spring-flowering bulbs that has come along in several generations.

BULBS, PLANTING DEPTH OF. As a general rule bulbs are planted at a depth equal to 3 times their diameter. (See adjacent table.)

Bulb Planting Table—Northern States

Arranged in Order of Flowering Period

Kind of Bulb	*Approximate Date Flowers Start*	*Height of Flowering Stalk*	*Inches to Plant Deep*	*Inches to Plant Apart*
Tulipa Botanical	*Apr. 1-30*	*5"-15"*	5	5
Muscari	*Apr. 10-25*	*4"-6"*	3	3
Narcissi Trumpet	*Apr. 10-25*	*18"-20"*	6	6
Hyacinth	*Apr. 15-30*	*8"-12"*	6	6
Narcissi Flatcup	*Apr. 15-30*	*16"-18"*	6	6
Narcissi Miniature	*Apr. 15-30*	*6"-9"*	2	3
Fritillaria	*Apr. 20-May 10*	*9"-12"*	4	3
Tulipa: Darwin (Ideal) Peony-flowered	*Apr. 25-May 5*	*16"-28"*	6	6
Tulipa: Cottage, Parrot, Lily-flowered	*May 5-20*	*20"-34"*	6	6
Scilla Campanulata	*May 5-20*	*10"-12"*	3	3
Anemone	*May*	*6"-10"*	4	4
Camassia	*May*	*24"-48"*	8	12
Lilium (Madonna)	*June*	*36"-48"*	1	12
Lilium	*May-Oct.*	*24"-48"*	7	12

Note: *In Southern states bulbs are planted as much as two months later than in the North—and they bloom as much as two weeks earlier. They should, however, be stored most of those two months in a refrigerator at 40-45 degrees F. Do not plant in direct sunlight and keep plantings moist. With only a few exceptions plantings become less and less perennial as the latitude moves south and the altitude drops. Southern gardeners should experiment with bulbs and use those types best suited to their location—or treat them as annuals. Soils for Bulbs everywhere: a good garden loam, but add bonemeal liberally to each planting, mixing it well in the bottom of the hole, plus ¼-teaspoon of sewage sludge.*

There are, of course, exceptions, the principal one being to cover the Madonna Lily with only 1 inch of soil. Also, if mice eat Tulip bulbs, plant them as deep as 10 to 12 inches in friable soils. They usually grow well at this depth, which hides them from all but the most determined mice.

BUTTERFLY BUSH—*see* Buddleia

BUTTERFLY WEED—*see* Asclepias

Campanula lactiflora Pritchard's Variety

Buxus

Bucks'us

Boxwood. Zone 5, southward, but zone 4 if protected. A fairly large genus of shrubs and small trees whose species are widely distributed over the world. Many of the species are hardy, including the famed English Box, which was brought to the American South generations ago. English or Common Box (*B. sempervirens* and its many varieties), although hardy in cold climates, must be protected against snow, the weight of which breaks the extremely hard but very brittle wood. It is, therefore, little used in the North. Korean varieties do not have this drawback, but most are coarse and unattractive. *Buxus Welleri,* immediately following, is a *sempervirens,* not equal to English Box but hardy in zone 4 and very good indeed. Plant spring only.

B. sempervirens Welleri. Leaves are glossy and growth is exceptionally compact. Unless plants get very large they do not require protection from snow. Late fall growth sometimes is killed back by icy spring winds, but it is easily clipped off in the spring. The variety shapes easily in any form and makes an ideal hedge that can be grown to almost any size.

caespitosa (*kas-py-tow'sa*) *growing in tufts*

CALLA LILY—*see* Zantedeschia

CALLIOPSIS—*see* Coreopsis

CALLUNA—*see* Heaths and Heathers

Camassia

Ka-mass'ee-a

Camassia. This hardy bulb produces flowers that resemble Scilla of giant size. The quantities of star-shaped flowers that appear on 2- to 3-foot stems are long-lasting. Blooming time starts with and continues after late Tulips. These bulbs can be used for naturalizing or in border plantings. Plant fall only.

C. Cusickii. Soft blue, tall and free-flowering.

Campanula

Kam-pan'you-la

Bellflower. A fine group of garden plants native to eastern and southern Europe, the Alps, and Asia Minor. Varieties range from dwarf to 3 feet tall and look superb in the perennial border. Some bloom continuously from June to October. Culture is not difficult, as they need only a moderately rich, well-drained soil. Be sure to give them protection each winter and divide half the stock every second or third year to keep it vigorous. Plant them only in springtime.

***C. carpatica.** This variety from eastern Europe grows in compact tufts never more than 8 inches high and throws blue blooms vigorously all summer. A perfect edging plant for the border or for a nook in the rockery.
***C. carpatica alba.** A pure white form of the foregoing.
***C. China Doll.** The flowers are delicate lavender on stems about 8 inches high. The exceptionally large blooms appear in June and intermittently afterward.
***C. garganica.** Bright blue, star-shaped flowers with small white eyes cover the plant's trailing stems in June. Ideal for the rockery. It grows best in partial shade.

Campanula carpatica

Campanula persicifolia Blue Gardenia

C. lactiflora Pritchard's Variety. These plants grow strongly to 3 feet. Colors are mixed and range from pale to deep blue. Plant in full sun, but this one can be grown in partial shade. Leave undisturbed for 3 to 4 years.

C. persicifolia Blue Gardenia. This lovely Campanula from Europe has large double blooms on 24-inch stems and its season of bloom is a long one—from June to October. It is most unusual and generally hard to find.

C. persicifolia grandiflora alba. This variety produces white flowers on 2-foot stalks.

C. persicifolia grandiflora coerulea. Same as the foregoing but the flowers are bright blue.

***C. Poscharskyana.** A species from Dalmatia with pale blue star-like flowers that is a vigorous creeper and entirely compact. Flowers bloom on 12-inch stems, not 4-inch as described in some texts. This gem blooms from June until cut down by frost.

***C. rotundifolia.** This European species throws dainty blue bells from July until September. It is ideal for the rockery, or for edging perennial borders. Plant it in full sun or light shade.

***C. Wedgwood.** This plant is difficult to get true to variety, for its flowers look like *C. carpatica*—but it is more dwarf. The flowers, a deep blue, bloom from June on.

***C. Wedgwood alba.** White form of the foregoing and just as pleasing and just as hard to find true to variety.

campanulata (kam-pan-you-lay'ta) bell-shaped

canadensis (can-a-den'sis) Canadian

canaliculatus (can-a-lick-you-lay'tus) channelled or furrowed

Canbyi (kan'bee-eye) in honor of Canby, U.S. amateur botanist

candidum (kan'did-um) white and shining

CANDYTUFT—*see* Iberis

carnea (car'nee-a) flesh-colored

CAROLINA LUPINE—*see* Thermopsis

carpatica (car-pat'ick-a) of Carpathian origin

Caryopteris

Carry-op'ter-is

Blue Spires. Zone 5, southward. This is a genus of low-growing Asiatic shrubs which blooms from August until frost—long after all other shrubs. It is covered with clusters of powdery blue fringed flowers. The plant, a nice rounded mound, grows from 18 to 24 inches tall and about 2 feet in diameter. Foliage is lanceolated and silvery green. Prune back to live wood in the spring. In zones 4 and 5 *Caryopteris* tops may kill back to the ground. If killed to the ground, protect the crown as you would perennials. New spring growth should be luxuriant and bloom heavily. Use *Caryopteris* in the perennial garden—it makes a great blue show with contrasting late-blooming annuals and Dahlias. Plant spring only.

C. clandonensis. This variation of the Asiatic species *C. incana* was first raised at Clandon, Surrey, England, in 1930, and imported here a few years later. Because of its difficult name it didn't sell. Then a nurseryman named it Blue Mist, called it his alone, and it's sold well ever since. A lovely plant under its botanical or promotional name.

Caryopteris clandonensis

Catananche

Cat-a-nan'chee

Cupid's Dart. It is beside the point that ancient Greek women used Catananche in love philters, but that is how it got its common name —Cupid's Dart. More to the point is that *Catananche* is a rugged plant, easily grown in ordinary garden soils, and that its flowers are both useful for cutting and everlasting. Plant spring only.

C. caerulea. Dainty cornflower-like blue flowers on stems rising above rosettes of foliage. It blooms from July to September. Height 15 to 18 inches.
C. caerulea alba. The white form of the foregoing.

CATCHFLY—*see* Lychnis

CATNIP—*see* Nepeta

caucasicum (*caw-kas'i-cum*) *of Caucasian origin*

cembra (*sem'bra*) *Italian for* Pinus cembra

Catananche caerulea

Chaenomeles

Key-nom'e-lees

Flowering Quince; Japanese Quince. Older botanical names, still in use for one species, are *Cydonia japonica* and *Pyrus japonica.* This is a small genus from China and Japan. Years ago Chaenomeles, tall- and low-growing species, were used extensively for hedges, and very lovely they must have been because the large flowers (up to 2 inches in diameter) appear on the stems before the leaves. Colors are gay reddish orange, scarlet, nasturtium red, and white. Fruit appears in the fall, but it can hardly be called decorative; it is not as big as orchard quince. But it is plenty big enough to be harvested and made into excellent jelly—its pectin content is high. There are many varieties hardy in zone 4; others with larger flowers are hardy only in warmer zones. Chaenomeles lost its popularity as hedging material when San Jose scale attacked it. Since then this scale has been controlled, and although the genus no longer is used for hedging (there are better plants) it is still widely popular—largely due to the fact that nurserymen find it an easy plant to produce. Because it is easily hybridized and grown from seed, its varieties are countless—the nurseryman who doesn't have his own "unique" variety is a lazy fellow. Most have long thorns, which makes for a good hedge but decidedly unpleasant maintenance. *C. japonica,* the Japanese Quince, is liked because it doesn't grow more than 3 feet. *C. japonica alpina* is a dwarf, a charming one rarely over a foot high, very dense and smothered with orange flowers over an inch in diameter. *C. lagenaria,* called the Flowering Quince, grows to 6 feet and throws its flowers, as do all Chaenomeles, in early May. Choice is a question of color preference and flower form; there are many double and semi-doubles, and, if I've failed to mention it before, flowers that are double tend to last longer than singles because they have more petals.

CHAMAECYPARIS—*see* Evergreens, Dwarf Needle

chamaedrys (sham-ay'dris) ground oak

Chaxii (shayks'eye) after Chaix, a botanist

CHERRY, FLOWERING—*see* Prunus

chinensis (chi-nen'sis) of Chinese origin

CHINESE LANTERN—*see* Physalis

Chionodoxa
Chi-oh-no-dox'a

Glory-of-the-Snow. These natives of Crete and Asia Minor bloom very early and produce dwarf 6- to 7-inch flower spikes holding 12 to 15 flowers. Plant bulbs about 3 inches deep. Excellent for rockeries. Fall planting only.

*f **C. Luciliae.** Very delicate blue.
*f **C. tmoli.** Clear blue, white center; blooms after *luciliae.*

CHIVES—*see* Herbs

CHRISTMAS ROSE—*see* Helleborus

chrysantha (kri-san'tha) yellow-flowered

Chrysanthemum

Chrysanthemum
Kri-san'thu-mum

Chrysanthemum. There are over 150 species of this most valuable plant, which ranges the temperate and subtropical lands of the world. The Chinese and Japanese have cultivated them for over 3,000 years. The value of Chrysanthemums in the garden is that they burst into color sensationally in the fall, the last of the flowering perennials. The choice of color and form is broad. Many gardeners buy Mums in bloom in the fall, not knowing, we suppose, that fall-planted Mums are not likely to winter well. It is easier to work with new stock in the spring. But this doesn't mean that one should resist good-looking Mums at roadside in September—the pretty things will sparkle in an otherwise drab garden and bunches of flowers can be stripped from their sides for arrangements indoors, and, if a gardener has a cold frame, he can probably winter them successfully.

Gardeners should remember that Chrysanthemums are tender when shipped, for they are greenhouse-grown plants, and, although hardened-off in cold frames, cannot survive sharp frost in late spring. They therefore need protection, if planted early.

Culture: Unlike most perennials, which grow from a loose crown and which can be left in the ground for several years, Chrysanthemums should be dug every year in early spring and divided. After digging, discard the center of the old root system and keep only the vigorous individual outside shoots. Each should have a good piece of root attached to it. These look like very small plants, and indeed they are, but they will grow beautifully during the season—just as well as the rooted cuttings you buy in the spring. After division there will undoubtedly be many more plants than needed, so give them away. Shoots or cuttings will need attention at various times during the growing season, for tops must be pinched back if one is to get a compact plant covered with bloom in the fall. The drawing shows how young plants are pinched. Keep inspecting and pinching back new growth (from the "breaks") until July 4 or a bit later. Then let them grow. Experienced gardeners have learned that "hardy" Mums are not as hardy as the ads imply—they winter their spring-planted Mums in frames. There are so many varieties of Chrysanthemums offered for sale today that it is impossible to pick the best for each locality in this country of so many different climates. Mums, which are particularly sensitive to the hours of daylight, are fooled by nurseryman who force them to bloom by artificially shortening the day with black-cloth shade. Football season Mums, if unshaded, probably would not bloom until late December. Fortunately, garden Chrysanthemum varieties have been developed so that they will rush into bloom in early September, others are bred to bloom in November. This makes it possible for gardeners all over the country to get bloom before the deep frosts that kill—light frosts do little damage to most varieties.

The following Mums do well in zones 4 and 5, but if one lives in zone 4 it is well to choose varieties that bloom before October 1. Blooming times noted were observed in Litchfield, Connecticut. I believe that the varieties described will be offered by the trade for a considerable length of time, for most of them have been performing well for a number of years.

Cushion Chrysanthemums are those varieties with low, compact growth which are very floriferous. They are excellent for cutting and for general display in the garden.

C. Apricot Sheen. All-America Award. This variety is a very strong grower with flowers up to 3 inches in diameter. Colors are a blend of apricot, peach and gold. Bloom starts in mid-September. About 20 inches high.

C. Astoria. Another Mum that grows to 24 inches. It's a yellow whose color is between canary and primrose. It blooms in late September.

C. Bonnie Blush. Some petals of the 2- to 3-inch blooms are spoon-shaped. Bonnie's blush is rose-pink in color. The plant itself is a 15-inch compact, and is in full bloom by Labor Day.

C. Bronze Bonnie Blush. The same form as the foregoing, but color is an apricot-bronze.

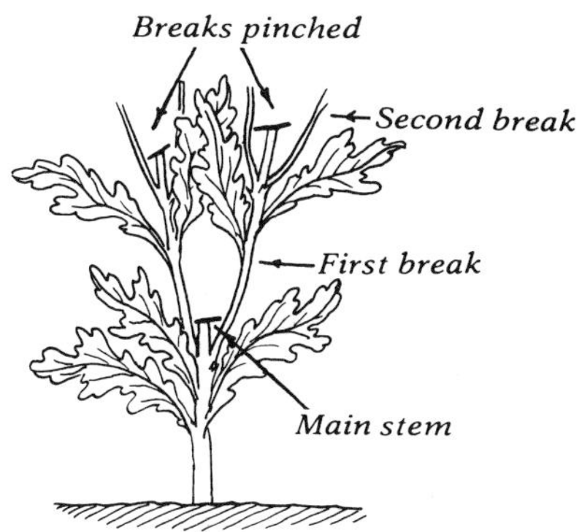

Pinching Chrysanthemums

First pinch back main stem to two to three leaves after Mum cutting or division is established. Growth (called a "break") appears above each leaf stem. Pinch back each break to two good leaves—keep pinching until July 4

C. Brown Eyes. This variety spreads well but is only 12 inches high. It is covered with bronze buttons from about September 15.
C. Gay Sun. Solidly covered with medium-sized yellow blossoms from September 20 on. About 15 inches high.
C. Grandchild. The blossoms are orchid-lavender with a red eye, and the bushy plant grows to about 15 inches. It flowers from mid-September.
C. Lipstick. A bright red, very showy, very compact plant. It blooms about September 25.
C. Little One. This very early Mum blossoms about September 10. The 12-inch plant carries masses of soft yellow buttons.
C. Minnautumn. A Mum that is reddish orange, grows to 15 inches, spreads nearly as much, and is a prolific bloomer starting the first week of September.
C. Muted Sunshine. The soft yellow blooms of this compact plant have a lovely Anemone-shaped center. It blooms from September 10.
C. Pancho. The blood-brother counterpart of Lipstick, and as fine a plant. It is orange, grows to 15 inches, and breaks into brilliant display the second week in September.
C. Preview. Orchid-lavender-pink blooms are 1½ inches across with a rose eye and show about September 10. It is 12 inches high.
C. Princess. A fine 14-inch dwarf with fringed salmon-pink flowers with a bronze cast that first show September 10.
C. Red Satellite. Waxen 3-inch blooms of a lively burgundy rose-red color on a 14-inch bushy plant. It's in flower September 10.
C. Ruby Mound. The name fits exactly. The plant itself grows to an 18-inch mound and is covered with ruby-red double blooms 2½ inches across in mid-September.
C. Sandy Sue. Here is a Mum that grows compactly to 20 inches and spreads farther. It is covered by September 20 with blooms that are terra-cotta bronze in color.
C. Sea Urchin. The flowers, which bloom by September 20, are about 3 inches in diameter; the plant itself is a tidy 15-inch mound. The color blends from yellow to chartreuse.
C. Snowbound. A fine little 12-inch plant whose 2-inch blooms open a pearly pink and change, as they develop, to glistening white. It is in flower by September 18.
C. Snowsprite. A very early variety growing 15 inches high. It has creamy white blooms with a canary-yellow eye which cover the plant in mid-September.
C. Sunloving. A 14-inch Mum that by September 20 is covered with 2-inch lemon to golden blooms.
C. Superior. Here is a plant 18 inches high with 3-inch orange-bronze blooms by September 18.

C. Tranquility. Soft primrose-yellow blossoms 2 inches in diameter cover this 18- to 24-inch plant in late September.

Decorative Chrysanthemums. Mums in this class are taller and more open in growth than Cushion types and the flowers are far larger—some are sizes usually found only on blooms of non-hardy varieties grown in greenhouses. The tallest varieties probably should be staked for them to make their best appearance. Decoratives make the best cut flowers and produce remarkably well outdoors.

C. Betty. A fine clear double pink with a darker pink tone showing in the center of its large flowers, which bloom about September 28.

C. Campaigner. An All-American Award Mum with bronze-gold flowers 3 inches in diameter. It blooms in mid-September on 24-inch plants.

C. Catherine Bauman. The 3-inch blooms are white with yellow centers. It flowers by September 15 and grows to 18 inches.

C. Chapel Bells. Pure white 2½-inch blooms on 24-inch stems. The plant grows tightly and is in flower about September 20.

C. Coppersmith. The color of this Mum's 3½-inch bloom is glowing burnished terra-cotta to deep amber. It grows to about 24 inches and flowers September 24.

C. Flameburst. All-America Award. Blooms are flame to deep rose-red overlaid on a yellow base. The 3-inch flowers open about September 22 on 24-inch plants.

C. Headliner. This All-America Award carries a 3½-inch flower with slightly recurving petals. The color is a very dark coral with the petals mostly gold-hazed on the reverse. It grows only 2 feet high in a most compact clump, and blossoms by September 25.

C. High Noon. Beautifully formed 3½-inch bright yellow blooms show on this vigorous 26-inch variety on September 15. The length of stem makes it splendid for cutting.

C. Juliet. Large sprays of 3-inch blooms, some with an anemone-like center. The color is rose-pink lightly shaded lavender. Growth stops at 2 feet and blooms come by September 15.

C. Lee Powell. A variety that produces masses of fluffy Chinese-yellow flowers with a slight orange tint at the center. It grows to 30 inches and blooms September 23.

Decorative Chrysanthemum

C. Martian. Here one gets huge, soft primrose-yellow recurving blossoms on a bushy 20-inch plant by September 25.

C. Mary Sue. Blossoms are rose pink with a coral eye and are 3 inches across; the plant itself is bushy and grows to 2 feet. It shows September 15.

C. Purple Waters. The crimson purple blossoms of this variety are more than 3 inches in diameter. Height is about 24 inches and it flowers in mid-September.

C. Red Headliner. This sort of Headliner is probably the best ruby-red decorative Mum. Blooms are 3 to 4 inches in diameter and the petals recurve. The plant itself is compact, grows 24 inches high, and blooms in late September.

C. Romeo. The 3-inch blooms of soft fawn, peach, and sandalwood, and 24-inch stems make this variety great for cutting. Flowers appear by September 20.

C. Soldier Bold. This variety is considered the best early red in the group. Blossoms are 3 inches across, recurved, and cardinal red. The plant grows to 26 inches and starts to show September 15. An excellent cut flower.

C. Sparkling. For a plant that grows to 22 inches this one is remarkably bushy in habit. Blooms are rose pink, lightly centered in gold, and 3 inches in diameter. It begins to flower at the end of September.

C. Sunny Glow. A very early Mum with 2½-inch orange blooms, which shade to maple-sugar brown then to soft bronze colors as they age. Height: 20 inches. It blooms by September 5, which makes it very early.

C. Trail Boss. This flashy thing combines peach, walnut, gold, and lemon and looks not at all like any TV trail boss one has ever seen. The flowers are cactus-type in form and 3 inches in diameter. It has 24-inch stems. The flowers show by September 20.

C. Yellow Glow. This 20-inch variety is covered with blooms of chrome yellow with slightly deeper centers by September 15. Fine for cutting.

Pompon Chrysanthemums. A distinct group of Mums that have small button-like flowers in unbelievable profusion. Their habit of growth is generally more open than the Cushions. Heights, of course, vary according to variety. These daintiest of Chrysanthemums are extremely valuable for table decorations.

C. Copycat. Its originator says that because the variety looks like a Marigold, he called it Copycat. It was helpful of him to point this out. Color is old gold to orange and it blooms from September 22. It grows about 15 inches high.

C. Spotless. The name, to us, seems more appropriately used to describe condition or character than color—particularly this 16-inch variety whose 2-inch pure white blooms have slightly creamy centers. It blooms by September 15. It's nice despite the name.
C. Sunset Pom. This English origination is bronze and orange in color and it flowers September 24 on 20-inch stems.

Spider Chrysanthemums. The flowers of this group of Mums have unmistakable characteristics—petals are tightly rolled, somewhat irregular, a few reaching out almost menacingly, as a spider's long legs might. They are prized as cut flowers and the bigger they are the better gardeners like them—some of the non-hardy Japanese types produced in greenhouses are sensational. These hardies, however, are satisfactory—just let them grow after pinching them when planted, but disbud side growth. Most spiders bloom late. These do well in zone 5, and in 4 in protected plantings.

C. Pink Pagoda. This variety blooms about September 25. Quills are 4 inches long, are darkest rose pink, and approach purple as they age. It grows to about 28 inches.
C. Star Trail. This spider often produces blooms 9 inches across, if it is disbudded. Bright yellow blossoms appear in late September.
C. Sunnyslope Splendour. Here's a white with a light green over-coat. It blooms in mid-October at a height of 30 inches.

Spoon Chrysanthemums. This group of Chrysanthemums is named after the shape of its flower petals. They are rather tightly rolled tubes in the center of the bloom, which then flatten out at the ends, spoon-shaped, most attractively. Forms range from single to semi-double and heights of plants from 18 to 24 inches. Spoons are airy things that make delightful bouquets. All are good cut flowers. A plant grown well is indeed a pleasant garden ornament.

C. Bauman Red Spoon. With soft rose-red petals and silvery tubes this 3-inch flower is a beaut. It stands early September frost well, grows about 18 inches high in rather loose form, and commences to flower about September 28.

C. Hansel. A deep rose-pink variety with silvery tubes. The blooms are 3 inches across. The plant itself grows to about 18 inches and spreads 18 to 24 inches. It is in flower by September 20.

C. Lemon Lace. It is creamy yellow outside, the center lemon yellow. Lacy pinwheel-like blooms are about 3 inches across. It's known as a spoon-anemone type. An excellent cut flower. A robust 24-inch plant that flowers in late September.

C. Shining Light. So far this is the earliest yellow spoon. The plant is a compact 18 inches and is covered by September 20 with 3-inch lemon-yellow blooms. Nice.

C. Starlet. An orange-buff spoon with coral tubes. The 18-inch plants are loaded with 2½-inch blooms by September 20.

Chrysanthemum maximum Alaska

Chrysanthemum Maximum. Shasta Daisy. Fine border subjects that like only a good rich soil and full sun. They should be planted 1 foot apart. Divide root stock every other year to keep plants compact and flowers large. All varieties must be protected in even moderately cold climates; the only protection in climates like Litchfield's (−20° and worse) is in a cold frame. Plant only in the spring.

C. m. Alaska. Large glistening white single daisy-like flowers with a yellow center. The 2-foot plants bloom heavily in June and July—and later, if the first flowers are cut back.

C. m. Little Miss Muffet. This variety is a fine dwarf for use in front of the perennial border. Its flowers are semi-double and daisy-like, the petals white, of course, with yellow centers, It blooms from June on and grows only 14 inches high.

C. m. Marconi. Double frilled sparkling white flowers from June onward on 2-foot stems. It is an excellent cut flower.

Cimicifuga

Sim-me-siff-you'ga

Snakeroot. Tall border plants that grow in ordinary soil in sun or part shade. They have large leaves and plume-like branching flower spikes. Plant spring or fall.

C. foetida intermedia. Spikes of white flowers 30 inches tall that come in bloom in September and October.

cinnamomea (sin-na-mowe'mee-a) cinnamon-colored

CINQUEFOIL—*see* Potentilla

CIRCLE FLOWER—*see* Lysimachia

citriodorus (sit-ree-oh-doe'rus) citron colored

Clematis

Klem'a-tis

Clematis. There are at least 300 species in this great family of vines, mostly natives of eastern Asia, the Himalayas, and North America. The varieties listed here are hardy, but the large-flowered ones are best planted in a southern exposure or otherwise protected from cold spring winds. A delight of Clematis is that most types flower all summer. Varieties climb 4 to 30 feet. Plant spring or fall.

Culture: Clematis are not difficult to raise, but they do require a bit of special treatment. Dig a hole and replace the earth with rich loam in which a cup of lime has been mixed. Before planting provide supports on which the plant can climb. After planting, cover with about 3 inches of peat mixed with a bit of well-rotted or dried cow manure. This supplies a cool rootrun, a requirement. Each fall use about ¼ cup of lime on each plant; in the spring fertilize lightly (2 tablespoons of an organic fertilizer). It is best to protect the base of the plant after deep frost with pine boughs or salt hay. Jackmanii types make a better show if the vines are cut back to 18 inches from the ground before new shoots appear in early spring. For *C. montana* varieties just thin out unwanted growth after flowering: *C. paniculata* should have unwanted growth pruned out in early spring. Sometimes a Clematis that has been doing well for

Chrysanthemum maximum Marconi

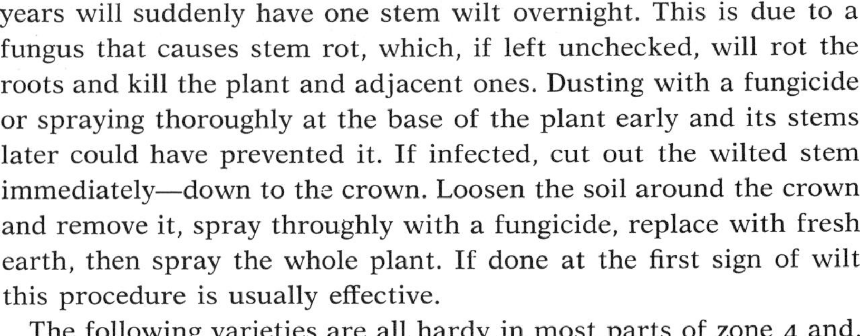

years will suddenly have one stem wilt overnight. This is due to a fungus that causes stem rot, which, if left unchecked, will rot the roots and kill the plant and adjacent ones. Dusting with a fungicide or spraying thoroughly at the base of the plant early and its stems later could have prevented it. If infected, cut out the wilted stem immediately—down to the crown. Loosen the soil around the crown and remove it, spray throughly with a fungicide, replace with fresh earth, then spray the whole plant. If done at the first sign of wilt this procedure is usually effective.

The following varieties are all hardy in most parts of zone 4 and, of course, southward.

Clematis

C. Comtesse de Bouchard. Satiny rose-pink flowers with curved petals.

C. Crimson King. This variety is the best red (with brown anthers) that we have seen in this lovely family of climbers. Also, the blooms, up to 7 inches in diameter, are of spectacular size. It flowers from late June to early September.

C. Duchess of Edinburgh. A large double white which causes no end of comment when in bloom in our gardens.

C. Jackmanii. The best deep purple Clematis, and it is very large-flowered.

C. lanuginosa candida. A giant single white variety which blooms most of the summer.

C. montana alba. This native of the mid-Himalayas, unlike some varieties, seems hardy anywhere. It is also remarkably vigorous and sends out scores of new shoots every year. Its blooms are smaller than the Jackmanii and other varieties, but there are literally hundreds of them—charming white star-shaped flowers with distinctive yellow stamens. The plant should be thinned out a bit after it finishes blooming in June.

C. m. rubens superba. Another Himalayan, just as hardy and vigorous as *C. m. alba,* but with clear pink flowers. Prune this after it blooms, too.

C. Nelly Moser. Mauve pink with a striking yet subdued bar of deeper pink on each petal.

C. paniculata. Called Virgin's Bower, this very hardy climber is a rampant grower that will reach 30 feet. A mature plant is a gorgeous sight when covered with pure white, fragrant flowers in August and September.

C. President. Flowers are violet blue in color and bloom freely.

C. Romana. A profuse bloomer. Its flowers are large, single, and pale blue in color.

C. recta grandiflora. This lovely Clematis does not climb. It is best used toward the back of the border or as a specimen elsewhere. It grows to 3 feet and is covered with masses of small fragrant star-like white flowers in June to August, which can be cut and used most satisfactorily in arrangements.
C. tangutica. A Chinese species that flowers all summer long and well into the fall. Its gray-green foliage is covered with masses of small yellow tubular flowers, followed by silver-gray seed clusters. Merely remove unwanted growth in the spring, rather than pruning it.

Clivia

Klee'vi-a

Clivia. This is a genus of 3 South African species, but only 1 is widely popular as a greenhouse or house plant. It is a member of the *Amaryllidaceae* family and practically a first cousin of Amaryllis, also a South African. Amaryllis grows from a bulb; Clivia develops from a bulbous root. Its leaves, unlike Amaryllis's, never die back during its dormant period, but stay a dark leathery-green the whole year. Its flowers come from an umbel atop a thick stalk, up to 20 of them on mature plants. They are shaped like the flowers of Amaryllis but are delightfully small. Many gardeners complain that Clivia does not flower. For this reason it is not popular, which is too bad, for they make spectacular house plants and their lovely blooms last a couple of weeks and longer if kept cool during the blooming period, which for mature plants generally comes in late spring. (Young Clivia tend to flower at any old time.) With the right environment, culture is far from difficult. They need considerable shade and a night temperature that doesn't fall below 65°—so a north window in a hot city apartment is fine. Too much light or a 60° temperature (if prolonged) causes leaves to yellow. The pot should be rested on a plate of moist pebbles for humidity. Feed with 20–20–20 (or any good liquid fertilizer) once a month during the growing season and keep damp, but don't let plants stand in water. Clivia needs a fairly large pot (about 10 inches), and the plant must be thoroughly root-bound. It will then flower regularly, sometimes twice. You will find that side shoots (baby Clivia) come up from the roots. Cut them off until the plant is established and blooming, then don't let more than one grow thereafter. And cut spent stalks after bloom to prevent seed development. When will young plants begin to flower? That would be nice to know. Some will bloom the first year, others take 2 years or more. Try to get as large a plant as possible to start with. Almost all Clivia are imported from Belgium as 2-year-olds. *C. miniata,* the species most often grown, has flowers, many to a scape, lily-like in shape, scarlet outside, yellow inside. This species won't be too difficult to locate, but *C. flava,* a stunning yellow, and other fine hybrids will be difficult to buy. They, are, however, worth a good search.

cneorum (nee-o'rum) resembles olive

coccinea (coe-sin'ee-a) scarlet

coeruleum (see-rue'lee-um) blue

COLD FRAMES. If one doesn't have a greenhouse, a cold frame is a great help in gardening. A 1-frame structure that can be covered snugly with a 6-foot by 3-foot glass or plastic sash will handle many plants. The height of the frame should be about 2 feet at back, about 20 inches in front; it's best to sink it about 1 foot into the ground. The back of the frame should face north. Total cost will be about $30 to $40 if made and installed by a carpenter; do-it-yourselfers will cut costs to bare materials, or $12 to $18. A cold frame has three principal uses: (1) starting seed (2) starting divisions into growth in very early spring and (3) holding over plants of doubtful hardiness—some of the Chrysanthemums, for example. You'll find lots of uses for it—but don't have too many frames.

Start with one, then add more if really needed. It should be placed in a sheltered location or unexpected winds will lift the sash and break it.

COLUMBINE—*see* Aquilegia

Comolii (kom-ole'eye) after Comoll, a botanist

compacta (com-pack'ta) close-growing

COMPOST. To build a compost heap, collect leaves, hay, weeds, and other vegetable matter, but not the tops of diseased perennials. Use about an inch of soil between layers of vegetable matter, which should be 5 to 6 inches thick. Build the heap about 10 feet by 4 feet and high on the sides—in other words, make it cup-shaped on top to hold water. To accelerate decomposition use a couple of handfuls of any nitrogenous fertilizer, as well as a few handfuls of superphosphate and an occasional one of lime. Keep on building the pile until you have one about 3 to 4 feet high, then start another, if needed. In a year the compost will be first-rate, but it must be screened for use in the garden. Use a coarse screen—½-inch mesh hardware cloth attached to two-by-fours. Place it in a level position about 2 feet above ground. Fork in compost, then drive it through the screen by pulling a hoe back and forth on it. Dump out rock and coarse undigested vegetable matter; refill the screen and repeat. All this, of course, comes under the heading of somewhat heavy work, but it's worth it.

CONEFLOWER—*see* Rudbeckia

conica (kon'i-ka) cone-shaped

conspicuus (kon-spik'you-us) conspicuous, easily seen

contorta (con-tor'ta) twisted

*[f]Convallaria

Kon-va-lair'ee-a

Lily-of-the-Valley. A genus of one species found in Europe and Asia and here in the high mountains from Virginia to South Carolina. Plant spring only, but pips can also be dug in one's own garden, separated and replanted in the fall.

C. majalis. An old and beloved garden favorite. If its pips (really individual root stocks from which the plant spreads) are of good quality, they bloom quickly and spread well. Imports are so well grown that they bloom the first year. Also, they can be shipped in late December or January for forcing inside in bowls. Later plant them outside. That's getting double use from a plant. Lily-of-the-Valley culture is that used for all woodland plants—a woodsy soil (one very rich in humus) and a location in half-shade or well-filtered sunlight. Tighten the soil firmly around the pips. In the garden fertilize annually after the tops, killed by frost, have been cut off.

CORAL BELLS—*see* Heuchera

cordata (core-day'ta) heart-shaped

cordifolia (cord-i-foe'lee-a) heart-shaped leaves

Coreopsis Sunburst

Coreopsis

Ko-ree-op'sis

Tickseed. A broad genus of daisy-like plants that are excellent for the border. Most species are American, but there are a few Africans. They are not the least fussy about soil, but thrive best in full sun. Annual varieties are known as Calliopsis. Plant them only in the spring.

***C. Goldfink.** This is the first really dwarf Coreopsis I have seen and it's a love. It came from Europe in 1967 and it performs wonderfully. The plant grows only 10 to 12 inches high, its stems are very strong, and it is literally covered with bright yellow blooms from late June to early August. It looks mighty perky and pretty in front of the border or in the rockery.

C. Sunburst. An excellent and showy border plant that provides golden double blooms on 30-inch stems from June until frost.

CORNFLOWER—*see* Stokesia

Cornus

Kor'nus

The Dogwoods. This most important genus of about 4 species is native to the North Temperate zone. They are shrubs which are generally hardier than the tree forms. The shrubs are important for their berries and the color of foliage in the fall. In winter the red tinge of the branches on most of them stands out in any garden. For no good reason, my own interest in the shrub species of Cornus has never been high, although I have admired greatly the ones I've seen in gardens. Many varieties are offered by American nurseries, probably too many, at least that is the opinion of Dr. Donald Wyman, Director of Arnold Arboretum. The mail-order nurseries offer few. I do have a deep interest in the tree forms. They are notably beautiful in bloom, change their coats to gorgeous reds and dusty pinks in the fall, and their berries, besides being colorful, are fine bird food.

Cornus florida is undoubtedly the finest ornamental tree native to North America and, because it demands little, it is planted everywhere it will bloom, which it does with abandon in zone 5 and southward, or in the decidedly warmer parts of zone 4. The tree lives on our hill (zone 4) and grows well, but it only blooms during the mildest winter—and then reluctantly. This is a great sadness. Planted in mass on highways or parks, *C. florida* is sensational, and our English friends shake their heads as sadly as we do—it won't bloom for them, either. It doesn't bloom in Litchfield because intense cold during the winter destroys the flower buds. Lack of bloom in England is due to the tree's desire to bloom at the *first* sign of warm weather. The freezing weather that inevitably follows kills the buds.

C. florida is the single white one sees most often. There is also a double form, *C. f. pluribracteata;* the red or pink form is *C. f. rubra; C. f. xanthocarpa* has yellow fruit. There are many named varieties, improvements (and some are) produced by selecting fine cultivars, which are grafted on ordinary understock. Mail-order nurseries offer many of these improvements at rather high prices, particularly when the cost of transportation is included. Good garden centers and local nurseries are better bets. *C. Kousa,* Japanese Dogwood, is hardy in zone 5 and southward. Its star-shaped blooms literally cover the tree, and they appear three weeks after *C. florida* has stopped blooming. If planted where it can be viewed from above—oh well, plant it even if you can't get this effect. It's a tree you'll have a hard time not looking at, and when its bloom is gone things won't seem the same around the place for a while. Note: using a dormant spray in early spring is a good idea in cultivating Dogwood, for it controls borers that sometimes attack when the tree is feeling out-of-sorts.

Corylus Avellana contorta

Corylus

Koe'ril-us

Hazel. Zone 3, southward. This is a group of about 8 species of trees, some of which bear nuts. They are from North America, Europe, and Turkey. Their lovely, broad, hairy leaves are generally dark green, but a few are purple. They are grown more for nut production than as ornaments, but nut quality except in Washington and Oregon is not good. There is one fine novelty noted below. Plant spring or fall.

C. Avellana contorta. Harry Lauder's Walking Stick. A large shrub, almost tree-like in some climates, with severely twisted branches. Leaves are lush, green, and hairy. The catkins that break out like Pussy Willow in late winter are interesting, but the black corkscrew branches are its chief interest and are particularly fascinating in winter when snow rests unevenly on them. The comedian Harry Lauder—if anyone remembers him—had walking sticks made from its fantastically contorted branches. Ultimate height is about 25 feet, but it takes years to grow that tall. Also, it can be contained by pruning. It is not difficult to find.

COSTMARY—*see* Herbs

Cotoneaster

Ko-toe-knee-as'ter

Cotoneaster. There are 40 or more species of this important group of shrubs and small trees, exceptionally fine garden plants, almost all from China. The flowers come in dense clusters in spring and are not the least important. The plant's great value lies in the masses of large berries, which range in color from black to brilliant yellows, oranges, and reds, in the fall. Some species are prostrate, others grow in the form of bushes up to 6 feet high. The more beautiful are evergreen and are not hardy north of zone 6. It is, however, unwise to be hasty about planting Cotoneasters in a prominent location, or making a hedge of them, because nearly all, no matter how well they have grown or how long, can be hit with fire-blight (a bacterial disease) and decimated in a short time. There are few satisfactory controls for it, if any; also, bacteria causing fire-blight strike suddenly, particularly in hot weather, and if they catch a plant in a weakened condition it has little chance of survival. Cotoneaster is also highly susceptible to red spider and to the lace bug, both easily controlled if caught in time. These three negatives are, of course, points one could not reasonably expect a vendor to promote.

C. racemiflora songarica, the hardiest of all the species, was a great favorite of E. H. Wilson, the famous plant hunter. It's a zone 3 southward plant. Species hardy from zone 4 south are *C. foveolata, C. horizontalis,* and *C. lucida.* Among those that thrive from zone 5 south are *C. bullata floribunda,* which has brilliantly colored berries; *C. divaricata,* a great spreader; and *C. microphylla,* which has the smallest leaves, is only 3 feet high, and is best for the rockery. Practically all others that are hardy in the foregoing zones are not desirable; most of the others are the beauties that survive only in zone 6 and southward. Not many of the foregoing varieties can be found in mail-order nursery catalogues; the best place to find them is in good local nurseries or in some of the large garden centers.

COTTAGE TULIPS—*see* Tulipa

COTTON LAVENDER—*see* Santolina

COWSLIPS—*see* Primula

CRABAPPLE—*see* Malus

Crataegus

Krat-ee'gus

Hawthorn. There are over 1000 species of these thorny trees and bushes native to the North Temperate Zone. Many are from North America, but only about a dozen are worth growing for ornament. Nearly all are hardy in zone 4 southward. Before planting one or a dozen it is well to remember that they are members of the Rose family, and therefore subject to its ills, all of them; but one dormant spray and two sprays to inhibit leaf-eating insects take care of this problem if done every year during the season. Also, Hawthorns are extremely thorny, more so than garden Roses, and hence unpleasant, to say the least, to maintain. As they resent being moved, be sure to calculate their location carefully so that a change will not be needed. The most floriferous ones are the English Hawthorns, named varieties that come from *C. Oxyacantha*. There are many thus derived. *C. Oxyacantha pauli* (Paul's Scarlet), with bright scarlet double flowers, is unsurpassed; *C. O. plena,* a double white, is effective. Hawthorns make inpenetrable hedges that can be beautifully cropped. *C. monogyna stricta* is the best species to use for hedging purposes, for it grows upright and is easy to establish. It is hardy in zone 4. Use young whips 1 foot apart.

*Crocus

Crow'cuss

Crocus. The large-flowered bulb of spring that everyone knows and loves. The bulbs, which multiply amazingly, can be planted any place except on a lawn requiring early mowing. An excellent location for Crocus is in Vinca or Pachysandra beds. Note that there are two types—the species, *C. chrysanthus,* and the hybrids; the former are notable for their unusual coloration. They bloom earlier than the hybrids, so by using both kinds one prolongs the blooming season. All can be used for the rockery or for forcing. Plant fall only.

Crocus

Hybrid Crocus. These are the large-flowered, spring-flowering crocus known so well to everyone. Bulbs should be the largest obtainable, for each will produce up to 6 blooms the first year. All varieties in this group except yellow are good for forcing.

C. Little Dorrit. Light blue bloom with a silver sheen.

C. Peter Pan. A very large, pure white flower, with orange stigmata.

C. Pickwick. Silver lilac in color with somewhat darker lilac stripes.

C. purpurea grandiflora. The best of the purple hybrid varieties. It is outstanding for forcing.

C. Yellow Mammoth. The name is quite descriptive—it has the biggest flower of the yellow hybrids.

Species Crocus. This is a large group of about 80 species, distributed from middle and southern Europe to Afghanistan, but fewer than 12 of them are represented generally in gardens. They flower most profusely, some varieties producing up to 20 blooms per bulb. Species Crocus, shorter than hybrids, have unusual blends of colors not found in hybrids.

C. crysanthus Balansae Zwanenburg. The inside of the flower is buff orange, the exterior a suffused brown.

C. c. Blue Bird. A soft blue flower with a white margin, creamy white inside, stigmata deep orange.

C. c. Blue Peter. The bloom is rich purple outside, blue inside with a golden throat.
C. c. Cream Beauty. Cream in color, shaded deeper at the base of the flower; stigmata deep orange.
C. c. Dorothy. A light yellow flower with bronze tones feathered on the outside.
C. c. Goldilocks. A deep, nearly golden yellow flower with a dark orange stigmata.
C. c. Warley. White with a yellow throat; outside shaded purple.
C. vernus Vanguard. The inside is Ageratum-blue; outside a neat French gray.

Autumn-Flowering Crocus. These charmers bloom in September, October and November, so gardeners can have Crocus at both ends of the growing year, which couldn't be nicer. They are also permanent plantings and increase wonderfully. Plant them as you do spring-flowering Crocus in locations that do not need mowing—around the bases of trees, in the rockery, and in open areas of the shrub or perennial borders. They should be ordered in the spring or late summer. Suppliers ship them immediately so they will bloom the first year. When delayed in the mails, you may find that some of them, if not all, have bloomed in transit. But just cut off the blossoms and plant them—they are perfectly good stock and will bloom the next year. Plant fall only.

C. Aitchisoni. The lavender-violet bloom is very large.
C. medius. This is the showiest of all the fall-flowering varieties and is slightly fragrant. The color is a uniform lilac blue and the large stigmata a deep orange scarlet.
C. sativus. It is called the Saffron Crocus in Kurdistan and Italy where it is native. The bloom is large and violet blue, the showy stigmata orange.
C. speciosus. It is deep blue with vivid orange stigmata. Outstanding.
C. speciosus albus. The large flowers are the whitest of white and the flower is very large. A beaut.
C. zonatus. The flowers are rose lilac in color and have a yellow throat. Excellent.

CUPID'S DART—*see* Catananche

CRANE'S BILL—*see* Geranium

cultivar (cull'ti-var), a horticulturist's term that applies to any variety not a natural variety of a species, a fact so obvious that a term for it hardly seems necessary for laymen to bother about.

CULTIVATION—*see* Weeding

CULTURAL INSTRUCTIONS. Some plants need special cultural instructions, but most require only good garden soil, full sun, and 1 inch of water a week. A few require special handling. The culture of the so-called tricky plants is described where they are listed in words or drawings. (*See* Iris, Lilies, Begonias, Roses, Fuchsia and Lantana, Fraises des Bois and Fraises Espalier, Gloxina, Azaleas, Tree Wisteria, Peony, Papaver, and Chrysanthemums.) Following is a list of short essays on gardening included in this work: Annuals, Baskets, Bonsai, Bulb Food, Bulb Planting Depth, Cold Frames, Compost, Dew, Double-Digging, Dried Flowers, Espalier, Feeding, Fertilizer, Flats, Greenhouses, Hand Tools, Hardiness Zones, Herbicides, Hill, Insecticides, Irrigation, Landscaping, Lawns, Lime, Manure, Mutation, Nurseries, Patio Gardening, Perennials, Perennial Gardens, *p*H Factor, Plant Family, Planting, Pots, Potting and Potting Soil, Preservatives, Pronunciation, Propagation, Pruning, Pruning Roots, Rock Gardens, Rogue, Sand, Shade, Soils, Staking, Sun, Thinning, Topiary, Topsoil Requirements, Tools and Machinery, Weeding and Mulching, and Winter Protection.

CUPID'S DART—*see* Catananche

Cusickii (koo-sick'eye) after Cusick, botanist

cyanea (sigh-an'ee-a) having blue tones

CYPRESS, FALSE—*see* Evergreens, Dwarf Needle

Cytisus

Sit'is-sus

Broom. It is indeed unfortunate that so few of these excellent evergreen shrubs are hardy north of zones 5 and 6. We suggest that gardeners who live close to the East Coast as far north as the coast of Maine experiment with the less hardy forms, which have a wide and lovely range of color. Some varieties will undoubtedly survive. Those in zone 4 will have to be satisfied with the following varieties, which are hardy on our sub-Alpine Litchfield hill.

Cytisus has pendulous, thin evergreen branches, its principal distinguishing characteristic. In May it is literally so covered with pea-like flowers that the green branches hardly show. The shrub makes a graceful, rounded mound and should be planted mid-border with other shrubs. Also use it as a specimen. Plants move best when pot-grown, and they must be small to move at all, for they are taprooted. It is best to "bundle" the plants in winter (tie them up with heavy twine or light rope) to limit snow damage to the branches. Plant them in the spring or fall.

Cytisus praecox

C. praecox. This variety is loaded with light yellow pea-like flowers in spring. Five feet is about its maximum height.

C. p. Lucky. This is a color break we found in Woodbury, Connecticut, and we named it Lucky for good reason. In May it is covered with large blooms, the basic color of which is peach. Each pea is flushed deep pink on both its keel and standard. It eventually grows to 6 feet.

DAFFODILS—*see* Narcissus

Dahlia

Dahl'ya, also Day'lee-ya

Dahlia. Not hardy. This tropical genus was introduced in Europe from Mexico in 1789 and has spread over the world. Just to count its many species would be difficult. We report here solely the bedding forms, which began to be developed in Europe in 1922 and which are now so extensive that they seem to form a separate race.

I am more or less acquainted with the giants, for I have seen them in bloom in climates where frost comes in December, but I've never grown them. Their culture should be no different from that used for bedders. Unlike the large forms, the bedders require no staking and have a longer season of bloom in temperate climates than Tuberous Begonias. They are at their best in late July, August, and September. In climates warmer than Litchfield's they show mightily through October, or until cut down by the first frost. They are extremely useful: put them in holes that develop in the perennial garden, edge a walk with them, grow them in tubs or large pots for the terrace or patio, or use them as they are used in Europe—in masses by variety. Mass-planting provides the most spectacular show, and because they are inexpensive few gardeners use less than a couple of dozen. To get the best results, give them full sun. Dahlias shouldn't be overwatered—irrigate and fertilize normally. They sometimes show virus, but it can be checked by feeding. If red spiders attack, they are easily controlled by regularly flushing the plants with water (using reasonably strong pressure) in very hot, dry weather.

If you have a greenhouse, pot the tubers about a month before the last frost, then set them outdoors. However, most gardeners get early flowers by planting directly in the ground after the last frost. The tubers should be covered with approximately 2 inches of soil. Bedding varieties are bushy. For mass planting use 2-foot centers or less.

To store tubers over the winter: dig them after the first light frost blackens the foliage, leave 2 inches of stem, wash, discard damaged tubers, put in sun to dry thoroughly, turning occasionally; when dry put each tuber in its own plastic bag, seal tightly, and store in a cool, frost-proof place. Plant only in the spring. There are many

Cactus-form Dahlia

Mignon-form Dahlia

other lovely bedders besides those following. I just haven't had the time to grow them.

Cactus Form. Cactus-form Dahlias, either single or double, have recurved petals that are quill-like in shape. They are showy flowers, usually up to 6 inches in diameter. Most of the varieties in this class grow as wide as they grow tall. All are compact and therefore excellent for bedding.

D. Autumn Leaves. The flowers are amber orange with rose tones on a 2-foot plant.
D. Border Princess. Double blooms in blending shades of salmon-rose-yellow. It is about 2 feet high.
D. Park Jewel. The color is a pleasant rose, a little on the dark side; the originator, for apparently no reason, describes it as "phlox rose." Another one 2 feet high.
D. Park Princess. A double of pure pink and a beauty that grows to about 30 inches.
D. Salmon Perfection. The double blooms are salmon red of an unusual shade. It grows to 2 feet.

Decorative Form. These Dahlias have flowers that are broad-petalled and flat and up to 6 inches in diameter. All make fine bedding plants.

D. David Howard. Although it grows to 48 inches at the end of the season, it stays nicely erect and bushes out only to 28 inches. Call the color orange yellow or old gold. The blooms are 5 inches in diameter, the foliage bronze.
D. New Drakestyn. The broad petals are a cerise red—wonderfully vital. The plant is very compact—24 inches in height with an even spread of 20 inches. The foliage is dark green.
D. Park Beauty. Its blooms are a bright orange-red—a flame color—and 5 to 6 inches in diameter. The plant grows to 24 inches and spreads that far. Foliage is nearly a mint green.
D. Park Delight. This has the same form and habit as the foregoing, but the flowers are white. It is a relief to find it *not* named Mount Shasta, or after any other snowy mountain you can think of.
D. Rocquencourt. The color of this variety is a warm red—one can't see the orange, but it is there. The plant grows to 24 inches and spreads about as much; the foliage has a deep reddish-brown cast.

D. Rote Funken. This beauty produces flowers that grow up to 4 inches in diameter and are deepest ruby red. The petals are iridescent in the sun. The foliage is a dark greenish purple and most attractive. It grows to about 36 inches but spreads only 2 feet. A gal with impeccable taste pointed to this variety and said, "If you did not follow the alphabet, you could put it first."
D. Yellow Cheer. It's a pale yellow beauty with a 6-inch flower. The plant is a compact 26 inches high, 22 inches wide.

Mignon Form. Charming small single blooms show on these Dahlias all season. They are fine for bedding. Some flowers are as large as 4 inches in diameter.

D. G. F. Hemerick. Masses of bright orange, single blooms on 18-inch plants.
D. Irene Van Der Zwet. Soft yellow single blooms in profusion on 18-inch plants.
D. Nelly Geerlings. Single bright red flowers, masses of them, show on this 18-inch variety.

Pompon Form. This class of Dahlia is perfectly described by its name. They are perky little balls that make delightful indoor arrangements. The plants themselves are large, but as they have very strong stems few need staking. They are useless as bedding plants because they tend to sprawl. Put a few in the cutting garden.

D. Albino. These nice balls are white and 2 inches in diameter. The plant grows to 40 inches and is about 28 inches wide; foliage is pale green, if you care.
D. Apropos. The most pleasant little yellow 2-inch balls imaginable. The plant grows to 36 inches and spreads as much.
D. Stolze von Berlin. Lavender-pink 3-inch balls on a plant that grows to 36 inches, but keeps a trim 20-inch figure, make this variety very useful indeed.
D. Zonnegoud. The flowers are a full 2½ inches in diameter and their color is deepest yellow. It is 36 inches tall and that much across.

dalmaticum (dal-mat'i-kum) of Dalmatia

Danfordiae (dan-ford'ee-eye) in honor of Mrs. C. G. Danford, a famous Crocus collector

Decorative-form Dahlia

Daphne
Daff'knee

Daphne. Zone 4, southward. A genus of about 35 species of evergreen and deciduous shrubs, many of which are not hardy. A few have excellent garden value in cold climates. The flowers bloom in a tight cluster at the end of graceful stems and have delightful fragrance. Soil should be lime-free, cool, friable, and well drained. Slight shade is desirable, but not necessary. Growth is slow. Even in the home garden they are extremely difficult to move after they are a few years old. Plant spring or fall.

***D. Cneorum.** Called the Garland Flower, this variety has a profusion of rose-pink bloom in springtime, delicately perfumed. There is a lesser flush of bloom in August. It rarely grows over 12 inches tall, but it spreads (the roots layer) as far as permitted. It is ideal for the front of the shrub or perennial border.
D. Somerset. This hybrid grows to 3 feet, spreads to about 4 feet—at least that has been the history of one I planted 15 years ago. Of course, if I had taken better care of it, it probably would have grown to 5 feet. Flower clusters are far larger than those on *D. Cneorum*, but it is not as compact. The blooms are flushed pink.

Separating Dahlia Tubers

Dig Dahlias before frost; cut stem to 2", wash—and follow directions on Page 111

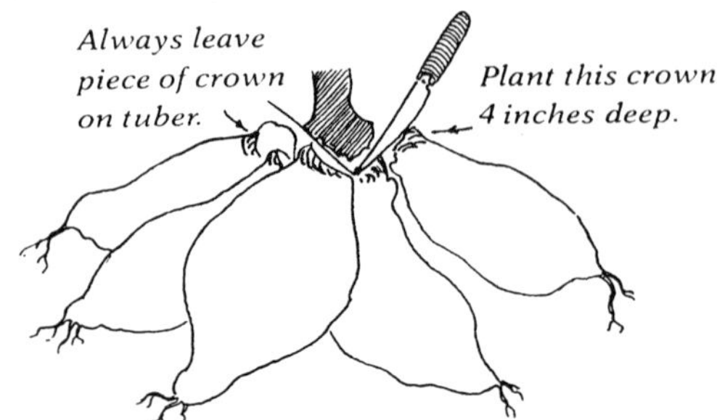

DARWIN TULIPS—*see* Tulipa

DAY LILIES—*see* Hemerocallis

deciduous (de-sid'yew-us) all woody plants, i.e., broad-leaf trees, which drop their leaves annually

DECORATIVE THYME—*see* Thymus

decussata (deck-us-sa'ta) at right angles

Delavayi (del-ah-vay'eye) after Delavay, a famous plant-hunter

Delphinium
Del-fin'ee-um

Delphinium. This is the queen of perennial garden plants. It is native to the North Temperate Zone of the world. Although many garden books and nursery catalogues say that large-flowering types of Delphinium, such as Pacific Coast, Blackmore & Langdon, Bishop, and other hybrid forms, are easily grown and are truly perennial—well, forget it. The hybrids are not truly perennial in the U.S., and they are easy to grow only if one knows how—about which more later. But no gardener worth his loam would stop growing Delphinium just because they are not as rugged as weeds. There is nothing more beautiful or more rewarding—getting just one plant out of twelve to mature to its 6- to 8- foot beauty is worth the trouble and the expense. Also it bucks up one's ego immensely.

Delphinium Border Planning and Culture: Delphinium require full sun and are best grown in a location protected from wind, for the flower head is so big that heavy rain will break it. Although the following applies to developing a garden composed solely of Delphinium, the preparation and culture is of course applicable to growing, say, just one Delphinium in an existing traditional mixed perennial border. In selecting a site one should remember that plants should not be closer than 24 to 30 inches from each other. This determines, obviously, the number needed. *Very high fertility is required.* (Italics, you know, are provided to stress words or ideas—and if it were possible I would have ordered double italics.) Normal fertilization, which is desirable for plants generally, doesn't work for *Delphinium* if you seek huge spikes—and why even bother with Dels if you don't strive for the spectacular. To achieve needed fertility do this: cover the planting area with 2 inches of well-rotted cow manure (or compost) and dig it 6 to 8 inches into the soil. Then spread 1 pound of 5–10–5 organic (or chemical) fertilizer per 100 square feet of border area, and put on an additional 2 inches of compost or manure. Dig (or mechanically till) this in as before. Irrigate the area thoroughly or wait for heavy rains (1 inch or more) before planting. Bed preparation may be done in late fall for

Daphne Cneorum

early spring planting, or in mid-summer for planting in the fall—it makes little difference. The point to remember is that a good interval is needed between preparation and planting. Preparation for Delphinium in an already established perennial border does not require a waiting period. After the plants start to grow in the spring, dig half a handful of organic fertilizer around each of them; repeat this twice before they bloom in July.

In succeeding years keep fertility high and continue to load the soil with manure, compost, or humus, as well as fertilizer. (Here I am, right back on feeding.) It is hard to kill a Delphinium by over-feeding it. I suppose someone will succeed in doing just this and say he's been misled; but I never have, although upon occasion I've actually tried. Note that Delphinium must be dusted or sprayed with green sulphur or *Bordeaux Mixture* to discourage blackspot on the leaves. (*Captan* is better, if available.) There is no cure for crown rot. And there is no cure for a Del that has fallen because it wasn't staked.

In choosing plants for an all-Delphinium border, we suggest *D. chinense* for the front, *D. Connecticut Yankee* or the species varieties in the middle, then a thick wall of the various tall hybrids in back. Because none of these plants will bloom at exactly the same time, the blooming period will be relatively long. Second blooms, about half as tall as the first flush, will appear in late September or October and continue until heavy frost. To get second blooms started, irrigate thoroughly after cutting back the first ones. One will also find that the amount of frost a Delphinium in full bloom can take without flower destruction, is remarkable.

What size plants should one buy? One-year-old field-grown stock is the size many garden books and nurseries suggest. And that's what I thought for years. But no longer. If one can get large plants growing vigorously in 6-inch containers, use them; but they will have to be found locally. Also, I know now what I long suspected, i.e., that 1-year-old field-grown Delphinium shipped bareroot are highly unsatisfactory. Few survive and they cost $1.50 or more. I got ridiculously low survival rates. But small plants started in late December in greenhouses become heavily rooted in their 3-inch peat pots (the roots actually break throught the pots) and can be shipped satisfactorily. You will have losses with them, too, but they are not extensive, or expensive. I find that the way to grow Delphinium by themselves in a border that has high fertility is to replace plants that fail every spring. Treat Dels as annuals, then one that lives over winter is a bonus. You will always find that some of them live several years. Plant spring only.

Bishop Hybrid Delphinium. This English series is grown from hand-pollinated seed. Bishop's Delphinium are known the world over and I find them a little hardier than large-flowered American hybrids. They only come in mixed colors. This strain is not easily found.

Blackmore & Langdon Hybrid Delphinium. B & L is the other outstanding English hybridizer of Delphinium. Fact is B & L have been working with this plant longer than any other English nursery and they have had some remarkable "firsts." Unfortunately, U.S. climate doesn't permit the growth of Dels from cuttings (as B & L produces them) and that is the only way to develop named varieties. Most plants from B & L seed are in lovely shades of blue, but you will occasionally get a pink or white one as a surprise. This series is also hard to find.

D. chinensis. Chinese Delphinium. This low-growing, branching Delphinium is a charming little fellow and blooms all summer if cut

Pacific Coast Hybrid Delphinium

back. The first blooms show late June or early July. Flowers keep a week in water. Treat it as a biennial. However, these should also be bought as bushy seedlings. Three varieties follow but they don't always come true when grown from seed.

D. c. album grandiflorum. Pure white. Height 24 inches.

D. c. Blue Mirror. Bright navy blue. Height 24 inches.

D. c. Cambridge Blue. A charming light blue, growing 18 to 24 inches high.

Connecticut Yankee Delphinium. The famous photographer Edward Steichen (also a famous amateur gardener) hybridized this pleasant new strain, which has an excellent color range. Foliage and height of plant resemble species Delphinium more than the modern hybrids. It is really a bush-type plant, hardly ever more than 30 inches tall, but a full-branching plant heavy with bloom. Colors are mixed.

Pacific Coast Hybrid Delphinium. This is the famous Round Table Series, which produces about the most beautiful Delphinium one will ever see. Individual flowers under good culture are huge. Spikes grow to 9 feet and must be staked even in protected places, for a beating rain with no wind can knock them over—even a heavy dew can hurt them. A second crop of smaller spikes (up to 3 feet) usually appears in the late fall. Unfortunately, the originator retired in 1969 and we do not yet know if his successor will keep the same high standards. It will be a great loss if the series disappears.

D. Astolat. Shades of lavender pink with a black or gold bee.

D. Black Knight. Shades of darkest violet (it shades almost to black) with a black bee.

D. Blue Bird. Shades of medium blue with a white bee.

D. Blue Jay. Shades from medium to dark blue with a black bee.

D. Cameliard. Shades of clear lavender with a white bee.

D. Galahad. Purest white. It blooms about 10 days later than other varieties in this series.
D. Guinevere. Outer petals light blue, inner petals lavender. It has a white bee.
D. King Arthur. Giant, dark royal-violet florets with a white bee.
D. Percival. Pure white with a black bee.
D. Summer Skies. Shades of lightest blue with a white bee.

Species Delphinium. These tried-and-true Dels are extremely hardy and will grow successfully under the worst conditions.

D. Belladonna. Light blue and long-lasting. Initial stalk may reach 5 feet. If pruned lightly, Belladonna blooms all summer.
D. Bellamosa. A dark blue form of *D. Belladonna.*
D. Casa Blanca. This is the pure white form of *D. Belladonna,* which grows vigorously to 5 feet. It is ideal.

Delphinium of the Future. There has been a great deal of work going on in Germany, Holland, England and Australia on new Delphinium strains. The hybridizers are all topflight. One of their objectives is to produce a red Delphinium, which is all right if one likes red in a flower that is normally a delicious blue or white in its native northern lands. When achieved it is sure to be a resounding success—the ad men will see to that. I, square that I am, reserve judgment—I have yet to accustom myself to the violet and mauve shades of two Round Table characters, Cameliard and King Arthur. However, the work is said to be coming along slowly—the new strains set little seed.

denticulata (den-tick-you-lay'ta) finely toothed

Delphinium Belladonna

Deutzia
Doot'zi-uh

There are about 50 species of this genus—all from Asia except 2 from Mexico. Actually, only about a dozen of them have garden value, and this is limited to their prolific, mostly white springtime

Dicentra spectabilis

bloom. Few pests attack them. As they have no fall or winter interest they bat .333 with no chance to do better. *D. gracilis,* which can reach a height of 6 feet but generally doesn't, is by far the most widely grown species and is hardy in Litchfield's zone 4 climate. *D. candelabrum* grows to 6 feet and produces a better display of flowers, but it is hardy only in zone 5 southward. Victor Lemoine, the great French plantsman, is responsible for originating 8 of the better Deutzia hybrids. *D. gracilis* can be bought anywhere; the Lemoine hybrids will be harder to find. Deutzias are all very friendly fellows—they'll bloom for anyone any place in the sun. They are perfect for home-owners who are just starting to garden. But the longer one gardens the more one is likely to tire of Deutzia, and also of *Spiraea vanhoutii,* the common Bridal Wreath, which also has little but a short period of intense spring bloom to recommend it.

DEW. The magic of dew, the result of the earth cooling faster than moisture-laden air, provides water that can be absorbed directly by the leaves of many plants and grasses. Fog can be considered as very heavy visible dew, and very foggy areas—California's Del Monte Peninsula, for example—grow very beautiful flowering plants, for the fog shades them and nourishes them with water until well past mid-morning. Dew and fog provide a neat water balance. One should note, however, that golf greens made of creeping Bent are massaged with a long bamboo fishing pole every time dew collects on them—the greens keepers know dew and fog encourage the growth of fungus. Heavy dews and fog, if prolonged, affect some perennials—black-spot mildew on Delphinium and white mildew on Phlox are examples. To protect leaves of susceptible plants from leaf fungus, dust lightly with green sulphur or *Bordeaux Mixture,* or better, with *Captan.*

*Diianthus

Dye-an'thus

Garden Pinks. A large genus of over 200 species, mostly from Europe and Asia, which includes Pinks, Carnations and Sweet William. Its garden species are beloved and are now grown all over the temperate zones of the earth. Dianthus should be planted in ordinary garden soil containing some lime. They make excellent rock garden or border plants. Most varieties bloom continuously from mid-June. Plant spring only.

***D. Allwoodii.** This is a hybrid of the old Garden Pink and the perpetual flowering Carnation. It's a grand cross, for the plant retains the compact growth habit of the Pink and has the wide range of color and perpetual-flowering quality of the Carnation. Flowers are very sweet-scented, mostly double or semi-double. *D. Allwoodii* blooms its head off from spring to frost and the more it is cut, the more it flowers. Colors are mixed. We suggest ordering a dozen, then choosing the pleasing colors and propagating them from cuttings. Thus it becomes your own private-label hybrid.

***D. Allwoodii alpinus.** This is a miniature of the foregoing variety with single flowers. It is a charmer for the rockery, stone walls, edging, or for whatever it is that you need a dwarf to do. It grows like a cushion—just 6 inches high. Colors are mixed.

Dianthus

Dicentra

Die-sen'tra

Dicentra. Only four species make up this small genus of garden plants which come from Asia and North America. Various hybrids have come to market the past few years. They are pretty but they collapse in misery if winters get a bit cold. They are also expensive. The following species is the only one I know of that is satisfactory on all counts. Plant it spring or fall.

D. spectabilis. Bleeding Heart. This old-fashioned species has been a garden favorite for years and it grows strongly for anyone. It's a fairly tall grower and has long racemes of heart-shaped pink flowers. Plant it in clumps about 24 inches apart. It shows best in partial shade and blooms in early spring. Its height is 30 inches.

Dictamnus

Dick-tam'nus

Gas Plant. A genus having only one species, which is native to Eurasia. It has a very long life. It has handsome ash-like leaves which have a delightful, tart fragrance. It is said that on hot, breezeless evenings, a gas forms on the leaves and can be ignited without damage to the plant. I once wrote I had never done this, knew of no one who had, thought the tale a pleasant myth. A surprising number of gardeners protested. It was not myth; *they* had done it, they said. They gave detailed instruction, which I followed with care one spring—and felt a little silly lighting matches in the garden at dusk. I got nary a pop nor a flash. Dictamnus should have a sunny, well-drained location. Never move it if more than 1 year old, for it will have grave difficulty trying to re-establish itself. Plant spring or fall.

D. fraxinella alba. Compact shrub-like growth and attractive spikes of pure white flowers during June and July. It is long lasting as a cut flower and grows to about 30 inches.

D. f. rubra. The same fine shrub-like growth as *D. f. alba,* with rose-pink flowers on 2½-foot plants.

Dictamnus

Digitalis

Di-ji-tay'lis

Foxglove. The name of the genus is Latin for the finger of a glove, but the reason the fox is associated with the name has nothing to do with the wily fellow. Fox is a corruption of folk—hence, little folks' gloves, or more exactly, fairy gloves. The species come from Europe and western and central Asia. Foxgloves are of easiest culture. They do best in a damp location in semi-shade. Some of the following varieties are biennial, others perennial. Plant them only in the spring.

D. ambigua. The true perennial type of this popular species. Flower spikes are 30 inches high. The tubular yellow flowers appear in June and July.

D. Excelsior Hybrids. The florets of this strain are carried at right angles to the stem, so one gets the full effect of the rich markings. Colors, though always mixed, blend beautifully. It is a biennial form that grows to 4 feet and blooms in June and July. It reseeds itself.
D. mertonensis. This is a perennial species of considerable beauty. The crushed-strawberry color of the flowers is most attractive. Use it in the border or in a shady position. It grows 3 to 4 feet and blooms in June and July.

distichum (dis-tick'um) with two rows

divaricata (div-are-i-kay'ta) spreading

DOGTOOTH VIOLET—*see* Erythronium

DOGWOOD—*see* Cornus

Doronicum
Do-ron'i-kum

Leopardbane. A most satisfactory genus of about 30 species from the Caucasus and southern Europe. Its leaves are heart-shaped, and daisy-like flowers show on it in early spring. One of the few good garden subjects in the group is *caucasicum magnificum,* which usually grows to 2 feet and makes excellent cut flowers. It prefers a moist soil and seems to do as well in partial shade as in full sun. It is easily propagated by division. When the plants go dormant in July and August gardeners who don't know them sometimes think the plants are dead. Plant spring or fall.

D. caucasicum magnificum. It has large, single, clear yellow flowers that are a joy. They also are excellent dried.

DOUBLE-DIGGING. Double-digging in gardening is a perfect way to start a perennial border. It is, however, horrendous work. If there is a man around the house who will undertake it, or a man who has become flabby and wants to toughen up, or hired labor is available and one can afford the expense—double-dig. The technique

Digitalis ambigua

is used to get a deep bed of topsoil for perennials, a precious thing few people find naturally on their grounds. Topsoil a foot or more thick exists naturally in few places other than rich river valleys. Topsoil on fields in the foothills of the Berkshires here is about 8 inches thick. After two decades ours is about a foot thick. By double-digging one can produce 2 feet of topsoil.

Here's one way to do it: Dig a trench the width of three spades and throw the topsoil to one side. With the topsoil out you'll be down in the ground about a foot. At this point spade out the subsoil and place it on the other side of the trench. You now have a trench about 24 inches deep, the width of three spades. At this point put a layer of topsoil in the very bottom of the trench and cover it with 1 to 2 inches of humus in the form of cow manure or rotted compost, plus 3 pounds of superphosphate and 1 pound of lime per 100 square feet. Mix all of this thoroughly with the soil. After all topsoil has been used, layer subsoil. It thus becomes topsoil because it now has humus. Now, start another trench 3 spades wide adjacent to the double-dug trench, and repeat. When the required area is double-dug put 3 pounds of superphosphate and 1 pound of lime per 100 square feet over the whole surface and fork it in. You will find that the bed, when finished, is 3 to 4 inches higher than the original soil level. It will slowly settle. Meanwhile it will provide drainage. Let the bed settle for a month before planting it. You'll get a grand result for the rest of your life with a double-dug bed. Of course, you may have a short life if you do it yourself.

Draba

Drah'ba

Draba. This genus of about 250 species, most of them dwarf, is as hardy as all get-out—and should be, for the plants are native to Greenland, the Alps and the high Himalayas. Some of them are also tufted or cushion-forming plants, and they've been neglected. We hope to find more varieties of this fine rockery plant. Draba is not the least fussy about soil, but insists that it be well drained and in full sun. Plant spring or fall.

***D. sibirica.** The growth of this species is prostrate, only about 2 inches high and it trails. In April and May clusters of small yellow flowers appear on pale green, grass-like stems.

DRIED FLOWERS. There are a surprising number of flowers that dry satisfactorily for winter arrangement. Drying is done by hanging fresh flowers, singly, upside down in a cool, dark, dry place. This keeps the flower straight, or at least straightish. (It's a good idea to dry some a bit crooked, otherwise a winter bouquet may look stiff.) If the drying area isn't cool the petals will mildew; if not dark, fading will be severe. There are only two rules about preparation before hanging flowers to dry: (1) start with a dry flower, freshly cut, and (2) strip off all leaves.

Some flowers dry better than others; however, the color of all of them is much duller than the fresh article. Delphinium make wonderful dried flowers but the darkest blue shades are the most attractive—the lighter blues and whites appear to have jaundice. One of the most successful flowers to dry is *Achillea Coronation Gold.* It has a big, closely-knit head that is gently rounded, and when dry it doesn't seem as fragile as others. It dries to a burnished gold. If placed blossom-to-blossom, rounding the head of the bouquet so that no stems are exposed after it is finished, the result is a pleasant, stylized arrangement.

Here are some other perennials to try: *Aconitum Fisheri, Catananche caerulea,* Echinops Taplow Blue, *Eryngium amethystinum,* Gypsophila Bristol Fairy and Perfecta, *Heliopsis scabra incompara-*

bilis, Lavandula Hidcote and Munstead, *Liatris, Limonium* (all perennial varieties), *Macleaya cordata* (its seed heads), and Rudbeckia Gold Drop and Goldsturm. Heather also makes an exceptionally good dried flower. Practically all Heath and Heather varieties, except the whites, can be used; most keep their colors well. Of course, Heather can be used with other dried flowers, but try massing them alone using only one variety in an arrangement. Heather is an exception to one of the basic rules for drying flowers—the needle-like leaves are not removed. Also, if arranged fresh, Heather will usually dry as arranged. A ball can be made by sticking the stems into a wire basket filled with dry sphagnum moss; it dries perfectly as arranged—no drooping regardless of angle.

Of course, there are lots of annuals that come under the general heading "ever-lasting," but except for Honesty and Statice they are stiff little things. Once arranged, dried flowers must be treated with respect, for they shatter dreadfully. Don't dust them with a vacuum; blow gently—with your breath, of course. Keep them out of sunlight or they will fade rather quickly.

Echinops

Dryopteris (dry-op'tear-is) a broad genus of ferns

dumosa (doo-moe'sa) compact, bushy

Echinops

Ek-in'ops

Globe Thistle. These are perennials from Europe with spiny white woolly foliage bearing handsome globular thistle-like flowers. They thrive in sun or light shade in ordinary soil, and bloom in July. Plant spring or fall.

E. Taplow Blue. The globular flower heads are deep blue. Height 4 feet.

EDELWEISS—*see* Leontopodium

Engleriana (en-gleer-i-aye'na) after Engler, plant-hunter

*Epimedium
Ep-im-ee'dee-um

Epimedium. This genus consists of about 10 species widely distributed over the North Temperate Zone. Only 3 are good garden plants, but they are the aristocrats of all ground covers. They prefer part shade and are so hardy in the warmer zones that, with a bit of protection, the tops remain evergreen. Epimedium's only requirement is a soil of half peat and half loam, light enough to let its creeping rhizomes spread readily. The flowers have curious, twisted petals and are borne in clusters on very wiry stems. Propagation is by division in July or August. Plant spring or fall.

***E. niveum.** Its pure white flowers bloom on 8-inch stems. Compact.
***E. versicolor sulphureum.** Charming, soft yellow flowers that dance on wiry stems. It is about 8 inches high and blooms in late spring. This variety is generally hard to find.
***E. White Flower Hybrid No. 1.** This hybrid has most unusual coloring—the flowers are red and yellow. It multiplies well and is very hardy.

epithymoides (ep-ith-i-moy'dees) similar to Epithymem

Epimedium

*Eranthis
E-ran'thiss

Eranthis. A Eurasian genus of about 8 species, of which only one, a tuber that some call a bulb, is widely grown. Eranthis is the Greek word for flower of spring. Plant fall only—as soon as the tubers arrive.

E. hyemalis. Winter Aconite. One of the most delightful of the spring-flowering bulbs and undoubtedly the earliest—which will surprise all those gardeners who think Crocus is the first bulb to bloom. Actually, Winter Aconite tosses out its lovely yellow flowers on stems 3 to 8 inches high two weeks before Crocus. One great feature is that it will flourish in shade, particularly on a woodland bank. It seeds very freely and for that reason increases its hold on a site rapidly and never has to be disturbed. If carpeted in a shrub border with Crocus, *Scilla sibirica,* and Chinodoxa, one gets a gorgeous early and long spring display. Plant 3 inches deep and 3 inches apart in a good garden soil that is well drained. Be sure to mix bonemeal and sewage sludge with them at planting time, and top dress them with the sludge each fall. The tubers should be planted as soon as received, so let other spring-flowering bulbs wait. They are ridiculously inexpensive—plant hundreds for mass display.

Eryngium amethystinum

Erigeron

E-rij'er-on

Fleabane. This genus has a large number of species, most of which have no horticultural interest. It is native to the high mountains of Eurasia and the Rocky Mountains. Varieties require no special treatment—just ordinary soil, sun and water. The species noted here are excellent border plants. Plant only in the spring.

E. speciosus. Single, Aster-like flowers show on 18- to 24-inch stems from June to September. They are blue in color, which makes them a great addition to those partial to blue or to growers of all-blue borders. It is an excellent variety for cutting.

E. s. Forrester's Darling. This has a bright pink flower, semi-double, with the same growth habits and qualities as *E. speciosus.*

Eryngium

E-ring'ee-um

Sea Holly. An attractive genus with serrated foliage. There are more than 200 varieties, all native in the North Temperate Zone, but only a few are considered garden plants. They are very valuable for the all-blue perennial garden, not an easy garden to grow. The species grow in ordinary well-drained soil and are desirable plants for any sunny border. They are also valuable as cut flowers. They may be planted spring or fall.

E. amethystinum. A metallic blue, thistle-type flower is borne on 2-foot stems. It blooms in July and August.

*Erythronium

E-ri-throw'ni-um

Dogtooth Violet. This highly usable genus of about 7 species is native to North America; most species grow from bulbs. They are highly useful in any partially shaded location. The soil must be well drained. Plant them 3 inches deep in bold groups. The bulbs multiply rapidly and are easy to grow. The hybrids, listed below, are the best bets. Fall planting only.

***E. revolutum hybrid Pagoda.** The canary-gold Cyclamen-shaped flowers appear on strong 12-inch stems—4 to 5 of them on each stem in spring. The foliage is marbled.

***E. revolutum hybrid White Beauty.** The large flowers are pure white. The center, however, shows a red circle and a creamy base; from this there grows a profusion of cream-colored anthers, which hang attractively. The leaves are marbled. An outstanding flower in the rockery or wild garden. Height is 12 inches.

ESPALIER (es-pal'i-yea) The art of training trees or vines to grow in exact geometrical shapes, usually against a wall or fence. French gardeners in the 18th and 19th centuries produced free-standing espalier that looked like huge 4- to 6-sided spears or tents.

Euonymus

You-on'i-mus

Euonymus. Zone 4—sometimes hardy farther north. This is a most versatile and easily grown group of shrubs. There are many varieties—some are trees, others shrubs, and some are climbers. Hybridizing has been done with the shrubs and climbers, but I haven't seen any that has attracted me—there are differences, of course, but they are slight to my eyes. So many of them are not hardy that I have had to leave them alone. Some of the vine species, although hardy, grow so devilishly slowly that all one can point to is rarity—to the few who find excitement in such slow motion. I do not seek vines that whoosh like Bignonia but they ought to look like something more than runts after a dozen years. The two following varieties seem highly useful. Plant them in spring or fall.

E. japonicus compactus. This bush, green and handsome and round, grows 1 to 5 feet. It is easily found.

E. radicans vegetus Sarcoxie. When trimmed, it can be grown as a shrub or hedge; when left uncut and planted at the base of old trees, it will climb 30 feet or more, densely covering the trunk; as a wall cover it is in a class with ivy. It can't be eaten, but that's about all one can't do with it. It is evergreen—and covered with orange berries in late fall. Nothing beats it.

Euphorbia

Eupatorium

You-pa-toe're-um

Eupatorium. A very large genus which is of North American origin, but few species have garden value. Those that have are prized for their profuse bloom that comes in late fall or early autumn—the time, we have often noted, when it is difficult to find showy perennials. They generally do best in light shade. No special culture is required. To increase your stocks of these out-giving plants, divide them in early spring. Plant spring only.

E. coelestinum. Hardy Ageratum. It grows to 2 feet, or well above the heavy growth of leaves which are thin and coarsely toothed. The color is an intense, deep blue and the flower heads will remind you of the annual Ageratum, from which it takes one of its several common names.

Euphorbia

You-for'bee-a

Euphorbia. A huge genus of over 1,000 species from Africa, the East Indies, Madagascar, Mexico, and Europe, but few are hardy. Plant spring or fall.

E. epithymoides. Milkwort, and numerous other common names. This is a showy, bushy herbaceous plant that grows from 12 to 15 inches high. The flowers appear in bracts which open yellow in late May and change to rose bronze as they age; foliage is a rich dark green. It is a fine accent plant for the border in a location more than normally dry.

EVENING PRIMROSE—*see* Oenothera

Evergreens

Dwarf Needle

Dwarf Needle Evergreens. Here are the varieties of unusual needle and needle-like Evergreens that are dwarf in form. Dwarf is a relative term applied to plants, and it does not always mean miniature. Some of these evergreens grow fairly large over the years, but compared to the species with which each variety is associated, those listed are indeed dwarf, for few will ever reach 15 feet. Some of their parents reach 120 feet or more. All of the dwarf forms can be contained by judicious pruning, or by planting them in restricted soil areas—a crevice of a rock garden, for example, to hold them to size by constricting their root systems.

We were attracted to Dwarf Evergreens because (1) we had seen and admired them greatly in estates here and in England (2) we found, to our considerable amazement, that few people knew anything about them as a group and (3) they were obviously ideal plants for today's smaller gardens. Finding the plants soon got to be a game, and trying to identify them after finding them proved to be particularly difficult and at times downright frustrating. We were told by various knowledgeable private and professional collectors that although it was a good idea, it was not commercially feasible, for the plants took too long to grow and gardeners knew nothing about them. So we blundered on and did a good amount of backtracking, but nevertheless got together about 30 varieties from cuttings. As soon as the plants were firmly rooted they were planted in a large border. The tiny 4- to 5-inch plants looked pretty ridiculous in the large space. Meanwhile we discovered that an English nurseryman had become engrossed with Dwarf Evergreens and had written a book about them. This proved very helpful in classifying them botanically. A trip to his nursery was less fruitful—he had too few plants to sell and we found that he knew no more than we did how the things would look at maturity. We will never know why no one mentioned the Gotelli Collection, the world's outstanding collection of Dwarf Evergreens, until 1965—probably because we didn't ask. We found it in Washington, D.C.

While we were rattling around hunting plants and trying to classify them correctly, the border of baby Dwarf Evergreen grew far beyond expectation. In 5 years the small plants literally jumped; in 10 years they were sensational. Today the border has slowed its growth—the picture gives one a good idea of its development. Many of the plants are also desirable as specimens in a lawn.

One great value in a border containing nothing but Dwarf Evergreens is that they do not defoliate in winter. A further feature is the wealth of different-colored foliage. They range from sea-greens to very dark greens, from shades of yellow to golden to beige, and are tantalizing as they change with the season. Dwarf Evergreens also make fine specimens for the terrace or patio when grown in containers. And many of them can be made into bonsai when trained only 3 or 4 years.

Also, they make unusual foundation plants. A foundation planting is strictly an American invention. I know of no other country that sits its houses on stone or masonry that juts as much as 2 feet above the surface. Because this way of building is unsightly, the foundation is hidden by plants—usually evergreens, so that it will remain covered in winter. This is done mostly with Yews and various broad-leaved evergreens. The result is satisfactory for a short time—well, say it provides the necessary cover, but to keep it from hiding the house, the stuff needs interminable clipping or pruning. Also, our factory way of life has produced local nurserymen with little or no imagination, for they all seem to put in the same kind of plants. The monotony is little short of dreadful. The use of these dwarfs for foundation work would go a long way to relieve the present monotony, because they have so many different forms and come in so many different colors. They, too, will require shaping, but because they are dwarfs there will be less need for it. Dwarf Evergreens occur in many genera. Each is discussed in this section for convenience. All of the following varieties are hardy in zone 4, some even in colder zones.

Abies (ab-eez) Fir. The Firs are known as the magnificent evergreens, because there are so many large species spread over the North Temperate Zone—some reach a height of 250 feet. The varieties of two species listed here are pygmies. Plant spring or fall.

A. balsamea nana Hudsonia. Dwarf Balsam Fir. A pygmy form of the Balsam Fir from the White Mountains of New Hampshire that grows from 1 to 2 feet high. It is perfect for rock garden or bonsai culture.

A. koreana prostrata. This beauty has rather open or spreading growth with often irregular branches; needles are a sea of gray green on top, distinctly silver underneath. We have 14-year-old plants that are about 2 feet in height with a spread of 4 feet. They make excellent specimens. Every All-Dwarf Evergreen border should have at least one in the front.

Chamaecyparis (kam-ee-sip′are-is) Two species selected from this large group of timber trees (both of Asiatic origin) make particularly valuable garden subjects. One, *C. obtusa,* is called the Hinoki Cypress in Japan and produces valuable lumber from trees growing to 120 feet. It has a multitude of other forms, many of which are fine garden plants, but only a very few are in cultivation.

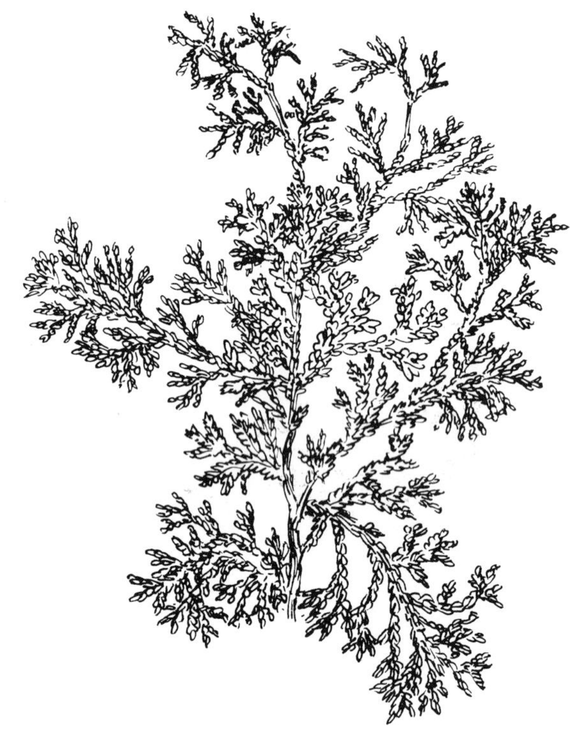

Chamaecyparis obtusa gracilis

C. pisifera, called the Sawara Cypress, is a Japanese tree that grows to 150 feet. Like *C. obtusa,* it too has a great many forms that have been neglected by gardeners for the good reason that very few nurserymen ever attempt to grow them. Both are hardy in zone 3 and southward. The other three species are not hardy. One, however, *C. Lawsoniana,* deserves mention. Some of its 80 garden forms are widely grown in the warmer parts of Europe. Some are grown in California, but this species dislikes drought and hot weather—as do all Chamaecyparis. Kammies, as they are nicknamed, are evergreen, but their leaves are needle-like—really minute scales pressed closely on tiny branches that remind one of fans. Some of the varieties can be grown successfully as bonsai; this is not to say that such bonsai is either easily or quickly achieved, but it can be done in from 3 to 5 years and the little plant looks completely respectable from the beginning. Kammies are the backbone of a Dwarf Evergreen garden because there are so many different colors, shapes, and heights. They may be planted spring or fall.

C. obtusa Crippsii. This lovely native of Japan, called Cripps Hinoki Cypress, has conspicuous, graceful, golden, fern-like foliage, and is remarkably beautiful even at 5 years of age. The 12- to 15-foot specimen in the famed Gotelli Collection, now owned by the National Arboretum in Washington, D.C., is a sight to see.

***C. o. gracilis.** Here is a most pleasant evergreen shrub. It has a very strong trunk and grows to 3 to 4 feet quickly. Its dark green fan-like leaves, all of them varied in size; attach to the main trunk on branches that look as if they had been specially placed there by some gifted Japanese gardener. For rockery work its roots should be sharply restricted.

***C. o. g. nana.** Its conformation is similar to the larger foregoing form and it is extremely useful for the rockery or for bonsai. It grows slowly to about 2 feet.

***C. o. Kosteri.** This variety's attraction is that its flattened foliage falls in folds with the dignity of old lace. They make rather rapid growth in the garden. Use it for the rockery, for bonsai, or as a specimen.

***C. o. lycopodioides.** Clubmoss Cypress. A most unusual Conifer, irregularly tufted, twisted and contorted—about as Japanese-looking as a Japanese tree can be. Thirty-year-old specimens are about 6 feet tall, and look many times that age. Foliage is a dark bluish green. It is an excellent bonsai subject.

C. o. tetragona aurea. A rare and most unusual shrub or small tree with pale yellow to golden moss-like foliage. A lovely Kammy.

C. o. torulosa coraliformis. This is a semi-dwarf, slow-growing Cypress with dark green twisted and irregular thread-like growth. Great for bonsai use.

***C. pisifera aurea compacta nana.** A neat dwarf with blue-green foliage—the new growth is yellowish. It is irregularly round in shape; 15-year-old plants, which are exceedingly rare, have 24-inch globes. Also fine for bonsai.

***C. p. filifera aurea.** This Japanese beauty grows very slowly. Its foliage in summer is yellow and turns golden in winter. It is a low, dense plant that can be used in the rockery by keeping its roots pruned, or developed as a specimen.

***C. p. plumosa aurea.** This lovely dwarf is golden in the spring and turns green later on.

C. p. p. lutescens. We haven't marked this for the rockery but it is nevertheless quite usable in large rock gardens. The plant is conical, very broad at the base, and crowded with plume-like branchlets. The color is golden yellow.

C. p. squarrosa. Heavily branched, this variety spreads beautifully to make a dense small tree or shrub. Leaves are blue green with a silvery underside.

C. p. s. minima. A most unusual Kammy. It is sea green in color, the form cunningly irregular and cushion-like, the foliage so dense that it is difficult to part with the fingers. The "feel" to the hand is soft, not prickly. It lends itself to topiary. Plants shipped look like 5-inch rounded cushions and are grown in 5-inch pots. They grow to a foot or more rather quickly. Very desirable.

Cryptomeria (krip-to-meer′ee-uh) Japanese Cedar. Zone 5, and 4 if protected. A single species of trees native to Japan and used there for centuries for planting the country's extensive temple gardens and ceremonial avenues. The Cryptomeria of Nikko on the Tokyo tourist route, and the Inner Temple of Ise, not well known to American travelers, have most impressive plantings of these 125-foot trees. The smaller varieties, suitable for garden use in America, are not extensively planted here. Plant spring or fall.

C. japonica cristata. This dwarf is all but unknown and it is one of the most beautiful. It develops the distinctive striated bark (marked with grooves) of the genus early and produces a strong trunk. The somewhat irregular branches are banded with bright green cockscomb-like growth. It looks exactly like Japan. A good subject for bonsai.

Juniperus chinensis pyramidalis

Juniperus (jew-nip′er-us) Juniper. A genus of many species of evergreen trees and shrubs widely distributed north of the equator, although one grows in mountains almost on the equator in Kenya. Many are trees of assorted sizes; others are shrub-like plants; still others are creepers. Only the hardy dwarf varieties and creepers need concern us. Both forms are easily established; the creepers grow particularly well on difficult slopes when provided with a moderately good garden loam and a bit of water in prolonged dry spells. Plant spring or fall.

J. chinensis pyramidalis. Hardy in zone 4, southward. An upright, compact and very slow-growing variety. It has glaucous needles, and, as the name implies, is pyramidal in form. Ultimate height is about 10 feet, but it makes nearly half of that growth rather quickly.

***J. communis compressa.** Hardy in zone 2, southward. A gem for the rock garden. It is probably the slowest growing of all conifers, taking 20 years to reach a height of 1 foot. The plant is cone-shaped and dense, with blue-gray foliage. Very rare.

***J. conferta.** Hardy in zone 5; if protected, zone 4. A prostrate species that forms a dense mat rather quickly by layering. It has bright green foliage. The variety is excellent for use in rock gardens or terraces and is superb hanging over walls. The vivid green color holds through all seasons.

***J. horizontalis Douglasii.** Hardy in zone 2, southward. The needle-like leaves of the long, creeping branches are steel blue in summer and change to plum purple in winter. It is a fine carpet plant.

***J. h. procumbens nana.** Zone 2, southward. This variety, known as the slowest-growing of the spreading Junipers, makes a compact, small mat of pale green. Use it in the rockery or in a small crevice where it will spread over a rock. Scarce.

***J. Sabina tamariscifolia.** Hardy zone 4, southward. This variety is native in the mountains of central and southern Europe and from western Asia to Siberia. It is prostrate, a good spreader for slopes. Leaves are needle-like and silvery green. This is a very popular plant in Europe but not known widely here.

***J. s. t. variegata.** Its hardiness and habits are similar to the foregoing, but its young tips in growth are variegated. Mix these two on a slope for an interesting effect.

Picea (pie′see-a) This is the regal Spruce family, but those which grow regally have no place in the average American garden. The Colorado Blue Spruce, for example, develops into a beautiful tree, but on small grounds it isn't long until it has taken over. Two dwarf forms of the popular species follow; others are dwarf or containable forms of other species. Plant spring or fall.

P. Abies Maxwelli. Zone 2, southward. The Norway Spruce, said to be the most widely cultivated evergreen in the U.S., grows to 150 feet and more, but provides gardeners with several delightful dwarf forms. This one is a rarity—20-year-old specimens, exceeding dense and rounded, rarely are more than 2 feet high and 3 feet across.

P. A. nidiformis. Zone 2, southward. Bird's Nest Spruce. A slow-growing Spruce forming a dense, flat-topped shrub with fan-like branches. Its spreads well—one in our garden is about 3 feet high and 4 feet across. From the time it was a little fellow 10 years ago it looked like a fine place for a bird to build a nest, but it has never happened.

P. A. pygmaea. Zone 2, southward. Pygmy Spruce. This variety is the smallest of all *Picea.* After many years it seldom grows more than 1 foot high, and is rounded and exceedingly dense; the needle-like leaves are a dark green. A rare plant that is hard to find.

P. A. repens. Zone 2, southward. A creeping Spruce with spreading branches that would have a hard time growing more than 18 inches high. It is dense, and when its branches root as they touch the ground, it spreads slowly but steadily.

P. glauca Albertiana conica. Hardy zone 3, southward. This Spruce, the dwarf form of the 100-foot Alberta Spruce, is an evergreen of great beauty. Its delicate needles are a delightful sea-foam green color, and are so compactly massed that the plant seems to be solid. Eventually it will grow to 15 feet and spread 8 feet at the bottom. Many take almost exact conical forms. In hot weather red spider may attack it, but this is easily controlled by dousing daily during the hot spell with water under pressure. Formerly hard to find, it is now available in good nurseries.

P. pungens glauca globosa. Zone 3, southward. As this globe-shaped dwarf form of the Colorado Blue Spruce rarely produces a definite "leader," it re-

Evergreen Planting

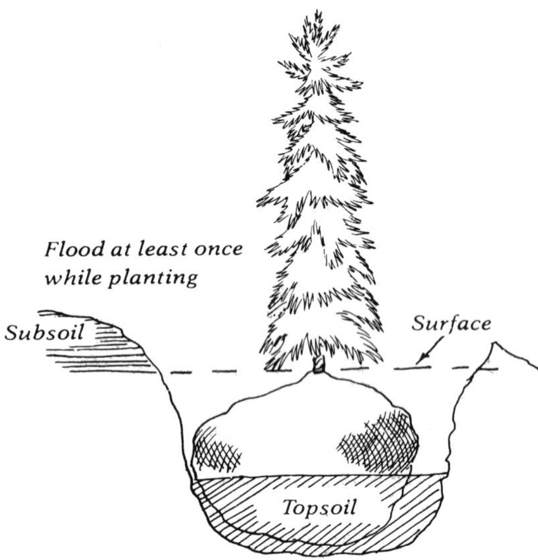

Do not remove burlap

mains compact and beautifully blue. It is an ideal accent plant for today's small gardens as it rarely grows 5 feet high; it spreads a bit farther.

P. p. g. pendula. Zone 3, southward. This is not a true dwarf—it's the lovely weeping form of the Colorado Blue Spruce, although it doesn't grow as high. It can, however, be held to a small tree by disbudding (remove the terminal bud of upward or lateral leaders) or by pruning carefully in August. The color is typically Colorado Blue.

Pinus (pie'nus) Pine. The name of this genus comes from the Latin "pix" or "picis," used by Virgil and others to describe plants exuding pitch. This is a huge family of evergreens, evidently useful for nearly everything. The genus also provides gardeners with several stunning dwarf forms, each very hardy. Plant spring or fall.

P. Strobus nana. Zone 3, southward. The dwarf and rounded form of the beautiful White Pine of the eastern United States. Its blue-green foliage is extremely dense. A specimen on the lawn in the gardens here is 12 years old and a nearly perfect 40-inch globe that has never been shaped. It is extremely hard to find.

P. Strobus pendula. Zone 3. This, the weeping form of White Pine, is not a true dwarf, but it can easily be held to small size by disbudding the leader or lateral branches. Left untended it will grow rather quickly to 35 feet. It should be grown as a specimen and held proportional to the space allowed it.

P. Tanyosho. Zone 3. Japan has thousands of forms of unusual Pines, most of which are not hardy here; but this lovely one is. It grows only to about 10 feet and becomes a beautiful, fully conical mound of green. No disbudding or shearing is required to form it.

Taxus (tacks'us) Yew. There are many species of Yew, but the forms everyone uses are the common spreading and upright varieties of *T. cuspidata,* the Japanese Yew, which can be called "foundation plants" because so many home owners use them to hide the American house foundation. Varieties of the English Yew, *T. baccata,* are also used for this purpose, as are various crosses between the Japanese and English species. There are a few dwarf forms.

The following one is, and it is also very slow-growing. Plant spring or fall.

T. cuspidata densa. Hardy in zone 3 with protection, and southward. This is a truly dwarf Yew, and if left untrimmed it is not likely to grow more than 3 feet. Its branches and leaves, as the name implies, are dense, even when compared to other Yews, which are themselves dense. Although very slow-growing, this variety makes the finest Yew hedge. As it grows in hedge form, it can be trimmed so that at least 2 inches of height can be added annually. It follows that a hedge of *T. c. densa* becomes a fine small hedge even in its early stages of growth, and becomes spectacular later as a large one. It can easily be held to any desired height by clipping.

Thuja (thoo'ya) The Arbor-Vitae Family. Extremely useful evergreens, many of needle types, others heather-like, make up this group. Plant spring or fall.

T. occidentalis ericoides nana. Hardy zone 2, southward; but not in hot, dry areas. The Royal Horticultural Society's *Dictionary of Gardening* remarks that this is "the dwarf broadly pyramidal form of Thuja, with slender branchlets clothed with needle shaped soft spreading leaves; dull green above, grayish green beneath—and a brownish tint in winter." It grows to about 4 feet at maturity.

T. o. lutea. Hardy zone 2, southward; but not in hot, dry areas. This golden Arbor-Vitae makes an ideal trimmed hedge plant or windbreak, for at maturity it rarely grows more than 8 feet high. It holds its golden color throughout the year.

T. orientalis aurea nana Raffels. Hardy zone 3, southward; but protect from strong winds. This Arbor-Vitae from China is treasured for its dwarf habit (it grows to 4 feet), and for the heavy-textured foliage of yellow green. The plant grows naturally in a somewhat oval shape.

Tsuga (sue'jah) Hemlock. There isn't a more beautiful evergreen than Hemlock, and the variety is endless so far as size is concerned. There is, however, really only one true garden subject, the pendulant form, although dwarf forms of tall-growing varieties do occur in plantings from seed. Plant spring or fall.

Evergreen Planting

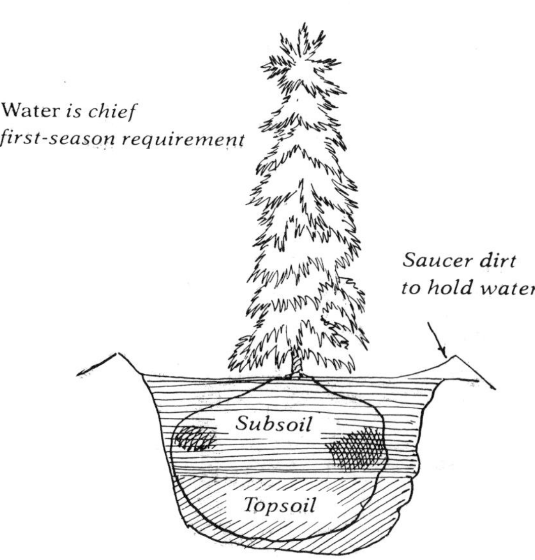

Be sure soil is tightly packed around ball

T. canadensis pendula Sargentiana. Zone 4. This is the lovely Weeping Hemlock that was found in Fishkill, New York, about 1860, and was introduced to horticulture by Dr. Charles S. Sargent, the first director of Harvard's Arnold Arboretum. The variety speads farther than it grows high—old plants 6 feet high spread 12 to 15 feet. The form is ever a delight. Young plants should be staked to grow upright for at least the first 6 years of their lives. Wise gardeners grow their own, for a large specimen cost several hundred dollars. Few, however, can be found, and when found are usually too expensive to move.

excelsa (eks-sel'sa) very tall

Fagus

Fay'gus

The Beeches. Zone 3. These are the royalty of shade trees, and the European varieties are by far the most beautiful. They also appear to have no known serious insect or fungus enemies. However, young trees (3 to 4 feet high) must be protected from deer, rabbits, and mice. The best protection for all is ¼-inch mesh hardware cloth, 3 or 4 feet high, buried 6 inches in the soil. It should be built up to 6 feet as the tree grows. (*See* Trees, Protecting Them.)

Most of the following varieties, we regret to say, are hard to find. Small sizes (3 to 4 feet) can usually be bought for from $12 to $20. Sometimes a few varieties are available in landscape sizes in fine nurseries. Plant spring or fall.

F. Engleriana. The extremely rare Chinese Beech. Leaves are a pale green with a glaucous hue.
F. sylvatica asplenifolia. This is the Fernleaf Beech, densely branched and dark green. One of the finest in the family.
F. s. fastigiata. The green columnar form of Beech. In fine nurseries one can generally find this available in large (balled-and-burlapped) sizes.
F. s. heterophylla laciniata. This Beech has finely cut green leaves and is one of the most effective of the large ornamental trees. Rare.
F. s. pendula. This is the superb and rare green weeping Beech. Can be found in large sizes, which are usually expensive, but worth the price.

F. s. purpurea pendula. The purple-leaf weeping Beech is as lovely as its green brother. Not easy to find and should only be used on extensive grounds—one is enough.
F. s. Riversi. River's Purple Beech leafs out red in the spring, turns deepest purple in the fall. Sometimes available in large sizes.
F. s. Rohanii. The purple-leaved form of the "Fern-leaved Beech." Very hard to find.
F. s. spaethiana. A new purple Beech. It leafs out purple and stays purple all summer. This is difficult to locate.
F. s. tricolor. An extremely rare Beech with copper-colored leaves tipped pink and white. It is effective even when very young. A very pleasant tree, but hard to find, even in small sizes.
F. Zlatia. This Golden Leaf Beech is a joy. Excellent. Use only for accent on large grounds. It is difficult to locate.

FALSE DRAGONHEAD—*see* Physostegia

FALSE INDIGO—*see* Baptisia

FALSE MALLOW—*see* Sidalcea

FALSE SUNFLOWER—*see* Heliopsis

Farreri (fahr′reri) of Farrer, a famous plant-hunter

fastigiata (fas-ti-gee-aye′ta) having erect branches

FEEDING (*See* Fertilizer) How to feed various classes of plants and lawns is a question always asked by inexperienced gardeners, and even experienced hands tend to forget quantities. So herewith how to feed trees, shrubs, hedges (which are shrubs), Roses, evergreens, perennials, and lawns—how much and when. In all instances organic fertilizers should be used, but use inorganics if organics are not available or too expensive. As explained elsewhere, fertilizers are made up of nitrogen, phosphate, and potash. These ingredients are present in varying amounts in all fertilizers, and the manufacturer by federal law must print the content on the outside of the package. Percentage of active ingredients are indicated by numbers,

Lilium

Fuchsia

thus: 8-6-6, 20-20-20, 5-5-0, etc. The first number represents the percent of available nitrogen, the second is percent of phosphate, the third potash. When you can't get a specifically balanced fertilizer, improvise. For example, if the dosage calls for 10-10-10, and you can only get 5-5-5, use twice as much. Also be sure to buy the new slow-release fertilizers to provide even fertilization throughout the season. Nitrogen provides good, strong leaf growth and healthy color, phosphate promotes root action; potash produces strong trunks and branches. Now, before pursuing this subject further, we warn against overfeeding. It is not true that "a little more" is better; it can mean death. Following are fertilization rates used in the gardens in Litchfield.

Evergreens (Broadleaf). Spread 2 pounds per 100 square feet of 7-7-7 over the soil evenly in April, another 2 pounds in May, repeat in June. But do not cultivate the fertilizer into the soil, for Broadleaf Evergreens send their delicate feeding roots to the surface and cultivation injures them. Irrigate it in thoroughly after each feeding. Treat Rhododendrons and Azaleas the same way. Use the same feeding rate, but put the first one on just after they have flowered, the second 1 month later, the third 3 months after flowering.

Evergreens (Needle). Apply 7-7-7 at the rate of 2 pounds per 100 square feet three times—first in March, then in April, and again in May. Work it into the soil from the trunk to where branches end; then irrigate thoroughly.

Hedges. Apply 3 pounds of 8-6-6 per 100 feet, half on each side, a foot from the base. Work in lightly and irrigate.

Lawns. Feeding lawns adequately is probably not done by most home-owners on a regular schedule and is probably more responsible for grass failure than any other reason. Feed 3 to 4 pounds of *Milorganite* per 100 square feet in the spring; in zone 4 and northward apply an equal amount every July. In zone 5 and southward feed in August. This heavy feeding keeps the grasses in strong growth even during summer dry spells. Lime should be used only on ground that has been newly prepared for seeding: authorities now agree that lime is harmful on established lawns. (*See* Lawns)

Perennials. If planted in good garden soil, very little feeding is necessary after a light top dressing of 5-10-5 (1 pound per 100 square feet) in early spring; a similar application in June is recommended if the spring has been particularly wet. Soak after each feeding.

Roses. Use one heaping tablespoon of 5-10-5 per plant and work it into the bed each month—but stop feeding August 15. Soak after each feeding.

Shrubs. In early spring drive holes 8 to 10 inches deep and 2 feet apart in a ring just inside the tips of the branches. Use a handful of 8-6-6 in each hole (must be organic "Tree Food"), fill with earth.

Trees. Feed before growth starts in spring. The amount is determined by estimating the diameter of the tree 2 feet above ground level. Use 1 pound of 8-6-6 fertilizer (organic "Tree Food") per inch of diameter. Now visualize 2 circles around the tree—one slightly beyond the tips of the branches, the other two-thirds of the distance from the outside circle to the trunk. Between these circles drive holes (with a crowbar) 12 to 18 inches apart and about 18 inches deep. Divide the fertilizer evenly; put it in the holes; fill with earth. Tree men do this work well and inexpensively.

Double Narcissus

Ferns

Ferns. More than 6,000 species spread through many plant families make up the perennial flowerless plants we know as Ferns. Except for the poles, there is hardly a place on earth where they are not found. We naturally restrict our interest to hardy Ferns and it is always best to grow those native to a locality. Native Ferns are easily found in the woods. But yank them out and they'll sulk, unless their new location has similar soil and exposure. Ferns need a woodsy soil, one high in humus—which can be manufactured by a gardener who uses a bit more peat or compost than he thinks he needs. Lime should never be used in preparing a bed, for Ferns require a very acid soil. A nitrogen fertilizer helps if given judiciously once every year or two. Semi-shade, which means full protection from burning sun at noon and after, is necessary. Besides acidity, moisture is a prime requirement; Ferns should never dry out. A Fern garden is a delight—and once established it needs little care. Fact is it could turn into a delightful pest. Plant only in the spring.

Adiantum pedatum. This airy, graceful variety is also called American Maidenhair, but it is quite different from florist's maidenhair, a greenhouse plant. This variety grows in clumps and spreads slowly. Fronds grow to 18 inches.

Asplenium filix-foemina. This is the Lady Fern. It needs moist soil so the clumps can expand quickly. It tolerates full sun. Fronds grow to 3 feet.

Athyrium thelypteroides. Known commonly as Silvery Spleenwort, its fronds reach 2 feet; its stalks are straw colored.

Dryopteris marginalis. The Heather-wood Fern. A handsome plant with fronds up to 2 feet. Fine for mass arrangements indoors by itself or with flowers.

Dryopteris spinulosa. Commonly called Toothed-wood Fern. It too is excellent when cut for arrangements.

Osmunda cinnamomea. Called the Cinnamon Fern because of the color of its fronds at maturity. Under ideal conditions it will grow to 6 feet, but 2 to 4 feet is about all one should expect. Fronds are the palest of green when young, and very slender. Properly placed and grown this is a decorative plant worth one's best efforts. It will tolerate considerable sun.

Osmunda regalis. The Royal Fern, as this is commonly called, is a highly ornamental fellow whose fronds push to 10 feet when it is under best culture. It is a very strong grower. It needs lots of moisture, and like the Cinnamon Fern, it can take some sun.

Polystichum acrostichioides. Similar in growth to the well-known Boston Fern, this Christmas Fern is also very easily grown. It thrives in shade, and fronds go to 6 feet or more under ideal conditions. Because it appears to be evergreen, quantities of it are used in Christmas decorations.

Pterestis nodulosa. Called Ostrich Fern commonly, this variety is very dark green in color and grows to 5 feet. It is unusual in that a separate plume-shaped spore stalk remains over the winter. Use it in woodlands, lowlands, or at shady foundation planting sites.

FERTILIZER (water soluble). Probably the best fertilizer for container-grown plants is liquid manure, but it's messy to make and smelly to use on indoor plants. There are many easy to prepare water-soluble chemical fertilizers—just mix them as directed. I like 20-20-20 water-soluble fertilizer, chelated. The numbers indicate that it is a high-nutrient fertilizer with equal amounts of phosphate, nitrogen, and potash. "Chelated" means that it contains all of the important trace elements so necessary to plant health. Many water-solubles are compatible with insecticides and can be used with them for foliar feeding. A pound lasts a long time. To use 20-20-20, dissolve one tablespoon to one gallon of water. Always irrigate plants before fertilizing them. For Fuchsia and Lantana use one cupful every two weeks. For Begonias use 1/4 cup once a month. Gloxinias and African Violets need little fertilizer—1/10 cup a month is enough. It is too expensive for lawn or general garden use.

Osmocote, a pelleted slow-release fertilizer, is also excellent for container-grown plants. It comes in different formulas, but 14-14-14 has been used for many feeding purposes here, including perennial gardens and shrubs. One application is good for a year. The material

Aster

is now available at most garden centers. It's expensive compared to other fertilizers. (*See also* Feeding.)

filifera (*fi-lif'ur-a*) *slender, thread-like*

filix-foemina (*fi-licks-fem-ee'na*) *lady fern*

FIRETHORN—*see* Pyracantha

Fischeri (*fish'er-i*) *after botanist Fischer*

FLATS. A flat is a shallow box, about 4 inches deep, used by gardeners to start seeds. It is also used for planting seedlings for further growth and to start dormant tubers of Begonias, Gloxinias, etc. A flat is a gardening necessity, and a nearly new wooden one can usually be bought from a florist or nurseryman for $1.50 or so. But a grape box from a greengrocer is a good substitute—just put some newspaper (1 sheet) in the bottom to close up the cracks when filling it with starting medium. Flats rot no matter what kind of wood they are made of, so one must be resigned to replacing them at intervals—coating a mere half-dozen or so of them with a wood preservative like Cuprinol is a waste of time. There are new flats made of plastic that are worth investigating—check locally. They, too, are sold for about $1.50 each, but they don't last much longer than wood—and get somewhat fragile as they age.

flavum (*flay'vum*) *nearly pure yellow*

FLAX—*see* Linum

FLEABANE—*see* Erigeron

FLEECE VINE—*see* Polygonum

florepleno (*flor'e-plee'no*) *having double flowers*

floribunda (flor-ri-bund'a) flowering freely

foetida (fee'ti-da) strong smelling

FORCING BULBS—*see* varieties of Narcissus, Tulipa, Chionodoxa, Crocus, Galanthus, Hyacinthus, Bulbous Iris, Muscari, and *Scilla sibirica* marked[f].

Forsythia

For-sith'i-uh

Golden Bell. This genus arrived in the United States from Europe a little over 100 years ago, not long after it had been imported to Europe from Asia. There are many species, but only a few of them have garden value. Forsythia is practically the first shrub to flower in early spring, a time when the landscape is looking particularly dreary. And it does this with such tremendous enthusiasm that one feels sure it is as pleased as punch to be alive and kicking after its bout with winter. Forsythia apparently likes everything—even New York soot—and it couldn't care less about soils. It just wants a little water every once in a while. It's a wonder this country isn't planted solid with it, for it's the easiest thing imaginable to propagate—force a few branches indoors, leave them after the flowers have dropped, and before you can say Jack Robinson they will have sprouted roots. It is even good-natured about being abused. Far too many home-owners attempt to restrain it by clipping it evenly, like a hedge, instead of cutting old canes out from the crown of the plant, but it still blooms. The weeping forms, such as *F. suspensa Sieboldii,* trail to the ground, root in, then push up and trail again, which make them ideal for covering banks that are impossibly steep. The improved upright forms are better than the species, for they are more floriferous and have larger flowers. *F. Beatrix Farrand, Lynwood Gold,* and *Spring Glory* are presently the outstanding hybrids. Another great plus for Forsythia is that insects avoid it like the plague, and so far as I know it is highly resistant to bacteria and fungus. It is not, however, as hardy as some writers indicate. The bush itself is probably hardy in most parts of zone 3, but the flower buds don't like really cold weather. In Litchfield we always know how tough the winter has been when Forsythia blooms. If it flowers only below the snow line, it's been a right cold season.

FORSYTHIA, WHITE—*see* Abeliophyllum

Fosteriana (fohs-te-ree-ay'na) after botanist Foster

FOXGLOVE—*see* Digitalis

Fraises des Bois

Fraises

Frez

Strawberries. It may seem a little precious to use the French name for strawberries, but two of the most precious strawberries in the world to us are French. One is *Fraises des Bois* (frez-day-bwah'), the wild strawberries of the woods, which produces the tiny, zesty berries that are the delight of gourmets the world over. The other is *Fraises Espalier*, whose fine, big, juicy berries grow on vines that can be trained upward. There is, however, an intruder from Russia demanding attention from woodland strawberry gourmets. It produces very interesting fruit.

Culture for Woodland Strawberries: Plant on one-foot centers, as edging plants in the perennial border, or in rows in vegetable garden. The soil needs no special preparation if the humus content is high. Like all strawberries, they must be kept damp—use the equivalent of 1 inch of water a week. Every other spring, dig, and cut or pull apart the crown in 2 to 4 pieces, being sure each piece has a good root system. Don't dig all of them at one time, for the roots may dry out before one can plant them. Separation is done only in early spring, just as the crown begins to show growth (*See* drawings). Plant spring or fall.

***Fraises des Bois Charles V.** Planted in early spring, Charles V will produce its first berries in late June; plants will be lush and in full production at the end of August. Fertilize with dry cow manure or compost. Charles V produces no runners, is ever-bearing and prolific; it is a charming edging plant for the perennial border. Charles V is named after France's famous king, who in about 1360 was the first Frenchman to bring wild strawberries from the woods and plant them in a garden. This variety is an open upright plant (no runners) with dark green leaves, about 8 inches high, 10 inches in diameter.

Catherine the Great. White Russian friends have always claimed that the berries from their woods put French *Fraises des Bois* to shame. We discounted this, putting it down to nostalgia for the good old days they had enjoyed in Imperial Russia. Then one of these friends visited a sister of hers in Moscow and was served her favorite berries, which the sister grew. She dried three and brought them here. From the seeds our friend gave us we experimented with hundreds of seedlings and found one that indeed was outstanding. The growth habit is truly upright like *Charles V*. The plant itself is slightly larger—it makes about a 14-inch mound. Hence it is just as usable as an edging plant as *Charles V*. In the garden it is propagated in the same way as *Charles V*—by division, as soon as growth starts in spring.

The fruit, somewhat larger than *Charles V*, is pointed. The berry is softer than the French one and far juicier. Its flavor, just as our

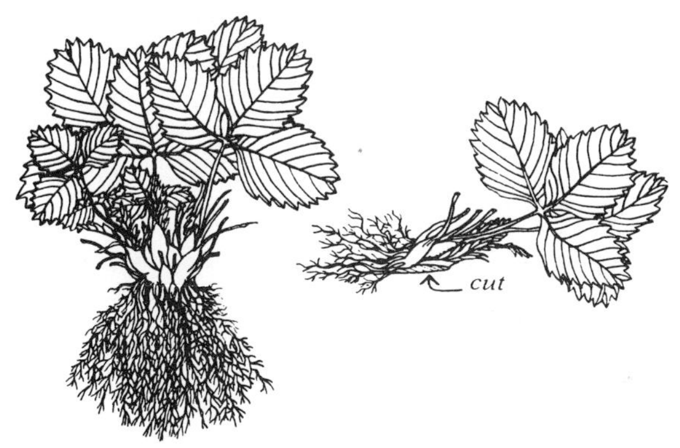

Separating Fraises des Bois, Charles V, or Catherine the Great

After a full season of growth, dig the plants in earliest spring, just as they begin to show green shoots. Shake off the earth; then either pull apart with care, or cut the crown, into two to four divisions, being sure that each has a good root system. Replant immediately. Do not dig and separate all plants at one time, for the roots dry quickly and losses result

White Russian friend said, is delicious, but if it is better than the French—well, that's not for us to say. Both *Charles* and *Catherine* are crops grown only by the writer's nursery—White Flower Farm, Litchfield, Connecticut.

Fraises Espalier. This is a relatively new strawberry developed in France and can generally be found under a variety of names. It has a most unusual habit. The plant throws long runners, and node after node after node—each of which, we'll have you know, produces strawberries in the air. So train, or *espalier,* the runners to a lattice, and you have not only an extremely interesting and good-looking plant, but one which produces quantities of large fruit like ordinary strawberries. They have excellent flavor. Actually, the variety was developed as a commercial strawberry in Europe to get better utilization of land.

We advise rooting a few of the nodes for use the following year, keeping, of course, the mother plants. If you tire of picking this luscious fruit off a fence, and the chances are you may, plant *Fraises Espalier* so it runs rampant on the ground. You will get huge pickings from one of the best conventional strawberries you have ever eaten—right up to frost. Full sun and plenty of water are the only cultural requirements.

Franklinia

Frank-lin'e-eh

Franklinia. The correct name of this unusually beautiful small tree is probably *Gordonia altamaha,* but practically every nurseryman in this country knows it as plain Franklinia. Actually, it is one of 2 American species of a genus having a largely Asiatic habitat. It was found by John Bartram, one of the earliest American plant collectors, on the banks of the Alatamaha River in Georgia and brought by him to his garden in Philadelphia in 1770. He named it after his good friend Benjamin Franklin and the river where he found it. So it's as American as apple pie. I doubt that James Gordon, an English nurseryman after whom the Asiatic group was named, ever heard of it or *G. Lasianthus,* the other native (Georgia). After 1770 it was never again seen in the wild state, so one has to believe that all stock since then has come from Bartram's garden. I saw one about 30 years ago in Delaware and was entranced. It had everything. At about 25 feet it was nearly mature, my host said. It was in bloom, in September, not smothered, just lovely nearly 4-inch cup-shaped white flowers, rather like single Peonies, at the end of enough twigs to jewel the masses of large oblong red leaves perfectly. Those leaves, my host said, had been green all summer; later they would turn to orange. It was rare and hard to find, but I got it. In fact I got it for several years—and got nothing. Too cold. I learned later that Franklinia will survive in the warmer parts of zone 5, but it grows like a shrub with many small branches from the base, and if one wants to be reasonably sure of keeping the roots alive it is best to protect them every winter, a dreary business. If you live where Franklinia will grow into a tree, by all means get one, if possible a fairly large one, balled-and-burlapped, from a good local nurseryman. A few mail-order houses offer stock a couple of feet high.

fraxinella (fraks-in-el'la) like a small Ash tree

*Fritillaria

Fri-til-lay're'ah

Snake's Head Lily. Old-fashioned, but a fine garden flower and a member of the Lily family. Roots are bulbous. Of the 70-odd species known only a few have garden value. These hardy spring-flowering bulbs bloom in April and May. Plant fall only.

F. Meleagris. The bell-like flowers, whose color is a mad mixture of bronze, gray, purple and white, are pendulant on 9- to 12-inch stems, and have curious checkered patterns of different hues. Use ordinary soil, but plant in groups in full sun and in a well-drained location, please.

Three-year-old Fuchsia Head

Fuchsia

Few'sha, properly fuke'zi-a

Fuchsia. This remarkable genus is named after Leonard Fuchs, who lived from 1501 to 1566. It is a tropical and *not* hardy. In his lifetime this German botanist published a book, now a collector's item, of very beautiful woodcuts of the plants. The genus has about 50 species and innumerable varieties of shrubs or small trees native to Central and South America and New Zealand. Fuchsia are hardy only in a few sections of America, principally in mild California climates.

For years I admired Fuchsia—from afar. Our California friends had them outside all year in profusion—not just the usual magenta-colored ones, the color most often associated with traditional Fuchsia varieties, which few people like. The Californians had Fuchsia in solid pinks (from little-girl to shocking), pink-and-white, red, red-and-white, delicate lavenders, and pure white. Blues, too—oh well, call them nearly blue. Then we discovered that they also grew Fuchsia in pottery in their very cold mountain homes. They wintered them in a 40° basement and brought them into a sunny window in early spring. The plants soon flowered. This storage idea, of course, solves the greenhouse problem. Now many gardeners in the East, the northern plains, and mountain states are growing this fine tropical plant on their terraces.

It is not so odd that the more spectacular the flower the better a variety sells; bigness seems to be a characteristic sought after by Americans as much in flowers as it is in cars. Many of the following varieties are spectacular in size of bloom. But there are also other varieties with very small flowers, charming and quietly spectacular in their own way—the plants are literally covered with blooms. Chances are that Fuchsia will be a very bright addition to your patio.

Culture: An excellent potting medium is 60 percent loam, 15 percent coarse builder's sand, and 10 percent leafmold. To each bushel add a 5-inch potful of bonemeal. Plants are usually received in heavily rooted 3-inch peat pots, the roots clearly showing through the pots. Plant at once (do not remove the peat pot in which they were grown) in a 5-inch clean clay pot that has been soaked in water a few hours previously. When planted keep them damp, never soggy. Hanging baskets need water every day; during windy, warm weather they may need it twice. At first grow them indoors in a sunny window; take them outside when all danger of frost is past and grow in filtered light.

As the plants grow, keep pinching them until a broad base has formed, then allow them to grow and produce flowering sprays. Further pinching will hold back bloom too long. Both upright and hanging forms can be shaped by judicious pinching later on with no apparent loss of bloom (*see* drawing on pinching and pruning fuchsia). When in full bloom, start fertilizing lightly (half strength) with liquid or soluble fertilizer once every two weeks. Fertilize hanging baskets every 10 days, because constant irrigation leaches out the plant food rather quickly. Be sure to pinch off seed pods as soon as bloom is finished, in order to keep them blooming. During hot weather syringe the leaves with water morning and afternoon

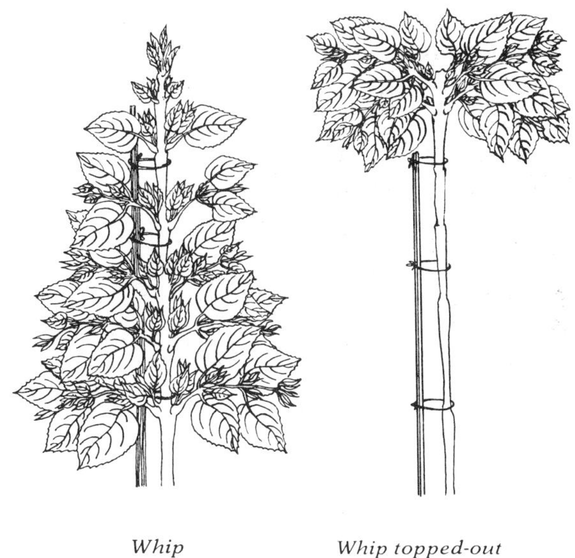

Whip *Whip topped-out*

Growing Tree Fuchsia and Lantana

Cut off all but the central shoot of a small bushy Lantana or Fuchsia plant in early spring to make a whip; train by staking. Allow side branches to develop (to increase trunk size) until desired height is reached. Then top-out the whip; later remove all side branches. Topping-out takes one year. Continue to pinch back breaks on head until desired size is achieved (opposite). Use 6-inch pot to start, transplant to 8-inch when topped, 14- to 18-inch pottery when mature and keep the plant out of the sun's burning rays. Fuchsias like warm days and cool nights, but as they do not tolerate prolonged periods of day-and-night heat they are not for gardeners who live in such climates.

Winter the plants in a 40° basement—water once a month, or just enough to keep the old wood from drying out. Bring them into sunlight indoors in February. When leaves just start to bud, cut them back severely to hard crown wood, for Fuchsia blooms only on new growth. What is meant by severely? If you are shocked by what you have done—well, that's severely. When you repot it, shake out some soil from the rootball, repot with new soil in a pot one size larger. If the plant is to be kept small, prune the roots back and return it to the same pot. I have found, after bringing back scores of varieties from the West Coast, that the varieties of Fuchsias that grow well in Los Angeles (it gets hot in summer) are more likely to do well in the East than those coming from San Francisco and the Bay Area, which has such an ideal climate for Fuchsias that all varieties do spectacularly. The following are the best Los Angeles imports. Plant spring only.

F. Bernadette. This Fuchsia has great quality. Its habit of growth is upright and compact, and the flowers, of medium size, are beautifully double. The corolla is violet blue, the sepals a charming blending rose. Bernadette can be grown in bush and tree form.

F. Chang. A charming variety which produces masses of small coral-scarlet blossoms with pert green tips that look a bit like some small Chinese firecrackers we have seen. Its Chinese name fits it perfectly. I have had this variety about 10 years and once offered it for sale. It went over like a lead balloon, but we kept the mother plant for our own joy and told it not to worry, for to us it was the prettiest lead balloon we had ever seen. It is best grown in bush form.

F. Checkerboard. Sepals of this strong upright grower are marble-white, the corolla is cherry-red, and tube shades to a lighter complementary pink.

F. Cotton Candy. A plant with delightful pink-and-white double flowers of considerable size. It grows upright.

F. Crimson Beauty. Huge single flowers with bright crimson tubes and sepals, and a rich, wine-red corolla. It is upright in growth and a prolific bloomer.

F. Display. This should have been called Pink Beauty, for pink it is and it's a beauty. It grows upright and is bushy. Floriferous as all get-out.

F. Jamboree. The corolla is rose, the sepals dawn-pink. The flower is semi-double but very large. Grow it upright or in baskets.

F. Mission Bells. This is an all-purpose single Fuchsia—grow it any way you like. Its corolla is an intense Aconite-blue; sepals are crimson.

F. Mme. Cornielson. This extremely free-flowering variety is literally covered with tiny blooms, which are single, but which give the effect of being semi-double because the corolla is swirled. The color is rose overall with white veins down the sepals. Delightful. Excellent for upright or basket use.

F. Mrs. Victor Reiter. A very floriferous single with marble white tubes and petals; the corolla is a vivid deep rose. It is an outstanding basket plant.

F. Muriel. Another floriferous hanging-basket variety. Its corolla is rose veined with crimson. The thing actually has a bluish edge; sepals are solid crimson.

F. New Fascination. Grow this in upright form. Flowers are huge doubles. The corolla is flared and pale pink, its veins cherry-red. The tube and sepals are cherry, too. It is a lovely big thing. Pick off seedpods or it stops blooming.

F. Orange Drops. This single may be used in upright or trailing form and is the best orange-colored variety produced thus far. The blooms drip on long stems in heavy clusters.

F. Southgate. This excellent variety can be staked into bush or tree form, baskets, or window-boxes. It has huge, double, pink flowers; the tube and sepals are a slightly deeper pink than the corolla.

F. Swingtime. Outstanding for basket or upright work. It has a fully double milky-white corolla and sharply red sepals. If you buy 1 or 20 Fuchsias, start with Swingtime, for this flashy red-and-white thing is best of the breed so far.

F. Voodoo. Basket or upright. Not only does the corolla of this variety flare magnificently, the huge flower is practically double-double, and the color is the deepest tone of imperial purple. Sepals are a glowing deep crimson.

F. Whitemost. Basket or upright type. Its attractive, delicate semi-double flowers have a pure white corolla; the sepals are palest pink.

Fuchsia Voodoo

fulgens (*full'jens*) *glowing, shining*

FUNKIA (funk'ee-a)—*see* Hosta

Gaillardia portola Hybrid

Gaillardia
Gay-lard'ia

Blanket Flower. A North American genus of showy perennials that are very popular garden plants. They require a rich, light, well-drained soil and full sun. The varieties bloom profusely all summer and seem to require little water. Blooms are highly satisfactory as cut flowers. Plant spring or fall.

G. aurea pura. This species has large yellow flowers on strong 30-inch stems.

G. Burgundy. A hybrid that has wine-red flowers 3 inches in diameter and grows about 30 inches.

G. Portola Hybrids. A strain with large flowers having dark red centers. The petals blend to copper and have golden tips. About 30 inches high.

*[f]Galanthus
Ga-lan'thus

Snowdrop. A genus of about 10 species that come from Eurasia, only one of which is widely grown. They share an extremely early blooming period with Eranthis and are very welcome. Flowers from the small bulbs are white. They like a rich, woodsy, well-drained soil and they show best in shade—under bushes, trees, or along woodland paths. Like all early-flowering small bulbs, hundreds or thousands are needed to make a show. Plant them 3 inches deep and 3 inches apart. If they like their home they will remain a lifetime. Plant Galanthus as soon as they are received; let other spring-flowering bulbs wait. They are very inexpensive. Plant fall only.

G. nivalis flore pleno. Very large, double white snowdrops.

G. nivalis simplex. White with large single blossoms.

GARDEN BOOKS. Unless one becomes an enthusiast, the purchase of a book on gardening is not warranted, for the simple basic cultural directions can be found in trade catalogues. Later on, when one's interest has deepened, a good garden book is a necessity for reference—for the pronunciation of botanical terms and names, species reference, sophisticated data about culture, border or landscape planning, or what have you. After having bought more than my share of garden books, I find now that those in encyclopedic form are the ones I most often use. Insist upon recent editions. Here are several.

America's Garden Book, by J. Bush and L. Brown, revised edition (New York: Scribners; 1966), 766 pages, $8.95. This one covers the waterfront, but don't read the section on plant diseases and insect pests (not in any other book either). If you are the least neurotic about your plants, it will curl your hair, or you will imagine that every disease in the book is afflicting your favorites. I recall reading widely of human ailments in the large volumes on medicine my great uncle bought in the 90's, and, at age 14, I had most of them. Then my mother found out what I was reading, and with considerable gaiety (forced, I thought), asked at breakfast, "And what disease do you have today, William," so many times that I gave up the whole business. *America's Garden Book* is arranged in categories, but its excellent index unlocks most of them quickly.

Taylor's Encyclopedia of Gardening, edited by Norman Taylor, fourth edition (Boston: Houghton Mifflin Company, 1961) 1225 pages, $15. Its alphabetical form makes it easy to use. Some 70 contributors, all experts, provide authority, and Mr. Taylor's editing makes points clear. It is not a bulky book. In using the book's hardiness zone recommendations be sure to check its maps against your location. Taylor's zones don't follow Harvard Arboretum's zoning, the first in the field. It is unfortunate that this important data comes in more than one standard.

The Royal Horticultural Society's Dictionary of Gardening, 4 volumes (London: Oxford University Press, 1951) Imperial $47.05, and Supplement, Imperial Quarto $15.50. This is really an encyclopedia and it is as horticulturally exact as it can be made. Its botanical language may disconcert those not familiar with it, but no one-upmanship is being displayed. The English gardener, for whom it is written, generally knows botany and understands its terms. As it is a dictionary, one can always look up the unknown words within its covers. Plant names, in Latin, are printed with the proper accents, but there is no truck with phonetic spelling, presumably because educated Englishmen already know how to pronounce Latin. Pay no attention to its comments on hardiness—England's climate is not ours, even if one lives on the Monterey Peninsula or on the coast of the Pacific Northwest. The volumes range the world of plants having garden interest.

In my opinion the outstanding American in the scientific horticultural field is Dr. Donald Wyman, Horticulturist for the last 31 years at Harvard University's great Arnold Arboretum in Cambridge, Mass. The books he has written for American gardeners carry his great authority, which is recognized abroad. He writes well. He doesn't write down. And his wry New England humor leaves no doubt about his opinion of genera which he thinks have little garden value but which are highly valued by nurserymen because they are easy to grow, inexpensive, and easy to sell. His 4 books, 1 published last year, 2 recently revised, are about all even the most sophisticated gardener really needs. They follow:

Trees for American Gardens, revised edition (New York: Macmillan Co., 1965) $10.95. A recommended list of 1200 species and varieties of trees now grown in America for landscape planting. Origin, size at maturity, habit of growth, foliage, blooming time, foliage color, hardiness zone, and common names, plus comment make this book remarkably useful. There are also 1800 additional species and varieties that are not recommended. Dr. Wyman's reason for writing this (and his other works) can be found in the foreword: "With the tremendous amount of plant material being grown in this country, it is time that someone indicated which plants are superior to others." He adds that he doesn't expect agreement.

Shrubs and Vines for American Gardens, revised edition (New York: Macmillan Co., 1969), $14.95. Approximately 1700 species and varieties, treated as they are in *Trees,* are recommended; a large number are not. For home gardeners this is more valuable than *Trees.*

Ground Cover Plants (New York: Macmillan Co.; 1970), $5.95. This is the best authority in this important field.

Wyman's Gardening Encyclopedia (New York: Macmillan Co., 1970), $17.50. This is Dr. Wyman's most recent undertaking. It is an admirable reference work.

There are literally thousands of garden books; scores are published here every year. For the gardener who starts to specialize in a particular genus or group, an entire literature already exists, neatly focused on his interest. There are innumerable books on Roses, probably the world's most popular flower. Name the genus and the literature on it is broad; it then becomes a question of selection, and, depending on the gardener's depth of interest, on funds. One can, however, pick up a lot of turkeys by merely reading the reviews. Horticultural writing is a tight little world, and a mighty polite one, too. There is also a startling sameness about general garden books.

Lilium

Part of this is due to the unavoidable repetition of having nothing new to say about a plant's cultural requirements, but a large part is caused by writing from research after the author has exhausted his first-hand experience. This results in petty plagiarism (phrases or sentences identical) and the handing down of errors so consistently that it is difficult for anyone except the dedicated scientist to know the truth. (I am told that this also happens in text books.) But even in the dullest of these garden books there are bits and pieces of such exquisite logic that one wonders why it wasn't developed before.

GARDEN CENTERS. The development over the past 15 years of the modern garden center, either independent or part of a local nursery, has been a boon to the home gardener. They come in all shapes and sizes, and because of the unprecedented boom in home building even small communities can support one. Generally they are good, particularly those established by local nurseries, for in them one can usually find a competent and helpful plantsman. The independent centers are strictly merchandising operations. Of course, the centers are aided in their selections by the large wholesale nurseries which supply them, but the personnel, sometimes including the boss himself, may not be well informed about culture or the subtle differences between varieties. Some stock the better-known perennials, but as unit prices of perennials are low and they take more care than trees and shrubs, balled-and-burlapped or put up in large plastic bags, the average garden center operator shies away from them. Also, they do not favor unusual plants, for turnover is low and selling time high. But for well-known ornamentals it is hard to fault the local garden center—the home gardener gets his choice, and doesn't have to pay the price of the plant again in transportation. He gets balled material that will grow, instead of bareroot ornamentals that come through the mails from far away and which must be nursed into bud. Also, most garden centers are loaded with big and small tools, insecticides, fertilizers, and bales of peat—perhaps too many kinds to choose from intelligently, but nonetheless a convenience. Many of these centers also devote an amazing amount of space to the display of "flowers" made in Hong Kong.

The hybridizers have been at work in the ornamental field and there are many new-new varieties of flowering trees and shrubs offered in the garden centers. These "news" are heavily backed by advertising, but only a very few are truly different from established varieties. Some have new forms, but many tend to be columnar and tight—uninteresting when planted on one's own grounds. Others, particularly very dark or red-leaved trees, used by landscape architects as accents on large estates or in highway planting because they are "different," are now showing up on 50-foot lots where they have no business being. For large-caliber trees, as well as for large sizes of unusual genera, we suggest shopping the best general nurseries one can find in the area—even as far away as 100 miles.

GARDEN MAGAZINES. There are 3 U.S. monthly magazines whose contents are exclusively about gardens and gardening. *Horticulture,* the official publication of the Massachusetts Horticultural Society, is outstanding. One difficulty with the horticultural periodical press is that writers are paid little or nothing, which obviously results in many second-rate articles or gushy ones. One monthly, *Organic Gardening,* deals more with vegetables than with garden plants; it is also headquarters for the organic gardening enthusiasts' cult. *House & Garden, Better Homes and Gardens,* and *House Beautiful*

Narcissus

are slicks which are superbly edited, but the accent is more on the house and its furnishings than on the garden itself. However, their garden pieces, usually one big feature to an issue, are beautifully illustrated and full of ideas. And there are plenty of ideas in their features about outdoor living. Quarterlies are published by some of the associations devoted solely to horticulture. Those issued by the Brooklyn Botanical Garden and the New York Botanical Society are outstanding; serious gardeners usually join both groups. Their articles are generally authoritative, for most of them are produced by professional horticulturists—or home gardeners who could be professionals if they so desired.

A surprising number of American gardeners are members of the Royal Horticulture Society of London. Its monthly publication is interesting, and an excellent source for spotting new foreign developments in plants. Readers, however, are warned that it reports on plants grown in one of the temperate zone's most benign climates —degrees of "frost" is a British measure of winter weather, not degrees below zero—so it often turns out that plants hardy in Britain ("it withstands 20 degrees of frost") turn up their toes here or hate our scorching sun. In passing I mention the quality of the work of English authors who write of gardens. They are in most instances those who write so superbly about all manner of things. Our fine American authors spend little time gardening and rarely write about it.

The daily U.S. press pays attention to gardening, and many garden editors on large and small newspapers are knowledgeable. They are aware of the miserable and often misleading garden advertising their papers carry (the notable exception is *The Christian Science Monitor*), and those I have talked to about it are resentful but resigned. It's a little hard to imagine a garden editor, or any editor now that *The New Yorker*'s Harold Ross is gone, being able to exert any pressure on his advertising department.

The national horticultural periodical press attempts to report on gardening in the enormous range of U.S. climates. Some devote sections to gardening in the South, the Southwest, the Midwest, and the Pacific Coast, in an effort to present sectional garden problems. The business of being all things to all gardeners in the U.S., just because a magazine is "national," isn't very rewarding to most home gardeners. What New Englander cares about Miami's problems? Or vice versa? *Home Garden* and *Flower & Garden* do as well as they can with sectional reporting, but both contain enough good articles on general gardening practice to have value to their subscribers. *Home Garden,* under a vigorous new management, seems to be moving as fast as it can into the home service field occupied by the 3 big slicks. *Sunset,* a magazine devoted exclusively to the Pacific Coast, goes its way with California outdoor living so single-mindedly that a reader would never guess there was another civilized spot for living on the face of the earth. For those who do not garden there, there is one major thing wrong with gardening in the Pacific Coast: envy.

GARDEN PINKS—*see* Dianthus

garganica (gar-gan'ick-a) from Gargano, Italy

GARLAND FLOWER—*see* Daphne Cneorum

GAS PLANT—*see* Dictamnus

GAYFEATHER—*see* Liatris

genevensis (jen-e-ven'sis) of Geneva

GENUS—*see* Plant Family

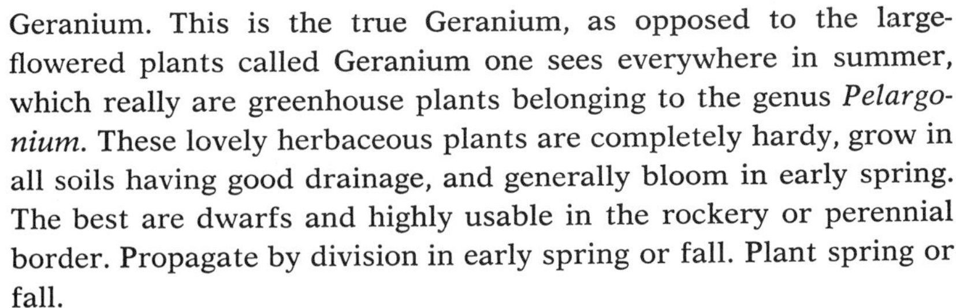

Geranium

Je-ray'ni-um

Geranium. This is the true Geranium, as opposed to the large-flowered plants called Geranium one sees everywhere in summer, which really are greenhouse plants belonging to the genus *Pelargonium.* These lovely herbaceous plants are completely hardy, grow in all soils having good drainage, and generally bloom in early spring. The best are dwarfs and highly usable in the rockery or perennial border. Propagate by division in early spring or fall. Plant spring or fall.

***G. dalmaticum.** Use this variety in the rockery or at the edge of the perennial border. It's a real dwarf with a spreading habit. Flowers, a delicate pink veined crimson, bloom on 6-inch stems all summer. Brilliant crimson foliage lasts into early winter.

***G. dalmaticum album.** The white form of *G. dalmaticum,* but there is a faint blush of pink in the center of each blossom.

G. grandiflorum. An excellent dwarf showing double purplish-blue blooms on 10-inch stems in May and June. As a border or rockery plant it is outstanding.

***G. subcaulescens splendens.** This crimson-pink dwarf is only about 3 inches high and is excellent for the rockery or in the front of the perennial border.

GERMANDER—*see* Teucrium

Geranium dalmaticum

Geum

Gee'um

Avens. An extremely hardy genus of about 7 species native to the cooler parts of the North Temperate Zone. The flowers and the foilage are both effective and they are not particular about soil. They do best in sun and thrive in light shade. They bloom early, but moisture will bring flowers all season. Plant spring or fall.

G. Lady Stratheden. This variety from a Chilean species shows golden-yellow double flowers on 2-foot stems.

G. Mrs. Bradshaw. Brilliant scarlet double flowers are on 2-foot stems.

G. Princess Juliana. Double, bright orange flowers on 2-foot stems. It is a profuse bloomer.

GINGER—*see* Asarum

Gladiolus. They are not hardy, of course, for these very valuable bulbous-rooted plants come from South and Tropical Africa. The very large ones do not make satisfactory border plants because most of them are too stiff—Gladiolus is Latin for a small sword. If a gardener plants corms in the cutting or vegetable garden as early as the ground can be worked, and continues plantings at 3-week intervals until July 15 (in zone 4; the last planting can be later southward), he can get cut flowers until frost. Giant Glads are not favorites of mine, but I do like named varieties of *G. primulinus*, the branching miniature Glad, for they are graceful, useful in arrangements and can be used in the border. With Giant Gladiolus varieties, which can be bought anywhere, care should be taken to chose proved older varieties, for current introductions are expensive and usually are not different enough to be worth the money. *G. primulinus* is somewhat hard to find. Plant spring only.

Culture for all Gladiolus. Plant corms at least 6 inches deep to keep flowering stalks from toppling. If put in rows in the cutting garden, keep the bulbs 3 to 4 inches apart. Spray early with *Sevin* to inhibit thrip, a common but easily controlled pest. In late fall dig the corms with a fork before the ground freezes, cut off the tops about ½ inch above the corms, then spread them thinly in flats to dry. When they are thoroughly dry pick off the little cormels, then snap off the new bulbs and store in a cool place in open flats. Next spring sow the cormels with the large ones to increase stock. Do this every year and you will soon have stock enough to sell.

Gladiolus

Gla-dye'owe-lus or Glad-ee-owe'us

Geranium grandiflorum

Butterfly-form Gladiolus

Butterfly and Miniature Gladiolus. The breeding of the following varieties is based on the species *G. primulinus.* All of the following varieties, except *G. P. Atom,* are from Dutch strains that have been awarded the highest honors by England's Royal Horticultural Society and by equally prestigious organizations on the Continent. The Butterflies seem to bloom a bit earlier than the Miniatures. Corms are 1½ inches in diameter, an ideal size—the very large ones are called platters and do not provide satisfactory flowers.

Miniature Butterfly Types—throat markings like butterfly wings:

G. p. Blondine. Pure white with a yellow blotch.
G. p. Donald Duck. This variety is creamy white with a red throat.
G. p. Femina. Deep salmon pink with a scarlet blotch.
G. p. Green Bird. A pale yellow chartreuse overall and heavily ruffled.
G. p. Greenwich. Lemon-yellow chartreuse overall that blends well with Green Bird.
G. p. Haute Couture. Ivory white with a cinnamon-orange blotch.
G. p. Mennon. Solid ivory in color but with a faint yellow throat.
G. p. Pertisan. It is orange scarlet all over.
G. p. Pirate. The color is solid scarlet and heavily ruffled.
G. p. Seqwin. Salmon pink is dominant, the two lower petals have a red blotch on a yellow ground.
G. p. Zenith. Pale pink overall and heavily ruffled.

Miniatures—blossoms conventionally marked:

G. p. Atom. A fine branching red, delicately edged with silver, bred in the U.S. and first introduced about 1941, has yet to be equalled. It is a "must," we add pontifically.
G. p. Candy. Cinnamon to peach with a brownish-red blotch does not adequately describe this variety's charming color.
G. p. Eridanus. Ivory white with a cherry-red blotch.
G. p. Page Boy. Somewhat similar to Atom in color but with a faint yellow edge.
G. p. Palermo. Palest of lavender with a blotch the color of a lavender Cattleya Orchid.
G. p. Sappho. Pure white, except for a faint sulphur-yellow blotch in the throat.

G. p. Tangiers. Brightest solid scarlet red.
G. p. Troef. Salmon pink with a yellow throat, ruffled.
G. p. White City. Every bit of it is pure white.

glau'ca (glaw'ka) gray or bluish green

GLOBEFLOWER—*see* Trollius

GLOBE THISTLE—*see* Echinops

GLORY-OF-THE-SNOW—*see* Chionodoxa

Gloxinia

Gloxs-in'ee-a

Gloxinia. To keep the record straight, the correct botanical name is *Sinningia* (sin-nin'ja-uh) *speciosa.* This plant is for indoor culture, and anyone who can grow African Violets can grow it. That is a lot of people, and I believe they will find Gloxinias more rewarding. The beautiful trumpet-like flowers may be obtained in many colors. Gardeners who are successful get great satisfaction growing these beauties—try to find a good one under $10 at a florist. Start the first bulbs in February or March, then plant at intervals for a succession of blooming plants.

Culture: Unpack tubers carefully and examine them for small pink buds on one side; plant those with largest pink buds first. Repack the remainder carefully, using vermiculite or completely dry sawdust and put in dry 50° storage. Leave the package or box open; every 2 or 3 weeks start another tuber. Leafmold (or compost) and loam with 5 percent coarse builder's sand makes a good potting soil. Fill a 5- or 6-inch clay pot with soil, tap it on the bench, then lightly compress. Press the tuber (the pink buds up) into the soil. Cover the buds—if small, only lightly (do not cover buds if ¼ inch or more high, but have the soil even with them). Syringe with water

Gladiolus primulinus

lightly until growth starts—the red buds become green leaves. Temperature should be 65°; place it in light but not direct sunlight. Plants require a reasonable amount of water as they grow (never allow water to stand in a saucer), but when they come into bloom, water only when the soil on top gets powder dry, or flower buds may blast. Fertilize lightly every two weeks. After all bloom is finished, continue leaf growth until they brown and show signs of going dormant, then withdraw water completely, but do not remove the stems (and dried leaves) until they fall away easily from the bulb. Put the potted bulb in dark, dry, cool 50° storage. When red buds appear again in late winter, put its pot back in the light, water it once to dampen soil, and continue as before. Unlike Tuberous Begonias, the bigger the Gloxinia Tuber, the bigger the plant and its flowers. Repot it in a couple of years to larger pottery.

There are several U. S. firms, most of them small, which specialize in Gloxinia. Some have interesting novelties. Most tubers, however, come from Europe. They are generally good; the prices are $1 or less. Gloxinia are shipped in late winter or early spring.

G. Blanche de Meru. Rose with white throat.
G. Emperor Frederick. Scarlet bordered white.
G. Emperor William. Violet bordered white.
G. Etoile de Feu. Solid scarlet.
G. Mont Blanc. Purest white.
G. Prince Albert. Darkest violet, heavily frilled.
G. Princess Elizabeth. Light blue with white throat.
G. Roi des Rouges. Solid crimson.
G. Violacea. Softest violet.

GLOXINIA (Hardy)—*see* Incarvillea

GOLDEN BELL—*see* Forsythia

GOLDEN CHAINTREE—*see* Laburnum

GOLDEN MARGUERITE—*see* Anthemis

GOLDENROD—*see* Solidago

gracilis (*gras'i-lis*) *slender*

grandiflora (*gran-di-floe'ra*) *large-flowered*

GRAPE HYACINTH—*see* Muscari

GRASS—*see* Lawns; Russian Buffalo Grass

GREENHOUSES. One can garden quite successfully without owning a greenhouse or a cold frame, but a gardener has far more latitude with one—he can winter non-hardy plants easily under its benches, and starting such plants as Tuberous Begonias indoors is better done in a glasshouse than a sunny window. The real joy of a greenhouse is in being able to raise such lovely plants as Orchids—as well as common annuals like Snapdragons and Stock—out of season and better than either can be grown outdoors. If one wants to fiddle with seedlings or cuttings, it should be done for the sense of satisfaction it gives—not to save money, because they'll be more expensive than those bought. Greenhouses, it need hardly be said, are not built for saving money. If good help is lacking, a greenhouse should be small and filled with every automatic device—to make it easy to run, and easy for you to run away from for a while without having to worry about the plants in it. If you do have help, build a larger house and equip it with two heat zones, so that almost any kind of plant can be grown—a 60° section (minimum night temperature) handles most kinds, but a 70° section is needed to handle the real tropicals, particularly most Orchids, which are great to have when grown in limited quantities. We suggest that you do not attach a greenhouse to a house unless it is to be used as a conservatory. Even then arrangements should be made for an outside door to move soil in and out. A detached greenhouse opening into a small shed (it's called a headhouse) is best. Any greenhouse under 18 by 25 feet is very small; a house more than 18 by 50 feet is probably too large for most gardeners.

GREEN THUMB. A green thumb, attributed to a gardener who grows plants effortlessly, is an old wives' tale. This ability comes from working with plants, from experimenting, personally, with their needs. It follows, I think, that a green thumb is a dirty thumb.

GROUND IVY—*see* Nepeta

GROUND CYPRESS—*see* Santolina

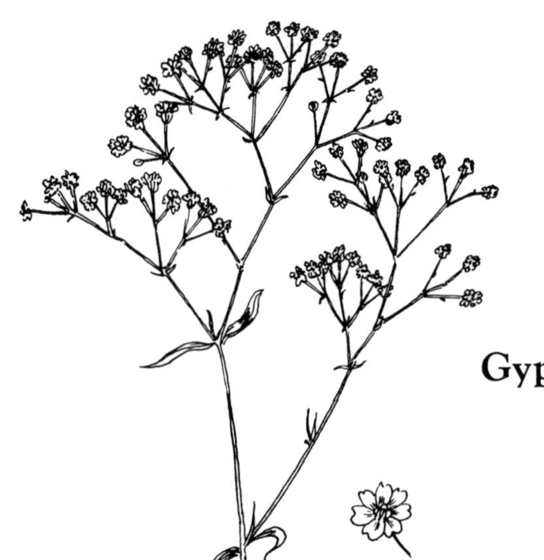

Gypsophila Pink Fairy

Gypsophila

Jip-soph'ill-a

Perennial Baby's Breath. An extremely popular garden genus of about 60 species from Eurasia. They are ever so useful in the perennial border and as trimmings for bouquets, for the flowers look like a delicate and beautiful veil. The flowers make sensational bouquets by themselves; mixed with other flowers they form background clouds of white or pink. They also dry well. Gypsophila likes a well-drained soil. It is a taproot and cannot be moved once established. Don't expect much the first season. Large-growing varieties like Bristol Fairy or Perfecta must be kept at least 6 feet apart. Blooms appear in June or July. Plant spring or fall.

Culture: Ordinary soil, full sun, and lots of water are about all that's needed to grow Gypsophila successfully. A handful of hydrated lime per square yard should be worked into the surface immediately surrounding the plant, for Gypsophila is a lime-loving plant. Repeat every third year. However, keeping the big varieties in a solid massive ball of tiny flowers is a bit of a trick. When an established plant grows to about 15 to 20 inches high, place finger-bamboo stakes closely around it—6 to 8 per plant. After all are in place, cut off the top of the stakes—24 inches of bamboo should show above the ground. Now take twine or a reel of *Twistem* and make the bamboo into a fence—really a tight corset, pull it 19th-century tight. This binds the branches tightly at the bottom part of the plant. As it grows, its heavily branching stalks will form a lovely feathery ball of bloom at the top and it will spill over to hide the tight fence made at the base. But be sure the fence is strong, otherwise the mature plant, drenching wet and hit by wind, will fall—fence and all. This good trick keeps Gypsophila stalks from being beaten to the ground in the first heavy rain.

G. Bristol Fairy. Pure white double flowers. It is a good idea to keep one or two plants in the cutting garden for floral arrangements as it blooms repeatedly if kept cut. Height is 4 feet.
G. Perfecta. A new introduction from Europe with double white flowers at least twice the size of Bristol Fairy. Perfecta is a far more vigorous grower than any Gypsophila introduced this past decade.
G. Pink Fairy. Flowers are extra large, fully double and a good bright clear pink. It grows to 18 inches, spreads, and it stays in bloom until frost.
***G. repens alba.** Here the creeping form which grows only about 4 inches high and spreads quickly. The plant is covered with a delicate cloud of tiny white blooms from June onward.
***G. repens rosea.** The pink form of the foregoing.

haematodes (*he-ma-toe'dees*) *blood red*

HAND TOOLS. An astonishing number of gadgets are produced for home gardeners, many of such low quality that they break, jam, or dull almost immediately. Experienced gardeners use a few hand tools of top quality—a trowel (balanced well and made of stainless steel), the principal hand tool for planting, and a small, stainless-steel hand-fork for roughing up the soil or digging individual plants.

Gypsophila Perfecta

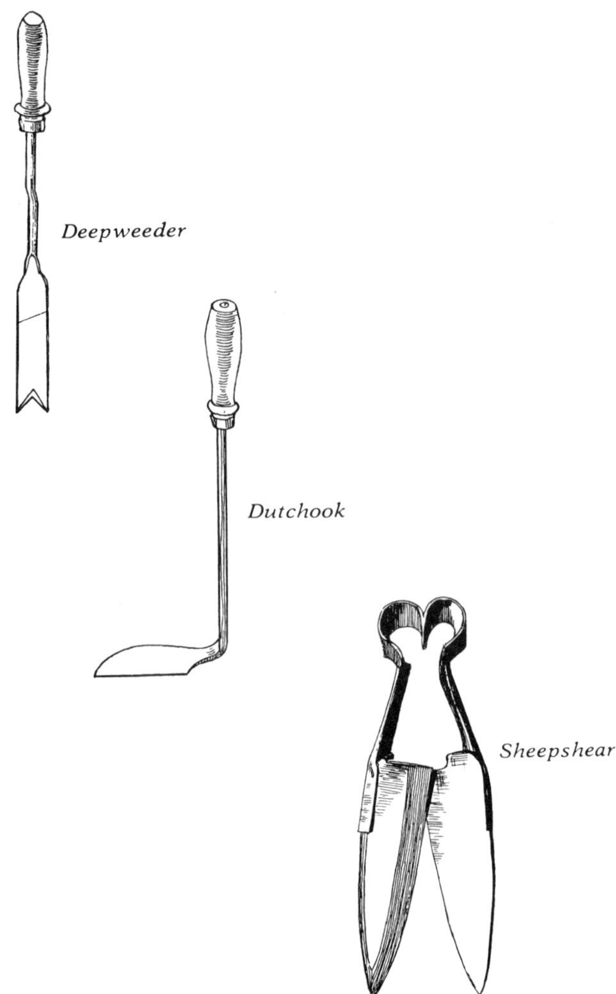

It is hard to get along without a really good pruner, and, of course, a stout pocket knife. Some gardeners think a dibble is helpful in transplanting, and it is; the blunt end is also useful for compacting plants in pots. It can be made from an old broom handle. A good idea is to paint hand tools red so that they are easy to find. (We once lost a green wheelbarrow for days in a shrub border.) All of these tools are easily obtained locally. Sheepshears are also a great help for cutting soft growth or edging a lawn.

HARDINESS ZONES. Little concerns gardeners more in the North Temperate Zone than the hardiness of plants. They also want to know what "half-hardy" means, as well as what is meant when a writer says that a hardy plant is tender. Half-hardy can be dismissed because it is apparently meaningful only to the user. Hardy plants, of course, are tender when they are very young or when they first come out of a greenhouse. Hardiness itself is a difficult term to define because so many factors besides temperature determine it. Temperature, however, *is* the ultimate determining factor of hardiness. The degree of maximum coldness, based on the range of the average annual minimum temperature, is the point of no return for any plant, be it an herbaceous perennial, a tree, or a shrub. Scientific work, first started by Harvard's Arnold Arboretum, now divides the United States and Canada into a series of 10 hardiness zones. Mr. Alfred Reheder published his first map of 8 zones in 1927; the present map is the work of Arnold's director, Dr. Donald Wyman, who is internationally known for his work in trees, shrubs, and vines. The Hardiness Zone Map on page 368 of this book is a copy of the most recent Arnold work. Before discussing other hardiness factors, let us first explore the temperature zones and set down the average annual minimum range for each.

Zone 1	*Below 50° below zero (F).*
Zone 2	*35° below zero to 50° below.*
Zone 3	*20° below zero to 35° below.*
Zone 4	*10° below zero to 20° below.*
Zone 5	*5° below zero to 10° below.*
Zone 6	*5° above zero to 5° above.*
Zone 7	*5° above zero to 10° above.*
Zone 8	*10° above zero to 20° above.*
Zone 9	*20° above zero to 30° above.*
Zone 10	*30° above zero to 40° above.*

Deciduous woody plants (trees, shrubs, vines, and evergreens) described in this edition are assigned hardiness zone numbers. Herbaceous perennials are not, because their culture, in most instances, requires winter protection to keep them from heaving and breaking their root systems in unseasonable winter thaws. Perennials, if kept frozen solid, can stand surprisingly low temperatures, particularly when covered with a blanket of snow. Perennials obviously have a point of no return from cold, but so far no measurements of this have been made. We doubt if gardeners would give them more than lip-service, anyway, for one of the great triumphs a gardener can experience is making a plant grow that others believe is not hardy, and it makes no difference what kind of plant it is. This happens constantly, and is due to local altitude, the protection afforded by a hill or woods or a house or by certain physiological factors that alert gardeners know about and try to alleviate and, of course, it is due to the skill of perceptive gardeners.

Some of these factors are far too complicated to encompass here, but one, the response of a plant to dormancy, is of major importance. If cultivated trees or shrubs respond to the rhythm of leaf-fall, as wild plants do, they, too, will survive. This rhythm is greatly affected by the water content of the cell structure—the wild plants hardly deviate more than days in the cycle, which is the reason they have not already perished. When entering dormancy, moisture content, particularly in the case of woody plants, is determined by the amount of summer rainfall or the use of irrigation. If there has been a slackening of rain as the season ages to September, the wood will start to ripen and the plant will begin to go dormant gracefully. But heavy rainfall will keep the summer's growth green and dormancy may come too late or not at all. When this happens the plant meets winter like a drunk, in the worst possible condition. When it dies because of this condition, it is said to be "not hardy," but this has little to do with temperature. Dormancy can be helped along by the gardener who uses sensible measures to counter unrhythmic conditions. For example, cultivation should be stopped in late summer, for it induces tender growth that does not winter; late pruning should not be done nor nitrogenous fertilizer used for the same reason. Summer drought, immediately corrected by irrigation, will keep the plant from suddenly shooting out tender growth—growth which won't winter—when the rains do appear.

Judicious planting on a site can provide plants of doubtful hardiness with good growing conditions. Shelter from prevailing cold winds plus a southern exposure will do wonders. Dogwood, for example, will not bloom where I live, although the tree itself is hardy. But a mile away—200 feet lower—at the edge of a woods close to Waterbury's principal reservoir, a small group of Dogwood blooms gorgeously every spring. They are in a porous soil, which proves the often-made point that fine drainage is a help to hardiness. Also, a plant of doubtful hardiness should never be planted at the lowest point of a site, for cold, early and late, will confound it. A further important point is that plants of doubtful hardiness are best purchased from places where the climate is known to be more rigorous than in the zone in which they are to be planted, for young plants taken from acclimated mother stock are more likely to survive.

By studying the Hardiness Zone Map a gardener can pretty well pinpoint his zone, but the height of his immediate terrain and exposure must be considered. Call your fuel dealer to get a better fix on the mean low temperature for your locality's coldest month. He works by degree days in delivering fuel and should be able to work this out for you. Even so, your home can be somewhat warmer or colder than his average, a problem only you can work out.

HARDY GLOXINIA—*see* Incarvillea

HAWTHORN—*see* Crataegus

HAZEL—*see* Corylus, Corylopsis

Heaths and Heathers

Heaths and Heathers. Several genera, all belonging to the great *Ericacea* family, are included in this heading in order to classify the many plants that have Heath- or Heather-like appearance but which in many instances are far from being kissing cousins and which rightfully belong in different parts of this listing. Practically, however, all belong under one heading. The genera included are *Bruckenthalia,* which has a single species called *B. spiculifolia,* also known as the Spike Heath because from casual examination it resembles Heath. Then comes Calluna, commonly called Heather and found wild all over Europe and Asia Minor. Next is *Daboecia,* with a single Heath-like species, which is also known as Irish or Connemara Heath. Last is Erica, true Heath.

Erica branches

I feel quite sure that this arbitrary bunching of genera of Heath- and Heather-like plants will be criticized by some of the experts. But we warn them that Mr. Harold Copeland of Chatham, Cape Cod, the outstanding U.S. authority on these fascinating plant groups, suggested it, and what is good enough for him is all right for us. His collection of Heath- and Heather-like plants from all over the world is magnificent.

Culture: Heaths and Heathers may be planted to provide bloom every season of the year. To get this effect select plants which bloom in each of the four seasons. The varying foliage colors of yellows, goldens, reddish tints, grays and greens add greatly to a garden's interest. Some varieties are shrubby and tall, others compact, still others are creepers. Most grow best in a bed consisting of 50 percent peat and 50 percent sand, or in a bed containing nothing but leaf-soil (soil from the floor of woods of deciduous trees). Some varieties detest lime, others merely tolerate it, some are completely indifferent to its presence. Lime-haters are identified in the following descriptions, but a principal point to remember about the culture of Heaths and Heathers is that all, regardless of genus, do better in acid than in sweet soils. How to tell if soil is acid? Get litmus paper from the local druggist, mix a bit of soil with distilled water (gas stations have it for batteries), plunge the litmus into the mixture. The druggist can read the degree of acidity—the *p*H factor (*see* *p*H factor)—from the litmus. To make soil acid, load it heavily with peat, plus some sand if it has a high proportion of clay. Full sun and good drainage are also required. Hardiness zones are indicated for each species, but it is nevertheless a good idea to place evergreen boughs over a planting to trap the snow, no matter how well the location is protected from unseasonably cold winter and spring winds. Many of the varieties listed will grow in a colder zone if planted protected from wind in a southern exposure and covered with evergreen boughs. Plant spring only in zone 4; spring or fall in zone 5 southward.

Bruckenthalia (brook-an-thay′lee-ah). Zone 5 southward, zone 4 with protections. A genus of evergreen shrubs native to southern Europe and Asia Minor. It has only one species.

B. spiculifolia. Spike Heath. This pretty little shrub stays extremely compact and has clusters of pink flowers on 5-inch stems in June and July. Not really a Heath, it looks so much like one that only experts can tell the difference. Place it in full sun, give it a gritty, lime-free soil, and it will be very happy.

Calluna (ka-loo′na) Heather, also called "Ling." Zone 3. These are the lovely shrubby evergreen plants, only a few over 18 inches high, that grow wild over Europe and Asia Minor and produce a profusion of long-lasting flowers from late June through November. It is particularly beautiful on the British Isles, where it covers otherwise bare hills and moors. It has also begun to grow wild in parts of the northeastern United States. Heather makes stunning dried flower arrangements that seem to last forever. Calluna is the Greek verb "to sweep," which harks back to ancient times when the dried branches and twigs of the plants were made into brooms. They are still made into brooms in some villages. The plants, which do well in poor sandy soil in full sun, are ideal for naturalizing. Nevertheless they grow much better in beds where their roots do not have to forage. Plants should be pruned each year after flowering to keep them in good form, but if this is neglected, cut back hard in the spring before new growth starts. The genus has only one species, *C. vulgaris,* but there are many forms, some dwarf, and innumerable hybrids. Depending upon size, plants sell from $2.50 to $6 and up.

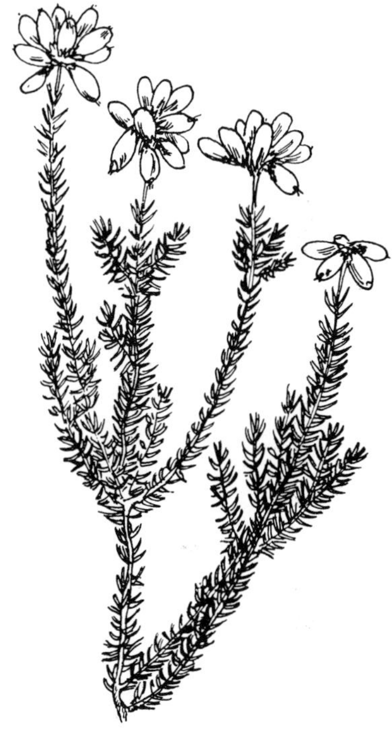

Erica Tetralix branch

***C. v. alba erecta.** This variety is white and blooms from June through August. It grows 24 to 30 inches high, which means that it will do well in a large rockery or mid-border in an all-heather planting.

***C. v. alba rigida.** This variety has an attractive habit of branching horizontally. It is covered with white flowers from July to September, and usually grows 12 to 15 inches high.

***C. v. aurea.** Because of its golden summer dress, this variety is called Golden Heather; in winter fringes of red, green and gold appear on the foliage. The lavender blossoms appear in July and August. Height: 15 to 18 inches. Use it in the rockery.

***C. v. County Wicklow.** A compact 15-inch plant that is loaded with sprays of of double pink flowers from July through September.

***C. v. Dainty Bess.** It seems odd that anything *vulgaris* (common) could be dainty, but this prostrate grower is. Foliage is a soft gray, the lavender flowers show in August and September. Height not over 4 inches.

***C. v. Foxii nana.** The tiniest of the tiny Callunas, this attractive thing looks like a 3-inch dark green ball of moss and paints itself with pinkish-purple flowers in August and September.

***C. v. Goldsworth Crimson.** This is one of the last Callunas to flower. It starts in August and continues to do so until November—with deep crimson blooms on 18-inch stems.

***C. v. H. E. Beale.** This is a strong, 24-inch spreading plant. Its branches are covered with largish, double pink flowers from August through November. It is excellent for cutting.

***C. v. Hammondii aureafolia.** This Calluna grows from 18 to 24 inches and has golden, plume-like foliage, particularly in the early stages of growth. Flowers are white and show in July, August, and September.

***C. v. Mrs. J. H. Hamilton.** This charmer spreads far beyond its 10-inch height. The deep green foliage is well massed with dainty, double, rose-pink blooms from July to December. It is ideal in the rockery.

***C. v. Mrs. Pat.** New growth is a delightful shade of pink, giving the effect of the plant being in flower in May and June. By late July the foliage becomes almost green, then the pinkish flowers appear. It grows 10 to 12 inches high.

***C. v. Mrs. R. H. Gray.** This variety is really dwarf—the bright green foliage is only 2 to 4 inches high. The lavender-pink blooms appear in August. A perfect rockery plant.

***C. v. mullion.** Deep pink flowers appear on this variety in late July. Its foliage is bright green. Height is 12 inches.

***C. v. Serlei aurea.** Foliage is bright golden on which white flowers appear in July. Height is 15 to 18 inches.

***C. v. Smith's minima.** A compact 6-inch dwarf with medium dark green foliage. Clear lavender blooms stay from late July to September.

***C. v. Tib.** Here is an unusual variety which grows to 24 inches. Its long spikes are covered with rose-purple flowers from June through October.

Daboecia (dab-ea'shi-a) Zone 5, zone 4 protected. Irish or Connemara Heath. Only one species, *D. cantabrica,* makes up this genus of low-growing, lime-hating, needle-like evergreen shrubs. It resembles *Erica,* but is distinct from it because of its shiny leaves and larger bell-shaped flowers. Failures with it are invariably due to lack of definitely acidity.

D. cantabrica polifolia alba. The bell-shaped flowers look like Lily-of-the-Valley. It blooms from June until November. Foliage is distinctly shiny green. The height is 12 to 18 inches.

D. c. praegerae. A compact grower, 12 to 18 inches high, with glossy green leaves and deep pink bell-shaped flowers which stand well above the foliage from June onward.

Erica (e'ri-ka) Heath. A very large genus of over 500 species of needle-like evergreens that come from South Africa and the Mediterranean region, although a few are found elsewhere. There are many forms, some tree-like, but most are bushy or prostrate—and it is from these that the best temperate zone garden varieties come. They range broadly in degree of hardiness and tolerance to lime. Because of this the approximate hardiness zone and lime tolerance is indicated for each species.

E. carnea. Zone 5, zone 4 protected. The following varieties of this species, called Spring or Winter Heath, come mostly from southern Europe and are tolerant of lime.

***E. c. Sherwoodii.** Sherwood Creeping Heath. It has carmine-red blooms in profusion from December to early spring. The foliage is brilliant green and the plant itself is a neat 6 inches high.

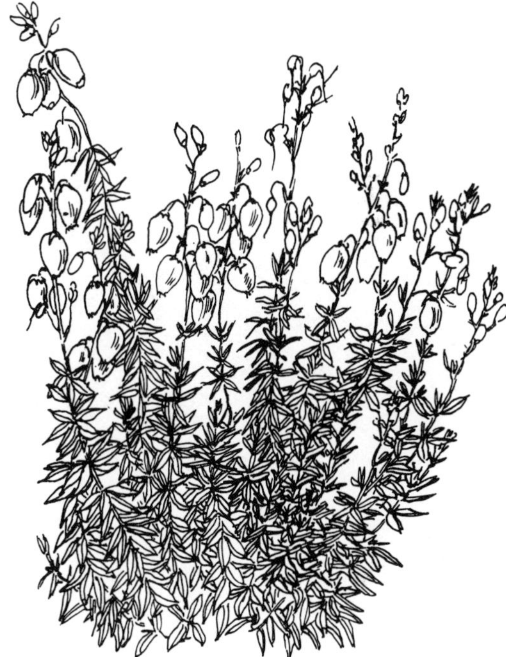

Daboecia cantabrica polifolia alba

Erica cinerea C. D. Eason

***E. c. Sherwood Early Red.** A very early variety that starts to bloom in late November or early December and then sends its bright red flowers through the snow. Grows to 12 inches.
***E. c. Springwood Pink.** This hybrid is an excellent ground cover, for it grows 6 to 12 inches high and its heavy root system spreads rapidly. It produces masses of clear rose-pink flowers during the milder days of winter and in early spring.
***E. c. Springwood White.** The same habit of growth and bloom as the foregoing. It is the best of all white creeping forms.
E. c. Vivellii. A truly little fellow—first it becomes a thick dark green mound only 6 inches high, later it spreads to about 2 feet. It flowers later than most *E. carnea*—it waits for spring and is then engulfed with carmine-red flowers which cause gardeners to say it is the finest dwarf Heath in existence.
E. c. Winter Beauty. During a mild autumn this hybrid will commence to flower and then continue throwing its bright rosy-pink blooms until early spring. It grows 6 to 12 inches high, and, of course, spreads.

E. cinerea. Zone 4, zone 3 protected. This species, the common "Grey Heath" of Scotland, is called Twisted Heath in other parts of Britain. It has naturalized itself in Nantucket. Color is reddish purple. Blooms come from June to September on wiry stems which grow 12 to 18 inches high. *It will not tolerate lime.*

E. c. C. D. Eason. Here is a choice Heath, about 12 inches high, that produces vivid crimson flowers in dense upright clusters during June and July.

E. mediterranea. Zone 6, zones 5 and 4 protected. This species of Erica is native to Western Europe and *is* tolerant of lime. It is a dense creeping evergreen shrub.

E. m. hybrida. Foliage is a very dark green, and grows as high as 18 inches. Blooms are a lovely rosy pink. They flower from late winter to early spring, which makes a pleasant sight when half covered with snow.
E. m. alba. Identical flowering and growth habit as the foregoing; blooms are white.

E. Tetralix. Zone 3. This European species is now busy naturalizing itself in the mild areas of the coast of eastern Massachusetts. It's called the "Cross-leaved Heath" abroad. The following varieties and hybrids *do not tolerate lime.*

E. T. George Fraser. A vigorous variety that grows from 12 to 15 inches high. From June to October it is covered with masses of deep rose-pink flowers; foliage is a grayish green.
E. T. Emollis. This variety grows to about 15 inches. The dark gray foliage is covered with white blossoms tinged pink from late June to October.

E. vagans. Cornish Heath. Zone 5, zone 4 protected. A species that has a spreading habit of growth but which is never prostrate. The height of varieties never exceeds 12 inches. Western Europe is its home. Its varieties *do not tolerate lime.*

E. v. Mrs. D. F. Maxwell. Outstanding. The clear cerise flowers are arranged in whorls on 6-inch stems. Blossoms from June to October.

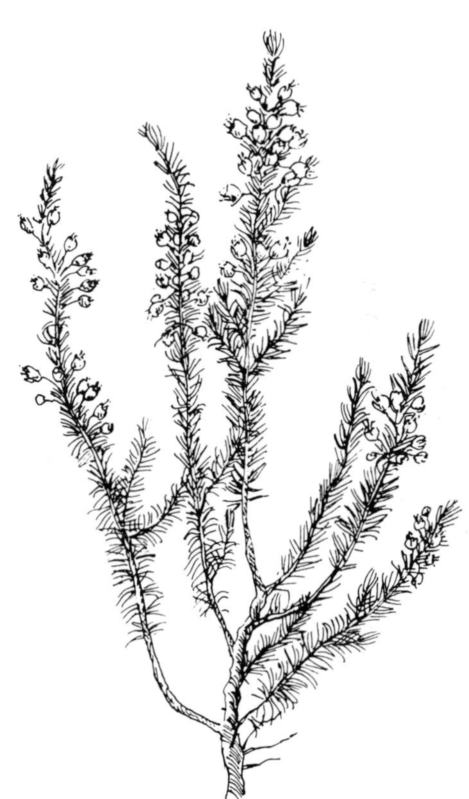

Erica vagans Mrs. D. F. Maxwell

Hedera

Head'er-ruh

Ivy. A genus of evergreen vines, native to Eurasia and North Africa, generally called Ivy. One species of English origin, *H. Helix,* provides the many varieties of English Ivy. They are most useful and it is hard to know what gardeners would do without them. The plant establishes rather quickly, and it is very easy to propagate from cuttings. Plant spring or fall.

H. Helix Baltica. Zone 5 and warmer parts of zone 4. This is the English species. Gardeners in zone 4 should test a few plants before trying a large planting.

Helenium

Hell-e'knee-um

Helenium. Named after Helen of Troy, this large genus is particularly valuable to gardeners with perennial borders, for it is a "bridge plant," i.e., it provides bloom between Phlox and Mums, the August–September period when few perennials are in flower. Rudbeckia,

Asters, and some Hemerocallis varieties are also bridge plants. Plant spring or fall.

H. Brilliant. This import is one of the most satisfactory of the late summer-blooming perennials. It starts blooming in mid-August and continues in profusion for nearly 6 weeks. The plant is a 3-footer, heavily branched (no pinching required), and it grows on a rugged stalk. Flowers are small but there are hundreds on each plant. The color—well, all the brilliant tapestry colors of fall.
H. Butterpat. All clear yellow. The best by far of the solid-color *Heleniums*. Excellent for cutting. It grows about 34 inches and blooms in August and through September.
H. Riverton Beauty. Bright yellow flowers highlighted with tints of orange. It blooms in August and September on very sturdy 4-foot stems.

Helianthus

*Helianthemum

Hee-lee-an'thee-mum

Rock Rose. This broad genus of low-growing and largely evergreen shrubs from the Mediterranean is made up of sun-loving plants that dislike shade and damp places. They grow well in a light soil heavily limed and are outstanding rock garden plants. Various species grow wild on limestone formations. Plant spring only.

***H. Buttercup.** Its golden-yellow flowers are on 10-inch stems. It is a pleasant dwarf. Blooms show from July to September.
***H. nummularium mutabile.** A dwarf shrubby variety that blooms from July through September. It likes full sun, and needs winter protection in very cold climates. It rarely grows more than 1 foot high. Colors are mixed.
***H. St. Mary's.** The white form of this excellent genus of dwarfs. July and September bloom. The height is about 10 inches.

Helianthus

He-lee-an'thus

Perennial Sunflower. About 60 species, most of them native to North America, make up this important genus. The name derives directly from the Greek (*helio,* sun; *anthos,* flower). One species is the common Sunflower, an annual. It requires full sun and gets along with little water, but does much better when irrigated normally. Plant spring only.

H. decapetalus multiflorus flora plenus. Delightful large sprays of almost double bright yellow flowers appear on the plant, which can grow to 4 feet in July, August and September, a time when few other perennials are in blossom.

Heliopsis
He-li-op'sis

False Sunflower. This genus is a native of North America. All of its perennial varieties are quite hardy. The blooms resemble small and perky sunflowers, and the plants are in flower from July until frost. *Heliopsis* do well in dry soils. Plant spring or fall.

Heliopsis

H. Hohlspiegel. This European import has 4-inch, golden-yellow, semi-double blooms from July onward. The petals are attractively serrated at the tips. It is an excellent cut flower. Stalks grow to about 36 inches.
H. Karat. A recent European import with very large single blooms of clear yellow on strong stems that grow to 4 feet. It will need protection from wind.
H. scabra Gold Greenheart. Its blooms are buttercup yellow with green centers and are 3 inches in diameter. They show from July to frost. It is fine for cutting or drying. Height is about 36 inches.
H. scabra imcomparabilis. The semi-double blooms are a rich golden yellow with dark centers and are about 3 inches across. It blooms from July until frost. An excellent cut flower; there is no better one for drying. Height is about 3 feet.

HELIOTROPE—*see* Valeriana

helix (hee'licks) old Greek and Latin name for a twining plant

Helleborus
Hell-e-bore'rus

Christmas Rose. This plant blooms in early or late winter (when the earth is not frozen). It requires a cool, moist, shady position (in the shade of trees or among ferns) and soil must be woodsy (mix it heavily with leaf mold and three-year-old cow manure; stay away from lime and inorganic fertilizers). Helleborus can be quite beautiful when grown well in the right location. Plenty of water is required in summer. Plant spring or fall.

H. niger. This is probably one of the most over-promoted plants in horticulture. Because Helleborus does bloom in cold weather it is hard to pick up a garden magazine in early spring or late fall without finding a headline, "Helleborus—it blooms through the snow." And it is so pictured—we feel it more likely that snow has fallen on it. Helleborus is, however, useful in a damp shady position. It takes a couple of seasons to get plants well established. The variety spreads rather slowly, but surely, and thereafter does better if it is seldom moved or divided. Flowers are white.

Hemerocallis

Hem-er-owe-cal'liss

Day Lilies. Each bloom lasts literally for a day, but the many buds on a scape provide a long period of bloom. The dozen species in the genus are mostly native to East Asia. They are of easiest culture, multiply freely, are permanent and apparently not palatable to insects. If one studies the approximate blooming dates of the varieties listed, a garden of Day Lilies can be built that will be in bloom from June to September. Hybridizers in this country have been very successful in creating new varieties—colors now range from softest yellow to almost fiery red. Move Day Lilies any time; they are the toughest plants we know.

Day Lilies make a very satisfactory plant for the perennial border. Also, if planted in mass close together, they require less work than any other kind of border, for little or no weeding is required. Put on 1-foot centers, in two years their arching grass-like leaves will shade the ground so heavily that weeds are inhibited. Scratching the soil around them in early spring and cultivating the front of the border hardly more than twice during the summer takes care of the weeding problem. Their heavy roots compete vigorously with tree roots. It is wise to fertilize them late each winter or in earliest spring. Later on, if one decides to propagate them by division, large divisions should be taken to get quick results. Plant spring or fall.

There are now literally thousands of varieties. New varieties are offered at horrendous prices—$100 and more—and some gardeners buy them. If they are bought as conversation plants—well, it's mighty expensive conversation. Within a few years prices tumble or one never hears of them again, which means that they weren't so good after all. We find the following varieties reasonably priced fine plant material:

H. Amber Wave. Ruffled amber flowers that look as if they were diamond dusted. Stalk grows from 30 to 36 inches. Blooms come from July onward.

H. Applause. This flower is solid cardinal red in color and has a green throat. Forty or more medium-large ruffled blossoms appear on 36-inch stems. It is well branched, and flowers mid-season.

H. April Dawn. The color of the 4-inch bloom is a blend of peach and pink. The throat is golden. The petals are broad, ruffled, and overlap. It's a nice thing. It grows to 30 inches and stands well. Flowers come a bit earlier than mid-season.

H. Big World. The flower is huge, its color apricot and it looks as if it had been brushed with translucent pink. The petals are creped and ruffled. The light green heart is a thoughtful addition. It blooms mid- to late-season; the scapes grow to 40 inches.

H. Bold Ruler. The color of the petals is a deep rose, but the sepals are a lighter tone. There is a cherry-red halo above its yellow throat. It blooms early. The height is 40 inches.

H. Bright Banner. Very large blooms, golden bronze in color, lightly brushed with red. The wide ruffled petals shade lighter at the center. Its long blooming period starts mid-season.

H. Carey Quinn. It is a lovely red flower of deepest hue with a velvety smooth look, and a small gold-green spot at the throat. It blooms early on 30 inch scapes.

H. Classic Simplicity. This well-named variety has 4- to 5-inch lemon-yellow blooms with a frilled, over-lapping petals. Its throat is touched with green. It branches strongly and blooms early- to mid-season on 36-inch scapes.

H. Colonial Dame. Flowers are a full 6 inches in diameter, light apricot in color,

Hemerocallis Colonial Dame

banded with pale rosy-tan; their throats are golden. It blossoms over a long period in mid-season. Height is about 36 inches.

H. Danish Duchess. This heavy bloomer (35 to 45 buds) is Majolica yellow with a rose overlay—on the clump the effect is pink. It grows from 35 to 40 inches and blooms from July onward.

H. Eagle Scout. Don't hybrids get the craziest names? Imagine, if you can, an Eagle Scout rose pink all over, with a clean cream throat. This scout's petals are ruffled and open to form a very large flower with a flat face. It's unusually beautiful and should be around a long time. It blooms mid-season on 32- to 36-inch scapes.

H. Evergold. This beauty is large, ruffled, and deep gold in color. Flowers are sun- and heat-resistant. It blooms mid-season, and is about 34 inches high.

H. George Cunningham. This variety, which has been extremely expensive in the past and which has won about every major prize, has now reached a far more reasonable price level. It can be bought for about $3. Color is melon (Casawba) with a gold to green throat; the thin midrib is lavender. The petals are ruffled, crepe-like in texture, and appear as lustrous as if powdered with diamond dust. Scapes are strong and bear from 30 to 36 buds. It blooms mid-season to late. Height under good culture is 36 to 40 inches.

H. Golden Wonder. This deep golden yellow is an excellent performer. Flowers are large and recurved. Blooms come mid-season. About 36 inches high.

H. Green Gold. The basic color is light primrose yellow overlaid with pale green; the green intensifies to lime green in the throat. The broad petals are slightly ruffled. Early to mid-season. Height 42 inches.

H. Holiday Mood. The mandarin-red petals are broad and ruffled. The blooms, which are sun-resistant, are a satisfactory size and there are lots of them. The plant, depending on culture, grows from 30 to 40 inches. It blooms in July.

H. Hyperion. Very large canary-yellow flowers. Although Hyperion has been around for 40 years it remains unsurpassed in its color class. It is one of the great performers. Flowers show in July and August. Height is 48 inches.

H. Illinois. The huge 6- to 7-inch flower is yellow; petals have the texture of crepe. It is sun-resistant. The flowering stalks start blooming in July and continue until frost.

H. Magic Dawn. This one blooms every day from late June until frost. The color is rose pink and the exterior of the bloom has a diamond-dust look. There are about 25 to 35 buds on each 36- to 40-inch stalk. It has won about every award in the book.

H. Nob Hill. The 5-inch-plus flower is lavender pink combined with yellow green. Its petals are gently recurved. It shows early on 36- to 38-inch scapes and continues bloom to mid-season.

H. Paradise Pink. When this variety opens in the morning the color is a deep but delicate pink, the throat greenish yellow. By evening the color changes to snow pink, the throat to pale gold. Superb. Mid-season to late; 34 inches high.

H. Peach Brocade. Like a ripe Elberta Peach, it's a blend of peach and rosy tones. Mid-season bloom on 34-inch scapes.

H. Petite Pink. The name is perfectly descriptive of its pleasant ruffled blooms. It branches well and flowers in mid-season on 35-inch stems.

H. Pink Prelude. Except for just a touch of cool yellow at the base of the sepals and petals, this lovely variety is all pink in varying shades. Height is about 39 inches. It blooms mid-season.

H. Pink Punch. This is a blend of coral pink with a deeper coral-pink halo; the throat is golden yellow to green. Height is about 38 inches. It blooms from mid-season.

H. Royal Command. This variety looks like bright red velvet and has an almost black halo above a small green-and-gold throat. It branches. Blooming period is early to mid-season.

H. Shining Plumage. The color of the widely-spread blossom is pure cardinal red. The flower is of medium size, but it is very floriferous on nicely branching scapes, which grow to about 3 feet. Blossoms come in July.

H. Shirley Wild. Here a truly colossal bloom on 34-inch scapes—flowers are a full 8 inches in diameter. Color is dandelion yellow from the tips of the petals to the throat, which shows a slightly green center. The fragrant blossoms show in July.

H. Snow Goose. The bloom opens cream yellow with white ribs—by evening the sun has turned it nearly white. Slightly frilled. Blossoms appear mid-season.

H. Sugar Plum Fairy. If you'd like to compare this beauty to a ballet dancer in a very ruffled orange tutu—well, that's the way it looks to us. Flowers are medium-sized and there are lots of buds on a scape. It grows to 30 inches and blooms early.

H. Summer Interlude. The ox-blood flower shows a velvety texture and possesses a yellow-green throat. Height is about 40 inches, and blossoms come from July onward.

H. Temple Bells. A variety that should have been called "musk melon," for the color is Majolica yellow. It shades to gold at the throat. The bloom has a crepe-like appearance. Scapes are 30 inches high; blossoms appear on them from July onward.

H. Theresa Hall. Here's a pink and gold gem that looks as if its slightly ruffled

Hemerocallis Paradise Pink

Chives

petals have been powdered with diamond dust. Scapes are up to 36 inches high; blooms appear in June and continue through most of July. Remarkable.

H. Three Cheers. A gay bi-color of medium size and quite floriferous. Petals are dark red, sepals golden, the throat a prominent green. Blooms appear mid-season to late. It is 36 inches high.

H. Whistling Swan. Its cool, pale yellow blooms turn almost white by evening; the throat is green. It flowers mid-season on a 36-inch scape which branches. It does not whistle.

HEMLOCK—*see* Evergreens, Dwarf Needle

HEN-AND-CHICKENS—*see* Sempervivum

HERB OF GRACE—*see* Ruta

herbaceous (*her-bay′sush*) *perennials which die to the ground annually*

HERBICIDES. The weed killers developed by the chemical industry are a boon to gardeners trying to maintain decent lawns. Their use is described in detail—*see* Lawns. Poison Ivy and other non-lawn pests are easily controlled with 2-*4D* mixed with kerosene or any other light oil. Herbicides are most effective when applied during hot weather, but follow directions carefully. Do not use them close to ponds or pools. If you use them devote one spray tool to this job, because cleaning a sprayer after using a herbicide is difficult and the residue can kill if the same sprayer is used for insecticides.

Unselective or total herbicides, used 2 to 3 weeks before planting, are now in general use in agriculture. They are particularly useful in the nursery business, for they almost eliminate hand weeding, a very expensive operation. These total pre-planting herbicides are also sold to gardeners in small quantities. If used exactly as directed, they are helpful, but we do not recommend them for the home garden, as they are so difficult to use and dangerous to user and plants.

Herbs
Hurbs

Herbs for Kitchen Gardens. All herbs in the list are perennials, and except for Rosemary are hardy; all are for eating—except Lavender. (Rosemary, which takes cold down to 10° to 15° above zero, is probably hardy in zone 6, and southward, if well protected.) You don't need many plants—herbs are strong stuff and should be used sparingly in cooking. One should seek a flavor, not a taste. There are many more culinary herbs, but the following kinds are the ones most generally used by cooks. Plant them in full sun in a garden convenient to the kitchen. They are not fussy about soils. Like all perennials they need winter protection. Plant them spring or fall. (The most important culinary herbs that are annuals and must be raised from seed are Basil, Dill, and Fennel. If you can buy plants from a nice "little" nearby herbalist, you are lucky; few nurseries or garden centers stock them.)

Chives. The flower, a small purple cluster on 10-inch stems, appears in early June and is decorative. It is an attractive and very inexpensive edging plant for a perennial border. The finely chopped leaves are used for flavoring salads or hors d'oeuvres. (To make chive bread: chop and mix with soft butter, spread one side of a slice of bread—homemade, *Pepperidge,* etc.—put slices back in loaf form, then bake 20 minutes in foil in a 350° oven. Serve immediately.) A strong grower; cut it back hard to induce new tender shoots.

Costmary. Use the whole leaves or chop them to brighten the taste of mid-summer lettuce or vegetable salads. A little does it.

Lemon Balm. Good in mint sauce when used with fish, lamb, beef or in salads. Use sparingly.

Lovage. Excellent for soup. It can be used either fresh or dried in

Satureia montana

Sweet Cicely

recipes that call for curry. But be careful—one leaf of fresh lovage flavors enough soup for four people.

Mentha piperita (Peppermint). This is the mint with strongest peppermint flavor.

Origanum vulgare (Marjoram). Use the fresh leaves sparingly to flavor soups and gravies. Dry them and young shoots for winter use. This perennial, it should be noted, is marjoram flavored. True marjoram is an annual called Sweet Marjoram. Grow it from seed or buy plants from local herb specialists; it is almost impossible to find in ordinary trade channels.

Rosemary. It is not hardy below 15°, but almost as important as Tarragon for cooking. Plant it in a large pot and winter it over as an indoor house plant.

Sage. The dried leaves are used for flavoring meats, soups, stuffings and dressings. One plant is enough of this strong stuff.

Satureia montana (Winter Savory). This flavors string beans and other vegetables, fish and meat, but use it sparingly. And, if you don't want it for your kitchen, remember that it makes an excellent edging plant for borders—clip it to form a low hedge.

Shallots. Shallots, which originated in Palestine, are bulbs having a delicate onion flavor widely used by gourmet cooks. Grow them in the vegetable or kitchen garden. Bulbs must be planted with the top just showing at the surface. They need good drainage and a soil rich in humus. Heavy clay soils are not suitable. When leaves yellow, growth is finished; lift and dry them in the sun for 2 or 3 days and then clean off old scales and leaves before storing them in a refrigerator vegetable bin or in a cool dry place.

Spearmint. The leaves provide mint flavor for beverages or meats, particularly lamb.

Sweet Cicely. A few chopped leaves added to salads and cold dishes give a delightful zest.

Tarragon. This is a basic flavoring in France. Fresh leaves are chopped finely and mixed with salads or used to garnish meat or fish. Dried leaves flavor soups or pickles in winter. And do you know about keeping Tarragon green in the winter? Stuff a large-necked gallon jar with washed green Tarragon leaves, fill it with red vinegar that has been heated to the boiling point. When decanted you have Tarragon Vinegar. To use the leaves fish them out of the vinegar and rinse in water. Stuff a chicken with it—the kind of chicken with a breast so big that if it didn't keep walking it would fall flat on its face—and you have Chicken Tarragon. A kitchen without Tarragon is almost in the same boat as a kitchen without salt or pepper. The best varieties come from France.

Thyme (Common *Thymus vulgaris*). Its fresh leaves are used in salads; dried leaves are important for meats, soups, and gravies.

heterophylla (he-ter-owe-fil'la) having leaves of different shapes

Heuchera

*Heuchera

Hew'ker-a

Coral Bells or Alumroot. Heuchera is an attractive genus of over 70 species native to the Rocky Mountains. They are stout plants with attractively shaped leaves; the bell-shaped flowers are carried on long stems. They make dainty cut flowers. Heuchera like a rich, moist, well-drained soil, but they'll grow in practically anything. Plant them 12 inches apart in the border in clumps, or use as edging plants or in nooks in the rockery. Divide about every third year. Heuchera bloom from June on. Plant them spring or fall.

***H. Pluiede Feu'.** Deep pink, almost cherry-red blooms that open wide on strong sprays about 18 inches high.
***H. Rosamundi.** Bright coral-pink bells on 24-inch stems. It is an excellent cut flower.
***H. sanguinea.** Bright crimson flowers on 12- to 18-inch stems. It flowers freely from June to September. It is also excellent for cutting.
***H. White Cloud.** White bells blending to cream on 18-inch spikes. It blooms from June through September if kept cut back.

Hibiscus

Hy-bis'kus

Mallow. A huge genus of more than 200 species having great horticultural interest but practically all native to the tropical areas of the world. The Mallows that are pictured in catalogues have great showy flowers and are delicious to look at—in the pictures. But most catalogues don't go to the trouble of indicating that these Mallows certainly are not hardy in these parts, or even in zone 5, unless protected or in the warmer parts of it. And even there a real tough winter will kill them. If one sees them growing consistently in a locality, it is safe to buy them, but check anyway with someone who grows them rather than with people who sell them. If you live in zone 9, or the warmer sections of zone 8, go ahead—that is where they are really hardy. One species, *Hibiscus syriacus,* is hardy in some of the colder parts of the U.S. and the southern portion of the Ontario peninsula. *H. syriacus,* Rose of Sharon or Shrubby Althea, is a tree that grows to 15 feet and is hardy from zone 5 southward. Its only garden interest is that it blooms in late August, a time when few other shrubs do. It sets no fruit and its fall foliage looks blah. We fiddled with it for a few years, pruned it to get larger flowers, and did, but the little tree's appearance was ruined for most of the summer. In cold areas like ours it needs protection; it needs protection the first couple of winters almost everywhere. But once established it *does* bloom in August.

HILL. "Plant a hill of this" is an instruction gardeners see regularly. Those who run vegetable gardens know what is meant, for corn is planted this way by putting several seeds in a circle 6 to 8 inches in diameter. A hill of bulbs means that up to 12 are planted in one hole, a large one if they are Daffodils, small if Crocus. The earth in the bottom of the hole should have bonemeal or sewage sludge mixed thoroughly into it.

HOLY FLAX—*see* Santolina

HOLLY—*see* Ilex

HOLLYHOCK—*see* Althaea Rosea

HONEYSUCKLE—*see* Lonicera

HORSE CHESTNUT—*see* Aesculus

Hosta

Hos'ta

Plaintain Lily or Funkia. This widely cultivated garden plant has 10 species, all of them from China and Japan. Most are very hardy. The species have many handsome leaf colorations and various colored lily-like flowers in clusters, which show in late summer on graceful stalks or racemes. *Hosta* likes any moist location in full or part shade. It dislikes sun but will grow in it. This truly delightful plant is great for mass plantings in heavily shaded areas. Plant close together for immediate effect. Also, in a year or two the plants' broad leaves will create too much shade for weeds to grow between the plants. Names of varieties in the various species are dreadfully con-

Hosta

fused. Because some varieties are sold under as many as three completely different names, the chances of duplicating what one has bought already is not slight. Plant them spring or fall.

H. decorata marginata. Well-formed oval leaves with a very pleasant white margin provide interest when the plant is not in flower. Blooms, which come in early August on 30-inch stems, are lavender purple with white veins.
H. glauca. This variety has large blue-green leaves and violet flowers on 24-inch stems. It blooms in July and August.
H. Honeybells. Fine, soft, lavender-lilac flowers on 3-foot spikes. The fragrant florets are about 1½ inches in diameter. They are marked with darting blue on a white underbase. The foliage is grass green in color. It blooms July and August.
H. lancifolia. A narrow-leaved variety which blooms quite late—in August and September. Foliage is a waxy green color, and the medium-sized bell flowers rise pleasantly to ring a lavender tone. Height is 2 feet.
H. subcordata grandiflora. Large, pure white, very fragrant lily-shaped flowers show in August and September on 2-foot stems. It is used extensively as a ground cover. If you live in zone 4, place orders for this variety for spring delivery. It is somewhat tender, but after it is established the cold weather does not bother it.
H. variegata. It has green and cream variegated leaves and violet-blue flowers. It blooms July and August on 18- to 24-inch stems.

HOUSELEEK—*see* Sempervivum

HUMUS—*see* Manure

Hyacinthus

High-a-sin'thus

Hyacinth. This great group of bulbs from the Lily family has about 30 species, most of them from the Mediterranean shores and from tropical and South Africa. They are used as spring-flowering bulbs all over the temperate world. The lovely flowers have a heavy perfume. Plant Hyacinth about 6 inches deep and be positive that drainage is excellent, for they are guaranteed to rot out if water stands on them. All are splendid for forcing. Plant fall only. There are many other varieties, but the following have a good range of color. Bulbs cost about $4.25 a dozen.

H. Anne Marie. The softest of pink.
H. Carnegie. Pure white bells of unusual size.
H. City of Haarlem. Soft yellow.
H. Delft Blue. Well, it's Delft blue.
H. La Victoire. Carmine rose.
H. Orange Boven. Excellent salmon orange.
H. Ostara. Dark blue.
H. Pearle Brilliant. A fine light blue.
H. Pink Pearl. Rose pink.

hybrid (high'brid) a plant produced by crossing two species or varieties. See *Plant Family*

hyemalis (high-em-ay'lis) of the winter, usually indicating plants flowering at that time

Hydrangea
Hy-drain'jee-uh

Hydrangea. This is an important garden genus of some 35 species, most of them native to North America and Asia, but there are some species in South America and Indonesia (Java). It is not at all hard to over-plant small grounds with them, a fact that is quite evident wherever they grow in the United States, for, as they show with a vengeance in late July and August (the time few shrubs are in bloom) there is always a tendency for the home gardener to plant "just one more" because they are so reliable. My own feeling is that most of them are gross, and my eyes get particularly beady at the sight of *H. paniculata grandiflora,* the one most used because it is inexpensive to buy and very easy to grow. Nurserymen can grow it from cuttings to a large bush in practically no time, and a plant that will do this is to them a jewel. (That's one reason why we see so very many Weeping Willows.) Hardy even in the colder parts of zone 4, this variety's huge white panicles, which change to dirty pink as they age, become as monotonous as pines closing in a Maine road. *H. macrophylla Hortensia* is hardy mostly in zone 6. In zones 5 and 4 it is a house or patio plant which needs winter protection. (It is over-planted outdoors throughout the South and the Pacific Coast.) Also, one can load the soil with lime, say abracadabra, and the flowers turn pink; add alum and say it again and they become blue. This is as close as I've ever come to magic and it's amusing—once. *H. macrophylla caerulea* is a Japanese variety brought back by "Chinese" Wilson. It is blue with no tricks. We have a couple of plants here, but it is really too cold for them. They are, however, protected, and the branches below the snowline usually bloom, one panicle to a stalk at its terminal. But one never sees them for long in the garden, for a girl called Grant cuts every one as soon as they show, because she has learned that they make fine large bouquets and last well indoors. *H. quercifolia,* the Oak-leaved Hydrangea, blooms better in zone 5 than here. It's a dense, handsome shrub with dark green leaves, comes up from the roots every year, and its greenery alone should be welcome in any northern garden. Also, it will bloom if winter has been mild. *H. petiolaris,* a vine that *is* hardy in zone 4, deserves a great deal more attention than it has had so far from American gardeners. It will climb to 60 feet, and when it blooms its masses of loose, delicate flower-clusters is a gardeners' kind of Soul.

Hypericum

High-pear'i-kum

St.-John's-wort. There are several hundred species in this North Temperate Zone genus, but only a very few varieties have garden interest. One is a fine, low-growing sub-shrub (means partly woody) that flowers brilliantly from early summer until stopped by frost. It can be used very successfully in the perennial border or in the foreground of shrub plantings. Spring planting.

H. Hidcote. A fine dwarf with bright yellow cup-like flowers 2 inches in diameter. In zone 5 and southward the top winters well, but it generally freezes back to the crown farther north. However, it throws new stems in the spring; blooms appear in late June to August.

*Iberis

Eye-ber'is

Perennial Candytuft. This rather large genus of about 40 species of annuals, biennials, and sub-shrubs are all natives of southern Europe and western Asia. The name is derived from Iberia, as you know, the ancient name for Spain, from which many of them come. Those listed are plants having woody branches which perish at the very tips over winter. They are also evergreen, but in the north, after a hard winter, they don't look very evergreen. Expect them to look beat up, but after the dead tips are cut off the plant regains its dark green color, new leaves form. They bloom gloriously in May. They can also be clipped into a very low hedge. Full sun and a rich, well-drained garden soil are their only requirements. Plant in the spring or fall.

Iberis Little Gem

***I. Little Gem.** Pure white flowers in May. A true dwarf; flowers reach 6 inches in height, foliage is about 3 inches high. A perfect edging or border plant; excellent for rock gardens.

***I. Purity.** Somewhat larger than *I. Little Gem.* Very uniform in growth, the plants look like miniature spreading evergreens after being a mass of white when flowering in May.

***I. sempervirens Autumn Snow.** This robust variety does its best to please: it blooms in spring, then again in September, and stays in bloom until frost. As it's compact, the variety works out well in the perennial border, in the rockery, or for edging. It is 7 inches high.

Ilex

Eye'lecks

Holly. Litchfield is too far north for most of 300 species of these fine trees and shrubs, which are widely scattered over the warmer parts of the temperate zones and the tropics. Bushy forms that are hardy (Black Alder, Inkberry, and Winterberry) are deciduous, and although their berries are attractive, they are not what most people think of when they think of Holly. What they have in mind is the beautifully shaped and lustrous evergreen leaf with red berries, the traditional Christmas Holly. That's what the English brought to America in early colonial times; its proper name is *Ilex Aquifolium.* As it has been grown for centuries, the number of named varieties are countless. Thus there is no way of knowing if a variety is abnormally dense, heavily berried, or beautifully shaped, unless one goes to the trouble of seeing a mature tree. It is best to buy a small specimen that is satisfactory, because moving a large tree is a tricky business, and expensive. Furthermore, one must plant a pollen-bearing tree in the near vicinity for the pistillate to produce berries. All of this also applies to *I. opaca,* the native form, which also has red berries. Its leaves, although shaped like its British cousin's, are not lustrous. Most forms are dense. Note that pollinate branches can be grafted on pistillate trees, instead of planting a pollinate separately, but it is wise to insist on a tree having several grafts, instead of one which might get broken.

Incarvillea

In-car-vil'lee-a

Hardy Gloxinia. These natives of Tibet and China insist on full sun and a well-drained sandy soil enriched with humus. The foliage looks somewhat like fern, the flowers resemble non-hardy Gloxinia in shape, but are much smaller. Plant spring only.

I. Delavayi. The blooms of this species are rosy purple in color and their throats are yellow. Blossoms start in late May and continue to June. We have succeeded in growing them here in zone 4 with special protection. From zone 5 southward the species is more permanent. This is a tender, borderline fellow, but more than worth trying to establish.

incomparabilis (in-kom-pa-ra'bi-lis) unequalled

inflorescence (in-floor-es'cens) the arrangement of flowers as they grow on a stalk, usually used in describing multiple blooms on a single stem, as, "the inflorescence of this Phlox is a tight mass."

INSECTICIDES. After reading Rachel Carson's book about the dangers of using modern insecticides—mostly derivatives of devilish gases which have yet to be used in warfare—the average reader is inclined to blanch at the thought of any spray material more powerful than pyrethrum or sulphur dust. Although we used some of the highly toxic stuff before *The Silent Spring* was published, we use none any more. The evidence is just too conclusive that the ecology of an area is upset when these insecticides are used for long. It is sad and surprising that these dangerous things are still packaged for home garden use; it is shocking that every horticultural magazine still prints stories by men with doctorates who continue to recommend them—at the same time various states are outlawing their use.

Here is some general information about the use of insecticides: use an all-purpose spray to cut work—one, in other words, that combines insecticide and fungicide (*Sevin,* an insecticide, and *Captan,* a fungicide, can be combined). The principal point about insecticides and fungicides is to use them *before* the plants need them. A stitch in time saves 9—leaves, stalks, plants, or what have you. Then keep a regular spray schedule going—every 2 to 3 weeks. If you do, bugs and fungus should give little trouble. Should you use insecticides in liquid or dust form? You choose; we think liquid best. Add one of the spreaders (also called stickers) to the potion. Do you have many trees? If so, call your local tree man, who has big spray equipment, and make a deal with him for the necessary number of sprays during the season—two is usually enough. Do you have fruit trees to spray? If you are an orchardist, you'll know what to do; if not we suggest a no-spray schedule and the purchase of the fruit from a supermarket—home-grown fruit is expensive, and purchased fruit is usually better, although we admit it does not taste as good as fruit off one's own trees.

Reference is made in this book from time to time to *Sevin,* an insecticide. It is a modern, low-residual contact insecticide and can usually be bought locally. *Captan,* a fungicide, is also mentioned. It, too, is generally available. Both are made by Stauffer Chemical Company. A substitute for *Captan* is *Bordeaux Mixture,* a satisfactory specific for fungus for years.

intermedia (*in-tur-mee'dee-a*) *between extremes*

involucrata (*in-vol-you-kray'ta*) *with the leaf edges rolled together*

Iris
Eye'ris

Iris. This huge genus of about 200 species, native to the North Temperate Zones, consists of herbaceous plants with rhizome, tuberous, or bulbous root stocks. Many have been garden subjects from early times. Those most generally used are the bearded species. There are many of them, including various sub-sections, but intensive inter-breeding has made classification far too complicated for home gardeners to follow—or to care about. The bearded forms used to be called German Iris, but this classification is being dropped by many horticultural organizations. Bearded, beardless, intermedia, dwarf, and Kampferi, etc. are more meaningful general classifications.

Common or bearded Iris is exceedingly easy to hybridize, and hundreds of "originations" are offered each year at prices up to $50 and more per rhizome. These originations may have such value to hybridizers, but in our opinion no bearded Iris is worth much over $5 as a garden subject, for the $50 origination, providing it is outstanding, will drop to half that amount or less the second year, and far lower in succeeding years as stocks build in the hands of growers. If one never hears of the variety again, the expensive origination turned out to be a dud. We have attempted to eliminate the duds by testing the new Iris that seem to have a chance to succeed. The result is the following list of highly satisfactory reasonably priced varieties. Planting times are noted under each of the following species, all of which are hardy.

Control of Iris Borers: There is only one sure way of keeping borers out of Iris. When new leaf growth in the spring is 3 inches high, remove all dead leaves and weeds, and dust or spray with a contact insecticide. Then dust or spray twice again at weekly intervals. This routine will keep a planting clean; it will not kill borers already infecting plants (*see* Insecticides).

Bearded Garden Iris. These sensationally showy creatures have remarkable coloring. Except for a few good novelties, the following varieties are all solid, blending, or two-tone in color. Use them in bold groups in the perennial border. A solid bed of Iris, no matter how colors are mixed, is a most satisfactory possession. They are very useful as cut flowers, but cut them in full bud so the display will last longer. Bloom comes in May and June. Move or plant in

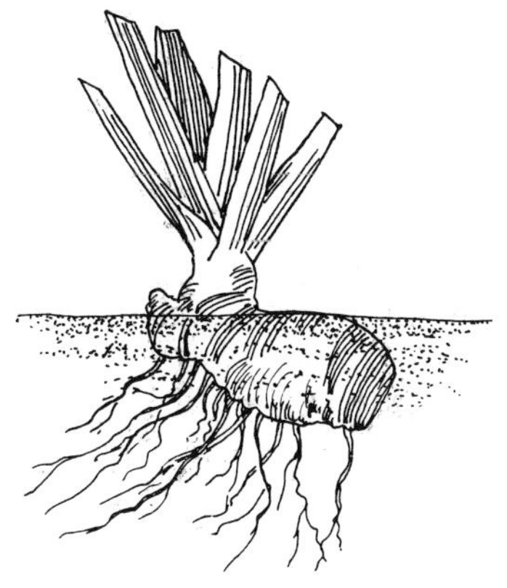

The Culture and Care of Iris

Drawing (left) is schematic of Iris in fourth or fifth year of growth, the time to replant. Discard old growth; cut and save only heavy tubers (called rhizomes)—use sharp knife and cut back past borer holes and soft spots. Leave in sun for a day to callus the cut (or dust with sulphur). Replant, making sure neck of tuber is just below the surface. Do this work from July through September. Soil need not be rich. Plantings flower little the first year, are sensational until crowding starts in fourth or fifth year early fall—before September 15 in zone 5 northward, by October 1 southward.

I. Accent. A flamboyant red-purple and yellow bi-color whose strong colors are glistening and fresh. It blossoms in June on 36-inch stems.
I. Amethyst Flame. Large ruffled blooms; the color falls between lavender and light violet. Outstanding. It grows to 38 inches and blooms mid-season to late.
I. Blue Baron. Massive marine blue and gorgeously ruffled with 15 to 18 buds on each 40-inch stem. It blooms mid-season.
I. Brasilia. A henna so brilliant it is hard to believe it's real. It blooms mid-season at 40 inches.
I. Bronze Bell. It is rich reddish copper with a metallic luster. Blossoms are massive and ruffled. Stalks are 36 inches high. Early to mid-season bloom.
I. Butterscotch Kiss. This variety is basically barium yellow in color with faint orange infused falls; the center and edges of the petals have gold tones. It blooms mid-season to late on 36-inch stems.
I. Captain Gallant. An unadulterated beauty—richest copper red inside and out. Blooms mid-season. It grows to about 34 inches.
I. Celestial Glory. Orange and gold falls; its beard is orange red. Ruffled, broad, flaring. It blooms mid-season at 36 inches.
I. Cloud Cap. The largest of the flamingo-pink varieties (often 7 inches across) with a showy tangerine beard. Height is 40 inches. Blooms mid-season to late.
I. Crinkled Ivory. A giant glistening ivory-cream flower, flushed light lemon in exactly the right restrained amount. Blooms early to mid-season on 34-inch stalks.
I. Eleanor's Pride. Powder blue all over and lovely. Height 40 inches. It blossoms in mid-season.
I. Frost and Flame. It is snow white with a brilliant tangerine-red beard. Blooms early to mid-season on 3-foot stems.
I. Green Quest. "Nearest to green" is one way to describe this beautiful thing—or say it's a bright primrose yellow with a chartreuse-green cast. It blooms late on 36-inch stems.
I. Happy Birthday. A flamingo pink. Blooms mid-season on 3-foot stems.
I. Helen Collingwood. Light lavender standards and brilliant purple falls. Ruffled. Blooms mid-season to late; 30 inches high.
I. High Above. Solid sky blue with a satin finish. The flowers are wider than usual and ruffled. Height is 36 inches. Early to mid-season.
I. Indiglow. Deepest of violet blue, velvety, brilliant. Gigantic blooms come early and continue to mid-season. Height is 40 inches.
I. Jane Phillips. A new light true blue. Blooms mid-season on 38-inch stalks.

I. June Meredith. Rich flamingo pink—every part of the beautiful thing. Blooms mid-season to late on 36-inch stems.

I. Lavanesque. Delicate orchid pink overall, ruffled, with a golden beard. Its height is 40 inches and it blooms early.

I. Lilac Festival. This one is light orchid and the beard is the same color. The thing appears to have a silver tinting, but perhaps only to our eyes. Height is 33 inches and it blooms early to mid-season.

I. Lynn Hall. Very deep shade of pink and a vigorous grower. Height is 36 inches. It blossoms mid-season.

I. Newport. Bluest of blue plicatas with a snowy background which is edged cerulean blue. All blue tones, but not a touch of Monday morning blue in them. It blooms early at 38 inches.

I. Olympic Torch. This torch glows a light golden bronze. It also branches well. Height is 40 inches; it blooms late.

I. Orange Parade. Orange Parade is a lovely variety, but difficult to describe. Its color is vivid, something between Marigold and Valencia orange; the beard is a deep—well, call it a fire-red orange. Height is 38 inches and it flowers early to mid-season.

I. Pacific Panorama. As impressive as the Pacific Ocean and a blue of a hue infrequent in the world of flowers. Height is 42 inches and it blossoms mid-season.

I. Palomino. The standards are a blend of ivory, soft amber copper, and pink. The falls are ivory with a narrow band of amber copper extending around the outer edges. Blooms early to mid-season at 3 feet.

I. Rainbow Gold. Spectacular because of the size of the bloom and the intensive yellow and tangerine colors. All the petals are heavily crimped. Blooms mid-season at 38 inches.

I. Ranger. Dark but very bright almost true crimson red overall. It has long, cone-shaped, closed standards, wide falls of glossy velvet texture, and a bronze-orange beard. A late bloomer at 36 inches.

I. Rococo. Snowy white with a clearly cut margin of violet blue. It blooms early and is 40 inches high.

I. Solid Gold. The deepest yellow imaginable; beautifully formed large flowers on well-branched stems. Blooms mid-season at 3 feet.

I. South Pacific. This famous light blue Iris was introduced in 1954 at around $100 per plant. Now, 7 years later, it is decidedly the best of its color and quite inexpensive. Height is 40 inches and it blooms mid-season to late.

I. Striped Butterfly. An outstanding Iris basically blue, but the veins of the huge, flaring flowers are a slightly darker blue. The beard is yellow. It blooms mid-season at 40 inches.

Bearded Iris

Dwarf Bearded Iris

I. Tall Chief. Glowing red with an orange beard—an excellent combination. Its height is 38 inches; mid-season bloom.
I. Top Flight. Color of the petals is apricot yellow, the beard is a fiery orange red. Blooms mid-season at 34 inches.
I. Trophy. Every bit of this variety is Lobelia blue, a most pleasant color. It has taken top awards here and abroad, and has now moved to a decent price. It blooms early to mid-season at 36 inches.
I. Whole Cloth. A bi-color with white standards and light blue falls. It is outstanding in its class. Blooms show early to mid-season and it is 36 inches high.

Bulbous Beardless Iris. These are excellent rock garden plants, best described as a small form of Dutch Iris. Many varieties can easily be forced into bloom in the house. Plant 6 to 8 of them in a 4- to 5-inch pot. The fragrant blossoms resemble bunches of violets. The bulbs are hardy with reasonable protection. Excellent for rockeries. Height of varieties range from 4 to 6 inches. They bloom in early spring. Fall planting only.

*f**I. Danfordiae.** Bright yellow.
*f**I. reticulata Joyce.** This is large-flowered for its class. The falls are pale blue with an orange blotch on white, the standards pale blue. A pleasant thing in early spring.
*f**K. Violet Beauty.** Dark purple with a velvet sheen and a well-placed orange blotch.

Crested Iris. This little gem grows only 6 inches high. The flowers (from May onward) are pale lilac, the throat and crest deep yellow. Use it in sun or partial shade in the rockery, the border, or any place not heavily grassed. It isn't the least fussy about soils. The species is called *I. cristata* and should be planted only in the fall.

Dwarf Bearded Iris. The various botanical authorities on Iris classification are currently in a quandary about the botanical categories of the many forms of dwarf herbaceous Iris. *Pumila,* of course, is the Latin word for dwarf, and, although there has been an *I. pumila* category for years, only a very few species have garden merit. Meanwhile, Iris of intermediate height have come along. Some authorities call them *Iris intermedia,* but others put them in the *pumila* category. We will call all herbaceous bearded Iris varieties dwarfs if they are smaller than tall ones, and will include recognized *pumila* varieties with them.

Certainly this new and expanding Lilliputian Iris world is a delightful one and deserves attention. One great advantage in using them is that, unlike common bearded Iris, best planted only in early fall, the dwarfs have no special planting season. Also, flowering tends to be early—in May in Litchfield—and some throw bloom a second time. They have delightful scents. All are quite hardy, and make excellent rockery plants.

***I. Baria.** Lemon yellow all over, with a deeper yellow beard. It grows to 12 inches.

***I. Blue Denim.** Both standards and falls are a clear sky blue. Delightful. It grows 10 to 12 inches high.

***I. Brassie.** Standards and falls are a deep yellow and have a slight bronze cast. It is 10 inches high.

***I. Bright White.** This little fellow should have a better name, for it is really white and yellow—standards are clear white, the white falls have a yellow tinge, the beard is yellow and white. It grows to 8 inches.

***I. Dale Dennis.** Standards and falls are white and streaked on the edges with a deep lavender blue. Excellent. It is 10 inches high.

***I. Dark Fairy.** Deepest purple. It blooms by May 10, and grows to 10 inches.

***I. Green Spot.** Again white standards, but the falls are a greenish yellow edged white. It is about 9 inches high.

***I. Lilli Bright.** Pure white standards, white falls tinted blue, and beard of yellow and white, make this one a pleasant tricolor. It grows to 9 inches.

***I. Lilliput.** The standards are a clear light blue, the falls a slightly deeper blue, the beard white. It is 12 inches high.

***I. Lilli Red.** Completely garnet-red flowers in early May on 10-inch stems.

***I. Lilli Var.** This variety is variegated yellow with red spots on the falls. Gay. It grows to 10 inches.

Japanese Iris Gold Bound

***I. Litchfield.** We named this one because it has an excellent form, as does our town. It's white with an edging of deep lavender blue.

***I. Sangreal.** The flowers of this variety are far larger than other *pumila.* It produces clear yellow blooms in the spring, and it blooms again in the fall. It grows 15 to 18 inches.

***I. White Autumn Queen.** A white variety that also blooms spring and fall on 8-inch stems.

Japanese Iris. *I. Kaempferi.* Japanese Iris are a distinct sub-section of beardless types—the lovely flowers resemble orchids. Japanese hybridizers are doing wonderful work with them; some of the better new ones are noted. Japanese Iris must have moisture, but water should not stand on them, for they like their feet damp, their ankles dry. Cover the crowns 2 inches deep and be sure the soil is acid. Lime is death to them. In Litchfield, all varieties bloom in late June through July and range in height from 30 to 36 inches—a few grow a little higher. Plant spring or fall.

I. K. Eleanor Parry. Rich reddish purple. It throws 5- to 6-inch double blooms on 3- to 4-foot stems.

I. K. Gold Bound. It is pure white double, and has a golden band on each petal in the center zone. It shows 5- to 6-inch blooms on 3- to 4-foot stems. This has been an outstanding *I. kaempferi* for a long time.

I. K. Great White Heron. The flowers of this variety are the largest in this group. Its semi-double blooms are pure white and are 9 to 11 inches in diameter. Stems are 4 to 5 feet high, and strong. It's hard to beat.

I. K. Kagari Bi. One of the loveliest rose-pink flowers to be introduced in this great group. Petals are veined silver. It has 5- to 6-inch blooms on 3- to 4-foot stems.

I. K. Lady in Waiting. A large double white with a delicate pink border; the 7-inch blooms are slightly ruffled and appear on 36-inch stems.

I. K. Over the Waves. One of the most intensely ruffled of the Japanese varieties. Color is pure white with a light purple border; the 5- to 7-inch bloom has a full tufted center. It is 4 feet high.

I. K. Pin stripe. A delicately veined 5- to 7-inch bloom, pure white, penciled bright blue; the white center has a bluish-violet halo. Height is 4 feet.

I. K. Pink Frost. A charming light pink; the double blooms are 8 inches in diameter and delightfully ruffled. Stems are 3 feet high.

I. K. Purple and Gold. Velvet-purple flowers with golden throat. Double. Its 5- to 6-inch blooms show on 3- to 4-foot stems.

I. K. Queen of Blues. This light orchid-colored flower has a blue cast and is veined white. Very pleasant to live with. Its 5- to 6-inch blooms are on 3- to 4-foot stems.

I. K. Reign of Glory. The bloom of this one could be described as silvery blue, or say it is white with very delicate striplings and markings of sky blue. The fully double 5- to 7-inch flowers are carried on 40-inch stems.

I. K. Tinted Cloud. The overall color is blue violet. There is a hint of pink in the outer portions of the 5- to 7-inch bloom; the center is a combination of yellow, ultramarine, and deep violet. No, it is not multicolored. Height is 4 to 5 feet under best culture.

Siberian Iris. *I. sibirica.* A truly tough group of beardless Iris. They produce spreading root systems and are extremely compact in growth, which makes them ideal for planting to hold the soil of steep grades. They are not fussy about soils and can be planted spring or fall.

I. s. Caesar's Brother. An extremely rugged variety. Color is blue to rich, nearly black pansy violet. June flowering, 30 inches high.

I. s. Snow Queen. A pure white, the beardless blooms large and well formed. An excellent border plant; or use it with *I. s. Caesar's Brother* on the edge of water. It flowers in June at 24 inches.

IRRIGATION. Soak, don't sprinkle, is the rule for keeping lawns, perennials, shrubs, or trees in growth. And don't wait for rain. If at least one inch of water doesn't fall from the skies each week, add it with the hose—more often if the temperature stays in the 80's. Plants should never go into wilt, for tips of the tender leaves will brown and be unsightly. Lawns, shrubs and trees may be watered at night in climates that are not too hot, but never Roses or perennials—continued night irrigation causes them to mildew. To con-

Siberian Iris

trol red spider, hose the tops of evergreens with full force twice a week during very hot weather. Otherwise, though you can't see the nasty little things themselves, you will see the result of their work: when they get out of hand the foliage browns. How can a gardener measure an inch of water? Put an empty coffee can halfway between the sprinkler head and the outer perimeter of the water pattern. When the container has an inch of water in it there is an inch of water on the ground. Then put the sprinkler where the can was, etc.

IVY—*see* Hedera

Jackmannii (jack-man'eye) from Jackman, a famous English Clematis originator

JACOB'S LADDER—*see* Polemonium

japonica (ja-pon'i-ka) Japanese

Jasminum

Jasminum

Jazz-mi'num

Jasmine. A large genus of vines (some reach 100 feet), all of them tropical or subtropical, so none of them are hardy. The species are largely evergreen and covered with flowers in winter. Gardeners adept at growing plants indoors in sunny windows are successful with these beauties, which can be kept bushy by pruning. Plant spring or fall.

J. polyanthum. A delightful mist of longish white flowers cover the plant in wintertime. Not least important, of course, is the delicate and well-known fragrance that can't be anything but jasmine. If planted in the greenhouse, don't let the plant get out of hand. Its vines can take up far too much room, very quickly.

Kaempferi (kemp'fur-eye) after Kaempfer, who wrote of Japanese Iris.

Kalmia
Kal'me-uh

Mountain Laurel. Zone 4 southward. This is not a broad genus, and only one of its species has garden value. *K. latifolia,* is a very beautiful shrub native to the northeastern part of the United States. It is Connecticut's state flower. To do well it requires an acid soil, a mulch of pine needles, and moisture. Its delicate clusters of pink or white flowers (or white blending to pink) appear in mid-June. New England, famous for its colorful autumnal beauty, should be visited in June as well, for literally millions of Laurel plants bloom then. Buy it anywhere.

Kaufmanniana (kowf-man-nee-aye'na) after botanist Kaufmann

Kelwayii (kel'way-eye) after botanist Kelway, Peony expert.

Kerria
Ker'ree-uh

Kerria. Zone 4 southward. This genus from China has only one species, but it has several interesting variations. *K. japonica* is a twiggy, low-growing shrub (4 feet) with pleasant, medium-green leaves. It is well covered with 1½-inch yellow flowers in mid-May. It is generally used in front of the shrub border. It requires pruning from the crown. Sometimes winter kills the tips of its green twigs, but this is a small problem. *K. j. aureo-variegata* has leaves that are edged yellow; its branches are marked by striped green and yellow, its winter feature; and *pleniflora* has double, ball-shaped flowers which last far longer than the singles of the species. (But don't let the flowers seed. If that happens the seedlings, pure green, gradually take over the plant.) They do best in the sun and are not the least fussy about soils. A few mail-order nurseries have them under more striking names ("Superba") so it is necessary to unravel the description to fit the prosaic foregoing botanical names.

The better nurseries and some garden centers stock Kerria, but few carry the whole line.

Kolkwitzia
Kolk-wit'zi-uh

Beauty Bush. Zone 4 southward. A genus with only one species, *K. amabilis,* which was brought to Arnold Arboretum by E. H. Wilson from China in 1901, and is now so widely planted over the country that one gets the idea it is a native. The Arnold's Dr. Wyman comments that "early commercial attempts at distributing it proved a failure because the plant was not sufficiently well known. In 1922 one enterprising nurseryman decided to distribute it as new. . . . The plant (became) popular almost overnight." It is indeed beautiful. In early June it is massed with flowers that shade from a pink off-white to deep pink. In the fall the leaves become reddish. The plant grows to 10 feet, and its branches arch gracefully. Kolkwitzia is easily forced into bloom indoors. That it is as common as pretty girls in California is not a point against it.

Kolpakowskiana (kol-pak-ow-skee-aye'na) after botanist Kolpakowsky

Laburnum
La-burr'num

Golden Chain Tree. The few species in this genus of small flowering trees come from southern Europe, and *L. alpinum,* called Scotch Laburnum, is somewhat more hardy than *L. Watereri* (sometimes catalogued as *L. Vossii*), a hybrid that originated in Europe shortly after 1850. The former survives in the colder parts of zone 4, the latter in zone 5. Both varieties are notable only for the masses of long yellow racemes that cover them during their 2-week blooming period in late May. *L. Watereri* is the better of the 2 because its flowers are larger and a deeper yellow. Both are stiffly upright. Mass planting not more than 8 feet apart on a fence line is a highly effective way to use them. *L. Watereri* has withstood our very cold weather for 15 years. It is alone on a windswept hill, but cold weather has killed bloom not more than twice in this time. The tree is now 14 feet high. Eventually, it should reach 30 feet, the proper height at maturity.

The most effective use of Laburnum I have ever seen is at Lord Aberconway's estate in Wales. Using heavy wrought iron, he constructed a quonset-shaped arch about 150 feet long and 25 feet wide (as I recall it). He then planted Laburnum at about 4-foot intervals and tied the soft young wood firmly to the arch. I saw it in bloom. The outside was solid green, inside the long yellow racemes hung down in profusion, each about 15 inches long, and the sun through the espaliered branches brushed the yellow blossoms with different intensity. It was fairyland.

laciniata (la-sin-ee-aye'ta) jagged

lactiflora (lak-tif-lowe'ra) with milk-white flowers

LAD'S LOVE—*see* Artemisia

Lalandei (la-land'ee-eye) after LaLande, horticulturist

LAMB'S TONGUE (or Ear)—*see* Stachys

lanata (lan-aye'ta) woolly

lanceolated (lans'oh-lated) lance-shaped, i.e., longer than broad and tapering to a point.

lancifolia (lan'si-foe'lee-a) spear-shaped leaves, narrowly elliptical, tapering at both ends

Centerpiece Detail

Centerpiece ideas are useful for accents on grounds, terraces, patios, or driveways. The low wall (above) can be brick or flagstone (cemented or dry), the pots planted or unplanted, the center grass, low perennials, or ground cover. The real eye-catcher, of course, is some unusual low-growing tree in the center

LANDSCAPING. Many gardeners, particularly beginners, sometimes appear to be bereft of ideas when it comes to landscaping their homes. The difference between the treatment of the landscape surrounding an *average* English home and an American one is marked. There is charm and grace in the former, and sometimes imagination; all three are generally lacking in the latter. This, however, is nothing for the American to feel hurt or inferior about—he just hasn't been planning his castle for as long as his English cousin, nor has he had the example of great estates and glorious public parks to educate him or help him develop style. Also, the more prosperous American has chosen to have his leisure time consumed by expensive sports, touring, or activities he considers more amusing than gardening, which to him is not so much work as mystery. So when he switches to gardening (usually somewhat late in life) there is much he doesn't know, not only about raising plants, which is not difficult, but about their arrangement on the landscape, which confuses him because he does not know how a tree or a shrub will look when it reaches maturity. If he is a typical American and finds gardening more to his liking than he had thought it would be, he will use his prosperity to employ a landscape architect, and buy specimen trees and shrubs. The rich think nothing of paying $2000 or more for moving large trees.

To the family with means the services of a good independent landscape architect are invaluable. The landscape people employed by most local nurseries use landscape planning to sell whatever stock their nurseries grow. Independents wed site and plants and find plants from as many nurseries as required. This result is usually excellent, and gets even better when the grounds get to be 10 to 15 years old, if the shrubs and trees fill the landscape without crowding it. Friends of ours bought a plan and plants from a "good local" nurseryman about 20 years ago. Their grounds were rather large. At one end of the property, bulldozers had gouged out the side of a hill to supply earth for the banks of a pool big enough to row a boat a respectable distance. At the back of a mahogany-floored pier they had built a charming bathhouse, complete with kitchen and bar. Although some trees had been saved, construction had left this pleasant haven-within-a-haven rather bare. The nurseryman worked out a pattern of different greens, trees and shrubs on the steep hillside, and on the walk around the small lake he planted Japanese Cherries—the lovely double-flowered *Prunus kwanzan*—and made it into a miniature Washington Tidal Basin. For five years it all looked fine, particularly a belt of Weeping Willows on the hillside. Today the Willows dominate the hill; they are now completely out of scale and hide other, slower-growing trees. Far too many Cherries were planted; they have grown together as they pushed up to 30 feet. Years ago I read somewhere that the man who would landscape his property but who has no idea of plants, would do well to insist upon seeing mature trees and shrubs of the kind he wants to plant.

Actually, gardening's greatest reward comes from viewing one's own landscaping (on any scale) and pronouncing it good. Praise from others is pleasant but not necessary. It's your taste. Your handiwork. You like it. I have never seen an ugly, well-tended garden or landscape. Some have not represented my taste, but that is of no moment. There are, however, some points to be made about a home-gardener's garden. There are two kinds. One is a man's own private garden, so-called because only he and his family can see it. The other is his public garden or landscape, which can be seen from the street by passersby. Idiosyncrasies, such as a hideously-painted plastic gnome fishing in a pool, are a proper part of his private garden, but such creatures can be obtrusive as part of the public landscape (a point Nan Fairbrother makes in her excellent book *New Lives, New Landscapes,* an examination of men's living relationships to man in his *own* ecology).

Unless one is blessed with structural visualization, an aptitude which permits the building of a sound and graceful structure imaginatively, one must work empirically. I have only a touch of this aptitude, so to guard against errors in landscaping, which are both costly and irritating, I have learned to plant trees and shrubs sparingly and far enough apart so that mistakes can be moved later, if need be.

It is obviously a good idea to lay out a plan for any landscape or flower border. Only a rough plan is needed, reasonably accurate as to scale, and dated; then it can be redrawn as it is changed. This is absorbing winter work in the garden, and rewarding, for it keeps things on the track. A reasonable amount of planning, I have found, is a great way to expose an idea to the realities of cost—and to find out ahead of time if it can be maintained.

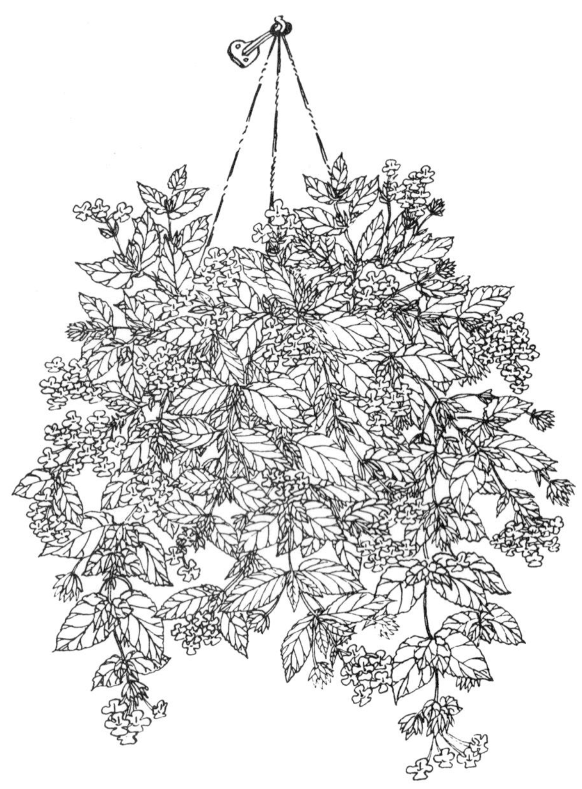

Lantana Semantha

Lantana

Lan-tah'na

Lantana. This genus is a native of tropical and subtropical lands. In zones 9 and 10 it is a hardy shrub. In sunny California and in the South, trailing Lantana is used extensively to cover banks. In northern areas of the country Lantana is not hardy, but it is nevertheless extremely useful, and northern gardeners who neglect it are missing a great decorative plant. Its outstanding feature is mass bloom all the time. Use it in baskets, in pots high on a terrace, in window boxes. Just use it. Like Fuchsia it can be wintered easily indoors. Lantana is best in the north in tubs or pots on a sunny terrace. There is one basic difference between Fuchsia and Lantana culture: Lantana requires full sun all the time. Otherwise follow directions for Fuchsia—cultural as well as for growing various forms. Plant out in spring after frost.

L. Confetti. An excellent tricolor. The individual flowers in each cluster are yellow, pink and a blending purple, which sounds impossible but isn't at all, for the effect is that of confetti on a green carpet.

L. Golden Redhead. Red and a very pleasant red at that, with a golden crown. Excellent shrub or tree form.

L. Gold Rush. Masses of solid gold all yours for the planting.

L. Pink Frolic. Some of the flowers in the large cluster are creamy with a yellow throat, but most of them are two-tone pink.

L. Selloviana. Here is the most prolific bloomer of all Lantana. Color is a dainty pinkish lavender. *Selloviana* has been satisfactory everywhere. It is primarily for basket culture.

L. Semantha. A brilliant tricolor of yellow-red to brown. This is one of the best Lantanas to grow in tree form. We have one tree specimen of it over 100 years old. It is a very old variety and we do not know its correct name. It is named after the woman who started it—the grandmother of Mr. Leonard Hanna of Cleveland, Ohio, now deceased, who gave us the plant.

L. Spreading Sunset. Vividly colored yellow-and-red flowers do indeed give it a sunset color. Leaves are a very dark green.

L. W. F. F. White. This truly purest white Lantana is a treasure. Other white Lantanas tend to be off-white with blue or yellow or gray tones. It is also very floriferous and seems not to rest a minute in the summer.

L. W. F. F. Yellow. We haven't the remotest idea where this vivid yellow (or the pure white) Lantana came from, and we have no knowledge of its correct name, but we suspect it is as old as *Semantha.* We don't even know where we got the plant; it just seemed to materialize several years ago in the form of a tree, not grown well. As it was hungry, we fed it, and it responded beautifully with a mass of bloom. The color is the most arresting clear yellow imaginable. *W. F. F. White, W. F. F. Yellow* and *Semantha,* none of them patented, are available now only at White Flower Farm, but chances are that other nurseries will soon be growing them.

Larpentae (lahr-pent'ee) after Lady Larpent

latifolium (la-ti-foe'lee-um) broad-leaved

Laucheana (law-chee-aye'na) after botanist Lauche

Lantana Semantha

Lantana selloviana

Lavandula

La-van'dew-la

Lavender. Many gardeners grow Lavender for its fragrance and put it in sachets for linen or with whatever they want to smell like Lavender. Our interest in Lavender is that the genus produces several excellent garden plants that should be used more than they are—as plants, not oddities with an odor. (We think sachets made by Lubin of Paris smell better.) Some varieties are small, others tall. They like a well-drained soil and lots of sun. Plant them in masses or form them into small hedges. Each year cut them back to just above last year's point of growth. Plant them spring or fall.

L. Hidcote. A variety with very deep, violet-blue blooms, extremely compact. It grows to about 20 inches. Excellent for small hedges.

L. Munstead Dwarf. This 12-inch dwarf is a deep heliotrope in color. It is the lowest-growing variety, excellent for a hedge or as an edging plant for a shallow border.

Grass-seed spreader

LAVENDER—*see* Lavandula

LAVENDER COTTON—*see* Santolina

LAWNS. "How can I have a really good lawn?" is the one question we are most frequently asked. To answer it we developed a lawn cultivation or refurbishing program, which, if followed even haphazardly season after season, will provide a velvety, largely weed-free turf one can be proud of. The five major steps are as follows:

1 *Seeding—the whole lawn area heavily in the fall, bare spots in the spring.*
2 *Fertilization—in early spring and mid-summer.*
3 *Weed control with herbicides.*
4 *Irrigation.*
5 *General Care.*

Each of these will be discussed in detail. They have been derived from our own experience with lawns in the gardens in Litchfield over the past 30 years.

Seeding: The cultivation or refurbishing of established lawns requires annual seeding. It is necessary because the grass plants tend to thin out if they are subject to drought or if fertilization is neglected—in other words, they die of their chlorophyll ills. Others disappear because the life gets tramped out of them by people. So just as dead Roses or perennials are replaced, new grass plants must be supplied to provide a lawn thick enough to inhibit annual weeds. This is particularly true of that worst of all lawn pests, crabgrass, which is shallow-rooted and germinates best in hot, bare ground. It is hardly ever successful in deep turf. Of course, broadleaf weeds will grow in a thick turf, but they won't be too numerous. Their control will be discussed later.

The seeding and planting procedure is uncomplicated. If possible, run a thatcher through the turf before seeding. This will loosen the soil a bit and provide the seed with a good bed. Seed broadcast by hand two ways—this gets the desired density—or use a spreader. Then broom the lawn hard with a bamboo or metal lawn broom to get the seed well down to the surface of the earth. At this point run a lightly weighted roller over it. This compacts the seed and helps get early germination. The compacting plus the shade of the grass provide ideal growing conditions. If the turf is fairly good, use 2 to 3 pounds of lawn seed per 1,000 square feet in the fall. New lawns, whenever they are seeded, require 5 to 7 pounds.

The time of seeding is more important than most gardeners realize. Advertisements in springtime offering grass seed for immediate sowing seem to goad an enthusiastic gardener into heavy seeding then. Of course one should seed in the early spring, but *only* in bare spots. The fall is the *only* time to seed the whole lawn heavily—in late August or September, for this is the time of the fall rains, the longer nights and the cooler days, all of which are ideal for grass plants. The little fellows will drive their roots down deep; most of them will laugh at winter, then whoosh next spring. It's impossible, as we said before, to overemphasize the importance of sowing grass seed in the fall. Those who live in the North where deep frost comes early probably should get their seed planted by September 1 to 15; along the mild Northeast Coast as far up as Maine, October or even early November should be satisfactory.

The kind of seed one uses is, of course, important. Read the small print on the seed package (a Federal requirement) to find out what kind of seed is in the mixture. Chances are that the least expensive brands will contain a fairly large percentage of annual rye grass. This stuff is cheap, but useless for permanent turf, for it dies in winter. (It can, however, be used in the late spring or summer to get a quick cover of green to hold new grading until permanent seeding can be done in the fall.) Somewhat more expensive seed mixtures will have little or no annual rye. They will carry a heavy percentage of Kentucky Bluegrass, probably small quantities of a Fescue. Kentucky Blue is a good grass and it's relatively inexpensive, but by nature it goes dormant in midsummer and browns. Still other mixtures will have some Merion Bluegrass, which is great grass, plus Kentucky Blue, Fescue or a Bent or two. If the Merion, Kentucky Blue, and Fescues add up to 80 percent or more of the total content, this is a good mixture; if the Merion and Fescues are a similar percent, it's an excellent mixture. Be skeptical of Bent grasses—the upright varieties do not perform well. If one decides to make a lawn solely of Creeping Bent, the gorgeous grass used on golf greens, be prepared to clip it daily with a special mower, to water it at the slightest sign of dryness, and to watch diligently for fungus, which can be inhibited only by expensive mercury compounds.

Lawn mixtures called *Shady Lawn Seed* are about the most expensive mixtures one finds in ordinary trade channels. *Shady Lawn* mixtures have a heavy percent of Fescue grasses, because Fescues perform well in rather heavy shade. Actually, this fine grass grows best in full sun. If you can find an all-Fescue mixture, one composed of Chewings, Creep Red, and Pennlawn (Pennlawn is the best and most expensive of all grasses) by all means buy it if you can afford it. Those Fescues complement each other almost perfectly, and because all Fescues spread by rhizome action the turf underfoot has an untufted, even "feel." Each Fescue has a different spreading rate. For example, Creeping Red spreads fast, and thus provides protection from heavy lawn wear, particularly in game areas. Chewings has finer leaves than Red. Pennlawn has an even finer texture. However, the Fescues will not do well in climates where the nights are devilish hot. You know your own climate, so act accordingly.

Fertilization: Probably the most important part of lawn cultivation during and after the time a turf is being built up is proper fertilization. We have heard experts in the field say that if 1 out of 100 lawns is properly fertilized they would be surprised. Old-fashioned fertilizers, with their ingredients immediately available, have little lasting effect even when the dosage is heavy. Today's slow-release fertilizers are put on in smaller amounts, and only 2 applications are necessary. The first application should be made in early spring (when Crocus bloom) and again in the first 10 days of July (in zone 4). Use 8 pounds of 15–8–12 slow-release organic fertilizer per 100 square feet each time. In warmer zones with longer growing seasons, 10 to 12 pounds will be a good amount; the second feeding should be moved to the last 10 days in July. If organic fertilizer can't be found, use inorganic, but the top of the grasses will burn unless it is washed off immediately (no permanent damage results).

For years garden writers have advised putting lime on an established lawn every four or five years. Some have recommended a sprinkling of it every year. We have stopped advising the use of lime on established lawns, for there is no evidence it does any good, and it may do harm by (1) bringing in clover and (2) releasing the nitrogen in fertilizers while letting the lime rest, unused, on the surface. The use of lime on lawns appears to have been started in areas having soils too acid to grow Kentucky Bluegrass, and as Kentucky Blue became the principal lawn seed, lime followed it only because it was the thing to do. Actually, to sweeten acid soils, lime must be incorporated evenly, for it has little or no lateral movement. It is needed on lawn grasses only when an area is being dug up for re-seeding or for laying turf—but not even then if the *p*H tests are satisfactory. Most grasses, including Bluegrass, do well in a slightly acid soil, and as most of our soils (there are notable Far West exceptions) are slightly acid and remain that way for years, it is to be hoped that gardeners with established lawns will just forget about liming them (*see* Lime).

For gardeners who are serious about lawns, there are two further points about fertilization. The first point has to do with "spiking." This operation is described by the word itself—holes (6 inches deep) are spiked into the turf. It is, however, tedious to drive a ¼-inch spike down 6 inches on 6-inch centers. Spiked rollers can be bought or rented to be pulled slowly behind small tractors.

Spiking should be done before fertilization, for it provides channels to get the nutrients to the roots and improves aeration. The second point has to do with top-dressing—raking humus or earth over the turf thinly enough to keep the grass growing but thick enough to fill in uneven places. Ideally, this should be done every fall before spiking and seeding. Over a relatively few years top-dressing produces an even surface. It also makes the turf more resistant to drought. In ordinary (or sandy) soils we suggest 1 part pure humus and 1 part topsoil applied at the rate of 2 to 6 pounds per square yard. In heavy clay soils 1 part humus, ½ part sand, and ½ part topsoil should be used. Admittedly, this is a considerable chore for the ordinary householder to undertake—but try to get it done on contract. The turf should be rolled lightly (do not weight the roller) after top-dressing. Note that ordinary humus carries some weed seed, but not enough to cause trouble.

Weed control: No matter how much a thick turf inhibits crabgrass—and it does—such broadleaf weeds as dandelions and plantain will pop up. Kill them with hormone herbicide sprays (2–4*D* and the like) without hurting the grass or upsetting the lawn's ecology. A herbicide called *Dimet-Plus* 2, a combination of materials that will destroy most of the weeds in a lawn including freshly sprouted crabgrass, is excellent (*see* Herbicides). *Dimet-Plus* 2 comes in concentrated liquid form, is mixed in water and sprayed at low pressure on the broadleaf weeds. For best results, apply on a hot day—the directions on the bottle provide correct dosage. Use a 2- or 3-gallon knapsack sprayer but fill it with only 1 gallon at a time—3 gallons of water weigh 24 pounds, and that's tiring to lift. Use this sprayer for herbicide applications only, but wash it out after using. Sprayers with stainless steel tanks last longer. We walk the

Narcissus

lawnmower marks, spot the broadleaf seeds, then douse each of them. If done in the morning one sees immediate results by late afternoon. The weeds will have actually sprouted up during the period, forced into rampant and deadly growth by the hormone. It's a fine sight. Go around the next day and douse the ones missed.

Irrigation: This subject should have been discussed first, for if one doesn't have an adequate water supply it doesn't make sense to try to grow good turf. Grass plants need at least 1 inch of water a week, and if the temperature stays about 70° they will need more. Naturally, lawns planted on very sandy soils need more than 1 inch. A good test for moisture is the spongy feeling of one's heel in the turf. There is enough moisture if the heel (not a spike heel) can be driven easily into the surface.

Soak, don't sprinkle. There is an old theory that watering gardens or lawns at night will cause mildew. Another equally old one warns that watering in full sun will cause plants to burn. These warnings stumped us for a while when we were rank amateurs. Then we decided to play it the way nature does rain—at any old time. That logic can hardly be breached. Night irrigation of lawns is the favorite time here because it conserves water, but night irrigation regularly in warm, moist climates will cause mildew. And a note for those gardeners bent on a lawn of Creeping Bent—get up at dawn and sweep the Bent with a 20-foot fish pole to knock the dew off the grass, or mildew will appear.

General care: How high to set a mower and what to do with grass clippings vexes, as we so well know, those new at gardening. Grass can be cut as short as one wants it, but if trimmed as close as 1 inch or less the turf must be fine, perfectly irrigated, and fertilized, and clippings must be caught as it is mowed—every day. Those who can afford help can do this and produce lawns for bowling or putting. The rest of us, more moderately endowed, set mowers at 2 inches (3 inches is better), and let the clippings drop. As the clippings decompose they help feed the turf and build humus, and it's a lot less work than picking them up. But grass should not grow too long, for the heavy clippings will heat and burn the turf underneath (they can even kill it). Don't mow when the grass is wet or has dew on it—this can also produce severe burns. Under bad growing conditions, i.e., drought, don't mow.

If clippings are permitted to fall, there will come a time, say in 4 or 5 years, when the ground under the grass should be examined to determine how well the clippings have rotted. If they have matted, it may mean that the grasses are in danger of being choked off by the mat. This mat can be removed in the very early spring (before spiking, fertilizing, or seeding) by using a thatching machine, which, as noted earlier, can be rented from a local lawnmower organization, garden center, or hardware store. Use the mat in compost.

A lawn is rolled lightly in early spring to compact turf that has heaved from frost. This drives the crowns back into the soil and gives them a chance to send out new roots. As noted, roll after seeding. We find that people can rarely be induced to do this for fun.

We know there are gardeners who will tire quickly at the thought of the work outlined in this program. But we promise that with fertilization built up in 3 or 4 years they can stop fall seeding. It's a wonderful feeling.

Ledebourii (led-e-boor'eye) after botanist Ledebour

LEMON BALM—*see* Herbs

Leontopodium
Lee-on-ta-poe'dee-um

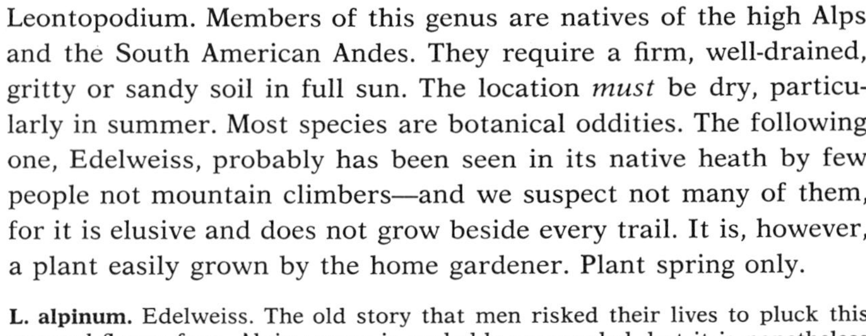

Leontopodium. Members of this genus are natives of the high Alps and the South American Andes. They require a firm, well-drained, gritty or sandy soil in full sun. The location *must* be dry, particularly in summer. Most species are botanical oddities. The following one, Edelweiss, probably has been seen in its native heath by few people not mountain climbers—and we suspect not many of them, for it is elusive and does not grow beside every trail. It is, however, a plant easily grown by the home gardener. Plant spring only.

L. alpinum. Edelweiss. The old story that men risked their lives to pluck this unusual flower from Alpine crags is probably apocryphal, but it is nonetheless a nice tale. The foliage is woolly-white, the flowers really floral leaves arranged in star-like clusters. It blooms in June and is only about 6 inches high.

LEOPARDBANE—*see* Doronicum

LEOPARD FLOWER—*see* Belamcanda

Leontopodium

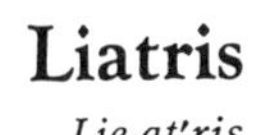

Liatris
Lie-at'ris

Gay-feather. Liatris, a North American genus consisting of about 20 species, thrives in light soils in sun or light shade. Plant it in groups. In our opinion Liatris has been neglected by gardeners. It is excellent for cutting, superb for drying, beautiful in the border. Some call it weedy, which is a libel. Plant it spring or fall.

L. Cobalt. For Liatris, this variety is a dwarf—only 18 to 24 inches high—so it can be planted well up in the front of the border. It flowers from July to September. Flowers are reddish purple.

L. scariosa September Glory. Purple flowers all come into bloom on 6-foot spikes in late August.

L. scariosa White Spires. The white form of September Glory.

LIGHT—*see* Shade, *also* Sun

LILAC—*see* Syringa

Lilium
Lil'ee-um

Lily. This is one of the great garden plants of all time. The genus consists of about 200 bulbous herbaceous species, all indigenous in the North Temperate Zone, many of them natives of the United States. They formerly were thought difficult to grow because of the failure of imported bulbs. We know now that this imported stock was diseased. Today, most of the Lilies sold in the United States are produced in Oregon by Jan de Graaff's great nurseries. Not only are they free of disease but in the last 35 years de Graaff has created new races of this lovely flower. It is not an exaggeration to say that de Graaff, born in Holland and now a naturalized U.S. citizen, will have a permanent place in horticultural history. In 1968 he sold his great nursery, but it is in good hands and the breeding programs will continue.

Culture: Lilies do not require special soils, but they demand locations which must not—repeat *not*—be too wet; water must never be allowed to stand on the bulbs. Lilies grow best in filtered light, for this brings out color and makes blossoms last longer. Half to ¾ sun is best. They like good air circulation; it is also a good idea to over-plant a Lily border with perennials or annuals to keep bulbs cool. Except for **L. Candidum** (The Madonna Lily), plant bulbs from 4 to 7 inches deep, and use one handful of bonemeal and a heaping teaspoon of *Milorganite* mixed in the bottom of each hole. (Exceptions to that planting depth are noted in the following list of varieties.) Cover Madonnas with only 1 inch of soil. Lilies mature late, and are usually shipped in late October or early November, except Madonnas, which are delivered in September and which should be planted immediately. Plant fall only.

The following list of de Graaff bulbs is extensive, and you may not be able to find them all at one source (de Graaff is a whole-

Liatris Cobalt

Lilium Bellingham Hybrid

saler). In the short section on mail-order nurseries are the names of 2 organizations that have a wide selection of these Oregon bulbs. We have grown all of them in Litchfield at one time or another, and a display planting in the gardens contains about 1200 bulbs of 70 varieties which bloom from July to September. You are invited to visit it. Note: in buying Lily bulbs, get the largest size possible—6 to 7 inches in circumference or better. How to tell if sizes are not advertised? The nursery quoting the highest price usually supplies the largest bulbs. Don't be misled by "flowering-sized bulbs." Small bulbs will flower—weakly—and fade away. Few soils in the U.S. are good enough to make "flowering-sized" bulbs grow large.

L. auratum platyphyllum. The sensational golden-rayed Lily of Japan. It has great, fragrant, waxy-white blooms, streaked golden and sometimes spotted crimson. It needs full sun and a rich, well-drained soil. It flowers in August and September. Height is from 4 to 6 feet. Plant 5 to 7 inches deep.

L. auratum platyphyllum virginale. A vigorous white form with a golden stripe infrequently found among the seedlings of the true *L. auratum platyphyllum.* The broad, dark green, glossy leaves and the immense stem are in proportion to the large, widely expanded flowers. Height is from 4 to 6 feet. It flowers in August.

L. aurelian African Queen. A strain. Each of these bulbs is slightly different, but all are vigorous and tall; blooms have warm apricot colorings. In very warm climates plant only in partial shade. Blooms come in late July on 5- to 6-foot stems.

L. aurelian Hybrid "Sunburst." Large lemon-yellow to salmon recurved flowers on tall wiry stems. Suitable as a cut flower. Plant 6 inches deep in rich soil slightly on the heavy side. The height is from 5 to 7 feet, and it blooms late July.

L. Bellingham Hybrids. The color range runs from clear yellow to yellow orange to bright orange red, some with scarlet-tipped petals. A wonderful cut flower—the pyramidal head (up to 20 blossoms) blooms in water if cut when the first bud opens. It flowers in June and July on 3- to 6-foot stems. Plant it 5 inches deep.

L. Black Dragon. The inside of the flower is purest white, outside it is a rich purplish brown margined white. It grows to 8 feet. Black Dragon bears a dozen or more huge blooms in perfect candelabra form in late July.

L. Bright Star. Orange and ivory-white blooms, almost Turk's cap in shape, but 5 inches in diameter. They are ideal for corsages because they last so long. Height is about 3 feet and blooms show in mid-July.

L. candidum. This is the Madonna Lily, a native of Greece and a favorite for years. It is pure white, June-flowering. Plant it in September. It must not be planted over an inch deep. Be sure it is kept damp after planting. It grows to 4 feet.

L. centifolium Olympic Hybrids. Its great trumpets bloom in July and August on stems 5 to 7 feet tall. The variety does well in sun or light shade. Colors run from pure white to deep ivory with soft green, greenish brown or wine tints on the exterior of each bloom. Plant 5 to 7 inches deep; leave undisturbed.

L. Corsage. A most unusual clone from the sparkling Harlequin strain. It has outward-facing flowers of ivory and pink. As many as 10 blooms, each about 3 inches in diameter, are carried on 3- to 4-foot stems in late June or early July. Its flowers are male-sterile (no pollen), so they are useful in bouquets and corsages.

L. Crimson Beauty. The impressive 10-inch flowers are bowl-shaped, pure white with a deep Bing cherry-red band in the center of each petal. In the pure white of the petal are vermilion spots which become papillae at the base. The very center shows a green star. It grows from 4 to 6 feet high and flowers in August.

L. Discovery. An outward- and downward-facing flower, and a lovely addition to the Harlequin clones. The flower is Turk's cap in form and the petals curl gracefully. The center of the flower is soft pink overlaying white, with deep crimson spots that are nearly black. The reverse of the petals is pink with a silvery sheen. The flower head is pyramidal in form with 16 or more flowers. Blooms are 4 inches in diameter. It flowers at the end of June or early July at 3 feet.

L. Empress of China. Chalk-white blooms with many small maroon-purple spots on the inside, but tips of the curling petals are unspotted. Outside is pure white except for a very pale green center rib. Flowers are very large, appearing in up to 8 blooms per stem, which grows from 3 to 6 feet high depending on location and culture. It blooms in August.

L. Empress of India. Stems stand 4 to 6 feet, carry 8 to 10 bowl-shaped blooms 10 inches across. Color inside is like ripe watermelon; outside is a warm pink. It is a sensational flower which blooms late in the season.

L. Empress of Japan. Here's another formidable empress—just the petals of the white blooms are 3 inches across, and the diameter of the flower itself reaches a full 10 inches. The center carries a golden stripe. Spots along the stripe area are deep maroon. Height 4 to 6 feet, depends upon culture and location. It blooms in late August.

Outward-facing-form Lilium

L. Enterprise. A clone from the Jamboree strain. Flowers are almost flat, yet form a graceful curve from base to tip of the petal. The crimson in the center of the petals is bordered by silver; there is an apple-green star in the center. The blooms are up to 7 inches in diameter, 8 or more flowers on a stem. August-flowering, up to 5 feet in height. It could be described as a "Giant Speciosum."

L. Everest. A strain of pure white, Jamboree-type hybrids. The center of the white flower has a hint of green, which varies in intensity from plant to plant. Fragrant. They grow 5 feet high and flower in August.

L. Fiesta Hybrid Strain. The bulbs come in mixed colors that range from straw yellow to vivid reds to orange to deep maroon red. One great charm of this strain is that the lovely blooms are on stems never over 3 feet high. It makes an excellent cut flower. Blooms show in July.

L. First Love Strain. This variety, a trumpet, has the lovely tints of Pink Perfection with gold. The pink is confined to the outside edges of the petals, fusing into the golden stripe in the center and the pale green throat. The long flowers are 6 to 8 inches in diameter when fully opened. It blooms from the second week of July on 5-foot stalks.

L. Golden Showers. Bright butter-yellow pendant blooms show in July and August with a brown reverse on 4- to 6-foot strong stems. Ten or more flowers on each inflorescence. As Golden Showers is a very heavy self-propagator, gardeners get big clumps of this beauty after a few years.

L. Golden Splendor Strain. These lovelies are show flowers; they are also sturdy, vigorous, and prolific garden plants. This is the newest strain of the golden-yellow trumpet type of Lily. They usually flower in late July, and if grown well, stand 5 to 7 feet tall. The color is a deep golden yellow. All show a deep maroon-brown stripe on the reverse of the petals.

L. Green Dragon. An outstanding trumpet, chartreuse and white in color. Grown well, the stems rise to 7 feet. A beaut. Blossoms show in July. Nine- or 10-inch bulbs.

L. Hallmark. It is a strain of chalk-white Lilies with such vigor that it is tolerant of adverse conditions. The plant, when mature, carries 15 to 20 recurved Turk's cap blooms on a 4-foot stem, each having a diameter of about 4 inches. It is an early bloomer.

L. Harlequin Strain. Pretty gay, this one, with as much of the rainbow as can be captured in Lily chromosomes—each bulb throws a different colored blossom. Vigorous, too. It flowers in June–July on 3- to 5-foot stems.

L. Honeydew. Mimosa yellow and lettuce green, the chart says—and that's Honeydew. Blooms hang down, a score or more of them, from the top of 5-foot stems.

L. Imperial Crimson. A strain. White with crimson centers. It flowers in August on 5- to 7-foot stems. A lovely thing.

L. Imperial Gold. A strain. This de Graaff strain is truly imperial. Each petal measures up to 3 inches in width, and we refuse to tell you the number of petals on each bloom, for you won't believe it. Color is purest white, heavily dotted with maroon spots; a heavy gold stripe shades down each petal. Height is 5 to 8 feet; it flowers in August.

L. Imperial Silver Strain. A huge all-white Lily in great size. Height is 5 to 6 feet; it, too, flowers in August.

L. Limelight. A heavy winner of awards abroad. It's fragrant. Color is almost true chartreuse yellow. Height is 4 to 5 feet; it flowers in July.

L. Magic Pink Strain. This is a strain of hybrids of *L. rubellum x L. auratum* with delicate shell-pink flowers which open wide to form a bowl-shaped flower 7 inches in diameter. The center of the flower is dark green, with a reddish-yellow stripe showing at the base of each petal. The lower parts of the petals are lightly spotted with deep crimson spots; the reverse of the petals is pink overlaid with a silvery pink; the silver often being very apparent toward the edges. It blooms in early July at 3 to 4 feet.

L. Midnight. These are selections from the darkest of the Pink Perfection strain. They are lovely.

L. Pink Glory Strain. Color is almost salmon pink in the center of each petal but diffuses outward leaving a narrow margin of white. The base of each petal is green and forms a star at the heart of each flower. The pink varies from plant to plant; in some cases it's very intense. Blooms are 8 inches in diameter. It flowers in July and at 4 to 6 feet.

L. Pink Perfection Strain. This strain, similar to de Graaff's great Olympic Hybrids, is shaded pink. The color extends over the inner as well as the outer surface of the petals. Experience with it indicates that while it is a true and definite Fuchsia pink in Oregon (and other cool moist climates), it shows lighter pink tones when grown in regions where nights are warmer. It blooms in July on 4- to 6-foot stems.

L. Royal Gold. Here is a mutation of the Regal Lily that is identical to that fine plant except that the color is golden yellow. Royal Gold has caused more comment in the gardens in Litchfield than nearly any other Lily.

L. San Gabriel. This recent de Graaff strain is startlingly beautiful. Stems up to 6 feet support 20 or more golden-to-yellow, scented blooms 3 to 5 inches across, the petals of which seem dusted with saffron through the small vermilion dots; large near-black spots are confined to the center of its Turk's-cap blooms.

L. Sentinel Strain. Purest of white with a soft golden throat. Up to 20 flowers

Upward-facing-form Lilium

Trumpet Lily

are expected from an inflorescence when grown well. Exceptionally hardy, so use it in cold climates. Height is 3 to 5 feet; it flowers in June and July.

L. Silver Sunburst Strain. Ivory or pure white with a golden throat. Exceptionally large blooms on strong 5- to 8-foot stems. It flowers in July and August.

L. speciosum album. White Champion. This improvement on the species is one of the loveliest of cut flowers. It is pure white with radically recurved petals on curving stems. It needs some shade during the hottest part of the day. Plant 6 inches deep. It blooms in August and September on 3- to 4-foot stems.

L. speciosum rubrum. Red Champion. The improvement in the species, always a delight, is marked so that's the reason it has been given a name. The blooms, like *L. s. album* in shape, are delightful shades of pink to blending reds. It flowers in August and September. Plant 6 inches deep.

L. speciosum rubrum Superstar. An even larger and more vigorous form of *L. speciosum rubrum.* The flowering period is very long—from August to late September—and its blooms will take 5 degrees of frost. If used as a cut flower, every bud opens. Height is 3 to 5 feet, but most stems tend to curve as they grow. Plant 6 inches deep.

L. Sprite. This Oriental, resulting from crossing *L. auratum* with *L. speciosum rubrum,* is extremely vigorous and produces a great number of flowers 7 to 8 inches in diameter. The broad petals have silvered edges and tips; the centers are a deep crimson. The flowers are flat. It blossoms in August, and when established reaches a height of 5 to 6 feet. Usually expensive.

f***Lilium Mid-Century Hybrids.** An entirely new group of hybrid Lilies were developed by Jan de Graaff from *L. umbellatum,* a very hardy wild Lily from the northeastern states. Mid-Century Lilies grow about 3 to 5 feet high, are tough in any climate, and should be planted about 5 to 6 inches deep in a well-drained location. These Lilies are not only the hardiest we know about, but they propagate like weeds—and that should be taken literally. One small bulb equals 10 in 3 years. All start to bloom in late June; some look good as late as September 15. Mature bulbs in this group vary in size from 4 to 7 inches in circumference, but all will produce heavily the first season.

L. Cinnabar. A strong-stemmed, upright-flowering type. The flowers, borne on long pedicels, are clear maroon red. This variety is fine for forcing or for growing in pots in a cool greenhouse. It likes light shade.

L. Challenger. A Mid-Century with a startling color between lilac and red, and it is *not* magenta. It is an upright-flowering type with large flowers.

L. Croesus. True yellow. Blooms are large, wide open, and upright with some black spots.

L. Destiny. Bright, upright-facing, canary-yellow flowers with brown spots in the center.

L. Enchantment. De Graaff describes this as the best Lily he has ever developed and others call it the best Lily origination of the century. *L. Enchantment* is a vibrant nasturtium red in color with upward-facing flowers which last for weeks. It blooms in June and July. When cut with the first bud open all other buds flower, some even after the leaves have browned.

L. Fireflame. Large outward-facing, rich Indian-red blooms with recurved petals on 30-inch stems.

L. Golden Chalice Hybrids. These vigorous hybrids range in color from clear lemon yellow through shades of gold and apricot orange. Some flower very early. Plant 6 inches deep.

L. Harmony. Upright-facing flowers of rich and brilliant orange with wide petals. Fine for cutting. It flowers early in July on 28-inch stems.

L. Joan Evans. Very broad-petalled, upward-facing flowers of bright golden yellow with maroon spots. From 6 to 9 blooms on wiry stems which grow to 3 feet.

L. Paprika. This sturdy variety has outstanding blood-crimson outward-facing flowers, which are borne horizontally on stiff, branched pedicels on stems from 2 to 3 feet high. It blooms in June and is specially good for forcing.

L. Prosperity. Cool lemon-yellow outward-facing flowers. The stems grow to 4 feet.

L. Tabasco. A very early upright-facing variety; chestnut red with black spots. It is sun-resistant. Early June bloom.

LILY-OF-THE-NILE—*see* Agapanthus

LILY-OF-THE-VALLEY—*see* Convallaria

LIME. Calcium, or lime, is basic to the health of most plants, primarily because its chemical presence helps make available other plant foods and it brings very acid soils toward a "neutral" condition (*see* *p*H Factor). Lime has been used since man started farming. Although its importance in farming (clover doesn't grow well without it) has not diminished, many herbaceous shrubs and trees tolerate a considerable degree of acidity and become acutely ill if limed too much or too frequently. It is not a fertilizer, hence it should never be added to a growing border, and established lawns should never be top-dressed with it (*see* Lawns). Its value is in its ability to help release plant nutrients. Rhododendrons, Azaleas, Heaths and Heathers, bog and woodland plants abhor it. *It should only be used on a bed (for lawns or perennials) being prepared for planting and not then without a simple soil test to determine need.* About the only kind of lime available to home gardeners is agricultural lime. If the sack's contents are 70 percent calcium oxide, it is satisfactory. Hydrated lime from a building supply house is all right to use, if it, too, is 70 percent calcium oxide. The misconception about the use of lime in home gardening is of such long standing and is so widespread that this paragraph will cause a flood of letters from limers, who are referred again to the foregoing to save their time and ours. Fie upon companies which advocate lime application on growing lawns and established flower beds!

*Limonium

Ly-moe'knee-um

Statice or Sea Lavender. A genus of many species that is broadly distributed throughout the North Temperate Zone. A few of the species produce good garden flowers. The species nearly all produce pleasant cushion-like blossoms which can be used as cut flowers or dried for winter arrangements. The following one is the best we have seen. Culture requires only full sun in a well-drained or sandy soil. Plant spring or fall.

L. latifolium. An excellent plant for the border or rockery. Coastal gardeners should note that it is not affected by salt spray. The compound flowering heads are large and lavender in color. Stems are about 15 inches high. Of course, it can be dried.

LING—*see* Calluna

linifolia (lin-ee-foe'lee-a) leaves like flax

*Linum
Lie'num

Flax. A very large group of species, many of them perennials. The fiber-yielding Flax of commerce is a *Linum* annual. A few perennials are good garden plants. They should be located in full sun and propagated by division. Plant spring only.

L. flavum. Profuse quantities of waxy yellow flowers with feathery foliage. Blooms recur all summer. Height is about 15 inches.
L. Heavenly Blue. The best of all blue Flax—luminous ultramarine-blue flowers on 12- to 18-inch stems. Recurring bloom all summer.

Lobelia
Lo-bee'lea-uh

Lobelia. Everyone, of course, knows the lovely annual called Lobelia, but not too many gardeners are aware that there are many other species in this genus, most native to the eastern United States, one of them a delightful blue perennial. Nothing special in soils is needed to grow it well, but it does like moisture and light shade. Plant spring only.

L. syphilitica. It develops long leafy stems up to 30 inches high; the sky blue flowers form singly at the leaf axil, which gives the effect of a leafy-blue raceme. Blooms appear at a perfect time of year—from September until frost.

Lonicera
Lon-iss'er-a

Honeysuckle. About 150 species make up this genus of shrubs and vines that are used all over the world in gardens; many are from the North Temperate Zone, particularly China and Japan. Others from warmer climates are not hardy in northern American gardens, which is unfortunate because many of them have blooms of spectacular size. The wide use of the hardy types is due more to their easy growth and relative freedom from disease or insect pests, than to any particular merit. The shrubs do make dense backgrounds, and, like the vines, produce many flowers, but there is a rankness to their growth that leaves them without the character one expects of garden plants. The hardiest and best species, *L. tatarica,* has many varieties. All grow to about 9 feet in full sun in almost any soil, and if treated to fertilizer and water they'll go higher. It's a great plant for home-owners who are just beginning to garden, for it just grows, grows, grows.

LOOSESTRIFE—*see* Lythrum *and* Lysimachia

LOVAGE—*see* Herbs

Lowii (lowe'eye) after Lowe, horticulturist

LUNGWORT—*see* Pulmonaria

Lychnis Haageana Hybrid

Lupinus

Loo-pine'us

Lupine. Another broad genus found in North and South America and the Mediterranean. It has many species, but few of them good garden plants. Lupine require lots of moisture, full sun, and protection from prevailing hot summer winds. Plant them in bold groups only in the spring.

L. Russell Hybrids. Pea-like blooms in rainbow shades of lavender, blue, pink, red, white, bicolor, and yellow on 30-inch stalks. This stock is from Bakers, the famous English nursery. This famous Lupine strain was developed by George Russell of Yorkshire, who, as a railroad guard at a quiet crossing, worked out these great flowers, now grown all over the world in temperate climates. Mixed colors only.

lutescens (loo-tes'sens) becoming yellow

Lychnis
Lick'nis

Catchfly. A large genus of the Pink family, some of whose species have been cultivated for centuries. The best are sunny border perennials bearing large heads of brilliant flowers in late May through July. Plant spring or fall.

***L. Haageana Hybrids.** These show-offs come in flashy salmons, orange reds and scarlets. Blooms are 2 inches across, stems are sturdy and about 12 inches high. It blooms from June to August. Use it in the border or rockery. Mixed colors only.
***L. Viscaria flore-plena.** Bright rosy-crimson flowers in June and July. In the summer the plants are neat mounds of green; they turn almost crimson in the fall. They grow from 12 to 18 inches high.

Lysimachia

Lysimachia
Ly-si-mack'ee-ah

Loosestrife. Another genus containing many species, but few are for the garden because they are weedy. They are widely distributed in the North Temperate Zone. Plant spring only.

L. punctata. Circle Flower. This charmer from Asia Minor is a great border plant. It has naturalized in parts of the eastern United States. It makes a fine show and it is very good for cutting. The lemon-yellow flowers have a light brown circle in the throat, hence its common name. Height of stems is about 18 inches; it flowers in June–July. Plant it in full sun or partial shade, and give it plenty of water.

Lythrum
Lith'rum

Also called Loosestrife. Tall border perennials, mostly from Eurasia, that form shapely plants. They are good for naturalizing, and useful in any shady, moist location, although they grow well in full sun.

Several species have naturalized in the eastern United States. Plant spring or fall.

L. Dropmore Purple. This rich purple variety blooms profusely from late June through September on 30- to 36-inch stems.

***L. Happy.** Lythrum varieties, as you know, have all been tall. This one, named after that most pleasant dwarf who was one of Snow White's seven henchmen, is only 15 to 18 inches high and a fine darkish pink. It is a very heavy bloomer that is useful for mass planting or as a neat hedge bordering a path. It is very hardy, and, like all its fellows, easily propagated by division in early spring.

L. Morden's Gleam. Flowers are a bright carmine, the nearest color to red in Lythrums. It blooms July to September at 40 inches.

L. Robert. An English origination. Flower spikes of bright rose red on a compact plant. Its foliage turns scarlet in the fall. It grows to 24 inches.

Lythrum Morden's Gleam

Macleaya

Mack-lay'a

Macleaya. A genus of two species, both garden subjects, but the unpracticed eye can hardly tell one from the other. These stately plants can't be beat where a bold planting is desired. Foliage is sculptured and quite lovely. Blooms come in showy clusters. Isolate a planting on a lawn or put it by frequented paths and these 6-foot plants give a sensational appearance. Grow them in big pots or tubs for use on the terrace. They like a rich soil which should be deeply prepared (2 feet) and given lots of water. Plant spring or fall.

M. cordata. This handsome decorative species produces creamy buff flowers in July and August. The elegant seed pods that follow are most useful for dried floral arrangements. Very weedy if not contained.

MADONNA LILY—*see* Lilium candidum

magnificum (mag-nif'i-cum) magnificent

Magnolia
Mag-no'lee-uh

Magnolia is a magnificent genus of about 30 species of shrubs and trees that are native to North America, the West Indies, Mexico, and Asia. Only a few are hardy in Litchfield. Our experience is limited to 2: *M. Soulangiana,* called the Saucer Magnolia by some, and *M. stellata,* known to everyone as the Star Magnolia. In warm climates, the former grows to a tree of considerable proportions. In this section of zone 4 (it is not supposed to be satisfactory north of zone 5) it grows into a large shrub. *Stellata,* which grows to 20 feet in warmer climates, is smaller here, but satisfactory. The deciduous Magnolias all tend to rush to bloom on the first warm days of spring, and can be harmed by late frosts. Some plantsmen suggest planting them in exposed rather than protected southern locations, reasoning that they will not respond quickly to warm weather and that, thus retarded, they will miss damage by late frosts and at the same time provide a longer season of bloom. I haven't tried it but it seems reasonable. Certainly a longer season of bloom would be highly desirable; as it is the things are open and gone far too soon. This does not happen when spring temperature stays cool. Good culture requires a site with excellent drainage, and once every 2 or 3 years a dressing of well-rotted cow manure is in order.

Malus
May'lus

The Flowering Crabapples. There is little doubt that this genus of small trees with many species and innumerable varieties is the most widely planted spring-flowering ornamental tree in the United States, if not the world. They are natives of the North Temperate Zone, including Siberia, the home of *M. baccata,* so hardy that it thrives in zone 2 where temperatures drop to −50° F. It is also one of the easiest plants to hybridize—the reason why scores of varieties go to market every year. Its literature cites many instances where

Macleaya cordata

chance seedlings or volunteers have displayed such admirable qualities that they have become cultivars. But before discussing the various forms and varieties, it should be made clear that the continued beauty of these plants can only be assured by care. They are subject to the ills of common apple trees: scale, insect, borer infestation, and fire blight. In practice this care is not as demanding as it is with fruit, if pruning, spraying, and borer control is done annually—a dormant spray in the spring, up to 2 general sprays during the summer. They cannot, in other words, be neglected.

Flowering Crabs have a wide variety of forms. A few will grow from 30 to 40 feet. Most of them reach 20 feet and have broadly-rounded crowns. Some are weepers; others are so small they might be called large shrubs. As all but the columnar forms spread, space must be allowed for their ultimate growth. A warning: some very beautiful varieties are alternate bloomers, which means that they are dazzling one year and put on little vegetative growth, and the next year produce few flowers and lots of vegetation (we have a couple like this). The qualities to seek, regardless of height, are massive annual bloom, maximum production of fruit for display and wildlife, and leaves which turn color satisfactorily in the fall.

I have no first-hand experience with the new varieties, but I have seen many and consider most of them superior to the dozen or so older models we still have in the gardens. However, one old one doesn't seem to get nearly the attention it deserves. It is *M. hupehensis,* the Tea Crab, brought from China to Arnold Arboretum in 1900 by E. H. Wilson. It has a vase-like form and looks every bit the Oriental it is. Its trunk produces long, single branches that reach out with exquisite grace. The flowers bloom prolifically from many small spurs, so that each branch is beautifully wreathed. It's a beaut and may be hard to find. Another one, quite new, called

M. Red Jade, originated in the Brooklyn Botanical Garden. It is semi-weeping. The flowers are white with a pink blush, but its name derives from its spectacular fall appearance—great cascades of bright red tiny apples cover it. It is patented, and has been released through fine nurseries, including some of the better mail-order houses (Wayside for one). *H. Hilleri,* originated by Hillier & Son of Winchester, England, the world's most prestigious nursery, and *M. Hopa,* far older hybrids, are hard to beat for intensity and density of bloom. In buying Malus one should insist that the variety selected be true to its name, not the name the nurserymen has selected to insure that at least one feature is unique to him. A lot of this goes on, for there are few patents in the field. It is a tactic far less likely to be used by a good local nurseryman who grows his own stock. Beware the nursery or garden center that does not carry *M. Hopa* because "this one is a better variation—or close to it." Maybe so, but get it in writing. Bareroot, most varieties can be bought in the $15 range; balled-and-burlapped a well-grown tree will cost $25 and more. Shop early to cover as many sources as possible—and to be able to select the best form in the lot.

It is a great temptation, if one lives in the country, to line a wooden fence or stone wall with Crabs. We found out that it doesn't work—they encroach the wall and make it look broken, and they are much harder to get into for effective pruning. Better to plant a single specimen at a strategic point, or several well-spaced in a small grove. They are tremendously effective in mass on a steep bank or hill, particularly if only one variety is planted or if 2 are alternated. An acquaintance in the Midwest has nearly 100 of them on the side of a rolling steep hill too far away to be seen from his house. Every spring he hauls out a large table, sets up a bar, and invites friends from all over to a party for them. I've never seen them in bloom. The pictures, however, are spectacular. I've heard that the parties, if the night is right and warm, can be spectacular too.

MALLON—*see* Hibiscus

MANURE. The addition of manure to a garden adds some plant nutrients to the soil, but its most valuable ingredient is humus—the soil factor which determines the ability of soil to retain moisture. Humus, which in its best form is thoroughly decomposed vegetable matter, also stimulates the growth of myriad soil bacteria, which break down soil nutrients and make them available to plants. To put it another way, humus mixed in mineral soil is topsoil; the subsoil one digs up is a mineral soil without humus. The former grows the world's trees, food, and plants; the latter grows nothing. Cow manure is the form most available in this country. If it is several years old and well rotted it can be dug into an established garden without fear of burning the plants. Fresh cow manure, pretty unsavory stuff, should be composted before use, but it can be used to great advantage in establishing a new garden if dug into it a month or more before planting. Dried cow manure is more readily available to most gardeners; instructions on the bag should be followed. Plant nutrients should be added when thoroughly rotted manure is used, for most chemicals have leached out. In preparing a new garden or lawn it's a good rule of thumb to use 1 ton of manure to each 2000 square feet of area.

Swamp humus, a substitute for animal manure, is available in some areas. It is a fine top dressing for gardens and lawns but fertilizer should be added. If swamp humus can be bought steamed, so much the better—no weeds.

Horse, chicken, pig, and sheep manures are also available, but seem more suited for farming than gardening. Horse manure, with its high straw and urine content, heats badly, will burn if composted improperly, and requires turning too many times to make its use practical. The other animal manures mentioned have very high plant food content and must be used sparingly before plants leaf out to keep from spoiling foliage. We know a gardener on the Atlantic Coast who never puts in a plant without burying a chunk of fish well under it. He has a fine garden, no humus or fertilizer to buy. That's the way the Indians planted hills of corn. This chap picks up fish that can't be sold at dockside, cuts them into chunks, then puts them in an old deepfreezer until needed. He admits having a little trouble with neighboring cats.

Producing green manures by plowing under a growing crop of buckwheat or other grains is a technique farmers use to build humus in a soil. It is rarely used by home gardeners.

marginalis (*mar-gin-aye'liss*) *having a margin*

maritima (*mar-it'i-ma*) *of the sea*

Marjoletti (*mar-joe-let'tye*) *after Marjollet, botanist*

MARJORAM—*see* Herbs, Origanum

Meleagris (*me-lee-ag'ris*) *from Meleagros*

Mertensianum (*mer-ten-si-a'num*) *after botanist Mertens*

Mertensia

Mertensia

Mur-ten'see-a

Mertensia. These herbs from the North Temperate Zone are generally low-growing, and make excellent subjects for the rockery, border, or in beds in light shade. Flowers are mostly blue and appear as racemes. Plant spring or fall.

***M. virginica.** Virginia Bluebell. You'll never see a prettier flower than this. It likes shade, as you probably know. The tubular flowers, blooming in early spring, are sapphire blue on 18- to 24-inch stems. It is native to the United States.

MICHAELMAS DAISY—*see* Aster

microphyllis (my-crow-fill'liss) small-leaved

midrib (mid-rib) the middle vein of a leaf or flower

MILKWORT—*see* Euphorbia

millefolium (mill-ee-foe'lee-um) thousand-leaved

minor (my'nor) small

missouriensis (miz-zoor-ee-en'siss) of Missouri

MOCK ORANGE—*see* Philadelphus

mollis (moll'is) soft

Monarda

Monarda

Mon-are'da

Bee Balm. An attractive North American family with fragrant mint-like foliage; for sunny border or light shade. Tubular petals form a globe-shaped head of brilliant flowers. Very hardy—and *very* attractive to bees. It gives a wonderful show, and has been a favorite in the garden for many years. It flowers in July and August. Plant spring or fall.

M. Cambridge Scarlet. It produces brilliant scarlet flowers from late June to September on 24- to 30-inch stems.
M. Croftway Pink. Rose-pink flowers. From 24 to 30 inches high.
M. Melissa. A charming soft pink variety.
M. Mahogany. This new Indian-red color is a valuable addition to this highly usable genus. It flowers over a very long period.
M. Prairie Brand. Fine salmon-red blooms on a 4-foot plant.
M. Snow Queen. White, of course. It's free-flowering too.

MONKSHOOD—*see* Aconitum

montanum (mon-tay'num) of the mountains

MOUNTAIN LAUREL—*see* Kalmia

MOUNTAIN PINKS—*see* Phlox subulata

MULCHING—*see* Weeding and Mulching

MULLEIN—*see* Verbascum

multiflorus (mul-ti-flowe'rus) a many-flowered thing

*Muscari

Mus-kay'ree

Grape Hyacinth. A Mediterranean genus whose bulbs are excellent for bedding or rock garden work. They should be planted immediately upon arrival and can remain in place, without division, for years. They thrive under trees or in full sun. It blooms very early. The bulbs are inexpensive and should be planted by the hundreds or thousands. Plant fall only.

M. armeniacum. Clear blue giant flowers.
M. a. Blue Spike. The double hybrid form of the foregoing. The unusually large flowers are sterile and, because they are, last much longer.
M. botryoides album. A delicate pure white.

Muscari

Mussinii (moos-sin'eye) after Mussin, horticulturist

mutabile (mew-tay'bill) changeable, as to color

MUTATION. It is believed that a miracle of the cosmos is responsible for a branch of a shrub, for example, suddenly showing a different characteristic, in color of leaf or flower or growing habit. It has mutated, and many a rare plant, the weeping form of Hemlock, for example, is considered a mutation. Indeed, the garden at Brookhaven Atomic Laboratory on Long Island is full of plants scientists have bombarded with man-made cosmic rays. This attempt to speed mutation has been successful, particularly in producing new varieties of grains and grasses, some of which have already proved to be invaluable in commerce.

myosotidiflora (my-owe-sowe-ti-di-flow'ra) flowers like Myosoties (Forget-me-not)

nana (nay'nah) dwarf

Narcissus

Nahr-sis'sus

Daffodil. Very important garden plants, chiefly hardy and bulbous, most of them from Southwest Europe and North Africa. In all of horticulture there isn't a finer bulb for naturalizing. Plantings do not have to be disturbed for years; the bulbs multiply amazingly; flowers come in profusion; few diseases attack Narcissus in this country. What more does one need from a flower? They are also extremely useful in the perennial border—they provide the first large flowers of spring. Gardeners now have many forms to choose from. In naturalizing Narcissus it is more effective to devote an area to just one form, separated from another one by 10 to 20 feet of woodland or grass. Fall planting only.

Culture: Daffodils are easy to grow. They seem to do as well in semi-shade as in full sun. They force their way up through any turf, and although they grow well in damp areas they do not like a location where water stands on them. Plant them 4 to 7 inches deep for fast propagation. If put down 9 to 10 inches the bulbs propagate far less rapidly. Be sure to plant Daffodils as soon as they are received

—they should throw a heavy root system before deep frost to produce large flowers the following spring. Instead of using only bulb food or bonemeal at the bottom of each hole, add to it a heaping teaspoon of sewage sludge and mix both thoroughly in the bottom of the hole. Plant the bulb, then top dress with sludge each spring after bloom. This sludge culture, recently worked out by Dutch growers, gives remarkable results. (*Milorganite* is a sewage sludge sold nationally.) Daffodils in the perennial garden can have tops cut back when they sprawl—it is not necessary to wait until they yellow. Gardeners who want to naturalize a meadow should hire a tractor, cut furrows following the contour of the land, load with sludge and bonemeal, plant the bulbs, and then replace the furrow. Dig up every fifth year, separate, and replant. I should point out that I have stayed with conventional Narcissi classification, a confession that will raise eyebrows among the many experts—amateur and professional—in this field. I have a tendency to keep up as well as possible with new horticultural classifications, but I don't believe that most gardeners care about them until they become expert in a field. I have no quarrel with the new Daffodil classification and consider it a great improvement over the old one—for the professional. But there are just too many classes for the amateur to worry about, for it's based on numbers. It seems to me to be enough for the government and A.T.&T. to complicate our lives with numbers; gardeners should not be burdened with them. They contend with weather, insects, marauding dogs, and destructive children, which is quite enough.

Note: The letters F. C. C. or A. M. found after the name of the following varieties are abbreviations for the First Class Certificate and Award of Merit, both top prizes at the best Dutch, English, and Irish shows, and hard to win.

Narcissus Apricot Distinction

Flatcup Narcissus. This is a modern form of Narcissus the varieties of which come in many sizes and colors. They result from a single bulb hybridized by W. F. M. Copeland, an English specialist living in Southampton, and shown by him in 1920. He named the flower John Evelyn (after an English writer who lived in the early part of the 18th Century), because Evelyn wrote so well about gardens. Copeland won an A. M. from the Royal Horticultural Society that year, and at Haarlem in 1921 and 1924. The Dutch (and others), impressed by its different form, have developed a remarkable strain from it. Instead of trumpets, this form has flat cups, some flaring, others ruffled and edged in various colors. The petals are very large, some with a semi-double effect. All have such strong stems that they have been called "Weatherproofs" because hard spring rains rarely damage them. All Flatcup Daffodils bloom mid-season. There are so many varieties I could not possibly know all of them. The following are excellent, but I am sure that many other varieties perform as well.

[f]**N. Amateur.** A. M. The large white petals overlap and are perfectly shaped. The cup is small, as flat as can be, and brightest scarlet in color.

N. Apricot Distinction. This variety is relatively new—18 years ago bulbs were quoted at $25 each. It is still relatively expensive—$9 will usually buy a dozen bulbs. However, it is very unusual. The petals, believe it or not, are delicate apricot in color; the strong, frilled cup a very deep matching shade. This may be the first new color break in Narcissi in the past 25 years. But if you get it be sure to put it in filtered shade to keep the sun from burning out the color.

N. Arguros. F. C. C. An outstanding new flower with creamy white petals, and of all things one doesn't expect, a greenish flat cup.

[f]**N. Burma.** It has large overlapping yellow petals; the cup is orange scarlet.

N. Delibes. A. M. The large petals are a rich golden yellow, the big shallow cup is tangerine orange. It is a heavy propagator.

N. Duke of Windsor. F. C. C. A sensationally large flower on a very strong stem. Petals are purest white, the large spreading cup is orange apricot. It is one of the best in the flatcup series and old enough to have reached a reasonable price—say a little under 25 cents each in 100 lots.

N. Eddy Canzony. A. M. The big cup is bright orange red, becoming gold at the base. The petals are large and white.

N. Galway. A. M. and F. C. C. This Narcissus has been heaped with awards in all countries. It's all golden yellow; with flaring petals and the large crown.

N. Iceland. A. M. An excellent John Evelyn seedling. The white petals are large and flaring and the huge cup is apricot.

N. Jezebel. The petals of this beauty are reddish gold, the medium-sized cup is the color of red lead. Unusual.

N. John Evelyn. F. C. C. The daddy of this strain and as fine a flower as any of its many offspring. Large white petals in beautiful composition. The huge flat cup is heavily frilled and pale apricot.

N. Lady Kesteven. F. C. C. The pure snow-white petals of this unusual flower form a perfect background for the cup, which is a solid cherry red.

N. Margaret Mitchell. A. M. and F. C. C. Another variety which has taken prizes everywhere. The pure white petals are broad and overlap; the smallish cup is soft yellow with a near-red margin.

N. Milk and Cream. A. M. This giant flower has pure white petals and an enormous flat crown the color of double cream. Nothing like it has been seen so far in this exciting group.

N. Missouri. A yellow-petaled variety with a flaring cup that is orange red throughout.

N. Mother Catherine. Very large white petals; the expanded cup has a sulphur-yellow edge followed by a broad band of soft orange yellow, the base is pale cream.

N. Muscadet. A flat cup with pure white petals and an ivory cup. It is the only Daffodil with the fragrance of Freezia.

N. Rococo. A. M. and F. C. C. This Daffodil has huge white petals; the flat crown is soft yellow with a broad ribbon of salmon orange on its edge.

N. Royal Crown. Petals are silvery white. The cup—large and heavily frilled—is a lovely soft apricot. It is a newish Evelyn seedling now reasonable in price.

N. Royal Orange. Very strong, overlapping white petals. The spreading, heavily frilled cup is enormous and deep orange throughout. It has the largest cup in this classification.

N. Spencer Tracy. F. C. C. This huge round thing has a cup of purest orange.

N. Sun Chariot. Broad, flat, rather pointed petals of deep golden yellow. The well-proportioned goblet-shaped cup is a solid glowing orange red. The flower seems sunproof and lasts remarkably well as a cut flower.

Narcissus Eddy Canzony

Narcissus John Evelyn

Miniature Narcissus. These are the botanical species types and their hybrids. Some are surprisingly little fellows, only a few inches high with delightful small flowers. They are rockery plants, of course, and most varieties are easily forced.

*[f]**N. Bulbocodium citrinus.** About 6 inches high with small sulphur-yellow flowers. Early flowering.
*[f]**N. canaliculatus.** It has a tiny flower with white petals and a yellow cup. It blooms mid-season.
*[f]**N. Liberty Bells.** Clusters of deep lemon-yellow flowers on reed-like stems; 3 to 4 blooms to a stem. Liberty Bells is the yellow form of *Thalia*, one of the loveliest small daffodils ever developed. Late-flowering.
*[f]**N. Little Beauty.** A. M. As you would expect from its name, this is a charming miniature. It is a perfect bicolor, the petals white, the trumpet a soft yellow. It flowers early at about 6 inches.
*[f]**N. Suzy.** This lovely is similar in form to *Trevithian* but with canary-yellow petals and a very clear orange-red cup. Late-flowering.
*[f]**N. Thalia.** A. M. Large pure white flowers on 6- to 7-inch reed-like stems;—3 to 4 of them to a stem, too, and very sweet-scented. Late flowering.
*[f]**N. Trevithian.** F. C. C. Broadly overlapping petals form the shallow crown in perfect proportion. A pale lemon yellow throughout, with 2 to 4 flowers dancing on each stem. Very fragrant. Flowers mid-season.
*[f]**N. triandrus albus.** Angel's Tears. A late-flowering silvery-white miniature; 2 to 3 flowers to each 5- to 6-inch stem.
*[f]**N. triandrus.** April Tears. This yellow, late-flowering hybrid has 3 drooping flowers with petals that reflex on each 5- to 6-inch stem. The small trumpet and the petals are a clear yellow and are very fragrant.

Mixtures. In the United States most home gardeners buy Daffodil mixtures instead of named varieties. A principal reason is that the bulbs are less expensive. However, the average mixture is not really a mixture. It is composed largely of bulbs in oversupply, and the bulbs themselves are in many instances of inferior varieties and sizes, and far too many of them are simple, small yellow trumpets. A few fine American retail organizations buy premium mixes, and the buyer will have no difficulty determining the real from the ordinary. The former cost, at retail, from 13 to 15 cents a bulb in

1000 lots, the latter cost half of that or, in some supermarket mixes, less. The real test is in the growing—the premium mixtures produce large flowers on long stems the first year and propagate heavily, the others do not. Some organizations also offer mixtures by types.

Poetaz Narcissus. Here is a group of charming Daffodils whose flowers cluster on strong stems. The first three are completely hardy. *N. February,* used largely for forcing in place of Paperwhite Narcissus, which is not hardy, is a tender bulb. Those who live in zone 5 and southward use them for forcing, then they naturalize them in the spring and get double duty from them.

[f]**N. Cheerfulness.** A. M. Never was a flower better named. Clusters of showy double white flowers bloom on exceedingly strong stems. When Cheerfulness first opens there is a suggestion of yellow in the center which soon fades. It is a late-season bloomer; a heavy multiplier.

[f]**N. Cheerfulness Primrose.** A. M. It has the same lovely double form of Cheerfulness but in a solid primrose yellow. Both of these Cheerfulness varieties are very sweet-scented.

[f]**N. Early Perfection.** Whitest of petals with a light yellow cup, and many flowers on a stem. It flowers in mid-season.

[f]**N. February.** F. C. C. Early Flowering (also known as Cragford). This delight in multi-flowered Daffodils has white overlapping petals and a yellow cup edged a bright orange scarlet. February, when started in December, blooms indoors in, obviously, February. Not hardy in zone 4.

Trumpet Narcissus. Trumpet Daffodils are the most familiar form of the genus and over the years have been naturalized by the hundreds of millions. Most naturalizing mixtures are largely composed of them. The hybridizers, however, have turned up some remarkable new varieties in the last 2 decades—huge things. Also, Irish and Dutch plantsmen have developed pink forms, different shades of gold and yellow, and bicolors. Here is what seems to be the cream of the crop:

Narcissus Lady Kesteven

Narcissus Spencer Tracy

[f]**N. Beersheba.** F. C. C. A widely known pure white flower and quite satisfactory. It flowers mid-season.

[f]**N. Lord Nelson.** A. M. A uniform soft yellow throughout, and a sensationally large flower to boot. Flowers show mid-season.

N. Louise de Coligny. Late-flowering. It is one of the best of the pinks: the petals are white and large and the trumpet shows its apricot-pink color immediately after opening. It is fragrant and a heavy propagator, so it's good for naturalizing.

[f]**N. Oklahoma.** This well-proportioned, large trumpet Daffodil is intense orange yellow, the petals white and flat. It is an outstanding bicolor that flowers mid-season.

[f]**N. Spellbinder.** A greenish-lemon, mid-season trumpet. As the flower develops the inside of the trumpet turns almost white.

[f]**N. Unsurpassable.** F. C. C. A gorgeous flower, large and of the deepest golden yellow throughout. It is as vigorous as all get out and flowers in mid-season.

neapolitana (nee-pol-i-tay'na) of Naples

Nepeta

Nee'pea-ta

Ground Ivy or Catnip. A rather large genus of Northern Hemisphere plants, first named by Pliny, probably after the Italian town of Nepi. Only a few species are worth growing. They like ordinary sandy soils. Plant only in the spring.

***N. Mussinii.** An extremely good edging or border plant with gray-green foliage. It is a compact grower 15 to 18 inches wide. Profuse, small, lavender-blue flowers appear from June to August. Full sun is the best location.

Newberryi (new'berry-eye) after botanist Newberry

nivalis (niv-aye'lis) snow white, or growing near snow.

niveum (niv'ee-um) snow white

nodulosa (nod-you-low'sa) having nodules

nummularium (num-mew-lay'ree-um) coin-like, circular

Nearly all of White Flower Farm's rare, unusual, or hard-to-find plants can be seen in the 2¼-acre gardens. Above: "The Mother Garden"—source of cuttings.

Left: *A vista rarely seen, from the experimental block. Day lilies* (front of fence) *are* H. Flava, *originally found in China 3500 B.C.* Right, clockwise: *Bulbous Lilies put on a splendid show from late spring to September; a tapestry hedge made of different colored conifers and only about 7 years old is shaggy in late April, gets a formal pruning in late May; the hedge is a visitors' favorite because of its year-round color; Fuchsia "mother" plants like their summer home in light shade on a cool stone wall.*

Counter clockwise: *Visitors cut through path separating two perennial borders, the spring-flowering one on their right shows bloom, the late-flowering border will take over in early July, bloom steadily until frost; 20-year-old Weeping European Beech; White Pine on left is a nearly-mature specimen with a 12-inch butt—at right dwarf conifers at various stages of growth.* Opposite: *Weeping Hemlock in front of a large Bird's Nest Spruce, rare Rhododendron on test in the large border—Tree Peonies in flower in front of tall hedge.*

Opposite: *Named Delphinium originated by England's Blackmore & Langdon, the world's leading hybridizer of this great genus. Plants are staked so spikes sway instead of breaking in the wind.* Left and clockwise: *Tuberous Begonia from the fine Langdon nursery—it is one of several hundred plants from the annual exhibition of them in Greenhouse 4; Dwarf Conifers in a 22-year-old border; Annually Litchfield shows some of its old houses, and we serve tea to visitors on a shady upper lawn.*

obtusa (ob-tew'sa) blunt, rounded at end

occidentalis (ox-se-den-tay'lis) western

odorata (owe-doh-rah'ta) very sweet smell

Oenothera missourensis

*Oenothera

Ee-no-thee'ra

Oenothera. The Greek name of the genus means wine-scenting which refers, it is said, to an ancient use of the roots. This is rather hard to credit, for all but one of its 200 species originated in the Western Hemisphere, most of them in North America. The exception is a species from Tasmania, hardly next door to Greece. But one or the other of them may have journeyed to this country that seems to prefer wine scented one way or the other—*retsina*, for example. The genus is widely distributed in North America and is fond of open ground and full sun—the prairies and the plains are favorite habitats. There is little to say about their culture, except to note that only a few species are hardy in cold climates. One species known as The Evening Primrose, is a weedy thing not worth growing. The two following are excellent border plants.

O. fruticosa. Large canary-yellow single blooms on a bushy 18-inch plant. It blooms from June through August, and is very showy, very hardy, very nice.
O. missourensis. This lovely Evening Primrose grows only 12 inches high. Its golden yellow blooms are 4 inches in diameter.

OLD MAN—*see* Artemisia

orientale (ohr-ee-en-tay'lee) eastern

ORIENTAL POPPY—*see* Papaver Orientale

ORIGANUM—*see* Herbs

Osmunda (oz-mun'da) a wiry moss used in orchid culture

*Pachistima
Pak-iss'-tim-uh

Pachistima. Zone 4, southward. A genus of 2 species of low-growing evergreen native North American shrubs that have been neglected by the natives of North America, which is rather too bad. Plant spring or fall.

***P. Canbyi.** This evergreen grows only about 8 inches high, spreads to 2 feet. It is not the least fussy about soils, but other shrubs should not crowd it. Full sun or part shade seems to make little difference. Put it in the rockery or border, or trim it neatly as a dwarf hedge.

Pachysandra
Pack-iss-and'ra

Pachysandra. A genus of 5 species from North America and eastern Asia. One, *P. terminalis* (ordinary green Pachysandra), is a very valuable ground cover for shady areas that will support nothing else. It is readily available—a friendly neighbor is a good source. The variety described below is not so easily found. Plant spring or fall.

P. terminalis variegata. This variety has a distinct silver edge. Plant islands of it in solid green Pachysandra for bright accents. It succeeds in brightening up shady spots considerably when used alone.

Pachysandra terminalis variegata

Paeonia
Pea-owe'nee-uh

The Peony. This is one of the garden's major plants. It has been grown in China for 2,500 years and the 25-odd species of the genus are of Asiatic origin. The soft flowers, which break ever so slowly from their tight round buds, reach a spectacular size and then, fully open and a joyous sight one day, shatter completely in the night. "Kissed by a moonbeam," a Chinese poet said.

Peonies were brought to Europe about 1800. Five of the species, with their varieties and later hybrids, make up what we know today as the garden Peony, although some, Tree Peonies, for example, are not common. Single and Japanese-type single Peonies are widely

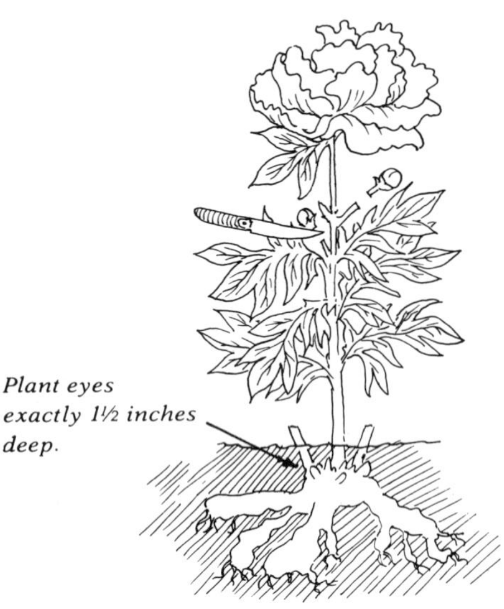

Planting and Care of Peonies

Disbud side shoots to get huge bloom; when blossom fades, snip off to prevent seed formation. After planting is 3 years old, two thirds of stalks can be used for cut flowers

used in Europe, but as yet they have attracted only the most knowledgeable American gardeners.

One great asset of Peonies is a very long life—there are plantings in Asian temple gardens 100 years old and more. (Practically every American gardener knows of flourishing Peony plants 15 to 20 years old—there are 6 plants that have been in the gardens here for 30 years.) These, of course, are varieties no one would think of planting today because the colors are mostly shades of *magenta.* One reason for the long life of Peonies is that they have no natural enemies—except man. With their many colors they have also been a symbol of beauty through the centuries. Not only are they very decorative in a garden but they have many uses. As a hedge along a driveway, for example, they bloom like no other hedge; afterward they stay a pleasant green until frost strikes them down. Then, after the dead tops have been taken away, the householder has an ideal open place to pile the winter's snows. The principal forms of this important plant follow. Many are lovely new varieties; some are older, but just as impressive today as when they reached market years ago. Plant only in the fall.

Culture: Peonies are not finicky about soils. However, they do better if the soil is slightly on the alkaline side (*see* pH Factor). They are also great feeders and should be lightly fertilized annually after bloom, but they go for years without additional food. They sulk when grass grows around them too densely, but they come back quickly after it is removed. Plant the eyes exactly 1½ inches below ground level, if possible (see drawing). When frozen in the first winter, mulch with evergreen, hay, or straw. Mulching is not necessary afterward. All Peonies make delightful cut flowers. When cut in heavy bud they will open and keep a week in water, but never cut more than two-thirds of a 4-year-old bush; cut only 10 percent of younger ones. Snip off any seed pods that develop on the remaining stems. Most types bloom in June. Wilt caused by fungus sometimes appears on stems of Peonies planted the previous fall during hot and humid spring days. Cut off the affected stalk and burn it. An early spray with a fungicide would have saved it. Spots on leaves are not usually encountered; simple fungicide sprays will arrest those that do appear (*Captan* or *Bordeaux Mixture—see* Insecticide). Peony roots can be divided, or you can get them from a friend or buy them. They should have at least 3 eyes, small soft reddish buds at the side toward the top of the root; a root with fewer buds takes too long to develop into a satisfactory plant.

Double Peonies. The following hybrids all owe their origin to *P. albiflora* and various crosses between it and other Asiatic species and their subsequent hybrids. They are intensely double, which means that as the bloom unfolds a center never appears, just masses of petals. Huge show-type blooms are easily grown by disbudding the side shoots, all of which have small buds at their ends. Obviously, disbudded stalks should be staked. It is well to stake the outside stalks of a plant; then the inside ones will be propped up and little flopping will result. If one fails to stake and the stalks fall over, just cut them off—neither the plant nor the visitors will ever miss them.

There are many varieties but, if the colors are satisfactory, it is hard to go wrong. Even though the double Peonies take extra care (they should, as noted, be staked), it would be hard to get along without them—if only because they provide such great bouquets. The following are the best double varieties we have grown in the last 15 years.

Double Peony

Pink to rose tones:

P. Emma Klehm. This variety is famous in the double group for its bright, deep pink color. Late season.

P. Jules Elie. A tall, free-flowering, light rose-pink variety long admired by fanciers.

P. Moonstone. Fully blush pink, and it's hard to think of a nicer color. Mid-season.

P. Mrs. F. D. Roosevelt. Deep pink with very long overlapping cupped petals which enfold a rosebud center.

P. Myrtle Gentry. A double light pink, fading with age to nearly white. Very fragrant late bloomer.

P. Nick Shaylor. A light or blush pink with occasional red markings in center petals. It blooms late.

P. Vivid Rose. And that's exactly the color, too. Quite fragrant. Blossoms come mid-season.

P. Walter Faxon. Mid-season light shell pink. Mildly fragrant.

Crimson to red tones:

P. Bonanza. Double and deepest mahogany red. Blooms mid-season on very strong stems.

P. Chocolate Soldier. Not really chocolate, but a deep maroon red. It blooms early. Some plants have blossoms with very small yellow dots on the center petals.

P. Inspecteur Lavergne. This variety flowers in mid-season, is tall and completely double. Blooms are globular in shape and crimson. The petals in the center are frilled.

P. Jay Cee. A remarkable mid-season variety with perfectly formed American Beauty-red flowers and bright green foliage.

P. Jean Bockstoce. Black red and about as desirable a Peony in its color class as we shall ever see. Early-flowering.

P. Kansas. Bright red blossoms carried on very strong stems. Use it as a show flower. It is a mid-season bloomer.

P. Karl Rosenfield. It is a fully double, brilliant dark crimson that blooms freely in mid-season.

P. Lowell Thomas. A remarkable double red that has no equal. Although the plant develops rapidly it is an extremely slow variety to propagate, which is why, no doubt, so few plantsmen grow it—and why it's so expensive.

Peonies Bloom All Summer

*They don't, of course, blossom on the plant itself, but you can have Peonies in bloom indoors for most of the summer if you will follow this simple routine. Cut the buds just before they open on stems about 6 inches long. Lightly wet the inside of a large plastic bag, place the buds inside, and seal the bag with a warm iron. Put it in your refrigerator (*not *deep freeze). Later take out the buds you need and float them in a shallow bowl of water (close the bag tightly). When a bud is about one third open, lift it, then cut the stem to one half inch and refloat.*

Blooms opened this way are more spectacular than those on the plant, where their beauty can be marred by wind, rain, intense heat or cold, or insects. All Peony blooms can be opened this way. Tree Peony flowers reach fantastic dimensions. Buds, however, must not be too tight when cut. Also, don't wait to get these results only off-season—do it this way when the plants are in bloom.

Single or Japanese-form Peony

White and off-white:

P. Bowl of Cream. And that is exactly what it is: huge, bowl-shaped flowers, creamy white, carried on fine strong stems in mid-season.

P. Carolina Moon. Early, very double, the petals yellowish white; the center a yellow bomb with white. Early bloomer and lovely.

P. Elsa Sass. White with a veiled pink overcast. Stems are strong and erect even during the blooming season, which is late.

P. Festiva Maxima. Large, pure white blooms with occasional flecks of crimson in the center of the petal's base. Vigorous and early. Very fragrant. This has been a great Peony for generations and no new variety in its class equals it.

P. Kelway's Glorious. The large, double flowers are glistening white and very fragrant. Mid-season to late.

P. Miss America. Huge sparkling white blossoms in mid-season.

P. Raspberry Sundae. Cream petals flecked and marked with raspberry red—so it's named after a raspberry sundae. It blooms mid-season.

Single and Japanese Herbaceous Peonies. For some reason American gardeners have paid little attention to this glorious form. They are extremely popular in Europe. This could be due to their slightly higher price in the past, but it is more likely that gardeners don't know them and feel that single means small. True, the flowers are not as heavy or ball-like, but they have great cushions of short staminodes surrounded with glorious petals, and they are anything but small. The color combinations are spectacular. They also have exceptionally strong stems, but we stake them anyway, for losing one would just be too much of a loss. The following varieties provide a rather broad look at the best in this class. Plant fall only.

P. Ama-No-Sode. Outer petals of this Japanese origination are a bright rose pink. The center petals, yellow at the base with the upper half chamois yellow edged gold, are faced with the pink tone of the outer petals. Quite lovely.

P. Gold Standard. The white petals are tinted yellow. The massive pillow of staminodes is yellow and overall it is as close as one can come to a yellow herbaceous peony. Although it is extremely difficult to propagate (only 2 or 3 divisions are possible from a 5-year-old root) we have worked with it for years because of its sheer beauty. It grows strongly in the garden.

P. Krinkled White. The crinkled white petals are specially large, the center a mound of golden stamens beautifully matted. Stems are slender but strong. It makes an excellent cut flower and blooms mid-season at about 2 feet.

P. Nippon Gold. Pink with a pure gold center of narrow crinkled petals. It blooms late.

P. Sea Shell. The color is not a delicate sea-shell pink but a strong pink with iridescent quality. The center is golden. It blooms mid-season and excels as a cut flower.

P. Sword Dance. This late-flowering, medium-dark red flower is very brilliant; the golden center is of extreme size.

Tree Peony. About 15 or 16 centuries ago the Tree Peony was discovered growing wild in the bamboo groves of the southern part of the province of Chekiang, China. It was named *Mushaoyas,* or Woody Shaoyas, after *Shaoyas,* the ancient Chinese name for the double herbaceous Peony we know so well. It had the characteristics of a tree or small shrub: it defoliated in the fall but did not die back to the ground like its herbaceous cousin. By A.D. 700 it had been given the name *moutan* and had become the principal flower of the Chinese Imperial Palace Gardens. Westerners who saw drawings of its flowers—huge, flat, fairy-like blossoms—on silk and pottery simply did not believe that such a flower existed, until plants were brought to England from Canton in 1787 by Sir Joseph Bank, who created Kew Gardens. The English sought Chinese *moutans* passionately until about 1840, when the vogue died. It revived in the 1890's with the advent of great new varieties the Japanese were producing. The boom hit France and then America in the early 1900's. It peaked out here during World War I, but revived for a while in the late 20's. Through the centuries Tree Peonies have been a plaything of the wealthy. Today there are some fine American varieties. This work was started by Professor A. P. Saunders of Hamilton College, in Clinton, and has been carried on by William

Gratwick of Pavilion, New York, and his associate Nassos Daphnis. This work is outstanding but it is not on a commercial basis.

There are other hybridizers in this country, but their work has not yet achieved importance. A good guess is that 99 percent of the Tree Peonies sold in the United States are grafted and grown in Japan. But as the species is no longer popular in that country, it has no hybridizers of note. However, there are many fine old varieties being produced in Japan. Getting them true to variety requires an horticultural agent who speaks idiomatic English. Some nurseries here claim to grow their own grafts, but visitors to such places get double-talked when they bring up the subject. They are told about the awful problems of importing from Japan, rather than being shown "own grafts" growing. If they are successful and being secretive, well and good, but growers of herbaceous Peonies who have tried it say that they quickly became discouraged with the extremely low percentage of successful grafts. There is not, however, any doubt about the difficulty of getting Japanese stock past customs (we used to lose whole shipments). This, coupled with the fact that to insure trueness to variety, a Japanese graft has to be grown until it has bloomed, keeps the retail cost of good stock rather high. As noted earlier, the Tree Peony, certainly the King of Flowers, frustrated us for years; but things are looking up now.

The literature on the culture of Tree Peonies is voluminous, old, and much of it is contradictory. A Tree Peony is a shrub, so let's start from there and treat it as a shrub—with a few important differences. The hole should be a big one even though the root is relatively small, so dig it 3 feet in diameter and 2 feet deep in a well-drained location. Test the topsoil, which should be rich, for *p*H. It should be a little on the alkaline side—6.9 *p*H is desirable, or a neutral 7.0. Gardeners in climates where rainfall is heavy may have to add a small amount of lime. In digging, place the topsoil at one side, the subsoil at the other side of the hole. Now put the top soil in the bottom of the hole and mix it thoroughly with an equal amount of damp peat, pure humus, or compost (never use manure) and 1 pound of bonemeal. Add lime if necessary. Cart away the subsoil and cart back enough rich topsoil so that after you have mixed it with an equal amount of humus and 2 pounds of bonemeal the soil will raise the surface of the bed about 3 inches. Again, add lime if necessary. The point of soil preparation is to produce a soil as rich as possible in humus. Irrigate to settle the soil—a week or more if possible. Plant the Tree Peony with the graft 4 inches below the surface. Try to have that measurement as accurate as possible. After deep frost, cover its branches with a 1-bushel wooden basket weighted with a rock. It should do well the first year. Our advice, which will be heeded only by strong-willed gardeners, is to snip off any buds that form, for you are after bush growth the first year, not flowers. After the second year work about 2 ounces of 14-14-14 *Osmocote* into the top 2 inches of the soil 12 to 15 inches around the branches. Repeat this, adding a bit more *Osmocote* each year and extending the circle as the branches spread. The plant should throw several flowers the second spring and put on 4 to 6 inches of growth annually. At maturity a Tree Peony under good culture should be 6 feet high, spread as much, and produce 50 to 100 great blooms. In zone 4 and the colder part of 5 it is well to choose a protected location.

A Tree Peony's principal disease is people—inexperienced help cut its branches back to the ground. Branches occasionally wilt. It is not true, as many once held, that this is of no moment because the fast-growing tops "compensate" for the slower-growing root system. The wilt is caused by a fungus that can be controlled, if it is not too far advanced, by spraying with *Bordeaux Mixture* or *Captan*. Be sure to sever the wilted branch and burn it. The foregoing detail may cause the faint-hearted to skip Tree Peonies. If they do they will miss having one of the most beautiful of all plants.

These varieties are listed by their English names, which are literal and sometimes fanciful translations of the Japanese names, which follow in parenthesis. One should not be misled by mere bigness of blossom in Tree Peonies. Bigness, flatness, and grace are attributes that all have. Plant only in the fall.

White varieties:

P. Five Continents (*Godaishu*, Japanese hybrid). Very large, double, pure white blossoms; the petals have a ragged edge. Blooms are 10 inches in diameter and heavy.

P. The Dictator (*Fuson no Tsukasa*, Japanese hybrid). The immense blooms of this pure white variety are ball shaped. Blossoms are 10 inches in diameter.

Pink varieties:

P. Cherry Two Two (*Yaegakura*, Japanese hybrid). The inside of the petals is a very dark cherry, shading to a lighter tone upward to the ends. Blossoms are double and 8 inches in diameter.

P. Camellia of Fortune (*Yachiyo-tsubaki*, Japanese hybrid). The nearly fully double blossoms are 7 inches in diameter and camellia shaped. The petals are deep salmon pink on the inside and shade to a light pink at the edge.

Red Varieties:

P. Cricket (*Higurashi*, Japanese hybrid). Early-blooming fully double blooms of bright scarlet crimson with darker crimson tones in the center. Blossoms are 7 inches in diameter.

P. The Sun (*Taiyo*, Japanese hybrid). The fully double, 7-inch flowers are bright crimson and the petals seem to have a satin finish.

P. Empress Brocade (*Tatsu Getsu Nishiki*, Japanese hybrid). Bright scarlet double blooms, 7 inches in diameter; the petal shades to white at the outside.

Yellow Varieties:

P. Alice Harding (French *lutea* hybrid). This variety is beloved all over the world. Blooms are fully double and ball shaped and the color is purest yellow.

They are fragrant. Blossoms are normally 7 inches in diameter, but are bigger under best culture. Give it plenty of room, for at maturity it grows about 3 feet high and can spread up to 5 feet.

P. Souvenier de Maxime Cornu (French *lutea* hybrid). The 8-inch double blossoms open orangy at the edges but turn to the yellow of the inside shortly afterward. The center has an orange shading.

Wisteria and Purple Varieties:

P. Wisteria of Kamata (*Kamata Fugi,* Japanese hybrid). This large double bloom is wisteria lavender in color and 8 inches in diameter. The name comes from *Kamata Fuji,* a mountain area of Japan famed for its wild Wisteria.

P. Bird of Imagination (*Rimpo,* Japanese hybrid). And that is exactly what *rimpo* means. It is the largest of all doubles—10 inches or more under best culture, 8 inches if grown carelessly. The color is black purple, the yellow stamens provide a most unusual effect.

PAINTED DAISY—*see* Pyrethrum

paniculata (pan-ki-you-laye'ta) any loose, diversely branched flower

Papaver Orientale

Pa-paye'var Or-e-en'tal

Oriental Poppy. These strong Poppies from the Mediterranean now come in an unusual and beautiful range of colors and forms, thanks to the hybridizers. The Orientals are extremely showy, and are best when planted in groups in the perennial border. But *not* too many of them, please—they are showoffs. They are of easiest culture: any soil, but they preen themselves in a deep loam and have a hearty distaste for transplanting. Place the crown 3 inches below the surface (see drawing). Mulch it the first winter to prevent heaving, and after that, do nothing at all—the finest instruction in horticulture. All varieties flower in June and range from 2½ to 3 feet in height. Fall planting only.

P. Barr's White. Free-blooming pure white with purplish black spots at the base of the petals. It is a very popular variety, but really should have been called Barr's Black-and-White because the black spots are large.

Papaver Orientale

P. Carmine. Striking cardinal-red flowers with black splotches.
P. Curlilocks. This variety represents a complete break in blossom shape—the petals are deeply laciniated. The flower is a deep rose-pink color and blooms on 30-inch stems that need no staking.
P. Helen Elizabeth. Pure pink, no dark spots. A lovely pink thing.
P. Lighthouse. The lovely blooms are a pastel or flesh pink, and are very large—10 inches across. There are well-defined blood-red spots on the base of the petals. It is 36 inches high.
P. Mahogany. The biggest mahogany-red flower we have yet seen.
P. Maiden's Blush. White, but the edge carries a pink band about 2 inches wide. The flowers are about 6 inches in diameter. Charming rather than spectacular. It grows to 30 inches.
P. Oriental. It has brilliant scarlet blossoms with a prominent black blotch. It puts on a gorgeous show.
P. Pandora. The clear salmon-pink bloom is 8 inches in diameter and has a blood-red basal spot. Strong stems.
P. Pinnacle. Petals are white in the center and shade to light pink. The edges are heavily ruffled and splashed scarlet red in the modern style.
P. Show Girl. Crinkled and ruffled and very big—and a bicolor. It's white in the very center, the rest is a bewitching pink, just as bewitching as any show girl you ever saw.
P. Spring Morn. A flesh-pink variety blending to a deeper pink in the center. It blooms on sturdy 36-inch stems.
P. Victoria Dreyfus. The salmon blooms, 7 inches in diameter, have a charming silver edge. The stems are so strong and wiry that the flowers stand erect even when heavy with dew or rain drops. Exceptional.
P. Watermelon. Just the color of the juiciest, pinkest watermelon you have ever seen—without any seeds.

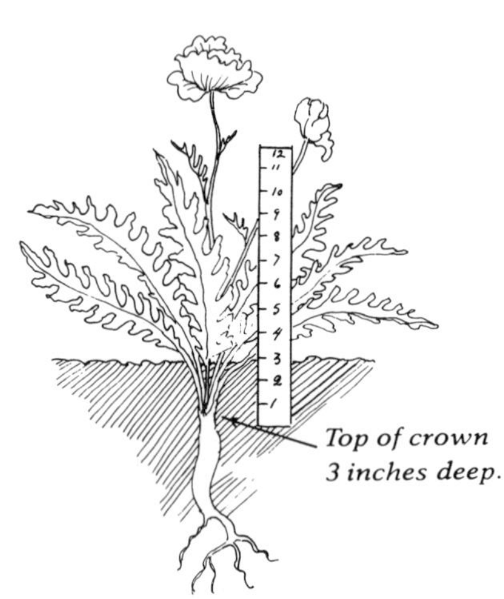

Oriental Poppy Culture

Most failures are due to shallow planting. Disbud after bloom to keep seed pod from forming. Once it is established, do not move it. Fall planting season: from late July through September

papillae (pap'ill-ee) a soft protuberance above the surface, usually found at the base of a flower

Parthenocissus

Par-then-owe-sis'sus

Parthenocissus. This genus of deciduous climbers, native to eastern Asia and North America, contains that great plant, Virginia Creeper, as well as a very small-leafed form commonly called small-leafed Boston Ivy. Plant spring or fall.

P. quinquefolia. Zone 4, southward. The true Virginia Creeper. It grows fast and is a lofty climber. Name your height, and if you are reasonable, this plant will reach it and thrive. The leaves are slender, pointed and rather coarsely toothed. It supports itself as it climbs. In summer the leaves are a lovely dull green, rather glaucous beneath. In the fall the whole vine turns to rich autumn tints.

P. tricuspidata Lowii. Zone 4, southward. This fine vine, which supports itself with tendrils tipped with adhesive, is another great climber. The very small leaves are dark green in summer and turn to glorious crimson before it defoliates in the fall. It is an ideal climber in climates unkind to evergreen ivy. It is not known well.

PATIO GARDENING. For "patio," read porch or terrace gardening, or any kind of gardening that largely dispenses with the conventional bed or border and in their place uses all kinds and sizes of pots, tubs and planters filled with soil and growing things. This is gardening in the outdoor room, a concept of living which has gone wild in sunny California, where it all started. Before World War II it was impossible for a visitor not to realize that Californians lived in rapturous weather and luxuriated in it, but then they seemed to spend a considerable amount of time indoors, like other people. Of course, the movie stars competed with each other in building bigger and bigger swimming pools, and if they held their orgies (the public's concept of movie stardom's parties) outdoors it wasn't so reported in the gossips or the tabs. Professor John Kenneth Galbraith (*The Affluent Society*) predicted in the mid-1940's that grass would grow on the streets of West Coast cities after the great war industries shut down, but this didn't happen; in fact, when the hordes of ordinary people began to invade California shortly after, they really started to live in outdoor rooms adjacent to swimming pools, which went from status symbol to necessity in a wink of time. In so doing they drove out an astonishingly large area that otherwise would have been grass. A visitor like me, who had known the West

Parthenocissus

Terra Rosa *pot*

Coast fairly well in the late 30's and then stayed away until the 1950's, couldn't help being impressed by the outdoor life or by the rapid development of the patio as outdoor living space. This style of living became great copy for the home-making magazines, whose editors at once attempted to transfer it to the rest of the country, in summer of course, the only time living outdoors elsewhere is possible. It seemed to me to be a nice way to live for even part of the year, so I set out to find out what kind of plants would provide bloom through the summer, and could be wintered over for use the following year, if grown in containers in the North.

A garden of potted plants I saw in 1950 near Lisbon, Portugal, on the patio of a house stuck on the side of a craggy mountain, went far beyond anything I had seen on the West Coast. That garden, in a climate similar to San Francisco's, was perfectly integrated with its house. There was no lawn. The surface of its terrace was stone, a few of them artfully omitted and planted with flowering plants (the English also are masters with this form of terrace). The place was protected from wind and it was beautifully "planted" with potted plants on various pleasing levels, in a form that reminded one of a great oak bookcase without doors. The three shelves were rich with plants in pots of various size. Small trees with heavy trunks grew from large pottery. They must have been 50 years old, or more. The cabinet beneath the "bookcase" had been turned into a bar. The garden had a quality of style that I had not seen on the West Coast; it was the gift, obviously, of age, and had none of the feeling one soon gets here of the awful conformity inherent in containers made on an assembly line and designed for machinery's efficiency rather than the eye's pleasure. To attempt to duplicate such a garden in a cold climate would of course require a great deal of peripheral equipment, as well as considerable labor; but it was full of ideas. It required that simple, basic pottery which in Europe doesn't look the least machine-made even when it is. We bought this peasants' pottery in many sizes in Italy—soft-paste pottery called *Terra Rosa* (rose-colored earth) made in northern Italy, largely by hand, and decorated with 3 simple rings. The stuff is a dime-a-dozen in Italy, but by the time the pots get here, crating, breakage (up to 75 percent), ocean freight, and duty shove the price up to a dollar a pound and more. But as nothing even close to it is made in the United States, even for double the money, it turns out to be inexpensive.

Square, octagonal, or oblong redwood planters made in the U.S. are fine in so far as the life of the wood is concerned, but the metal banding is shoddy. It is a light-weight iron strap which glitters like brass or copper and rusts out in 3 or 4 seasons. These containers have an indefinite life if the new iron bands are removed and carefully replaced with copper or aluminum wire.

The basic idea of gardening in pots or tubs is to have plants available for bloom at different seasons, or to produce green forms that are pleasing on a small stage. Pot culture also provides mobility impossible when plants are grown conventionally. It also requires a small area for use as a nursery or for storage, in a working section or enclosure. A small lath house will produce plants like Tuberous Rooted Begonias and Fuchsias for the shady parts of the patio. A small greenhouse is a convenience for starting them and other non-hardy plants, but not necessary to pot-gardening. An inexpensive garden house (with an earth floor and a wide door) is necessary to store hardy plants in pottery over the winter. This is done by moving them indoors, well-watered, before deep frost, then supplying them with enough water during the winter to keep the stems from drying out.

Redwood planter

There are an astonishing number of flowering trees and shrubs that do well under these conditions. Crabapples, Cherries, Peaches, and Almonds thrive. Varieties having small flowers and dense dwarf forms are best—the large double blossoms of the Kwanzan Cherry, for example, are too big to look well even when planted in a pot or tub so big that 2 men can hardly move it. A lavender Wisteria in tree form planted 18 years ago in a 20-inch *Terra Rosa* ring pot 17 inches high has assumed a dazzling Japanese form and has only failed to bloom once. Its trunk at ground level is more than 4 inches in diameter. It could be called big bonsai now. One envious fellow offered $425 for it—after he found it wasn't for sale. A pair of Dwarf Alberta Spruce planted 15 years ago in pots of the same size have grown to a neat cone 4 feet high with a 30-inch spread at the bottom. Their tiny needles make delicious greenery. A third one, planted at the same time, was removed one dark night by some appreciative thief. Four years ago we bought 20 different varieties of Rhododendron, lovelies hardy in southern England and the Pacific Northwest. They're hardly hardy, and we wintered them over in a 30° apple warehouse. They have grown well and flowered perfectly since then. Our customers, who had never seen the like of them, lost their enthusiasm when they found out how they had to be cared for. However, some of the David Leach originations (*see* Rhododendron) have done well inside tight buildings where the temperature drops to zero, so almost anyone in zone 4 should be able to grow them. After a Rhodo blooms it isn't necessary to move it from the terrace, for its waxy green leaves make a very satisfactory summer display; when they are kept in half-shade they set next year's flower buds nicely.

Lots of hardy perennials do well in pots. Any of the 3 Alyssums afford a gorgeous shower of yellow flowers in early spring and, if the weather stays cool, keep showing spectacularly for a couple of weeks. Artemsia shows its silvery foliage all summer. Astilbe does well in half-shade. Instead of a long list of hardy perennials that do well in planters, it will be better at this point to specify the characteristics necessary for both growth and looks in containers. High growers, like Delphinium, are far too difficult for most gardeners to attempt. Varieties should have heavy, vigorous roots, heavy foliage, and flowering stalks not much higher than 24 inches. Some of the Sedums grow taller than that, but as they flower on top of thick columns of very fleshy green leaves they are more than acceptable. *S. spectable Meteor* and *Star Dust* are spectacular. *S. telephium Autumn Joy* is less tall but equally spectacular.

And all of the Dwarf Needle Evergreens, a highly colorful group, are candidates for pot-growing for the terrace. Ditto Boxwood, Japanese Yews, and *Euonymous vulgaris Sarcoxie*, all of which are evergreen, all of which can be prettied by shearing. If one doesn't really feel up to trying hardy perennial plants, a carefully grown collection of green plants provides an excellent display with a minimum of work—and a lot more variation in color than one would think.

Some of the fine, free-flowering non-hardy perennials certainly should be grown. They are little trouble. For full sun there is nothing to beat Lantana in upright and trailing forms. The flowers show constantly, although a spell of very cool nights, such as we have in Litchfield late June and early July, will stop bloom and turn the leaves brown for a while. Fuchsia, on the other hand, like this kind of weather. They, too, are great bloomers. Wintering Lantana or Fuchsia is not difficult—put them inside in north light, in a cool greenhouse—or in a dark basement that doesn't go below 45° F. Tuberous Begonias are great producers over a long season; their favorite spot on a terrace has full light with little or no sun.

Of the annuals, Petunias are most satisfactory. They will bulge over a pot and spill in a satisfactory, uneven way. If dead flowers and seed pods are picked off daily—well, it's no more work than weeding, which you will have little of in pot-growing. Impatiens is the only plant I know of (it's an annual) that comes close to blooming in darkness. Not darkness of the kind you think of, but very, repeat very, shady places—like, under trees where there is no grass. There are always such spots on a terrace. They bloom better in full light.

At least half the satisfaction of pot culture comes from experimenting with plants you've never seen grown in pots. This obviously doesn't include Chrysanthemums, which take to pot culture so readily that it is hard to remember the last time you saw them growing in the ground. The culture is not tricky. One needs rich, loamy soil. For Rhododendron and Azaleas (Azaleas are, you know, really Rhododendron) the loamy soil should be woodsy, or on the acid side, which can be effected by loading it liberally with leafmold or peat. Soil for Tuberous Begonias requires leafmold rather than peat. Drainage is, of course, vital to the success of pot-gardening, so place several pieces of crock (broken pottery) in the bottom of each container, and—it should go without saying but let's say it—all containers must have holes in the bottom of them. (How's that for downsmanship?) If the bottom of a perfectly flat pot is to sit on an equally flat surface (wood or stone) put small pebbles under the pot to insure drainage. A final point: pot-gardening requires close attention to the water supply. Hit the side of the pot sharply. If it goes "plunk," it needs water; "plink" indicates it doesn't.

See also Ferns.

pauciflora (*poh-si-flowe'ra*) *with few flowers*

PEACH, FLOWERING—*see* Prunus

pedatum (pe-day'tum) resembling a bird's foot

pedicels (ped'i-cells) said of a flower cluster, each flower of it having its individual stem

pendula (pen'dew-la) drooping

Pentstemon

Pent-stee'mon

Beard Tongue. This very large genus of herbaceous perennials, most of them from North America, are nice and it is unfortunate that there are so few hardy members. Flowers are always tubular and are borne in profusion close to the stems. If given drainage, full sun, soils that are not soggy in winter, and lots of water in the summer, they are easily grown. Pentstemon have a long season of bloom and make excellent cut flowers. Plant only in the spring.

***P. heterophyllus.** Brilliant true-blue flowers on 15-inch stems. It blooms from June through September, and is excellent for the rockery or border or anywhere one wants a blue flower.

***P. Newberryi.** This excellent plant produces several 12-inch spikes covered with rosy-purple tubular flowers in June. If pruned back after the first flowering, the reward is a second crop of flowers on shorter stems in late summer. Foliage is a deep shiny green.

P. Prairie Fire. As one would expect, this variety is a vivid orange red, and like most varieties in this genus it blooms well from June until frost. It grows from 15 to 18 inches.

P. Rose Elf. A compact 18- to 22-inch grower throwing clear rose blooms.

Pentstemon Prairie Fire

PEONIES—*see* Paeonia

PEPPERMINT—*see* Herbs, Mentha Piperita

PERENNIALS. Perennials are deciduous plants which reappear from the roots year after year. This characteristic is obviously the

Artemisia

opposite of annuals, which have to be re-seeded every year. Some perennials, of course, are longer lived than other, but all of them are perennial in the sense that if, at decent intervals, they are dug and separated and the old crown is discarded, they will live on and on—so it follows that most perennials have to be worked with to get the best perennial result from them.

PERENNIAL GARDENS. The growing of plants did not start with man's advent on earth, for earliest man either ate the edible green things of nature or killed and ate the animals that lived on what he couldn't eat. Man did not stop being a nomad until he discovered how to raise, cure, and store his food. Then, only a relatively few generations ago, man began to garden for the sake of the look of a tree or a bush and the sight and smell of a flower, instead of for food, and in so doing turned gardening from a purely material activity to a form of art. (More factually it was woman, not man, who first grew plants for the love of the sight of them.) As we have been told so often, man's only state of innocence was in a garden, which he lost when he lost his innocence. Chances of his regaining paradise seem small, but those who garden today, arranging and growing plants for their beauty, find at least fleeting moments of Paradise again. For civilized man this is the lure of the garden.

It can be argued that the degree to which nations or communities garden for beauty is a key to how civilized they are. It is also a key to how civilized just one man is as compared to another. Of course, this is not a whole answer, for nothing ever is, but the man who gardens for beauty is likely to be the broader man, more interested in other forms of beauty than the man who does not. Compared to Europeans we Americans are rather far behind in appreciating these cultures, but we have made great strides in all of them this last decade. And even greater strides are coming, for we've chucked our frontiersman's clothes, and with them inhibitions about culture. Who would have thought 10 years ago that the production of symphonic music would so soon become a major industry—larger than baseball?

Unlike most arts, the art of the garden requires no special skills, only those simple ones that are inherent in human existence—the skills needed for the growing of plants for food. And the growing of things, helping them, coddling them to maturity, is a most pleasant human trait, not completely selfless, but almost. This business of growing things in the earth is bred into us, a fact that the man raised on the macadam of cities soon finds out when he moves to the country. Stick a plant in the ground; such is the persistence of living things that it will grow unless shabbily treated.

On the other hand, the growing of plants for beauty requires studying color, texture, and composition, which are basic to it. In final form the garden is realistic art, yet the impressionistic and the abstract are apparent from the way nature lights it, from the way she forms plants. Also, a garden is never static, for there is hardly a moment when the lovely thing is not at least in gentle motion, is not subtly changing its composition.

One man's perennial border is rarely another's. So bear in mind that the borders diagrammed here are solely for stimulating imagination. The idea, of course, is to try to work out a compromise between the 1000-foot perennial borders of 19th- and early 20th-century England, which today's gardeners couldn't tend even if they had the land, and the lawns and bare foundation plantings which many Americans seem willing to settle for today.

Only 3 of the perennial gardens shown cost more than a largish deep freeze, one probably would equal the price of an automatic

Aquilegia

Lilium

transmission, the rest of them cost about as much as second-hand television receivers. And who, these days, buys those? In growing perennial gardens, money doesn't count for much—that's the nice thing about them.

When it comes to shapes and diversity of material, the plans merely scratch the surface. The shapes or forms gardens can take are endless, principally because perennials generally can be planted anyplace where there is light and water. There are walk-around gardens, or walk-along borders which can be constructed beside a path, straight or meandering, of any length. A border need not be more than 18 to 24 inches wide as it follows the path, and its season of bloom can last from earliest spring to frost. Hard to take care of? No. Work it from either the path or the lawn.

The white border illustrated is easy to care for, too; note the 1-foot pathway left at the wall to work it from back as well as front. Also, it represents a form of what is called balanced planting. In other words, the exact center was chosen for one outstanding group of plants, then different groups were placed to balance the center. It is a rather easy form to follow, but if carried too far it can be monotonous. In this border there is one great Gypsophila west of center, a superb Tree Peony to the east. Lilies planted out of balance also break it up and give the eye far more than just one point to fall upon. This border produces a series of white flower shows from early spring until September, after which it reverts to varying shades of green. And there's nothing wrong with this; greens are fine colors. Some excellent gardens are composed solely in green tones. This white border isn't big enough to be stocked with late-blooming perennials—it can't be all things to all seasons. It has a somewhat limited objective. Other gardens should be used to meet other seasons—smallish mass plantings, for example, of perennial

Asters, another of only Chrysanthemums, still another of Hemerocallis.

It should be noted that the use of water as part of a garden plan is neglected in America. Spain's gardens at Granada make gorgeous use of water in quiet pools and sparkling fountains framed with masses of evergreens. We do not propose that you produce Alhambras, but we do suggest that more gardens should use water as a theme—not just a pool, a fountain or a bird bath, but water meandering in a miniature flume built of fieldstone or flagstone, or water racing down a series of small steps, captured here and there in quiet pools along the way. It can't be cost that drowns a water theme, for it would be a mere fraction of, say, a $75,000 home. Maybe it's because our landscape architects get to say so little about the garden so late in the planning of a home.

As noted earlier, the narrower the border the more it is restricted in terms of display. The typical English herbaceous border is at least 14 feet wide—18 feet is better, but the length of an 18-foot border should exceed 100 feet to be in proportion. In the portfolio of Perennial Garden Plans there is a border about 15 feet wide and 75 feet long that would be better if its length were closer to 100 feet. It is provided with a high background, which means, of course, that groups of tall plants are required for the back of the border, plants of medium height are necessary for the middle, the dwarfs go in front. Following is a guide to the heights of the principal herbaceous plants included in this book.

Front-of-the-border plants: dwarf to 15 inches. Ajuga, Alyssum, *Anchusa myosotidiflora,* Anemone, Bulbous Anemone, Arenaria, Armeria, Artemisia, Asperula, Dwarf Asters, Calluna, Campanula, Catananche, Chionodoxa, Cushion Chrysanthemum, Convallaria,

Digitalis

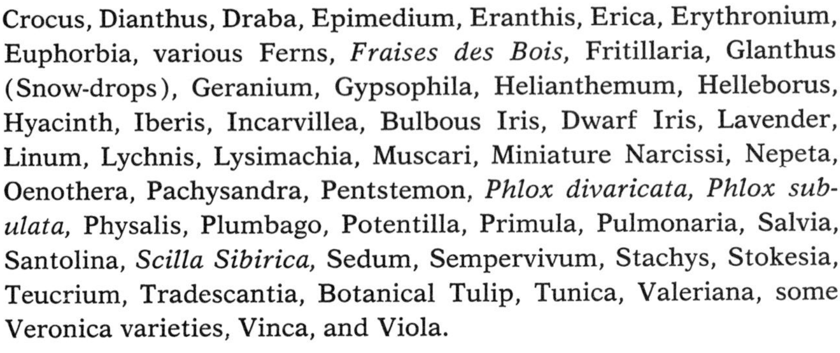

Crocus, Dianthus, Draba, Epimedium, Eranthis, Erica, Erythronium, Euphorbia, various Ferns, *Fraises des Bois,* Fritillaria, Glanthus (Snow-drops), Geranium, Gypsophila, Helianthemum, Helleborus, Hyacinth, Iberis, Incarvillea, Bulbous Iris, Dwarf Iris, Lavender, Linum, Lychnis, Lysimachia, Muscari, Miniature Narcissi, Nepeta, Oenothera, Pachysandra, Pentstemon, *Phlox divaricata, Phlox subulata,* Physalis, Plumbago, Potentilla, Primula, Pulmonaria, Salvia, Santolina, *Scilla Sibirica,* Sedum, Sempervivum, Stachys, Stokesia, Teucrium, Tradescantia, Botanical Tulip, Tunica, Valeriana, some Veronica varieties, Vinca, and Viola.

Middle-of-the-border plants: 15 to 30 inches. Achillea, Adenophora, Allium, Anthemis, Aquilegia, Artemisia, Astilbe, Belamcanda, Campanula, Chrysanthemum, *Chrysanthemum maximum,* Coreopsis, Chinese Delphinium, Connecticut Yankee Delphinium, Dicentra, Dictamnus, Doronicum, Dracocephalum, Erica, Eryngium, various Ferns, Gaillardia, Geranium, Geum, Gypsophila, Heuchera, Hosta, *Iris Kaempferi, Iris Sibirica,* Lavandula, Liatris, Mid-Century Lilies, Limonium, Lysimachia, Lythrum, Mertensia, Monarda, Narcissi, Paeonia, Papaver, Phlox, Physostegia, Platycodon, Polemonium, Rudebeckia, Ruta, Salvia, *Scilla Campanulata,* Tradescantia, Trollius, Tulips, and Verbascum.

Back-of-the-border plants: 30 inches and up. *Althaea rosea,* Anchusa, Asters, Baptisia, Camassia, Campanula, Hybrid Delphinium, Species Delphinium, Digitalis, Echinacea, Echinops, various Ferns, Gypsophila, Helenium, Helianthus, Heliopsis, Hemerocallis, Iris, Liatris, Lilium, Lupine, Lythrum, Macleaya, Phlox, Salvia, Solidago, Thermopsis, and Verbascum.

You will observe that some genera appear twice. It will be necessary to turn to the genus to find which varieties can be used in front, middle, or back of the border.

perianth (pear'ee-anth) the outer, non-essential part of a bloom, including sepals and petals

PERIWINKLE—*see* Vinca

persicifolia (per-sis-ee-foe'lee-a) peach-leaved

"pH" FACTOR. Sweet or sour, that's the question you will ask of your soil many times. And it's an easy question to answer, for soils can quickly be measured for alkalinity or acidity—for sweet or sour characteristics, in other words—by determining their *p*H factor. A completely neutral soil, one that is neither acid (sour) nor alkaline (sweet), has a *p*H of 7.0. Below 7.0 (to 0.0) soils are acid, above 7.0 (to 14.0) they are alkaline. Most soils are slightly acid and most plants, including grasses, grow well in this environment; a few, like Clematis, like their soil a bit alkaline. An uncomplicated test for *p*H is done with litmus paper (your druggist can supply the paper and instructions, and then read the results for you). Or send a soil sample to your state agricultural college for examination. The school will tell you how much lime to add to increase alkalinity, how much alum (aluminum sulphate) or sulphur to make very alkaline soils more sour. Actually, nature pretty well takes care of the *p*H factor by itself. Good topsoil that is rich in humus and is well drained is usually on the slightly acid side; boggy soils are generally very acid; very alkaline soils are usually found in the dry Middle West or Mountain States; moderately chalky or alkaline areas are found everywhere. Old or new lime kilns are evidence that soils may be chalky, and in this case a test is necessary because all but a few plants and grasses are not tolerant of lime.

Small quantities of ground limestone (a pound or so per 100 square feet) or even smaller amounts of hydrated lime (one gets this from a building supplier) can be added to ordinary acid soils. The presence of a bit of lime, as previously noted, encourages the activities of soil organisms, which in turn help release the plant nutrients in a form acceptable to it. Also, soils with a very high clay content also work better if limed a bit. Old hands at gardening generally play *p*H by eye and nose. Good healthy growth means a satisfactory *p*H; and though the smell of good garden loam is indescribable, on a warm spring day, when a handful smells very good indeed, your nose *knows* the *p*H is just dandy, which should be signal enough to your head that all's well with the myriad molds and other infinitesimal bugs living happily unseen in that handful of good earth.

For many years, as we said earlier, professionals have advocated the use of lime on established lawns—some suggest as much as every year or 2. We suggested this treatment every 4 or 5 years. We have been skeptical about this advice for a long time, and now the evidence is in: established lawns should never be top-dressed with lime, because (1) it encourages clover, a pest to those who seek grass and (2) the lime lies on the surface, with no lateral movement and no ability to penetrate, and quickly releases any nitrogen, pending it uselessly. To be useful, lime must be incorporated thoroughly into the soil. A seed bed for a new lawn may need lime, but it should not be applied without testing.

Philadelphus *Fill-uh-dell'fuss* Mock Orange. In America it is also called Syringa, the botanical name for Lilac, which makes for considerable confusion. These

North Temperate Zone plants, like Crabapples, have many species and countless varieties. They are valued for their masses of white, single or double flowers, which bloom, depending upon variety, in late May or mid-June. Many varieties are very sweet-scented; a number of them are hardy in zone 4. It is a good idea to stay away from the tall, stiff kinds. Their bloom is magnificent, but they do little to dress up a shrub border after the flowers are gone. Those with arching branches or mound-like forms are more satisfactory. An early affair with them cooled rapidly after I discovered their limitations, including the beat-up look and the dead branches that appear after most of our winters. But those I've seen farther south perform beautifully. The originations of Lemoine, the French plantsman, are excellent and still offer the best values in the market place. Some of their names are: *Belle Etoile,* single white flowers, 6 feet; *Avalanche,* single, very fragrant flowers on arching branches, 4 feet; *Boule d'Argent,* 2-inch double flowers, 5 feet; *Innocence,* single and most fragrant, about 8 feet; *Mount Blanc,* single blooms on a 4-foot mound (a miniature Mt. Blanc, obviously) and very hardy; *Girondole,* double on a 4-foot plant. A more recent variety, *Minnesota Snowflake,* is extremely floriferous, but its form is a good example of how Philadelphus should not grow—twiggy and stiff to about 6 feet. In this climate the branches get clobbered year after year. *P. coronarious aureus,* contrary to our other experience, has proved most satisfactory. It does have a few dead twigs after a heavy winter, but otherwise it is little trouble. Its small white single flowers don't amount to much, but the cover of its coat certainly does. In the spring its leaves are a blend of bright yellow and faint green. Then it darkens as the season passes. The green fades; the yellow becomes stronger. It's a very pleasant plant.

Phlox
Flocks

Phlox. This is another genus important to gardeners. Of the 50 species, most are from North America, but a few are Asian. Most garden Phlox are hybrids of the species *P. decussata* (sometimes called *P. paniculata*) and no perennial border can be considered complete without them. They require good garden soils that have been heavily enriched, lots of water, and a location in full sun. Damp, warm weather causes mold to grow on the leaves. This is unsightly, but not a danger. As sprinkling in the sun also has the same effect, it is best to soak the soil. Phlox is another of those plants that like their feet wet, their clothing dry. Plants should be set far enough apart—at least 2 feet—to provide good air circulation. They react well to thinning. Even when setting out newly-purchased Phlox, pinch out half of the new shoots, and always thin old plants heavily each spring. The reason—the roots can support any number of stalks, but not well. Not more than 3, at most 4 stalks to a plant will grow strongly. They will stand well and make a finer show than the Phlox plant that is not thinned. Also, thinning will do more to prevent the growth of fungus than sprays of sulphur, *Bordeaux Mixture* or *Captan* (*see* Thinning). Phlox should not be planted close to stone or brick walls, which hold moisture, or fungus may appear. Divide the roots every 3 or 4 years to keep the plants vigorous and flowers large (*see* Propagation.) And be sure to cut off flower heads before seeds mature. Be sure to destroy any seedlings that do grow—they turn to ugly magenta colors and are so vigorous they crowd out named varieties. Plant spring or fall.

Symons-Jeune Phlox

Symons-Jeune Phlox. This strain of Phlox is a remarkable one. It was developed by a captain in the British Army who made it a point to breed not only for great flowers on huge panicles, but who insisted upon color brilliance and fragrance, neither of which existed when he started. He also bred for resistance to fungus and for exceptionally strong stalks. There are, unfortunately, no pure white Symons-Jeune varieties. Whites, with a few other good American varieties, are listed under Standard Phlox Varieties.

The habits of the following Symons-Jeune varieties have been carefully observed here. In each instance the height of the variety is given for good culture. Blooming periods are indicated by numbers —blooming period #1 is the earliest. But as Symons-Jeune Phlox are in flower for a long period (from July until nearly frost), all will eventually be in bloom together.

P. Ann. Blooming period #3. Call this very late bloomer rosy lavender or mauve. It has great heads, and the plant grows to 36 inches.

P. Blue Ice. Blooming period #3. The eye is somewhat pinkish when the flower first opens; except for the tube it quickly turns to white as it ages. The plant grows to 40 inches, but it is compact.

P. Bonny Maid. Blooming period #2. A fine dwarf that rarely grows to 30 inches. The heads are large, the color pale blue with a rosy-violet tinge.

P. Bright eyes. Blooming period #3. The pips are a pale pink with a fine crimson eye. At 24 inches it is a dwarf, so place it in the front of the border.

P. Cecil Hanbury. Blooming period #3. One of Symons-Jeune's "older" varieties, popular in England because of its compact, free-flowering habit and its glowing salmon-orange flowers with carmine centers.

P. Charmaine. Blooming period #3. The color is a bright cherry red with an ivory blaze—and it is lovely. It grows to about 36 inches.

P. Dodo Hanbury Forbes. Blooming period #3. Here is a magnificent clear pink. Its huge head is rather pyramidal in form—a full 16 inches across. The individual flowers are large and stand up well under adverse weather conditions. It grows to about 36 inches.

P. Dresden China. Blooming period #4. Exquisite soft shell-pink deepening at the eye. A fine addition to the pastel group.

P. Dramatic. Blooming period #3. Dazzling white flower with a faint rose-colored eye. It is vigorous and the pips are exceptionally large.

P. Excelsior. Blooming period #4. A big fellow. With good culture, it grows to 4 feet on exceptionally strong stems. It's a doge purple—not magenta, although there will be those who call it that. Its heads are huge.

P. Fairy's Petticoat. Blooming period #2. A variety with immense, pale pink pips with darker pink eyes. Its huge heads have an unusually long flowering period. It grows to about 42 inches.

P. Fall Days. Blooming period #6. Hybridized and tested in the U.S. Color, according to Royal Horticultural Society color charts, is Bengal rose, whatever that means—probably tiger-rose, dark, in other words. But the outstanding feature of this variety is its very late blooming period—it starts to bloom when others finish and lasts until the end of September.

P. Gaiety. Blooming period #1. Flowers are a brilliant cherry red suffused with orange. It grows to 42 inches.

P. Inspiration. Blooming period #2. Light crimson with a slightly deeper eye. It is a 42-inch plant.

P. Juliet. Blooming period #3. A real dwarf in Phlox as it grows only to 2 feet. Color is palest heliotrope pink.

P. Lilac Time. Blooming period #4. A fine new Phlox with large heads which have huge individual flowers of clear lilac blue. It grows to 48 inches.

P. Olive Symons-Jeune. Blooming period #2. Captain Symons-Jeune named this after his daughter. Trusses are huge, so are the pips, and the form is all one could ask. Color is a rich rose, illuminated with orange. Height is about 40 inches.

P. Olive Wells Durrant. Blooming period #4. This variety received a Royal Horticultural Society Award of Merit. Trusses are huge and ever so compact. The pips lie flat and close together. Color is a clear light rose, the eye carmine. It grows to 48 inches.

P. Prince Charming. Blooming period #3. It glows reddish scarlet—and really glows. Excellent. It grows to 4 feet.

P. Roland Smith. Blooming period #2. Its rich salmon-pink pips are perfectly circular. Height about 36 inches. It is named after the well-known British plantsman, now deceased, the father of White Flower Farms horticulturist.

P. Royalty. Blooming period #1. Hybridized and tested here. Color, as you would expect, is imperial purple of richest hue. Height is about 40 inches.

P. Vintage Wine. Blooming period #1. This variety is claret red. It grows to 36 inches.

Standard U.S. Phlox Varieties. Here are standard strains of white Phlox—offered because there is no pure white as yet in Symons-Jeune. They do well throughout the country. Three recent colored varieties are also included.

White Varieties:

P. Mary Louise. Blooming period #4. Startlingly white; large flowers at 30 inches.

P. Rembrandt. Blooming period #1. A pure white and an excellent performer. It grows to 36 inches.

P. White Admiral. Blooming period #2. Enormous white heads with side branches that prolong blooming beyond the normal season.

P. World Peace. Blooming period #5. Pure white, having dark green, glossy foliage; it blooms in late August and September.

Colored Varieties:

P. Fairest One. Blooming period #2. A pale salmon pink having a cerise-red star effect at the eye, surrounded with a white halo. It's an exceptionally good U.S. hybrid.

P. Sir John Falstaff. Blooming period #2. This has a rich, luminous salmon-pink head of giant size, which one should expect from the name. The individual pips or blooms are a full 2 inches in diameter. It blooms on a very strong 30-inch stem.

P. Starfire. Blooming period #1. A brilliant, brilliant red that blooms very early. It is a strong grower. You'll be seeing it around a lot.

All-Phlox Gardens. As short a time as 10 years ago gardeners who planted all-Phlox borders, even though they had a wide choice of colors, found that most of the varieties reached the same height (about 40 inches) and that the plants massed bloom for hardly more than 2 weeks. Today they can choose plants that grow as low as 24 inches, varieties can be chosen to extend the display to a month, and if they will cut off the spent heads as soon as they fade, side-growth will continue in heavy bloom for another 2 weeks or more, and 2 varieties, *Fall Days* and *World Peace,* do not even start to put on their main shows until late August and September. An all-Phlox border is a nice possession and it doesn't have to be large to be effective.

Phlox divaricata. A species of dwarf phlox that blooms very early—with Botanical Tulips in April. It grows about 15 inches tall, has heavy, small, broad leaves, and is covered with clusters of flowers. It enjoys some shade. Plant spring only.

***P. divaricata.** The color is blue.
P. d. alba. Here is the very unusual and not easy to find white form of *P. divaricata.* It does well in full sun or partial shade; use in the rockery or for edging the border. The plant increases in size rapidly.

Phlox subulata. Mountain or Moss Pinks. These highly usable plants have evergreen, moss-like foliage and when in bloom in early spring are covered with flowers. Most varieties spread rapidly. Use them to cover bare spots, as edging plants, or as individuals in the rock garden. Varieties are free of fungus in most locations. They require full sun; the soil should be dry and sandy and not too rich. Red forms are too close to magenta to be useful. Try to find local sources for *P. subulata* as they are difficult to ship. Plant spring only.

***P. s. alba.** Covered very densely with pure white flowers.
***P. s. Emerald Cushion Blue.** Blue form of foregoing and just as free-flowering.

Phlox suffruticosa. The ever-popular early species of Phlox with long, loose, tubular flower heads. Varieties must be sprayed with *Bordeaux Mixture* or *Captan* to inhibit fungus. Blooms from June until late summer. Plant spring or fall.

P. s. Miss Lingard. Extremely good white and very early. Height is 30 inches.

phoeniceum (foe-niece'ee-um) deep red with a tinge of scarlet or carmine

Physalis

Physalis
Fiss'a-liss

Chinese Lantern. This well-known genus has about 100 species, only a few of which have garden value. Best known are the types whose seed pods produce the Chinese Lanterns that are in demand as dried decorations in the late fall and winter. Plant spring or fall.

***P. Franchetti pygmea.** This very hardy dwarf form is from Japan. It does best in a light, well-drained soil in full sun. The "lanterns" are orange scarlet. Contain it, for it can become a noxious weed. Height is 8 inches.

Physostegia
Fie-sos-tee'gee-a

False Dragonhead. A genus native to North America consisting of only 3 species. They are excellent in a wild garden or sunny border. Flowers appear on terminal spikes from July to September. Plants should be dug and divided every 2 years. Plant spring or fall.

P. grandiflora Bouquet Rose. The flowers, a lovely shade of rose, bloom from August to October and brighten up the border immeasurably during this slow period. It is one of the last perennials to flower and is colorful even after frost. It grows about 3 feet high.
P. virginiana alba. Pure white, a charmer which flowers from mid-July until September. Height is 18 to 24 inches.

Physostegia Bouquet Rose

PICEA—*see* Evergreens, Dwarf Needle

picotee (pick'oh-tea) edge suffused with darker tone of the base, or self, color, or a complementary color.

PINE—*see* Evergreens, Dwarf Needle

PINKS—*see* Dianthus

pinnately (pin-nate-ly) leaves arranged in segments, like a bird's feather

pisifera (pie-sif'ur-a) pea-bearing

PLANTAIN LILY—*see* Hosta

PLANT FAMILY. A plant family consists of a very large group of plants that resemble each other, although in many instances the

General Rules for Planting Flowering Shrubs or Trees

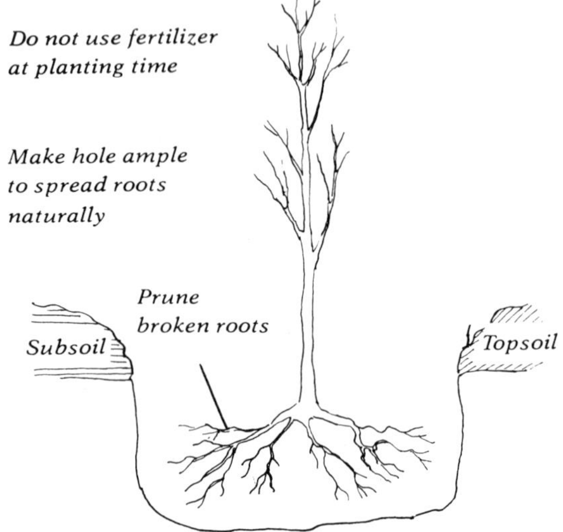

resemblance is so technical that it is clear only to a botanist. This book does not tabulate families. It lists genera—which are the main subdivision of families—their species and varieties. Some families are composed of scores of genera; and, as one genus can itself have many species, one who studies them will find that most plant families are as huge, say, as the Smith family of the world. A genus consists of plant species whose resemblances within the family identify it, and has been given the dignity of a name. Each member of a species has its own even closer, nearly unique, resemblances. At the species level, the plants which gardeners grow, we find varieties which differ largely in form and color. The species level is the level at which hybridizers work, through complicated plant breeding programs (including crossing species within a genus), to develop the many garden plants we all know. This is a highly simplified account of plant classification. The point, of course, is that horticultural classification strives to be exact, and with a few exceptions it is. This is why gardeners should ask for plants by their horticultural names, for their common names are so common that a plant can develop one name for nearly every section of the country where it grows. A Chinese proverb puts it succinctly: "The beginning of wisdom is to call things by their right names."

Following is an example of how this family, genus, species, and hybrid classification works. *Compositae* (kom-poz′ee-tea) is the Smith family of the plant world, the largest. It consists of better than 800 genera, 12,000 species, and no one knows how many hybrids.

If one equates genera with the races that make up the human family, one understands better the enormity of *Compositae,* which includes Asters, Cosmos, Daisies, Goldenrods, Dahlias and Rudbeckias, to name just a few of the 30-odd genera most important to gardeners (there are at least 50 others that have secondary garden importance). Races in the human species have to do with pigmentation and possibly language differences, but there are not 12,000 differences—and this is just as well, considering how people act. Of course, the human race has it all over the plant world when it comes to varieties—each human is a hybrid, few planned. Plant classification, we should add, tries the patience of the most dedicated gardener if it is carried too far. Ours, too, particularly when we find our British colleagues calling plant families "orders."

PLANTING. Put a $1 plant in a $5 hole, so that a plant's roots can be properly spread, not jammed down *en masse* in a little one. Depth of planting a perennial or shrub is usually indicated by the plant itself—plant it a little deeper than the soil line on the plant, which was the depth at the nursery. Some herbaceous plants have no soil line—Peonies, Oriental Poppies, etc.—but instructions for planting them and other plants requiring special culture are included in this book, usually close to the description of the genus.

A principal cause of failure in bareroot planting comes from neatly putting each plant where it is to be planted, then planting them later (after proper time out for Coke or coffee, discussion, of course, about location). The first plants in the ground grow, part of the middle group survives, but the last ones planted have their roots so thoroughly dried out that they die. A plant's roots must always be kept wet and protected from wind. More Roses are killed this way every year than we care to contemplate. Roses and shrubs should be carried to the border with their roots in pails of water.

Planting without thoroughly firming the soil also results in losses. Don't be dainty—drive the soil down hard with your fingers (use all of them), right down to the roots, then firm the soil carefully

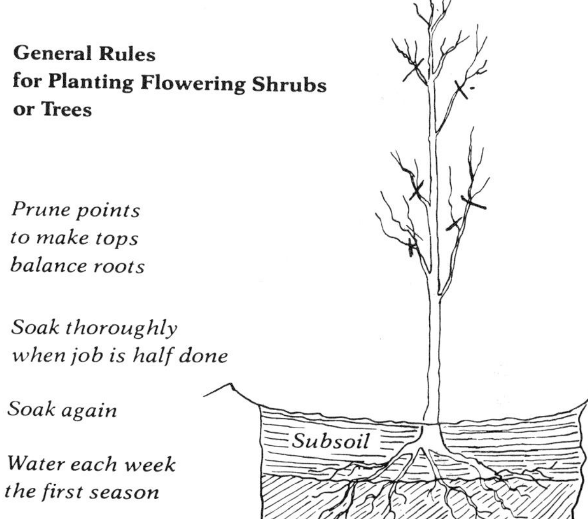

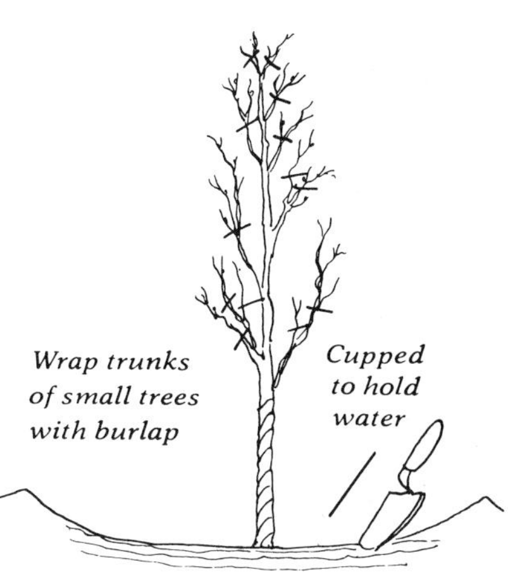

with your foot. The importance of the foot in planting can't be overemphasized in dealing with perennials, Roses, shrubs, trees—or grass. If you have ever planted a new lawn, you've surely noticed that the new grass comes up first on your footmarks. Be sure to "water in" plants after planting, but don't plant in gooey wet soils.

Chemical fertilizer should not be used in a planting hole, even if thoroughly mixed with the soil. It is too strong for the delicate roots. Use bone meal or *Milorganite* thoroughly mixed with the soil at the bottom of the hole. Fresh cow manure is dangerous if the roots come into direct contact with it. Well-rotted or dried manure is safe.

Now, to get back to the $5 hole you are to dig: place the topsoil to one side, the subsoil on the other; when planting use the topsoil at the bottom of the hole around the roots, the subsoil to finish off.

Nothing tries the patience of a good gardener more than getting plants from a nursery at the wrong time of year. It is true that many plants can be moved either spring or fall, but it is also true that some genera should be planted only in spring, others only in the fall. The obvious ones that come to mind for fall planting are garden Iris, Peonies, and Oriental Poppies. Dianthus and Campanula, on the other hand, should be moved only in the spring. In this book, proper planting time is noted at the end of the description of each genus. This is also the time plants should be shipped.

There is the basic problem of how early or late to plant. The books, for example, argue that Oriental Poppies and German Iris should be moved or planted in late August or early September. That is desirable in northern states, but either can be successfully planted in most climates for a far longer period. Go too strictly by the book and you may fail to get the necessary planting done at all. Fall, even though the first frost scares most beginning gardeners, is really a long period in any year. The pressure a gardener feels to plant early in the spring is understandable—but hard frosts do occur late and they kill plants put in too soon. So the overeager gardener loses plants that patience would have saved. Transplanting in one's own garden can be done, literally, at any time—but to do it a solid ball of earth must be taken, a ball that does not shatter when the plant is moved.

Platycodon

Platee-coe'don

Balloon Flower. This Eurasian genus of a single species is widely cultivated. It requires a light, sandy, well-drained soil. Put it in full sun and do not disturb after planting. It is a rewarding perennial. The colored bells, on 20-inch stems, are excellent cut flowers; the plants bloom all summer. Note: this is one of the latest perennials to show growth in the spring. It is best to mark them with a wire stake to be sure they are not hoed out with early weeds. Spring planting only.

Platycodon

P. grandiflorus. Deep, single blue bells or balloons on 20-inch stems.
P. g. album. The white form of the species.
P. g. Shell Pink. A variety that is a soft shell pink. The coloring is at its best when grown in semi-shade.

platyphyllum (pla-ti-fill'um) broad-leafed.

plicata (pli-cah'tah) petals folded lengthwise, pleated

*Plumbago Larpentae

Plum-bay'go Lar-pen'tea

Plumbago larpentae. This is a very desirable border or rock plant. It is dwarf, spreads 6 to 8 inches, and is covered with brilliant blue flowers from August through September, a time when blue flowers are at a premium in the garden. It likes sun or part shade. Plant spring only.

plumosa (*ploo-mow'sa*) *feathery*

Plumbago Larpentae

Polemonium

Po-lee-mow'nee-um

Jacob's Ladder. A genus of about 20 species mostly native to North America, with a few from Europe and Asia. It is a very hardworking and hardy group of plants—some are useful in the border, others in the rockery. They flourish in a soil that is neither very wet nor dry. So any good loam, fairly rich, suits them. All like full sun. Plant fall.

P. coeruleum album. This is the white form of Jacob's Ladder.
P. c. Blue Pearl. Clear, light blue, May-blooming flowers and attractive foliage make this plant a good one for use in the rockery or border. Height is 12 to 18 inches.

POLYANTHUS (pol-ee-an-thus)—*see* Primula

Polygonum

Pol-lig'owe-num

Fleece Vine. These excellent vines and ground covers for sunny locations are found throughout the world. *P. Reynoutria,* a ground cover, will do as well in sun as Vinca or Pachysandra does in shade. It is ideal for a bank too steep to mow—its vigorous root system keeps the soil in place. They require ordinary soil. Plant about 18 inches apart. Other forms are excellent climbers. Plant spring or fall.

P. Aubertii. Silver Lace Vine. A vigorous and rampant climber. As it grows quickly to 40 feet, *P. auberti,* which comes from western China, is invaluable for achieving immediate screening effects. Plant at the base of an old tree that has an unsightly trunk—or any place where it has room to spread widely.

It is covered with small white flowers for a long period, but its lacy leaves remain ornamental long after the flowers are gone.

***P. Reynoutria.** Light green foliage (12 inches high) which turns bright red in autumn. It spreads rapidly. Fleece-like sprays of pink flowers appear from September until killing frost.

Polygonum Reynoutria

Potentilla

Poe-ten-til'ah

Potentilla. Here largely the "Shrubby Cinquefoils," which are full of quality. As they are native to the Far North they are very hardy. *P. fruticosa* is by far the most important garden species in the genus. Its various woody forms range from dwarf to 4 feet high. They thrive in any soil, in sun or partial shade. Their flowers are like small single Roses, and are in full display on most varieties from late June until frost. Some of the herbaceous perennial forms are also listed here. They are excellent in the front of a border or in the rockery. Plant spring or fall.

***P. aurea verna** (perennial) This trailer is scarcely 3 inches high with strawberry-like leaves. It is covered with a profusion of yellow, single, rose-like flowers in June, July, and August. Its home is in the European Alps and Pyrenees.

P. fruticosa Everest (shrub). The best white form of these highly useful shrubs. Foliage is dark green. It flowers heavily in June and blooms recur until frost. It grows to about 40 inches and spreads well.

P. f. Katherine Dykes (shrub). This variety is a heavy producer of extremely bright yellow flowers, but it can be controlled easily by pruning. It grows to about 40 inches and can be used in the back of the perennial garden.

***P. Miss Wilmot** (perennial). This has strawberry-like leaves on a very compact plant that rarely grows more than a foot high. Color of the profuse blooms is soft cerise, a very pleasant shade of this violent color. It blooms all summer.

***P. Mons Rouillard** (perennial). This interesting variety has large, single, maroon-crimson flowers on 18-inch stems—all summer long. It is very hardy. Use it in the perennial border or give it a home in the rockery.

P. White Gold (shrub). In the summer of 1953 we were walking through the experimental gardens of Hillier & Sons, the fabulous English nursery founded in 1864 which propagates nearly 100,000 different plants (but catalogues only about 35,000 of them). With us was Harold Hillier, head of the firm. There we saw a low-growing *Potentilla* that was covered with light golden flowers twice the size of any other variety. Later we found that the plant had been bred for 2 important characteristics: low, compact growth, and those wonderfully large, golden flowers. Growth here has been even more satisfactory than in England, due to our hot summer sun. The first flush of bloom is followed by recurrent blossoms straight through until frost. The lovely dark green leaves are attractive, and its very compact spreading growth makes it very useful. It needs a rich loam and a well-drained location in full sun.

Potentilla White Gold

POTS (peat) In recent years the growing of small plants has changed radically. They used to be produced in tarpaper bands, small crockery, or plastic cups. Today they are grown professionally in peat pots. Peat pots are a decided improvement, for the roots, instead of cramping themselves in an impervious pot, strike through a peat pot, completely uninhibited. Plants grown in peat pots should be planted as received, with the pot. Some gardeners peel off the peat pots, thinking they are cardboard. But this peels off the fine roots, which inhibits early growth. If peat pots are broken with the fingers on one side, roots get out easily. Those who have their own greenhouses should use peat pots for cuttings or seedlings. The pots can be bought in small quantities from local florists and garden centers.

POTTING AND POTTING SOIL. Any good garden soil may be used for potting (*see* Soils), but if one is fussy—and many gardeners are —a prepared mixture is more satisfactory. Here's a good and an easy one: ⅓ topsoil put through a ½-inch mesh screen, ⅓ peat moss (leaf mold is better if you have it, or a well-rotted compost, screened), and ⅓ builder's sand. (No seashore sand should be used, for it is usually too fine and may be salty.) Mix all this well, adding 1 cup of hydrated lime if a *p*H test indicates the need (get this from any builder) and ½ cup of superphosphate per bushel. The stuff should be damp, not wet, when finished. A gardener can get even fussier with potting mixtures if he wants to, but we find this grows everything except orchids well (go to books or orchid experts for that data). If you are going to use this mix for plants inside the house, add a handful of mashed charcoal to keep the mixture sweet.

Now to potting. Pottery should be clean. Put broken pottery (crock) or coarse stones in the bottom—enough so that roots won't quickly clog the drainage hole. The size of pot should be just big enough to take care of the plant. We can't explain why, but little plants in big pots do not grow well. A baby seems happier when it fits places snugly, and we guess a plant does, too. Later on, move the plant to a little larger pot—from 3-inch to 5-inch—still later move it up to a 7-inch pot. When placing your plant, spread the roots and work the soil around them (bumping the pot up and down on the bench helps). By using a small stick with a blunt end, firm the soil—pot fairly hard, in other words, and leave enough room at the top to hold water. After potting, water, of course. If the plant droops, put it in a shady spot until it stands up again. A plant that needs staking (Tree Fuchsias and the like) should be planted with the stake; driving the stake into an already tightly packed pot can break the pot or damage the roots. When watering later, be sure to give the plant a full drink, but don't let it stand in water in a saucer. It won't like that. Over-watering is a common fault, an act of loving care; under-watering is obviously neglect. To determine a plant's dryness, thump the pot with a stick. If it goes "plunk" it has water enough; a "plink" calls for water. It's sort of like testing watermelons. Earlier we said we didn't know why small plants do badly in large pots. There are, however, two points that may help explain this nurseryman's ancient axiom. One is that small plants in big pots have a good chance of getting drowned—big pots stay wet too long around roots that are then again thoughtlessly flooded when the soil surface dries. Another reason is that a small plant in a large pot can easily be over-fertilized. We are pleased if this logic satisfies you; we shall, however, continue to believe that little things are more congenial living in little things, be they plants or animals.

It is ever so important to fertilize only when the rootball is completely developed, in other words, when the roots wind around the inside of the pot. Tap the plant out of the pot to see if this has happened.

praecox (pree'koks) appearing earlier than most of its genus

praestans (pree'stands) excellent, distinguished

PRESERVATIVES. There are more trade-name wood preservers than can be counted. *Cuprinol* is the best known, and its salts are not harmful to plants. However, preservative formulas based on creosote are harmful, particularly when plants are young. Soaking boards, flats, of tubs with preservative is best practice, but not very practical for most home gardeners, who have no facilities for soaking anything but their gardens. Put preservative on with a brush—literally douse it on a couple of times or more in order to get the stuff down into the cracks where pieces of wood are nailed together.

PRIMROSE—*see* Oenothera *and* Primula.

***Primula**
Prim'you-la

Primroses, Cowslips, Polyanthus and about 300 other plants in the Primula family are mostly natives of the North Temperate Zone. This huge family has one common trait—nearly all members require peaty soils and lots of moisture, and an astonishing number of them like partial shade. Some are devils to grow, and with them we have no traffic. Primulas in the U.S. are susceptible to red spider, which is easily controlled by flushing the plants with water. This should be done at the start of a hot spell and continued; when the plants have red spider it is harder to control. The following varieties will grow well in nearly any climate. All bloom very early in the spring. Plant spring only.

P. denticulata. A shade-lover, but it likes lots of light, no sun. Flowers are mostly lavender, white or purple. Height is up to 12 inches.
P. polyanthus. This fine strain of Primula is grown from specially selected seeds. Colors include shades of blue, crimson, flame, gold, pink and white. They should be planted in partial shade in a good, rather moist loam. Shade is very important.

primulinus (prim-you-lee′nus) primrose colored

PRONUNCIATION. Pronouncing botanical names is not as hard as it looks. Take a look at one—specifically, Abeliophyllum. Now run the eye over it, noting how neatly the thing splits up: a-be-lio-phy′llum, with the accent on the "phy." So you now listen for the sounds and rip through it like a professional as you say (and hear) a-bee-leo-fill′lum. Easy? Well, a bit easy. Phonetics follow the bold upper- and lower-case letters of the genus. Other words, horticultural descriptives, e.g., *millefolium, taggeta, cordifiolium, genevensis,* etc. are also phonetically spelled. In some instances they are briefly defined—for example, *millefolium* (mill-ee-foe′lee-um), *thousand-leaved.*

PROPAGATION. To keep the expense of a garden in line, it is well to know a few of the simple methods used to increase or to revitalize plant stock. The most practical method is simple division. To

Primula polyanthus

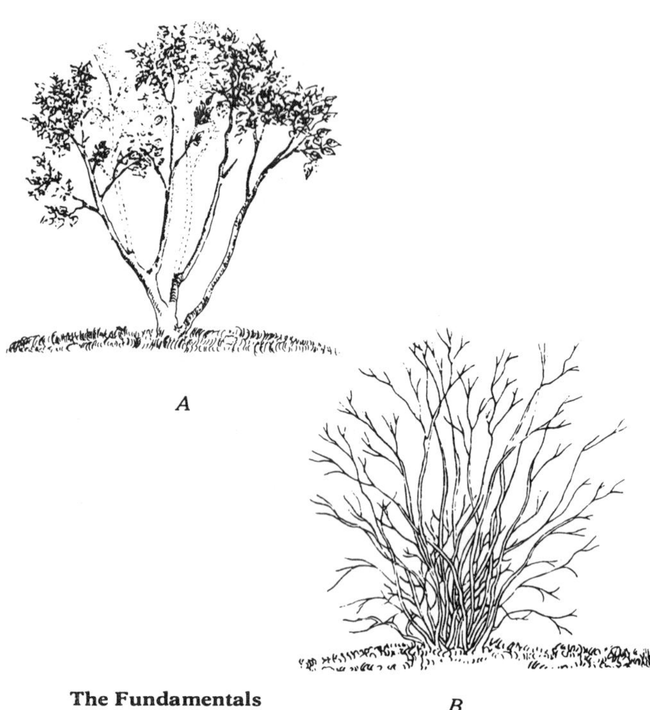

The Fundamentals of Pruning

For overgrown shrubs (Lilacs, Rhodos, etc.) take out two big branches annually (A), otherwise shrubs will drown in own sap. For twiggy shrubs (B), remove from base (C), crew-cut (D), undesirable. To force twigginess at bottom, prune as in (E). Yews should be pruned as growth starts

get experience, handle the plant itself. We won't name specific plants because nearly all are divided by one of the following methods, and as you dig them it is easy enough to decide which method to use. (1) *Spreading crown that shoots out runners close to the crown:* cut the new outside shoots for planting, throw away the woody middle parts. (2) *Roots that have discernible eyes and cannot be pulled apart easily:* cut them apart with a knife, leaving a goodly piece of the hard crown with the eyes along with any roots that can be saved on each section. (3) *Massive roots so tightly packed that they defy the hands:* don't cut or hack at them; instead, drive two ordinary tined digging forks into them back-to-back, then force the forks apart. Repeat if necessary to get small pieces, but always discard the woody center. (4) *Plants that grow from rhizomes:* cut them apart cleanly and discard the old woody ones. Cutting tools should be sharp; the cuts can be cauterized by dusting with a fungicide or by exposing them to sunlight for an hour. Perennials, we have said elsewhere, are truly perennial, and will grow year after year only when gardeners work with them. Left alone they become smaller and less vigorous, and eventually they will die.

pruinatum (proo-i-nay'tum) covered with glistening particles, as though frosted

PRUNING. Pruning causes trouble largely because if it isn't done regularly, each season, one forgets the rules. It is like planting vegetable seeds each spring—how deep do you put the things? One can guess, but it's better to know. The object of pruning is to get the best possible form and show of flowers from a shrub or tree. To do this, prune regularly; if one waits 3 or 4 years shrubs will become a thicket and the work difficult. When you are pruning, be deliberate. Try to visualize the look of a plant after you have pruned off a branch, because it can't be stuck back with Scotch tape.

To start, cut out the dead wood, then the weak shoots; afterward thin the twiggy areas. This thinning out of weak and twiggy branches provides light and air, both of which are good for the plant—but don't provide too much light and air or the plant will look mighty forlorn for a while. If you do prune too much, don't worry: nature will correct the fault before too long. Severe pruning must be done when a shrub gets out of hand. When this happens don't cut every large branch back the first year. Cut some back to the first main side shoot, then next year cut the rest. Afterward, shape.

Pendulous-growing shrubs, like some Forsythia, Weigela, etc., should have old wood cut out at ground level. Also, a plethora of shoots grows from the crowns of shrubs each year, and should be cut back, leaving 2 or 3 sturdy ones to take the place of the big old branches you will later have to take out. Shrubs that throw leggy stems and twiggy tops should have the tops cut back to side buds, for this will make them twiggier at the bottom, where you want a solid effect. And never give a shrub a crew cut, for then you have a monster (*see* Drawings). For how to prune the different kinds of Roses, turn to Rosa, *Culture*.

Besides shape, pruning is done to produce the best crop of flowers for the next year. To do this remember *when* the flowering buds form on the wood. Here's a good general rule: on shrubs and trees that bloom after July, the flower buds form on new wood that grows the same year—so prune these after-July bloomers *in winter* or very early spring to induce them to throw as much new wood as possible. Spring-blooming shrubs and trees (these that flower before July) generally form flower buds on new wood produced the previous year—so prune Forsythias, Almonds, Quince, Spireas, etc. immedi-

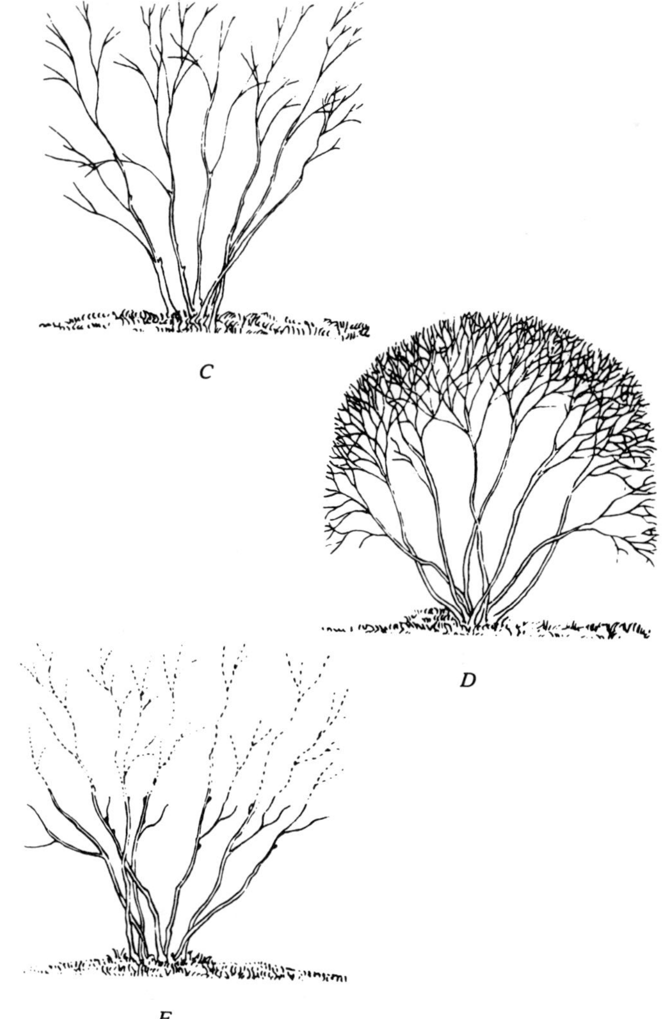

C

D

E

Pinching and Pruning Fuchsia

Pinching young plants to induce heavy bloom

ately after the flowers are gone. And always remember to cut off all of the spent flowers you can reach, for this stops seed production, which saps energy if allowed to go on.

If broadleaved evergreens have gone rampant, prune severely. To keep new broadleaf plantings fully leafed to the ground, prune lightly after flowers are spent. Rhododendron, which many gardeners hesitate to prune, is easily handled thus: observe that new growth starts only at the base of the old flower head, and that these new shoots are usually 5 in number. Trim out the shoots that grow *inward* or in an *undesirable* direction; keep those that will continue to make the Rhododendron bushy—most times you'll only keep 1 or 2 of the 5 new shoots. Form Holly by cutting back side branches; this induces growth and bushiness from the trunk.

Prune needle evergreens just as growth starts. This is particularly important for Yews. Keep pruners away from Firs, Arborvitae, and Spruces—cut only the sporting branches that could spoil shape. Wood even just a year old on Pine has very few living buds; the few that can be induced to form are only in new wood, so prune these soft new branches sparingly to induce budding and branching. As for hedges of all kinds, prune them to form an upright wedge—this lets light get to the bottom and keeps them green to the ground.

Pruning roots. Pruning the roots of deciduous shrubs and trees is standard procedure in the nursery business. In this instance the idea is to produce as heavy a root mass as possible in the least possible space before lifting the plant for transplanting. But root-pruning can also be used to keep shrubs and trees small. With small trees or shrubs a sharp spade is driven into the earth at an angle, the starting point far enough away from the crown of a shrub or the trunk of a tree to keep from damaging the plant (*see* Drawing). Judgment rather than rule is the determinant. Keep back far enough to avoid injury to the plant—the top and the root mass should be in reasonable balance. This is why one prunes back the branches on a newly-planted tree or shrub. The roots of such broadleaf evergreens as Rhododendrun and Azaleas are never pruned.

Our advice, unless the gardener is really experienced, is to bring in a tree man to do such work. Once he has watched the process, it will be easier for the inexperienced do-it-yourself gardener to try it himself.

Prunus

Proo'nus

The Flowering Cherries, Peaches, and Almonds. Next to the Flowering Crabapples, this genus of more than 150 species and innumerable varieties is full of plants very desirable for gardens. There are also many lovely bush forms, and I like them, but my own experience has been that they run out quicker than experts in the field admit. They do say that many are short-lived—10 years or so. I'd buy that, but the "less" for me is about half of that. Winter doesn't seem to get them; it's galloping old age. Two that were supposed to perform were *P. glandulosa,* a double-flowering dwarf almond, and *P. triloba,* also a double almond that is supposed to reach 12 feet or more. There probably aren't more beautiful spring flowers, but shortly after the third year here they deteriorated so quickly that there was nothing to be done but dig them out. The best of the genus are the tree forms, and decidedly the best of these are the Japanese cherries, which have been under cultivation for centuries.

Those who plant them will save themselves future disappointment by knowing that all of them are subject to the same ills that plague commercial cherry trees (but to a lesser degree). They are subject to scale and borers. Their leaves are delectable to the many insects

Pinching and Pruning Fuchsia

Pruning back hard to induce branching when plants begin spring growth

Root Pruning

This schematic drawing shows how a root system develops (lower right, in and out of circle). The spade (be sure to sharpen it with a file) should be driven at an angle. Although the drawing shows a small deciduous tree being root-pruned, the same technique is used for shrubs

whose mission in life is to eat as many leaves as they possibly can. However, these leaf-eaters are easily controlled with 2 sprays a year; some years once is enough. Scale and borers are kept under control with 1 dormant spray a year. So one can relax if these simple schedules are followed.

There is considerable literature available on Japanese Flowering Cherries for those who decide they want to know about the many fine varieties in the group. Dr. Wyman's recommended list in *Trees for American Gardens* isn't the last word, but it will do for most gardeners. He lists 17, the majority hardy in zone 5 southward, a fact that has made us cautious about even attempting to grow them. However, 2 specimens of *P. serrulata Kwanzan,* the variety with the largest clusters of the most double blooms of all Japanese cherries, have grown well in completely exposed locations on our cold hill for 15 years. *Kwanzan* also has a very long life—an impressive planting in the Brooklyn Botanical Garden is 55 years old. There are 300 *Kwanzans* in the famous planting around the Tidal Basin in Washington. That it doesn't produce fruit (no double-flowering trees do) is said by some bird-loving gardeners to be a negative. Others say it is too common—everybody has one. Okay. But if you don't have it, get it. *P. yedoensis* is the proper name of the Japanese cherry most used around the Tidal Basin. Nine hundred were planted there in 1912.

Pulmonaria

Pul-moe-nay'ree-uh

Lungwort or Blue Cowslip. The name is derived from the Latin word for lung. Indeed, one old tale relates that the plant was thought beneficial in the treatment of lung disease. The Royal Horticultural Society's *Dictionary of Gardening* says that "the species are difficult to distinguish and interbreed promiscuously." Promiscuity in plants is not all right with us, so we offer but one species—it must be propagated by division in early spring. Plant spring or fall.

P. angustifolia. A dwarf, 8 to 10 inches high. The buds of the flowers start out slightly pink, then burst into a fine bright blue in April and May.

pulsatilla (pul-sa-til'la) to shake in the wind

pumila (pew'mi-la) low or small

punctata (punk-tay'ta) dotted

pungens (pun'jens) ending in sharp point, as does a Holly leaf

pura (pew'rah) clean, pure

purprea (pur-pew'e-ra) purple

PYGMY SPRUCE—*see* Evergreens, Dwarf Needle

Pyracantha

Pie-rah-can'tha

The Fire Thorns. This genus has few species, but it is highly regarded for its large clusters of red, yellow, orange-red berries that show in the fall and last well into the winter months. The species are deciduous in the North and evergreen in the South, where they do best. It is a cousin of Cotoneaster, also a member of the Rose family, and unfortunately it is subject to fire blight, for which there is no specific. However, those that are well cared for (fertility kept up and watered regularly) seem to be able to fend off this nasty disease better than those which get the lick-and-a-promise treatment. Pyracantha is very beautiful when espaliered against protected walls; this is the way most of them are grown in these parts, for they are not hardy north of zone 6. They can be grown here (zone 4) if espaliered in a tub or large pot and moved to a closed building where the temperature does not drop below zero. The many small white flowers that appear in the spring on all

Pyracantha

Pyracantha make as good a showing as many small white flowers can make, but it's not the least spectacular. *P. coccinea Lalandei* is by far the most popular variety, and when it does well it provides a better winter show than any other shrub. *P. Oxford,* developed by the University of California in 1941, is only hardy in zone 7 southward, but it is said to be more resistant to fire blight than others. Grown in pottery and thoroughly protected in winter, it can be used farther north. Its berries are bright orange-to-red. As noted, Pyracantha are fine shrubs, but when a specimen several years old gets fire blight and its owner goes back to the nurseryman to find out what's wrong, the answer, "Oh, many do that," is not satisfactory, because it was information he should have had at the beginning.

pyramidalis (pi-ra-mi-day'lis) conical

Pyrethrum

Pyrethrum

Pie-reeth'rum

Painted Daisy. Pyrethrum is the very old name for this daisy from Persia. Botanists now call it *Chrysanthemum coccineum,* but by any name it is one of the useful perennials—and most rewarding in the border. Plant in full sun in ordinary soil about a foot apart. Plant spring only.

P. Giant hybrids. This group is grown from specially selected seed, and generally produces giant blooms. Some are double, others single. Colors are in shades of red and pink—and some are white.
P. Robinson's Crimson. Flowers are large, single, and crimson red. Excellent for cutting. Height is 18 to 24 inches.
P. Robinson's Rose. Its habits of growth and quality as a cut flower are equal to that of the foregoing Robinson. The color, obviously, is rose. It grows to 24 inches.

QUINCE, FLOWERING—*see* Chaenomeles

quinquefolia (sang-ku-foe'lee-a) having five leaflets, colors, spots, etc.

raceme (ray-seem) an elongated flower cluster blooming from the bottom up, as does Lily-of-the-Valley

radicans (rad-ee'cans) rooting as it creeps

regalis (ree-gay'liss) royal, stately

repens (ree'penz) creeping, flat upon the ground

reptans (rep'tans) crawling

reticulata (ree-tick-you-lay'ta) netted

Rhododendron

Roe-do-den'drun

Rhododendron. It is unfortunate that there are not lots of these fine shrubs that combine the colors of the new tender hybrids one sees in England (and in mild climates here) with the ruggedness of the Rhodos that will withstand the rough climates of zones 4 and 5, but so far there are only a very few. Several of the best, the result of the work of David Goheen Leach, the American hybridist who is internationally respected in the field, are now available. Among his hybrids are *Janet Blair, Vernus, Mist Maiden* (a selection from a species discussed later), and *Tang.*

C. O. Dexter, Joseph Gable, Guy Nearing and Edmond Amateis are others whose work on Rhododendron in the last 40 years will become better-known in the next decade. Although this new work has been good, only a few of the varieties will do well below −10° F. When one considers that most of the real beauties from mild climates catch cold at 10° to 20° above, one understands the magnitude of the problem confronting these patient people. They have, however, moved far in just a couple of generations.

There is one very beautiful Rhodo, a Japanese species called *R.*

Centerpiece Detail

This centerpiece features a Tree Wisteria. The sloping sides of the centerpiece are composed of heavy pieces of wide (10 to 12 inches) flat stone supported by the earth fill. Note that a great variety of rock-garden plants can be placed in openings left irregularly for them. Height should not be more than 4 feet. This arrangement needs irrigation regularly, for the holes for rock plants provide almost excessive drainage

yakusimanum, that withstands temperatures of −15° F. on the Japanese island of Yaku Shima, in southern Japan, where it grows at altitudes from 1,500 to 6,500 feet. Obviously, the variations within the species in this nearly perpendicular temperature range are great, and the chances of one of the lower altitudinal strains being more tender than those higher up are very good. Colors of all of them are similar—a delicate pink. The habit of the plant is spreading. *R. yakusimanum* rarely grows more than 3 to 5 feet high; old plants spread 12 feet and more. We have about 125 of them, some are seedlings, others, it is claimed, came from a very famous English specimen as cuttings. About 30 older ones have grown 6 to 8 inches in 2 years; a few have bloomed. I have my fingers crossed, and worry about them in this climate, but if they are hardy it will be a great bit of luck for cold-zone gardeners. In the 2 years they have withstood −20° F. temperatures, but they have been protected—and 2 years do not make a decade. Mist Maiden, a Yak cultivar chosen by Leach, is probably a good bet for adventurous gardeners. Baldsiefsen, a fine Eastern Rhodo grower, will sell you a *R. y. Mist Maiden* with a 6- to 8-inch spread for around $30. Write him at Bellvale, N.Y. 10912. Other responsible growers of unusual Rhododendron, including *R. yakusimanum Mist Maiden,* are The Bovees, 1757 S. W. Coronado St., Portland, Oregon 97219; Rainier Mt. Alpine Gardens, 2007 South 126th St., Seattle, Washington 98168; and Oliver Nurseries, 1159 Bronson Road, Fairfield, Connecticut 06930. By the time this is published it may be that some of these growers will be reluctant to ship retail orders—many fine growers have already given up shipping because of losses resulting from slow transport (the material is usually too heavy to ship parcel post). Of this David Leach comments, "The great gray Orwellian world is almost upon us in horticulture."

rhyzome (rye-zom) a creeping underground root, thick and swollen, which sends up leafy shoots and flowering stems.

ROCK GARDENS. Rock gardens are a relatively new form of garden in the Western World. They originated in China and Japan, but when brought to Europe their construction resulted in grottoes, cascades, and caves; the idea seemed to be that the rocks, rather than the plants, were the important thing. About the middle of the 19th century various European landscape specialists got the idea that there was a connection between rocks and Alpine plants, and the development of rock gardens since then has been rapid. The most remarkable ones are in England. Kew has a famous garden, started in 1910; the more beautiful and far less formal rock garden at Wisley (The Royal Horticultural Society's lovely gardens) was started about the same time. Both are very large. Gardeners in all walks of life in Britain and the United States have taken up rock gardening on scales pleasing to them, with the result that many gardeners have space set aside for what they lovingly refer to as their rockeries.

If one really wants detailed information about rock gardens, he should buy *Rock Gardens,* by E. B. Anderson, for $1.50 (includes postage) from The Royal Horticultural Society, Vincent Square, London, S.W. 1, England. It is a satisfactory small manual. Here is some general guidance about building such a garden. (1) The site should be in full sun, never close to a large tree, for its roots will soon take over. (2) Use rocks of the neighborhood, for then the artificial outcropping (your rock garden) looks natural. Remember that it's a garden of plants in rocks, not a garden of assorted rocks. (3) Use large rocks; you may need the help of a contractor to place them. Bury each two-thirds deep. (4) Tilt rocks toward the top of the

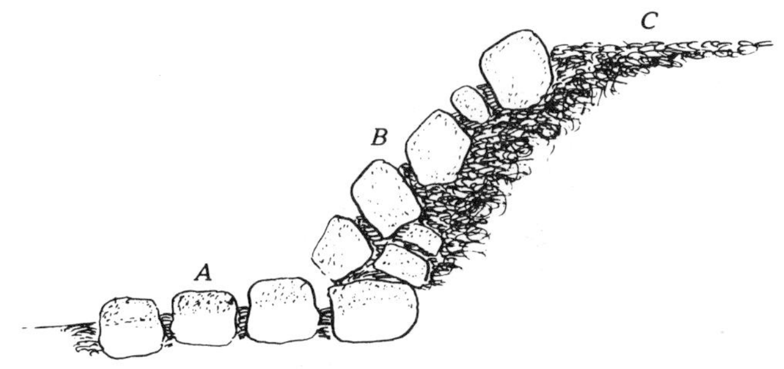

**Schematic View—
Rock Garden Construction**

The principal error most gardeners make in rock-garden construction is in using rocks that are too small and placing them on top of the ground. Use only native rocks that are large and bury three fourths of each rock to form proper planting pockets. Section A (above) shows rock placement on level ground. B indicates building on a sharp slope. C is a plateau area atop the slope, and rocks there should be placed as in A. Note that rocks on the slope are positioned to channel water inward. Ideally major rocks in the design should be so large a contractor is needed to place them (see rock gardens) grade to make the outcropping look more natural and to channel water down to the subsoil (*see* Drawing). (5) Supply drainage. (6) Soils, which should be deep in the many pockets between the rocks, can be specially prepared to suit plants, but we recommend for beginners ½ part garden loam, ½ part humus, 1 part of ½-inch crushed rock, and 1 part of coarse sand. (7) A scree, a heap of fine stones representing a rockslide or the tip of a glacial moraine, used for plants requiring perfect drainage, should be about a foot thick, the lowest 3 inches made of 2- to 3-inch stone, the "ground" a mixture of ½-inch crushed rock (2 parts) and soil (1 part). (8) Most rock plants require water in abundance—soak them when the weather supplies less than an inch of rain a week. Also, it is possible with careful hand-watering to give each plant the amount of water it needs—sedums need less, for example. (9) The size of plant material used depends on the size of the garden. Almost any plant can be used as a rock plant. The test is, how will it look in the composition? Unusual dwarf evergreens are excellent if planted in pockets to restrict their root-runs so that they remain dwarf (*see* Evergreen, Dwarf Needle). The foregoing admittedly is oversimplified. But a rock garden is great to work with, particularly if started small and then developed to a point that does not exceed the time the owner can afford to care for it well.

ROCK ROSE—*see* Helianthemum

ROGUE. In gardening, a "rogue" is a plant associated with other plants that differs in color (or variety) from them. For example, a red appearing in a solid planting of yellow Chrysanthemums is called a rogue, and indeed it is. In a well-conducted nursery, blocks of plants are "rogued" during the blooming season to rid them of these undesirable citizens. This is important work, for nothing infuriates good gardeners more than receiving a plant with a color that doesn't harmonize in a planting scheme; when that happens they have lost a season, a serious loss. No nurseryman can guarantee the color of plants grown from seeds; but if one gets seed directly from the originators, the chance of receiving a plant with a completely undesirable color is small. A new factor is also causing more rogues in American and British nurseries than ever before: the turnover in manpower. No longer do young men serve long apprenticeships to master the many details of this complex business. As a result few learn plant material, and, not knowing it, gather the wrong plant.

Climbing Rose

Rosa

Roe-zah

The Rose. The Rose tribe is huge and well it should be, for its history traces back to pre-Babylonian times (before 2300 B.C.) and, in China, a bit earlier. There is no doubt that the Rose in its many forms is civilized man's favorite flower.

There are some major Rose classifications to be considered. The first are the Tea Roses. They are gorgeous big bushes with huge, conventionally-shaped blooms that are grown in the South, Southern California, and in the mild climates of the Pacific Northwest. They were developed before the turn of the century in Europe. They are not the least hardy in our more rigorous climates. Little or no work has been done with them in the last 2½ generations, because hybridizers all over the world have fixed their attentions on the Hybrid Tea Rose and other small bushes that are for bedding. Although I have seen the lovely things, I have never attempted to grow Tea Roses, don't know the names of the varieties, and so must refer gardeners who live in those mild places to their local sources for information. As plants, they are considerably larger than Hybrid Teas and they do not bloom, as do the Hybrids, for long periods.

The Hybrid Teas, another major classification, have been a chore in my climate. For some reason those who sell Roses fail to mention the fact that most Hybrid Teas, Floribundas, and Polyanthus are of doubtful hardiness, although they nevertheless give buyers elaborate instructions about their care over winter. Gardeners in cold climates like ours—not so cold that the lot will be murdered every year, but cold enough to cause extensive damage in 9 out of 10 seasons—are so convinced that they can grow Roses that they refuse to blame the weather for losses. Their dead Roses are the result of their own failure to provide proper winter care for the bushes. They think nothing of blaming a perennial for lack of hardiness if it dies in a cold winter, but not Roses. This can only be called the ultimate in compliments to them. Of course, gardeners who grow them in the impossible climates of the far northern states have no such illusions—they know that if they don't dig up every last one every fall and put them in a root cellar or very deep pit, they will die. And they do just this and think nothing of the work involved. Also, Rose merchants push the sale of Roses heavily in the fall, which is another cause of failure. My feeling is that to deliver a Rose in the fall to gardeners in cold climates is like pushing the sale of grass seed in the spring—the season is not right for either.

Years ago I noticed that the Hybrid Tea, Peace, lasted many more years than others in my garden, and when I visited the originators, the Meillands, in Antibes, France, in 1947, they said that they were developing a strain of Hybrid Teas based on Peace, that they thought they could produce every color except possibly white, and that in their opinion the new race would be more resistant to cold than others. (Madame Meilland, incidentally, was the hybridizer of Peace and of all Meilland Roses; both she and her husband are now deceased.) Since then this great nursery has produced many Peace-strain Roses which are described later. As predicted, there is no white variety in the group. However, let me emphasize that these varieties, like all other Hybrid Teas, will still die from intense cold —they merely stand more of it, but only with the same winter protection prescribed for all Hybrid Teas.

It doesn't take long for a gardener, when he first starts to buy Roses, to discover that there is a considerable difference in their prices. One reason is grade. No. 1 grade has a strong root system and at least 3 heavy branches from above the bud. No. 1½ has noticeably smaller branches from the bud, and sometimes only 2 of them. This is the quality sold by many supermarkets and price-conscious merchants. Another reason is the plant patent—patented Roses sell for from $.75 cents to $1 more. This does not mean that the patented Rose is better than the unpatented one. It means that the variety has been considered good enough to patent. Growers who patent Roses always sell budding wood to other growers—freely to all comers in order to be sure the patent is not being used in restraint of trade. But with so many Roses under patent to so few growers, it is easy to see the effect that patented Roses, heavily publicized, have on the industry's price level. Peace, whose patent has expired, now sells for from $2.25 to $2.50; under patent it sold as high as $3.75.

Culture: Rose culture follows precise rules, but it is not difficult (see drawings for planting and winter protection). The soil should be rich in humus (compost or rotted cow manure) and at least 18 inches deep. Roses are great feeders and require fertilization at intervals until late July. They should also be sprayed every 2 weeks

Roses: Planting and Care

Dig big to spread roots naturally

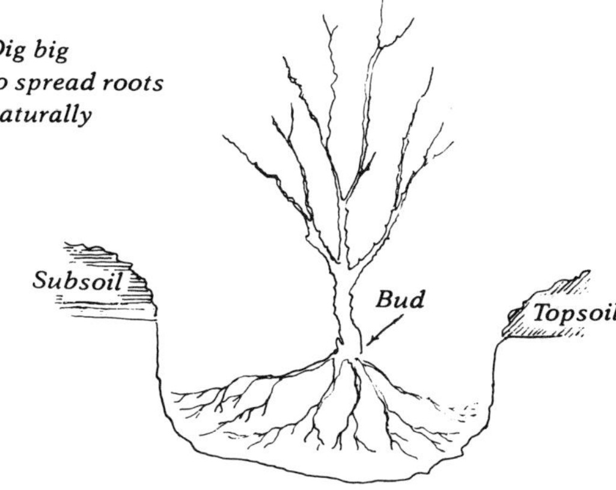

Put topsoil in bottom of hole. Enrich with bonemeal and old or dried cow manure or compost

Plant immediately. Do not expose roots to wind or sun while planting

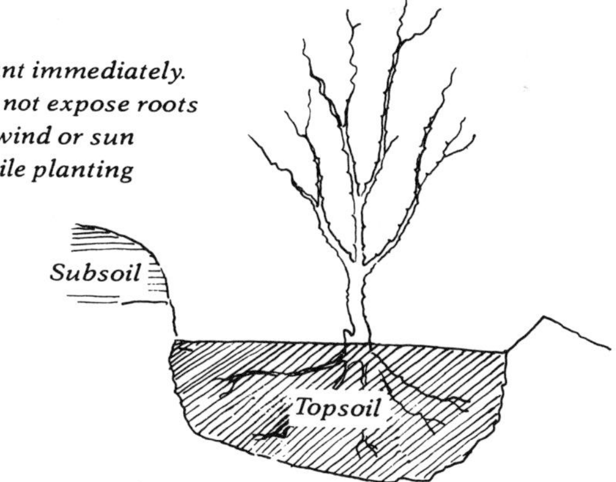

Roses:
Planting and Care

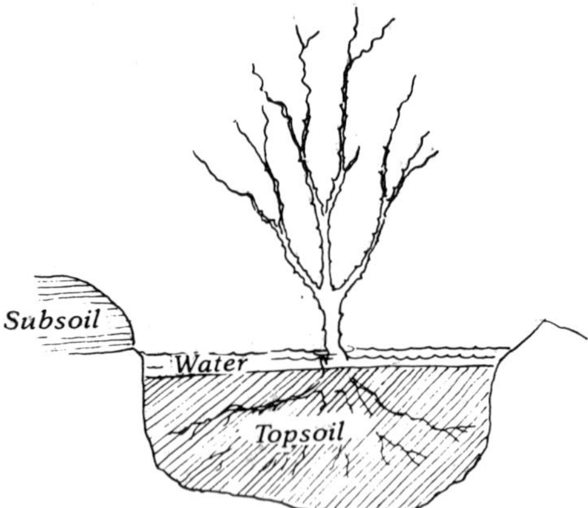

Flood, then put subsoil on top

Plant in full sun. Dig in handful of fertilizer first of each month, stopping August 1. Water heavily each week (soak ground). Spray every ten days with any good rose spray or dust for insect control with an all-purpose formula

In warm climates bud (or graft) should be slightly above ground level. In cold climates cover it 1 inch to 3 inches—depending upon the severity of winter

to inhibit fungus as well as sucking and biting insects. The bed should have thorough drainage but should not be allowed to dry. The gardener should note that in very cold climates the bud should be planted at least 1½ inches below the surface. Shrub Roses will survive in −20° F.; many grow well below that point. Climbers should be planted on southern exposures to provide protection from icy winds, and the canes should be laid on the ground and mulched with pine boughs over the winter.

Pruning practices: For climbers, prune back side growth on the canes in early spring, but remove only weak and aged canes from the crown—do not cut back strong new ones, for they will replace the aged ones that have been cut out. For *Floribundas* and *Grandifloras,* cut the canes back a third in early spring. Summer pruning requires cutting off about 4 inches of stem when taking off the spent cluster. For Hybrid Teas, cut canes back to within 8 to 10 inches of the ground in early spring. In summer prune back hard by taking about 4 inches of main stem when removing a spent flower—prune back close to 5-leaf growth, for the next flower will break at that leaf, never from 3-leaf growth. For shrubs, prune out dead canes or very old ones; canes can be shaped and strengthened by cutting them back about a third in early spring.

Following are the major Rose classifications. Varieties selected have the highest ratings given by the American Rose Society. As it takes several years for a Rose to perform in all parts of the country, which is the basic used for rating, many of the newer Roses are not included in these lists. The perfect rating is 10, a score no Rose has ever achieved. A Rose rated 7.0 to 7.9 is considered good, 8 to 8.9 is excellent, above that a Rose is outstanding. Judges, however, take so many factors other than the beauty of flower into consideration that it is difficult for a gardener who likes Roses, but is not expert, to tell the difference between a Rose rated 5.9 or less (of doubtful value) and one rated 7.0 or 8.0. The point is that if you like the bloom of a Rose with a low rating, don't be inhibited. Buy it, and you'll probably do better with it than with a Rose rated highly but not particularly appealing to you.

For more complete descriptions of the majority of the following varieties, I suggest that you consult catalogues issued by the major Rose growers. Some varieties may even prove somewhat difficult to find. Ratings follow each variety.

Climbing Roses. The climbers are highly useful on fence, wall, or trellis. There are many varieties. All are profuse bloomers, many of them will throw recurrent bloom if culture has been good, all are root-hardy everywhere, but in very harsh climates, as noted earlier, canes should be protected by placing them on the ground in December and covering them with evergreen boughs. For best effect against walls and fences, plant 1 variety or alternates of complementary colors. Spacing depends upon taste. We think 10 to 12 feet seems close enough, for after 2 or 3 years the tips of the canes from each plant will almost touch. Plant spring only.

Blends:

Royal Sunset, apricots, 8.1; Sutter's Gold, oranges, 7.9; Margo Koster, oranges, 7.7; American Pillar, reds, 7.4; Peace, yellows, 7.3; Circus, yellows, 7.4; and Mrs. Whitman Cross, oranges, 7.4.

Pink:

Pink Cameo, medium, 8.7; New Dawn, light, 8.4; Dr. W. Van Fleet, light, 8.1; Clair Matin, medium, 8.0; Cecil Brunner, light, 8.0; Blossom Time, medium, 7.8; Picture, light, 7.8; Inspiration, medium, 7.8; Mary Wallace, medium, 7.8; Coral Dawn, medium, 7.7; and Columbia, medium, 7.6.

Winter Protection for Roses

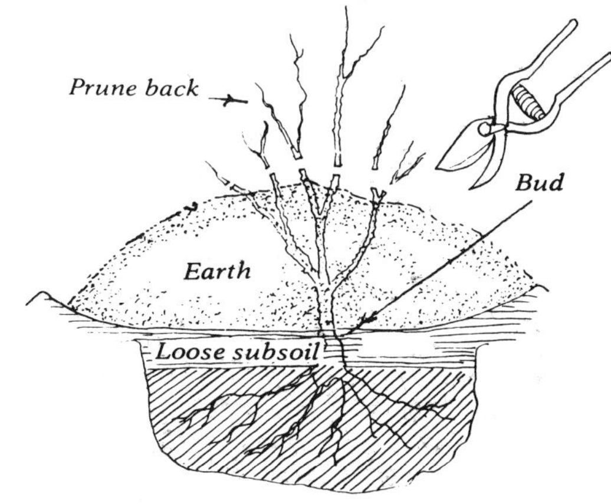

Build an earth mound to keep branches from dying out

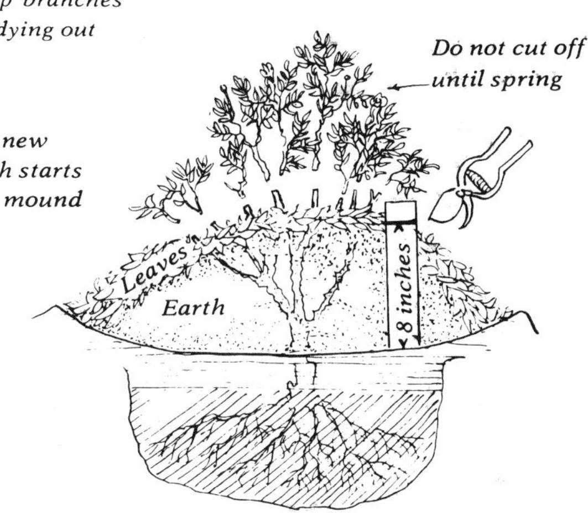

When new growth starts brush mound away

Red:

Paul's Scarlet, medium, 8.3; Heidelberg, medium, 8.2; Chevy Chase, dark, 8.1; Don Juan, dark, 8.1; Texas Centennial, light red and deepest pink, 8.0; Blaze, medium with recurrent bloom, 7.9; Carousel, dark, 7.7; Crimson Glory, dark, 7.7; Spectacular, orange red, 7.5; and Chrysler Imperial, dark, 7.4.

Yellow:

Mermaid, medium, 7.7; Elegance, medium, 7.6; Paul's Lemon Pillar, medium, 7.5; Royal Gold, medium, 7.4; Golden Showers, medium, 7.3; Zeus, medium, 7.3; and High Noon, medium, 7.0.

White:

City of York, 8.6; Glenn Dale, 8.0; Silver Moon, 7.8; Summer Snow, 7.6; Colonial White, 7.2; and White Dawn, 7.0.

Floribunda Roses. This is not only a charming but a highly versatile Rose form. Because *Floribundas* flower in large clusters, they are very showy plants and their continuous bloom produces a show all summer. Mass them in a single variety in beds 18 inches apart, or alternate with contrasting or blending colors. They also produce charming low hedges—2½ to 4 feet is as tall as they grow. A clump of them in the mid-section of the perennial border is effective. Varieties of the relatively new Rose class called *R. grandiflora* are included in this heading, but separated from the *Floribundas.* Spring planting only.

Blends:

Little Darling, yellows, 8.6; Border Gem, pinks, 8.4; Cupid's Charm, pinks, 8.4; Showboat, yellows, 8.2; Vogue, pinks, 8.2; Summer Song, oranges, 8.1; Circus, yellows, 8.0; Fashion, pinks, 8.0; Apricot Nectar, apricots, 7.8; and Woburn Abbey, oranges, 7.4.

Pink:

Betty Prior, medium, 9.0; Vera Dalton, medium, 8.3; Pink Rosette, medium, 8.1; Rosenelfe, medium, 7.9; Else Poulsen, medium, 7.8; Pink Bountiful, medium, 7.8.

Red:

Spartan, orangy, 8.4; Frensham, dark, 8.2; Ginger, orangy, 8.2; Orangeade, orangy, 8.2; Sarabande, orangy, 7.9; Permanent Wave, medium, 7.9; Red Pinocchio, medium, 7.9

Yellow:

Small Talk, medium, 7.9; Moonsprite, light, 7.7; Starlet, medium, 7.4; All-gold, medium, 7.4; Conrad Hilton, medium, 7.0; and Golden Garnette, dark, 7.0.

White:

Iceberg, 8.5; Ivory Fashion, 8.0; Shasta, 7.7; Summer Snow, 7.7; Saratoga, 7.6; and Snow Fairy, 7.6.

The Grandifloras:

Queen Elizabeth, medium pink, 9.3; Montezuma, orange red, 8.6; Carousel, dark red, 8.4; Olé, orangy red, 8.2; El Capitan, medium red, 8.0; John S. Armstrong, dark red, 7.9; Mount Shasta, white, 7.9; Camelot, medium pink, 7.9; Pink Parfait, pink blend; and Janzen Girl, medium red, 7.8.

Hybrid Tea Roses. This group of Hybrid Tea Roses, by color, are more sensitive to cold than Peace strain varieties, but all the plants produce blossoms of exceptional quality and are particularly useful in the warmer parts of zone 5 and southward. Some go back to the days before patents were thought of, others are patents that have expired. These are the high-rated Hybrid Teas and are arranged by color. A separate section follows that describes Peace strain Hybrid Teas.

Blends:

Tiffany, pinks, 9.1; Miss Canada, pinks, 8.6; Confidence, pinks, 8.4; Isabel de Ortez, pinks, 8.3; Helen Traubel, pinks, 8.3; Swarthmore, pinks, 8.2; Mexicana, reds, 8.2; and Granada, reds, 8.1.

Pink:

Pink Favorite, medium, 8.5; Royal Highness, light, 8.4; Dainty Bess, light, 8.3; First Love, light, 8.0; Blithe Spirit, light, 7.8; Memoriam, light, 7.8; Show Girl, medium, 7.8; South Seas, medium, 7.8.

Hybrid Tea in Full Bloom.

Red:

Chrysler Imperial, dark, 8.9; Tropicana, orangy, 8.7; Charlotte Armstrong, light red and deepest pink, 8.4; Crimson Glory, dark, 8.3; Rubaiyat, light red and deepest pink, 8.2; Mister Lincoln, medium, 8.2; Oklahoma, dark, 7.9; Prima Ballerina, light red and deepest pink, 7.9; Lotte Gunthart, medium, 7.8; Christian Dior, medium, 7.6; and Josephine Bruce, dark, 7.6.

Yellow:

King's Ransom, dark, 7.7; Golden Glow, dark, 7.6; Eclipse, medium, 7.5; Summer Sunshine, dark, 7.5; Golden Wave, dark, 7.4; and Town Crier, medium, 7.3.

White:

Pascali, 8.3; Matterhorn, 8.0; Burnaby, 7.6; Innocence, 7.5; Dresden, 7.5; Sweet Afton, 7.5; and White Queen, 7.4.

Peace Strain. As noted earlier, it is my belief that this strain of roses, developed over a period of almost 40 years, performs well in cold climates. This is an important difference. Moreover, they have exceptional beauty—some of the varieties will undoubtedly become classics. Most are still under patent. All ratings are high.

R. Candy Stripe. 7.3. Dusty pink with pleasant streaks of off-white and light pink on the inside of the petals. It is a sport of pink Peace. The blooms are 6 inches in diameter. It is a strong, upright grower with medium green foliage; very fragrant.

R. Chicago Peace. 8.1. This sport of Peace is a rich pink touched with shades of yellow and copper.

R. Christian Dior. 7.6. Crimson red and a beauty.

R. Garden Party. 7.9. Here's a sensational cross between Peace and Charlotte Armstrong, also a Rose of unusual stamina. Flowers are huge, petals creamy ivory tinted a delicious apple blossom pink at the outer edges. Foliage is olive green.

R. Kordes Perfecta. 7.6. The color of the cream-white buds edged with carmine spreads through the flower as it opens. It's a delightful combination of pink, white and yellow.

R. Lady Elgin. 7.4. Orange-apricot blossoms of great size.

R. Memoriam. 7.8. Huge pastel pink blooms, the like of which you've probably never seen.

R. Peace. 9.4. The patriarch of the family and the most important Rose in generations. Plants are huge and hardy. Chameleon-like flowers open yellow, edged pink, and they deepen in color as bloom matures. Its rating tops all others.
R. Pink Peace. 7.7. Flowers are enormous, dusky pink in color. A free and continuous bloomer whose flowers do not fade.
R. Royal Highness. 8.4. This lovely rose is a clear and light solid pink; very fragrant.
R. Swarthmore, 8.2. Two-tone—the petal is clear rose red and deepest pink. Its exceptionally long stems make it excellent for cutting. Very fragrant, too.
R. Tropicana. 8.7. An absolutely non-fading, exceptionally fragrant, orange-red Rose that stays in heavy bloom. It is the most popular Rose since Peace, its great relative.

Shrub Roses. This group of Roses almost dropped out of culture when the Rose world went mad about Hybrid Teas about 70 years ago. They have remarkable qualities. Here are Roses that require no winter care; they will live through −20° F as well as Hybrid Teas survive at +20° F. Flowers range from heavy clusters of singles and doubles to those nearly as big as dinner plates. Many bloom constantly throughout the season. When I first became acquainted with them in England in 1948 I hardly believed what I saw. But there are few U.S. growers. Because shrub Roses are unruly in the growing fields and carry no patents, none of the large growers will mass produce them. In 1950 there were about 10 small growers, now there are only 2 or 3. By far the most interesting of them is Tillotson's Roses, 972 Brown's Valley Road, Watsonville, California 95076. Their catalogue, written by Dorothy Stemler, is a booklet with charm. It costs $1, which can be deducted from a first order.

Some shrub Roses, particularly those that bloom perpetually, make very attractive hedges for suburban properties. None, however, are useful as living fences on farms, a use that was highly publicized by nurserymen about 15 years ago and which was applauded by agricultural schools over the country. The fences turned out to be a menace—the seed spread into plowed field and meadows and caused *Rosa multiflora,* the variety so widely publicized, to turn into a vicious weed. Some companies even promoted *R. multiflora* for home use, neglecting to mention that although mature fences would keep out dogs, the plants also produced strong and exceedingly sharp thorns about 1½ inches long that were dangerous to man and beast.

ROSE OF SHARON—*see* Hibiscus syriacus

rosea (roe'zee-a) rose colored

ROSEMARY—*see* Herbs

rotundifolia (roe-tun-dee-foe'lee-ah) round-leafed

rubens (roo'benz) blush red

rubra (roo'bra) red

Rudbeckia Gold Drop

Rudbeckia

Rude-beck'ee'ah

Coneflower. Highly decorative North American perennials that bloom in July and continue blooming until frost. This long show period makes them particularly valuable in the perennial garden, for few perennials flower at that time. Nearly all of the species are too tall, their stems too spindly to withstand wind and rain. The varieties listed here are short, strong, and disease-resistant. None are demanding. Plant spring or fall.

R. Gold Drop. A Dutch import of great merit. It barely grows to 30 inches—24 inches is the height in Litchfield. Its stems are very tough and sturdy. The golden-yellow flowers are big and very double.

R. Goldstrum. Large, deep golden-yellow flowers in daisy form. It blooms prodigiously in July, September, and part of October, which is a blessing. The plant itself grows compactly. No insects seem to touch it and it is very hardy.

rugosa (rue-go'sa) rugged, rough

rupestris (rue-pes'tris) growing on rocks

Russian Buffalo Grass

Russian Buffalo Grass. Mint in the summer to a man with a bottle of bourbon spells julep. To a Russian or a Pole with a bottle of vodka, the addition of not more than three stems of Russian Buffalo Grass changes vodka to zubrovka. It gives vodka a smoothness with which it was not born. Russian Buffalo Grass is no trouble to grow. It likes full sun, lots of humus (mix plenty of peat into the soil), and a damp location. One clump is enough to take care of heavy drinkers. Contain it, or it will become a weed in the garden. It can be bought only at White Flower Farm. Plant spring or fall.

Ruta

Rue'ta

Herb of Grace, or Rue. A genus of about 40 species from Eurasia and the Canary Islands. They consist of shrubs, sub-shrubs, and perennials whose leaves generally exude a pungent odor. It is called Herb of Grace because it was associated with repentance. Only one species has garden value. Plant spring or fall.

R. Blue Beauty. Seldom does one find a plant named for the outstanding characteristic of its foliage. This one is grown for its blue-green leaves. Remove the flower heads, for they are of no value. It is compact and grows 18 to 24 inches.

rutilans (rue'ti-lans) glowing deep red

SAGE—*see* Herbs, *also* Salvia

ST. JOHN'S-WORT—*see* Hypericum

Salvia

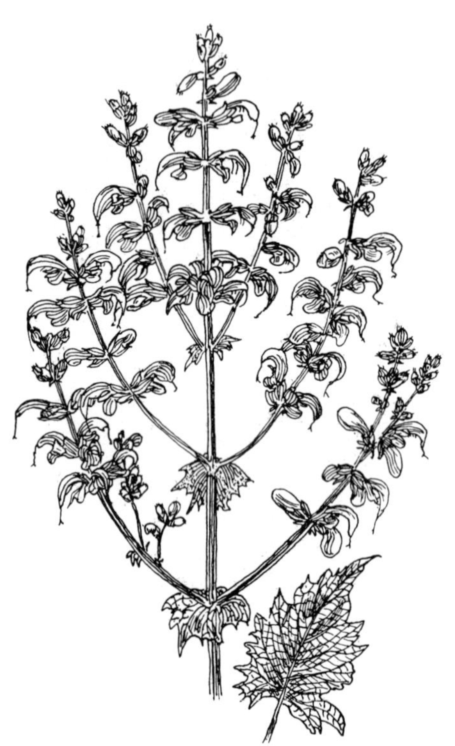

Salvia haematodes

Salvia
Sal'vee-a

Sage. A very large genus of showy annuals and biennials—and a few hardy perennials. They are natives of many countries—hot and cold. Plant spring or fall.

S. haematodes. It features strong, 36-inch sprays of bluish-violet flowers from a neat basal rosette of leaves from June to September when plants with blue flowers are hard to find in the border. It is not fussy about soil and requires little attention.

***S. Jurisicii.** This fine dwarf from Serbia is only a little over 8 inches high. It has violet-blue flowers that bloom from June onward. Use it in the rockery and in the front of the perennial border.

S. Oestfriesland. This variety produces 18-inch sprays of violet-blue flowers from July until September. Growth is strong and upright.

***S. officinalis tricolor.** The leaves start out gray green, veined yellowish white and pink, but turn to pink or red. The spikes of blue flowers appear in early summer on 15-inch stems.

SAND. The kind used in gardening is important. When coarse, sharp sand is called for buy builder's sand. It is washed and the only kind desirable for horticultural use. It feels sharp when rubbed between the fingers. Sand fresh from the seashore is likely to be too fine and will therefore compact, and it often contains a killing amount of salt. Builder's sand should also be used to lighten heavy muck or clay soils—and for working and draining them.

SANDWORT—*see* Arenaria

sanguinea (san-gwin'ee-a) blood-red

Santolina
San-toe-lee'nah

Santolina. A small group of very satisfactory shrubs and herbaceous plants whose home is the hills of the Mediterranean region. They do not require a rich soil, and rather intensely dislike a wet condition at the roots. A light sandy soil and full sun are the main requirements. In extremely cold climates they need a protected, southerly location or wintering in a cold frame. Plant spring only.

***S. chamaecyparissus nana.** Lavender Cotton. A charming deciduous dwarf shrub with close-packed, silver-gray foliage, highly useful in the rockery, for edging, for a path, borders, or anyplace. The variety make charming standards not over 14 inches high. Left to grow it reaches a height of about 8 to 10 inches, but it is largely used trimmed to a neat 6-inch miniature hedge. The flowers are of no importance.

S. virens. Holy Flax. A small, dark evergreen bush that grows to a height of about 2 feet. Flowers are creamy yellow and appear in July at the top of slender, erect stalks 8 to 10 inches high. An attractive plant for the perennial garden. Cut it back sharply each spring.

Sargentiana (sar-gen-tee-aye'na) after professor Charles S. Sargent, founder of the Arnold Arboretum

sarmentosum (sahr-men-toe'sum) having long runners

saxatile (sacks'ah-tile) growing among rocks

scabra (skay'bra) rough

scandens (skan'dens) climbing

scape (skape) a long, naked—or nearly naked—stalk rising from a plant's base, whether single- or many-flowered

scariosa (scare-ee-owe'sa) thin, dry, shrivelled

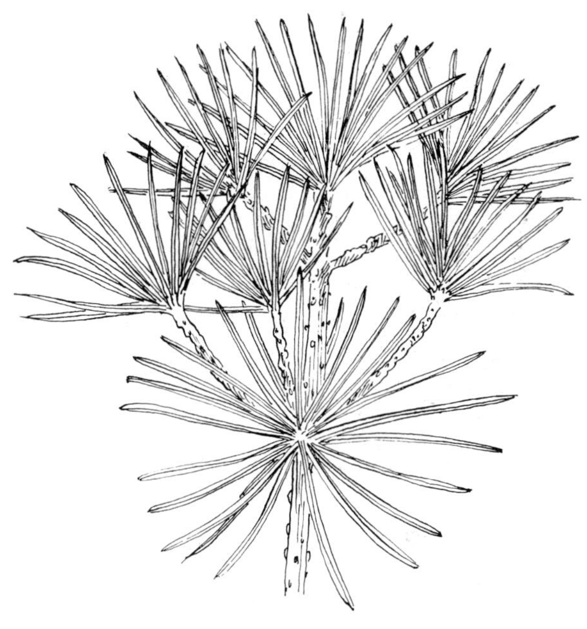

Sciadopitys verticillata

Sciadopitys verticillata

Sy-a-dop'ee-tis ver-tis-sil-lah'tah

The Umbrella Pine. Zone 4, southward. This Japanese evergreen of only 1 species is not easily found. It is not a pine—its long evergreen needles, formed like umbrella ribs, supply its common name. The tree grows to 120 feet in Japan, and its great and even base shapes it generally to a huge cone. Few specimens in this country are higher than 40 feet. Small trees should be planted in a location big enough so that its large, upright cone form will have plenty of room. The plant grows well, but very slowly, as far north as Stockbridge, Mass., with little protection, and is probably hardy farther north if more protected. As large plants are difficult to obtain and hard to move, one must start, like it or not, with babies—4-year-olds with a heavy earth ball, about 6 inches high and a 6-inch spread. But they take hold quickly and before long grow to 4 feet. Plant spring or fall.

Santolina Chamaecyparisus nana

SCILLA CAMPANULATA—*see* Scilla hispanica

Scilla
Sill'uh

Scilla. Bulbous plants of many species native to Europe and Asia that are cultivated for their spring bloom. The predominant color of all the garden species is blue, but whites, pinks and different shades of blue have been developed over the years. They are inexpensive. Plant fall only.

S. hispanica. The Scots and the Spanish each claim this late-blooming spring species as their own native bluebell, and although the claims are true, there is no difference in them botanically. Years ago they were called *S. campanulata,* and that name is still used more in commercial catalogues than *S. hispanica.* Flowering stalks are 18 to 22 inches high and covered with clusters of flowers; leaves are grass-like. The bulbs like deep shade and do extremely well planted under dense evergreens. Excellent cut flowers.

S. h. Blue Giant. Dark blue.

S. h. Blue Queen. Pale Blue.

S. h. Rosabella. A dark pink.

S. h. White Triumphator. A giant white.

Scilla sibirica

S. sibirica. Blue Squill. Excellent bulbous rockery plants that are wonderful for naturalizing. They bloom very early and should be planted in a sunny location about 3 inches deep. They produce delightful little flowers, rarely over 4 to 6 inches high, and they bloom in April. Plant them by the hundreds or thousands, fall only.

***S. s. Spring Beauty.** Bluest of blue in color, this variety's blossoms are large and free-flowering. Height is 4 to 6 inches.

***S. s. Tubergeniana.** Silver white with a bluish undertone.

SEA HOLLY—*see* Eryngium

SEA LAVENDER—*see* Limonium

*Sedum

See'dum

Stonecrop. This genus of fleshy-leafed plants which covers the north temperate, colder parts of the earth, has many fascinating and lovely forms and is invaluable for the rockery. Colors are nearly the rainbow. They demand drought and like poor soils. Sedums also propagate faster than rabbits; indeed, if not contained, many species can be pests. But good and bad points aside, if Sedum wasn't available, the stuff would have to be invented for gardeners. All are useful in rockeries; a few can be used to advantage in the perennial border. Plant spring or fall.

***S. kamtschaticum.** The foliage is deep green and scalloped. It's 3- to 4-inch height makes it useful for rockery work, or in the front of the border. The orange-yellow blooms are about ¾ inch in diameter. It flowers from July through September.

***S. k. variegatum.** This variety has the same growth habit and flowering time as the preceding one, but the dark green foliage has a broad band of white. The 2 varieties planted alternately provide pleasant contrast.

S. maximum atropurpureum. Mahogany Plant. It has cream-rose flowers on strong ebony stems. Leaves are mahogany tones to bronze purple. The plant makes excellent material for unusual flower arrangements. Use it in the perennial border. It grows to 24 inches high.

S. s. Meteor. This spectacular thing grows to 18 inches or more on strong stems covered with soft grey-green fleshy leaves. The flower appears as a large, flat umbel covered with small carmine-red blooms. It's a fine sight. It is also fine for growing in large tubs or pots for the terrace and is effective in the border—or anyplace you put it, for all of that. It keeps well as a cut flower.

S. pruinatum. The foliage is blue green and the dainty star-like yellow flowers show in July. A specimen growing on a stone wall looks very good, indeed. It has the long trailing characteristics gardeners like.

Santolina virens

***S. Sieboldii.** Leaves are round, thick, and silver gray in color. It shows bright pink flowers on 6- to 9-inch stems in early September. Use it in the rockery, or pot it for the terrace.
S. S. variegatum The variegated form of *S. Sieboldii.* The leaves carry a yellow blotch. It, too, is a rockery or pot plant.
S. spectabile Star Dust. The foliage is blue green. It produces bold heads of ivory-white flowers in August and September at 18 inches.
S. spurium coccineum. This variety is trailing and shows crimson flowers on 6-inch stems in July and August.
S. s. Dragon's Blood. Its foliage is reddish bronze, dense, and only an inch or so high. The dark carmine-red flowers appear in June and recur thereafter. It is highly promoted by many nurseries though over-promotion, which it certainly gets, many times results in disappointment when the gardener sees the plant. Some of the claims made for this variety are exaggerated—it doesn't spread as fast, for example, as the ad men say. However, most things said of it by the hucksters are true.
S. Telephium Autumn Joy. Leaves are bright green, thick and fleshy. The rust-brown flowers appear in August and September on 12- to 18-inch stems. It keeps a very long time as a cut flower, and makes a bold bouquet when used alone in a vase.
S. ternatum. This variety forms a pale green tuft and produces pure white flowers on 4-inch stems in May.

SEED—*see* Annuals; Lawns

sempervirens (sem-per-vie'rens) evergreen

Sedum Sieboldii

*Sempervivum

Sem-per-vie'vum

Hens-and-Chickens or Houseleek. The name of this genus was derived by Pliny from *semper vivo* and means, literally, live forever. And these fleshy plants, just as valuable for rockeries and walls as Sedums, seem to do just that. There are about 25 species. Only the good Lord knows how many varieties there are, for all of them can not be listed in botanical encyclopedias. Here is a broad selection of the best of the hardies of the tribe. All are excellent rockery plants. Plant spring or fall.

S. arachnoideum. The rosettes are reddish and green, and the flowers, which are on 6- to 8-inch stems, turn bright red in July.
S. atropurpureum. This variety shows sprays of pink blossoms on strong 6- to 8-inch stems in July. Excellent.
S. atroviolaceum. Rosettes are a shaded violet. The flowers, on 8-inch stems, are a rosy pink and show in July.
S. calcareum. Rosettes, 3 inches across, are vivid green, their points red. Pale red blooms come in July on 6- to 8-inch stems.
S. Commander Hay. This is a large variety of English origin. The rosettes, stained pink, grow 8 to 9 inches across; dainty pink blooms on 10-inch stems appear in July.
S. Laggeri. This variety is also somewhat similar to *S. arachnoideum,* but its blooms, on 6-inch stems, are yellow. It is a neat and compact plant.
S. regenae amaliae. Green rosettes are purplish at the tips; the flowers are pale yellow.
S. r. glaucum. The rosettes are dark green with blue-red tips; its deep pink flowers appear in July on 6-inch stems.
S. rubicunorum. The big rosettes reach 4 inches in diameter. The red flowers are on 6-inch stems.

Senecio

Sen-ee'si-o

Senecio. A very large genus of over 1200 species found throughout the world, but few have garden value. Plant spring or fall.

S. Desdemona. It is not known to many gardeners. The leaves are extraordinary. In early spring they are purple and turn to green as they open. On an established plant, leaves grow up to 12 inches across, so it needs room. Bloom comes in late summer and early fall. Flowers, which are nearly 2 inches across, are beautifully disordered and are orange yellow with a brown center. The stems are branched, and, depending on culture, grow 30 to 48 inches high, and are so strong they do not need staking. It has an enchanting perfume, almost like Heliotrope. Plant it in full sun in good garden soil. It's a wonderful addition to any border.

serphyllum (sir-fill'lum) mat-forming

SHADE. Shade means light without direct sunlight; we shall have to discuss it in terms of light to make the points gardeners need to

Sedum Telephium Autumn Joy

Sempervivum Commander Hay

know. Light is necessary even to the most shade-loving plants. What they don't like is direct sunlight. The annual Impatiens is a shade-lover, a sun-hater. It should be used when one seeks bloom in deep shade, but it still needs light—lots of it—to do well. Gardeners fail with Tuberous Begonias largely because they are told that these beauties love deep shade. They don't. The more light they get, the better they grow; but they rebel at direct sun. Another warning about shaded sites: many times they are too damp (dank is probably a better word), so be sure shaded areas are well drained. Many Lilies like part or filtered shade—the kind one gets under a Locust, not the kind of shade an Oak or Sugar Maple throws. A good rule to follow is that light without direct sunlight is the principal requirement of shade-loving plants. The rule can be broken to this extent: 2 hours of morning sun won't hurt any of them. So you may conclude that writers on gardening delight in confusing trusting gardeners—and you may be right. For convenience the genera in this book that like light-in-shade are: Ajuga, Anemone, Arenaria, Astilbe, Begonia, Cimicifuga, Convallaria, Dicentra, Digitalis, Epimedium, Ferns, Hedera, Helleborus, *Iris Kaempferi, Iris sibirica,* Lilium (see varieties), Mertensia, Pachysandra, *Phlox divaricata,* Platycodon, Plumbago, Primula, Tradescantia, Trollius, Vinca, and Viola. And all of the spring-flowering bulbs except Tulips. Roses also do better in filtered light (but lots of it) than in full sun.

SHASTA DAISY—*see Chrysanthemum maximum*

sibirica (*si-bye'ri-ka*) *Siberian*

Sidalcea *Sigh-dall'see-uh* False Mallow. Here a genus of about 8 species, natives of western North America, with flowers similar to Hollyhock. Indeed, one species is sometimes called wild Hollyhock, but the spiked form is quite different. The named varieties, which have been developed by hybridization, must be propagated by division; they should be separated and replanted every 3 or 4 years for best results. Plants do well in full sun in ordinary garden soil; irrigate thoroughly in dry weather. Plant spring or fall.

S. Rosy Gem. The leaves of this variety are medium green and pleasantly shaped. Depending on culture, the spikes grow to heights from 18 to 36 inches, and are well covered with rosy-pink, single blooms up to 1½ inches in diameter from July through September. They are valuable to the middle flowering season of the perennial border.

Sieboldii (*see-bold'eye*) *after botanist P. F. von Siebold*

SILVER LACE VINE—*see* Polygonum Auberti

simplex (*sim'plecks*) *undivided*

SNAKEROOT—*see* Cimicifuga

SNAKE'S HEAD LILY—*see* Fritillaria

SNOWDROP—*see* Galanthus

SOIL. Many experts give gardeners lots of firm commands about the specific soils they'd better use for specific plants. This isn't exactly true—you don't really need a different soil for each class of plant. When we ask for "a good garden soil," we ask little: topsoil to a decent depth, and that's about all. It should have a considerable amount of humus. If you have leaf mold, well-rotted manure (which is hard to get), dried cow manure or compost, use it instead of peatmoss, the most readily found but most expensive form of humus. A small amount of humus dug lightly into the soil each year gradually builds up humus content. But such vegetable matter should be fully decomposed, otherwise it will rob the soil of nitrogen. "A good garden

Sidalcea

soil" should be moderately sandy for drainage, which also provides a modicum of ventilation close to the surface, where most of a plant's finely divided feeding roots collect. Good garden soil should also receive superphosphate each year, an ingredient nearly always deficient in soils in damp climates. The use of chemical fertilizers is not recommended for the soil or the plants, but one must use them if organic fertilizers are not available. Don't buy expensive chemical soil-testing sets because most gardeners will have difficulty finding out for sure what their neat tests are saying. If your plants aren't lushly green, they need a shot of nitrogen; if their root systems aren't strong, phosphates are lacking; if stems are weak, the soil is low in potassium. That's highly over-simplified, but in essence true. Very small amounts of fertilizers combining these elements (plus trace elements—*see* Fertilizer) will correct this. There's one fact you can't get away from about soils—if they'll grow weeds lushly, they'll grow flowering plants. Don't worry about soil—if it turns out to be substandard it can be fixed.

"Friable" is another word used to describe soils, and it stumps some gardeners; it refers to a soil's physical condition. A soil is friable if, when damp, it crumbles easily after being squeezed in the hand. If it doesn't crumble it has too much clay. Add sand until it finally becomes friable. If it crumbles too quickly, it probably has too much sand—so add some more topsoil and more humus. Important: *see p*H Factor.

Solidago

Solidago

Sol-i-day'go

Goldenrod. A very large group of plants, mostly North American, which everyone knows because Goldenrod is such a common thing in the autumn. Also, its pollen was long considered a major cause of hay fever, and it still is by those who do not know that ragweed, which sheds its pollen the same time of year, is the cause of most of that suffering. "Why should I grow Goldenrod? It's a noxious weed," is the reaction most American gardeners have—until they see the gorgeous varieties the English have hybridized from this common American weed, which actually is a right pretty thing in itself. The Goldenrods are obviously very hardy and easily propagated by division. They should be grouped in the border with perennial Asters, which bloom in August and September, the months that must be bridged with plants like these to keep a perennial border in color until Chrysanthemums show. Plant spring or fall.

S. Golden Mosa. This variety is deep yellow. It branches strongly and has tapering trusses. Excellent for cutting. It grows to 36 inches.
S. Leraft. Buttercup yellow with a bushy habit. Makes a nice counterpoint to *S. Mosa* and is about the same height.

SOUTHERNWOOD—*see* Artemesia Abrotanum

Spathiphyllum Mona Loa

Spathiphyllum

Spath-i-fill'lum

Spathiphyllum. Not hardy. Several of the species of this genus (about 27 of them from tropical America and various Malaysian islands) are probably some of the most useful of all house plants, for they have qualities possessed by no other—when properly grown they provide luscious greenery and flowers the year around. The very dark green leaves are long, graceful and undulating; the flowers bloom above the foliage and are shaped like Anthurium and well they should be, for they are cousins in the same family, *Araceae*. Spathiphyllum is the only flowering plant we know of that grows beautifully in a city apartment. We have a plant that has flourished in the elevator vestibule of a New York apartment with absolutely no daylight, just a somewhat dim incandescent electric lamp which stays on 24 hours a day. The temperature in the small space stays well above 90° night and day during July. It is watered so heavily that it is soggy all the time. But these conditions are those (except constant light) under which Spathiphyllum grow normally—on the floor of tropical jungles. Stove heat and high humidity, in other words. Blooms come in flushes, but the flushes come regularly; moveover, blooms last a long time, like those of Anthurium. Keep the plant well watered, never place it in sunlight; temperature should be 70° or above (leaves yellow at 60°). Transplant to a pot one size larger every 2 or 3 years. It is not used nearly enough. A few nurseries offer it. Also, it is available from time to time from good florists.

S. hybridum. It is also called Mona Loa. Extremely long leaves make a shapely, large, very dark green head that can grow from 14 to 16 inches high. Flowers open white, turn green as they age. The blossoms are 4 to 5 inches long, about 2 to 3 inches wide on 14- to 18-inch stems; under good culture flowers on mature plants are 8 inches long or more.

SPEARMINT—*see* Herbs

speciosum (*spees-ee-oew'sum*) *good-looking, showy*

spectabilis (*spek-tah'bill-iss*) *worth seeing, admirable*

SPEEDWELL—*see* Veronica

SPIDERWORT—*see* Tradescantia

SPIKE HEATH—*see* Heaths and Heathers, Bruckenthalia

spinulosa (*spin-you-lowe'sa*) *having small spines*

SPIRAEA—*see* Astilbe

SPRING-FLOWERING BULBS. For those unfamiliar with the names of the many spring-flowering bulbs, all of which are shipped for planting in September and October, we round them up here by their botanical names, followed with their generally recognized common names. They are Allium, Anemone (the bulbous form), Camassia (a type of Bellflower), Chionodoxa (Glory-of-the-Snows), Crocus, Erythronium (like Cyclamen but called Dogtooth Violet), Eranthis (buttercup-like flowers on 3-inch stems, also called Winter Aconite), Fritillaria (pendulant and bell-like, known as Snake's Head Lily, but as unsnake-like as can be), Galanthus (the lovely Snow-drops), Hyacinth, Iris (only the bulbous form), Muscari (the delightful Grape Hyacinth), Narcissus (Daffodils, of course), *Scilla hispanica* (Wood Hyacinth or *Scilla campanulata,* its old botanical name), *Scilla sibirica* (Blue Squill), and Tulipa (which are obviously Tulips).

SPRUCE—*see* Evergreens, Dwarf Needle

SPURGE—*see* Pachysandra

spurium (*spew'ree-um*) *false*

squarrosa (*square-rowe'sa*) *having overlapping leaves with pointed tips which are very spreading or recurved*

*Stachys

Stack'iss

Betony or Woundwort. There are several species in this genus native to north temperate climates, but few are garden plants. They thrive in poor soil. Plant spring only.

S. lanata. Lamb's Tongue or Lamb's Ear. The leaves, gracefully shaped, are persistently woolly white, flowers are insignificant. It's a pretty foliage plant and deserves more use in front of the perennial border or in planters on the terrace. Height is about 8 inches.

Stachys lanata

STAKING. Plants that grow tall in locations poorly protected from wind should be staked. Finger-size bamboo (get it almost anywhere) is excellent for most plants. A stake can be pushed down close to an established plant, but if it's a tree it's better to place a large stake when the tree is planted. The best ties we know are strips of plastic with a small wire inside called *Twistems,* a perfect name. They are inexpensive. Buy the big roll almost everywhere. Wire stakes made of galvanized wire with a twist at the top (see drawing) are the easiest way to hold stalks in place. Shove them into the ground close to the crown, then guide the stalk into the twist at the top by simply turning the stake. The stalk finds it hard to escape. Also, because the stake is made of wire it "gives" a bit in the wind—rides it out gracefully, as sailors say. They can usually be found in garden centers.

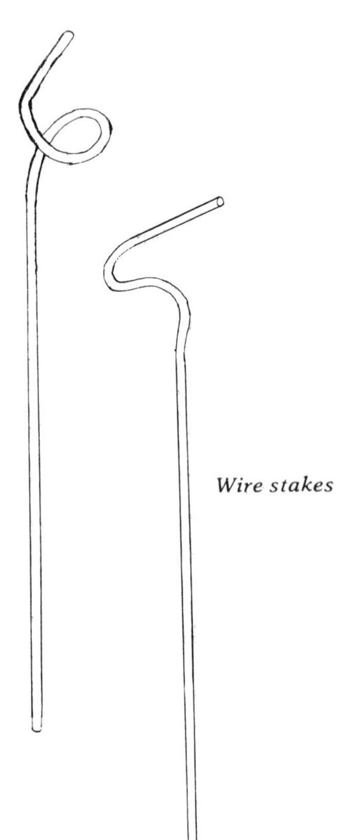

Wire stakes

staminodes (*stam'i-nodes*) *rudimentary stamen, producing no pollen*

STATICE—*see* Limonium

stelleriana (*stel-lee-ree-aye'na*) *star-like*

Stokesia
Sto-key'zee-uh

Stokesia. A hardy American perennial in the form of the annual Cornflower (it also bears a resemblance to Asters); a highly decorative border plant and good for cutting. It needs full sun and is not fussy about soils. There is only one species. Plant spring only.

S. cyanea. Light blue, disc-like flowers appear in late August and last well into September. Height of bloom is 12 to 15 inches.

stolonifera (*stowe-lon-if'ur-a*) *having runners that root*

STONECROP—*see* Sedum

STRAWBERRIES—*see* Fraises

strain, plant stock selected for general basic characteristics and breeding true to them

subcordata (sub-core-day'ta) slightly heart-shaped

subulata (sub-you-lay'ta) awl-shaped

suffruticosa (suf-froot-i-kowe'sa) low and shrubby at the base

SUN. When full sun is a stated cultural requirement, just that is meant—exposure to direct sunlight all day. Half sun can be found (1) under light foliage through which sunlight moves intermittently or (2) in a location in direct sun for half a day, shaded the rest of the time, but in full light—a side of a building, for example. But sun in the afternoon is stronger than morning sun. Terraces or patios usually provide all light conditions. Half morning sun is ideal for Fuchsia, Azalea, or Rhododendron. Tuberous Begonias like constant strong light, not direct sunlight (*see* Shade).

SUNFLOWER—*see* Helianthus and Heliopsis

superba (soo-purb'a) magnificent

SWEET CICELY—*see* Herbs

SWEET VIOLET—*see* Viola

SWEET WILLIAM—*see* Dianthus barbatus

SWEET WOODRUFF—*see* Asperula

sylvatica (sil-vah'tick-ah) of woods or forests

Syringa

Si-ring'a

Lilac. Syringa, which is native to the Old World, is a most confusing name for Americans. We call the Mock-orange, Syringa. It isn't. The Mock-orange is known properly as *Philadelphus* and has no relation-

Syringa microphylla superba

ship to Syringa, the Lilac. The familiar garden Lilacs are derived from *S. vulgaris.* They are the single and the double hybrid forms known as French Lilacs, which once were rare but now are common. Every garden center carries them. They are beautiful and most are extremely fragrant. The lovely species varieties, which one would think are common, are actually hard to find. Here, except the first one, is a short list of them. Plant them spring or fall.

S. James MacFarlane. Zone 4, southward. This new hybrid, developed by the University of New Hampshire, is a cross between *S. reflexa* and *S. villosa,* both of Chinese origin. The former is 12 feet high, the latter about 10 feet. *S. MacFarlane* matures at about 8 feet. Its heavy panicles, characteristic of the Chinese types, are a delightful pink.

S. microphylla superba. Zone 5, but zone 4 protected. This so-called "Rock Garden Lilac" seldom grows over 7 feet tall. Its mahogany-red buds open to soft pink. The short panicles have a dainty lace effect, and it invariably blooms twice a year—in late June and mid-August. It is intensely fragrant.

S. Palibiniana. Zone 4, southward. This variety is known as the Dwarf Korean Lilac and was named after the Russian botanist Palibin. It arrived at Boston's Arnold Arboretum shortly before World War II. Now it has moved into the better nurseries. It is an attractive shrub with compact, small, dark green leaves. It flowers profusely. Panicles are about 6 inches long and although very dark in the bud, they open a lavender lilac. Arnold's first description called for 3-foot growth and it is still generally described as being that height. But our plants seem to be maturing at 5 feet, and under warmer conditions we suspect they will grow higher. But that is still a dwarf compared to common Lilacs, which grow to 20 feet. It can be contained by pruning. It makes an excellent specimen in the front of the shrub border; an uneven hedge of them is a fine possession.

S. yunnanensis rosea. Zone 4, southward. The Chinese "Yunnan Lilac" with slender panicles of pink flowers. It grows to about 10 feet. Because it is not known it is not bought. Plants will be hard to find but they are worth hunting for.

taggeta (ta-gee'ta) tacked on

tangutica (tan-goo'ti-ka) from Tangut

TARRAGON—*see* Herbs

Taxodium
Tacks-owe'dee-um

Taxodium. A genus of 3 gorgeous species of trees—only 1 of which is deciduous and hardy—with fine-cut fern-like leaves and open foliage. The bark is brown and it curls and peels most interestingly on the trunk and branches—almost like Redwood. Because Taxodium is related to southern Cypress, it does well in quite moist locations, but specimens can be seen in locations here the gardens which are not the least damp or swamp-like. Plant spring or fall.

T. distichum pendulum. Zone 4 (and sometimes in zone 3), southward. This grafted deciduous evergreen has dancing pendulant branches. It is unusual. Height in zone 4 may possibly reach 30 feet. It is a rare tree and worth finding.

tectorum (tek-towe'rum) of roofs

telephium (tel-lef'ee-um) from the herb telephion, once used to determine if love was reciprocated

terminalis (tur-min-aye'lis) said of a plant having flowers that terminate on the ends of its branches

ternatum (ter-nat'um) whorls of 3 or having 3 parts arranged around a common axis

tetralix (te-tray'licks) 4 leaves arranged crosswise

Teucrium
Too'kree-um

Germander. A large genus of about 150 species, few of them worthwhile in gardens. A few dwarfs, however, are very valuable, for they can be used as miniature hedges. One is described below. They prefer well-drained locations in full sun. Plant spring or fall.

***T. Chamaedrys.** Zone 5, southward, but zone 4 with protection. A sub-shrub that can be formed into a delightful miniature hedge. Leaves are nearly oval in form, toothed and hairy. Height is 12 to 15 inches.

thelypteroides (*the-lip'tur-oy'dess*) *similar to* Dryopteris *species* thelypteris

Thermopsis caroliniana

Thermopsis

Ther-mop'sis

Thermopsis. Showy species of North American and Asiatic origin make up this genus, but only a few are used decoratively in gardens. Flowers are pea-like. Plant spring or fall.

T. caroliniana. Carolina Lupine. A species with attractive, deep green foliage and long yellow spikes of lupine-like flowers in June and July. Height is 3 to 4 feet.

THINNING. Everyone knows that vegetables or annuals planted from seed must be "thinned" to prevent crowding. To thin such seedlings one merely pinches out baby plants, leaving only enough to make a good crop of vegetables or a good show of annuals. Not nearly so well known is the practice of thinning established perennials so that the remaining shoots develop into strong stalks. Thinning perennials is a simple gardening technique to be practiced in early spring. It can be used on most perennials that grow from a crown and that do not have to be dug up, separated and replanted each year, as do Chrysanthemums.

Ordinary garden Phlox is a case in point. In the spring many shoots arise from the crown of the plant. When they are 3 to 4 inches high snip off all but 4 or 5 of the strongest. Snip shoots even on new plants. You might, of course, cut off more shoots than you save, but those left get all the strength the crown provides. As a result the 4 or 5 remaining stalks are strong, the flowering heads large, the leaves (because of the increased air circulation) are far less susceptible to mildew, and the side shoots become almost as large as the original head. In terms of size of plant one does not miss the destroyed shoots—a well-thinned plant is generally a larger plant. Moreover, its stalks don't topple because of weakness. Herewith a list of the principal perennials that can be greatly improved by thinning after they have been in place a year: Aster (fall bloomers only), *Chrysanthemum maximum,* Delphinium, Gypsophila, Helenium, *Paeonia,* and Garden Phlox.

THUJA—*see* Evergreens, Dwarf Needle

THYME—*see* Thymus *and* Herbs

Before

Thymus

Tye'mus

Decorative Thyme (*see* Herbs for the culinary variety). These easily grown plants form dense mats that are ideal for spaces between flagstones. They require full sun and that is about all. It is a perfect, low-growing cover for hot, dry places. When planting any of the following varieties, the gardener must be sure that the extremely fine roots are not exposed to sun or wind. Even a slight exposure will result in enough damage to the root system to cause failure. Plant spring only.

***T. citriodorus.** It is also known as Lemon Thyme because of its distinct lemon fragrance. *T. citriodorus* grows from 6 to 8 inches high and is covered with small rosy blooms in June. The foliage occasionally becomes variegated. Like all Decorative Thymes it needs full sun. It makes a delightful dwarf border for an informal path. It needs light protection in winter to keep its stems from drying out.
***T. Serpyllum album.** Its dense mats of dark green foliage have small white flowers.
***T. S. coccineum.** This variety forms extremely dense mats of fine evergreen leaves covered with reddish-purple flowers in late June. The leaves turn bronze in the fall. It is extremely hardy. This is the best variety for planting between stones in a terrace or walk.

TICKSEED—*see* Coreopsis

After

Thinning Perennials

Pick a few strong shoots, cut those around them out with a knife down to the crown of the plant. The Phlox so thinned above (bottom) will be mildew-resistant, its heads large, its stems strong

Thymus Serpyllum coccineum

TOPSOIL. The owner of a spanking new home, invariably interested in putting in a lawn, his first gardening project, almost always wants to know how much topsoil he needs. The answer is, a minimum of 6 inches—but 8 to 10 inches is a good seed bed. To spread 1 inch of topsoil over 1000 square feet, 3.1 cubic yards are required. Perennial borders should have 2 feet of topsoil, but most gardens do well with 10 to 12 inches. Topsoil varies greatly in quality. The best is the top 3 inches of a dry and fertile meadow, and it should contain little or no stone. Because it should have been shoved into a pile at least a year before, the turf in it should be thoroughly rotted. In small quantities (10 cubic yards or less) this ideal topsoil costs about $10 to $12 per cubic yard in rural areas, more in the suburbs.

TOOLS AND MACHINERY. The enthusiastic beginner quickly becomes fascinated with garden gadgets. This is a phase probably every gardener experiences. There are, however, a few things to bear in mind while loading oneself down with garden implements. One, of course, is to stay away from sheer gadgetry; it usually is junk. It is important to buy tools that last, and to buy single-purpose tools. Who has ever seen a good golfer depending on one club with a swivel head to provide the proper angle of all the irons, including the putter? Such things are made. People buy them. Few use them.

Here is a short list of hand tools a gardener generally needs: a 2-blade knife with a pruning blade; a trowel made of stainless steel, strong but not too heavy; a weeder (the best is an asparagus knife); 3 pruning shears (a light pair for cutting flowers—but without a trick stem-holder—a heavy pair that will slice through a ½-inch branch, and a big 2-hand job for heavy work. *Wilkinson Sword*

Tools are tops in pruners. A pair of small hedge shears (Wilkinson makes 2 stainless models) about completes the list of hand tools. If you have big hedges you'll need power shears (Black & Decker make a good cordless one). Also, there's nothing that beats gasoline-powered rotary lawn-edgers.

There is, of course, the business of selecting such mundane tools as shovels, rakes, spades, and forks. Since their use in your hands is limited, you want them light. Stay away from tools with painted wooden handles, for the paint is probably put on to hide defects in the wood. Wax the handles every so often during the season and when putting them away for the winter.

Power lawnmowers are a necessity. It is difficult today to buy a mower one pushes, but they are useful to cut grass power mowers won't reach. We have strong feelings about power mowers, and can't bring ourselves to use one having a rotary-knife. They are dangerous. Toes can fall to them, and the blade can hit a pebble and turn it into a bullet. The worst part about cheap rotaries is the way they shave slightly uneven parts of the lawn. To us that's equal to losing a toe. So we stick to reel types, but we know of only one make that really lasts. It is called a *Locke.* Even the 70-inch model turns easier than a car with power steering. *Lockes* never wear out—we have a 32-incher bought in 1945. *Locke* makes all sizes. Size-for-size a *Locke* mower always costs more but it's a beautiful mechanism. It must be bought from a *Locke* dealer; discount houses do not have them. If a dealer is not close by, they are expensive to service. *Locke,* a stuffy old Connecticut company, refuses to sell parts to responsible local repairmen—only their precious, over-protected dealers can buy them or get service manuals. I don't know if this is against the law, but it's an abominable trade practice.

The major farm-tractor makers have entered the home-tractor market with machines that differ little from farm tractors, except for size. They are fast, heavy, efficient, and have many accessories, all expensive. International Harvester makes one of the best (regular gears and clutches instead of v-belts). All are luxuries, status symbols, or whatever it is that causes the American male to preen as he guides sheer power on road or lawn.

All-purpose tools do jobs better and quicker, although they cost more. *Rotovator,* an English import, is the name of a single-purpose tool, made in several sizes, which does a good job chewing up soil. There are about 3 good single-purpose snow blowers on the market. Besides keeping such tools clean and the bolts tightened, the gasoline engines on them should be sealed between seasons. To do this, remove the spark plug, squirt in a little light oil to lubricate the piston rings, put back the plug. Then tightly seal the exhaust openings with aluminum foil. Don't use polyethylene—it's porous. Dow's *Saran Wrap* is a better plastic to use for this purpose. When you are putting away hand tools for the winter, don't drench them with oil or coat them with heavy grease, for rust can appear underneath. Clean them off with soap and water, dry them, smooth down stains or rust spots with emery cloth, then give them a light coat of wax.

If you can get a can of *IT* (an abominable trade name), by all means use it instead of wax. The stuff's a silicon and repels moisture. Also, it is the best thing we know for locks and squeaking hinges, and ideal to spray on ignition systems of garden tools. Spray the ignition system of your car with it—then very wet snow or drenching rain won't stall the engine. Grand stuff, except the name (Garry Laboratories, Buffalo, N.Y., is the maker).

We have yet to see a light wood wheelbarrow beaten as a toting tool in the garden. Good ones have a fat pneumatic tire that makes pushing nearly a pleasure. Keep the tire pumped up hard, and give the wood a light coat of paint every 2 or 3 years. Don't let junior play with it, and don't let it sit out in the weather—the wood will warp even though painted.

To wrap up this discussion of tools, let's say that if one buys quality, the tools will be around a long time, particularly if a little common-sense care is added. (*See also* Hand Tools.)

TOPIARY. Topiary is the clipping of living plants into such readily recognizable forms as chairs, animals, and other shapes that the topiarist fancies. The ancient Romans were experts, and the English are not far behind—even little cottage gardens there have a few examples, and some contain nothing else. Topiary is not popular in this country. Privet, which grows fast, is easy to train; Boxwood is more beautiful but slow to shape, as are the Yews, Arbor-Vitae, and dense-growing Chamaecyparis. The beginner should be sure the plants he starts clipping are completely hardy. Topiary is called grotesque by some, and like every other form of art it can be if the practitioner has little sense of beauty. We rather like some topiary we've seen on great English and American estates. They look completely artificial, but they are saucy and amusing when used with restraint. I have worked with a few, not too successfully, but the doing is enjoyable—even to telling our friends the shape we hope to achieve, not for a moment believing or caring for all of that, that the things will come out as planned.

Tradescantia

Tradescantia

Trad-es-kan'tee-a

Spiderwort. Before the hybridizers took over *T. braeteata* and *T. viginiana,* the 2 hardy species of this native North American genus, about all one could say in their favor was that they were interesting.

Protecting Young Trees

In many suburban areas deer and rabbits menace young trees and shrubs. Hardware cloth (below) buried a few inches also repels field mice. Add another band of the cloth as the tree grows. Protection is generally required for several years

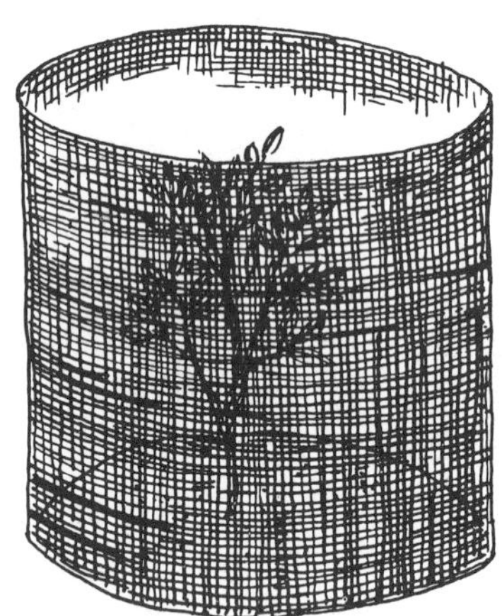

They are lovely today, but because they were namby-pandy for so long very few gardeners grow them, and fewer even recognize them now that they have been so remarkably transformed. The plants are strong, the long, narrow leaves very beautiful, the flowers most unusual in form and color. The blossoms close on a hot day by mid-afternoon, but a fresh crop opens shortly after dawn each morning. All varieties grow to about 24 inches in sun, about 30 inches in half shade. It is a perennial that deserves far more attention. Plant spring or fall.

T. Blue Stone. This European import is a lovely solid blue—the originator calls it a soft Moorish-blue, if that's any help.
T. Iris Pritchard. White flushed with blue.
T. J. C. Weguelin. Delightful pale blue flowers.
T. Pauline. Pale pink.
T. Purple Dome. Brilliant purple flowers all summer. Somewhat taller than other varieties.
T. Red Cloud. This variety is a rosy red and grows in the 15- to 18-inch range, which almost makes it a dwarf.
T. Snowcap. Blooms are large and purest white, a delightful addition to this genus.

TREES, Protecting Them. A drawing describes this technique.

triandrus (try-and'rus) having 3 stamens

tricuspidata (try-kus-pi-day'ta) narrowing to 3 sharp points

Trollius

Trol'le-us

Globeflower. A fine genus found throughout the temperate regions of the Northern Hemisphere, having beautiful, large globular or buttercup-like flowers and attractive dark green leaves. It should be used in a moist, partially shaded location. It thrives in rich soil with plenty of humus. It does well in full sun, too, but it needs moisture. Blooms keep exceptionally well in water. The various species and varieties seem to have all the best attributes one looks for in herbaceous plants. It is hard to praise them too highly. They bloom grandly in May and June, but continue to flower intermittently during the summer. Plant spring or fall.

T. Brynes' Giant. Deep, large lemon-yellow blooms on 24- to 30-inch stems.
T. Ledebouri. This variety has large, rich orange blooms and is an excellent cut flower. It is about 30 inches high.
T. Prichard's Giant. Enormous, deep golden-yellow flowers are on strong stems that grow up to 30 inches high.

TSUGA—*see* Evergreens, Dwarf Needle

tuberose (*too-bur-owe'sa*) *having tuberous roots*

Tulipa
Tew'lip-a

Tulip. Everyone knows this fine bulbous plant. Many are acquainted with the fact that the wild ones are native to the Mediterranean, and that "Tulipmania" was a spectacular speculative fever caught by Dutch burghers in the 17th century; but few realize that Tulip species are found as far east as Japan, or that *Tulipa* is the Latinized version of the Turkish word for turban, an allusion to the shape of the bloom. And not too many American gardeners are aware that in the past 35 years the hybridizers have achieved great changes in them. Blooms have become more colorful, the stems of many varieties are now as strong as sticks, and the color range is the rainbow. The newer varieties are not as well known as they should be, although they are priced in the range of the older ones. We have tried to pick the cream of these flowers by testing hundreds of varieties in the gardens; but holding down the list is difficult. If possible plant Tulips in mass by variety, or in 2 varieties whose

Trollius Brynes' Giant

colors are complementary. To mix Tulips successfully in mass, colored bulb should be surrounded with 3 or 4 of a white variety.

Culture is not difficult, but the best results always come from a deeply prepared bed, rich in humus, decidedly light or sandy in texture. A new Dutch cultural development, mentioned previously, and said by them to be the most important growing technique of the last 50 years, is the incorporation of sewage sludge in the soil at planting time. When preparing a bed for mass planting, mix in thoroughly 2 to 3 ounces of sludge per square yard with a fork. If spotting bulbs, use a teaspoon mixed into the soil at the bottom of the hole. And while you are at it, throw in a half a handful of bone-meal, too. I really don't know what bonemeal does, and authorities disagree; but it's traditional bulb food and being somewhat of a traditionalist, I'd rather have it there than not. For mass displays bulbs should be planted on 9-inch centers, all placed at exactly the same depth, which, except for the species or botanical forms, is ideally 9 inches.

Moles are grub-eaters and do not molest Tulip bulbs. It is mice running in mole tunnels that cause the damage. It is best not to plant Tulips next to stone walls or close to foundations, because mice run along the base; also, borders should be cleaned of trash, which provides ideal nesting places for mice. Evergreen boughs used to protect perennial borders do not harbor mice if placed on the border after it is completely frozen. When planting Tulips in the garden here we violate these "don'ts" by planting the bulbs 12 inches deep. Few mice dig down that far, and we have had little trouble.

We view with not a little apprehension horticultural writers who advise digging up Tulip bulbs after the tops have dried back, taking off the small bulbs, storing them in a cool airy place, and replanting them in the fall. This advice has been handed down in garden manuals for generations and we bet that the fellow who started it never did it himself—well, certainly not more than once. We gulped down this tale years ago and found it completely unrewarding. It is extremely difficult to fork a bulb out of a perennial border without disturbing valuable plants. Moreover, the bulb and bulblets are very hard to find. And the business of storing the bulbs in a "cool airy place" is beyond the facilities any home gardener can provide. Tulip bulbs of top grade are inexpensive—so why not dig up and throw out bulbs immediately after bloom, when they are easy to find, and cover the ground with annuals? All right, heel them in the cutting garden, if you must, for blooms next year. Let bulbs stay where they are in a perennial border. They will throw smaller and smaller blooms and then disappear. The point is that few gardeners live in the areas of America which have soils capable of propagating Tulips. We think the Dutch should propagate them. We chose to enjoy the small luxury of planting new bulbs annually. Plant fall only.

Botanical Tulips. Here are Tulips that are very different, and few gardeners know about their exotic forms, which range from the flamboyant to extremely delicate. Note descriptions and heights carefully. Some of these bulbs are quite small, but plant them all at least 7 inches deep. Like all Tulips they require good drainage and full sun. Botanicals (also called species) are more perennial than the conventional Cottages and Darwins. Almost all of them bloom before Daffodils.

T. Batalini Bright Gem. Cup-like blooms of soft yellow flushed with buff cinnamon. Height is 6 inches.

***T. Clusiana.** Only 8 inches high, the outer petals cherry red, the inside creamy white. A delightful flower.

T. Fairy Tale. This is a strain that produces a fine mixture of pastel flowers from apparently identical bulbs. It flowers the same time as *T. Red Emperor*, and grows about 15 to 18 inches high. This is a startlingly lovely plant. Plant in hills of 6 bulbs.

T. Fosteriana albas. Immense ivory-like flower with a yellow base on 18-inch stem. It seems to be unknown.

***T. f. Cantate.** It is vermillion red, 14 inches high, and the perkiest little fellow you will see.

ᶠ **T. f. Red Emperor.** If you don't know this variety, with its huge flaming red blossoms on 18-inch stems, you have been missing early spring everywhere Tulips grow. It's as flamboyant as a circus press agent's prose. It blooms very early.

ᶠ**T. f. Yellow Empress.** The yellow form of the foregoing variety, which blooms at the same time and at the same height. A mixed planting of this royal pair is a fine early spring sight—ring a mass of the reds with yellow or plant alternately.

T. Greigii Cape Cod. The outside is orange-red-yellow, inside bronze yellow with a black base. It sounds impossible, doesn't it? The leaves are a mottled green. It is 14 inches high.

T. g. Donna Bella. The outside of the petals is cream blazed with soft carmine; inside it is cream yellow with a prominent black base. The leaves are beautifully mottled; stems are 14 inches high.

T. g. plaisir. It is carmine red and cream outside; inside it is vermillion red touched sulphur at the edges; the base is a shiny black with yellow. Flamboyant to say the least. Height is 12 inches.

***T. g. Red Riding Hood.** This variety has vivid oriental-scarlet blooms on 6-inch stems that rise through very dark brownish-purple leaves.

T. Kaufmanniana Ancilla. The blooms of this charmer have a rose-red exterior, but the flowers, amazingly, open white and then show a distinct red ring in the center. As the bloom develops, a lovely soft pink flushes the white inside. Blossoms are large, and because they appear on stems only 4 inches long, they seem to rest directly on the foliage.

***T. k. Cesar Franck.** A bright crimson-scarlet flower edged with clear rich yellow on the outside; the interior is deep yellow. It is the earliest of all Tulips. Height is 8 inches.

***T. k. Fritz Kreisler.** This one is salmon pink, which is a very unusual color in Botanicals; large flowers are on thick 8-inch stems.

***T. k. Gaiety.** The Waterlily Tulip. The color is pure white inside, the outside is striped red. It is very dwarf—the flower practically rests on the foliage. Height is 4 inches.

*[f]**T. k. Shakespeare.** This is rosy red with a silvery shine, and no one has to believe it. It is 7 inches high.

*[f]**T. k. Stresa.** Blossoms are blood red broadly margined deep yellow; the foliage has black stripes. It blooms at 18 inches.

*[f]**T. k. Vivaldi.** Here one finds a soft yellow blossom with carmine-rose spots outside; the foliage mottled. Height is 8 inches.

***T. Kolpakowskiana.** The bloom is deepest yellow, and shaded rose on the exterior of the petals. The flower is long-lasting. It is 8 inches.

***T. linifolia.** Brilliant vermilion red, long-lasting, and a very dwarf 4 inches.

***T. Marjoletti.** Its flowers are soft primrose shaded carmine red at the base, and they appear in mid-May. Height is 14 inches.

***T. praestans Fusilier.** Fire-engine red flowers—3 to 5 of them on each stem, which is 14 inches high.

***T. turkestanica.** Each bulb produces 6 or more small, white flowers shaded yellow inside. Charming. It blooms at 8 inches.

Cottage Tulips. May-flowering. Many uses are found for this group of lovely Tulips, which everyone knows. They are excellent for the garden or for table decorations. For the most part, the flowers are oval with recurved petals. The stems are less stiff than Giant Breeder and Darwin Tulips. All are early bloomers.

T. Blushing Bride. It is creamy white with a fine, soft carmine-red band—the bride blushing, as brides still sometimes do. The large flower lasts a long time. Height is 26 inches.

T. Bond Street. Buttercup-yellow blooms flushed orange in this variety's lovely color combination. Height is 26 inches.

T. Elsie Eloff. The blossoms are soft buttercup yellow deepening in color toward the edges. Its flower is long and oval-shaped like *T. Renown*, a tulip famous for its size and exceedingly strong stem. Its height is 28 inches.

T. Gen. de la Rey. A large salmon flower shaded lilac rose and buff. It has a distinct orange center and a cream-white base. This variety has never been surpassed for its blended beauty.

T. Halcro. The large long blooms of carmine red are on exceptionally strong 26-inch stems. It lasts a long time in the garden or as a cut flower.

T. Marjorie Bowen. This is a buff and salmon beauty that won the Award of Merit at R. H. S. and Haarlem shows. It is 28 inches high.

T. Marshal Haig. Here is a glowing red flower that over the years has performed perfectly. Height is 28 inches.

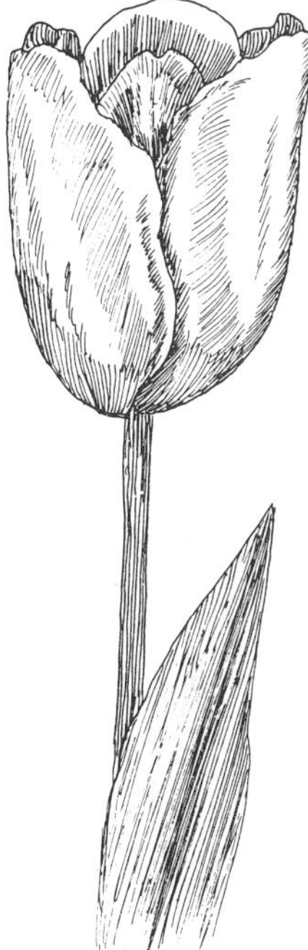

Cottage Tulip

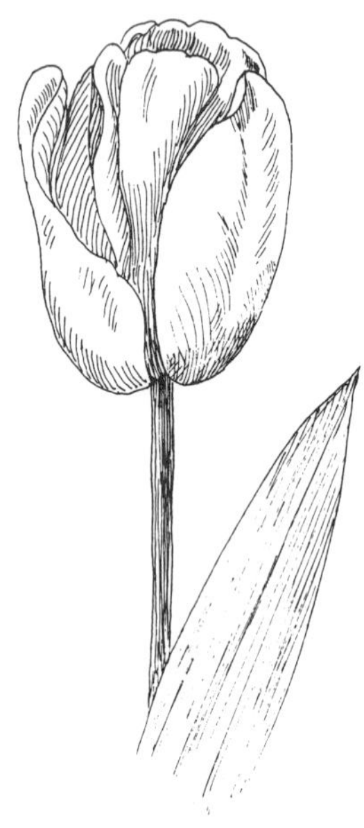

Darwin Tulip

T. Maureen. Oval-shaped, large marble-white blooms on 28-inch stems.
[f]**T. Mrs. J. T. Scheepers.** This is the best yellow Tulip that has ever been produced. It is 26 inches high.
T. Renown. Tremendous American Beauty colored blooms on 26-inch stems of such great strength that blooms stand through savage spring storms. Edges shade lighter in the same tone. It has no equal.
T. Rosy Wings. This variety is a fine delicate pink with a Forget-me-not blue base. Its long, 5-inch buds open fully in sunlight. It is earlier than most Cottage Tulips, but it lasts as long as others do. Height is 26 inches.
T. Smiling Queen. A lovely clear pink with a silvery edge and a satin sheen. It is 28 inches high.
T. White City. This pure white has been showered with awards all over the world. Height 27 inches.

Darwin Tulips. The new Darwins, first introduced in Holland in 1927, have been given many strain names by various growers, but they are all first cousins to the famous Darwins, although much improved. They have graceful form, sturdy stems, and the blooms are long-lasting. The improved types provide lovely new pastel shades not found in other Tulips. The colors are generally solid, so blending them in plantings is easy. Plants usually grow to 30 inches. They bloom after Cottage Tulips.

T. Ace of Spades. This is probably the darkest of all Tulips, for it is nearly black. The stem is exceptionally strong and 24 inches high.
T. Arlington. Blood red. A lovely solid-colored Tulip 26 inches high.
T. Balalaika. This variety has a very large Turkish-red flower with a yellow base and black stamens. Height is 27 inches.
[f]**T. Blizzard.** A remarkable white introduced about 1950. It has a huge alabaster-white blossom on the toughest of 28-inch stems. *T. Renown,* a Cottage, and this Darwin are the strongest-stemmed Tulips we have seen.
T. Blue Perfection. A clear violet blue. It is 28 inches high.
T. Cum Laude. Color is deep campanula violet. The flower is exceptionally large, the petals somewhat waved at the edges. It blooms at 28 inches.
T. Desiree. Vermilion red. Yes, a solid color 28 inches high.
T. General Eisenhower. A glorious scarlet-red tulip of remarkable size on very strong stems. When open it discloses a brilliant black-and-white bordered base. Height is 26 inches.

T. Glacier. An exceptional white that grows to 26 inches.
T. Golden Niphetos. This is the gleaming golden sport of *T. Niphetos.* The center is soft yellow. It blossoms at 28 inches.
T. Helen Madison. The bloom is rose pink outside, the inside claret with a white base. It has very strong stems 28 inches high.
T. Insurpassable. A very large flower of solid lilac, the color as delicate as can be. It is 28 inches high.
T. Jewel of Spring. The large flower is cream with slight tracings of red on edges of the petals. Height is 28 inches.
T. Lafayette. Violet purple. Height 27 inches.
T. Lefeber's Favorite. The bloom is glowing scarlet with a yellow base. It grows to 24 inches.
T. Little Queen Bess. The oval-shaped blooms of soft rose are on a white ground. Very strong 28-inch stems.
T. Margaux. A very, very, deep wine red all over. It is 28 inches high.
[f]**T. Niphetos.** Ivory yellow—a pastel-colored flower of great size that blends beautifully with Darwins of strong colors. One of the best. It grows to 28 inches.
T. President Kennedy. A deepest yellow hybrid that develops a deeper golden undertone as the flower matures. It is 26 inches high.
[f]**T. Queen of the Bartigons.** As pure a salmon pink all over as can be imagined. It is 24 inches high.
T. Snowpeak. An excellent pure white flower of great size on 27-inch stems—with white anthers, a most unusual feature.
T. Sweet Harmony. A lemon yellow with an edge that shades to white; 28 inches high.
T. The Bishop. The color is clear, deep violet with a blue base inside and a white edge that reminds one of a halo. It blooms at 28 inches.

Lily-Flowered Tulips. Graceful is the word for this class of Tulips, which has blooms that resemble Lilies. They are the result of crosses between Cottage and *Tulipa retroflexa,* and produce a sturdy flower with reflexed, pointed petals that are completely unlike any of the other Tulip forms. They are neglected by American gardeners. All of the following varieties bloom on stems in the 2-foot range.

T. Aladdin. The flower is brilliant scarlet edged with yellow.
T. Alaska. Pure yellow, very graceful, and sweet-scented, which is unusual in Tulips.

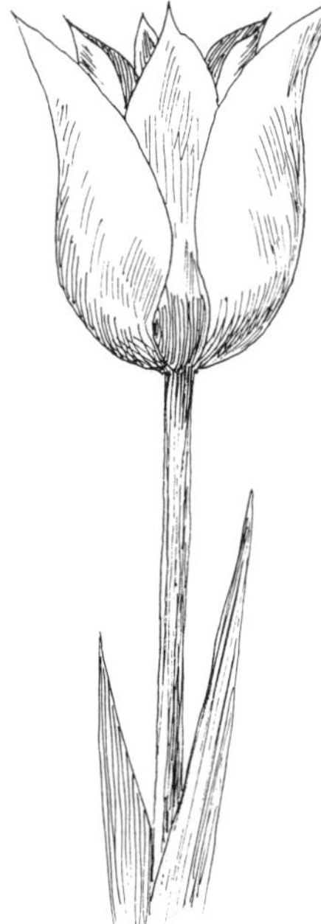

Lily-flowered Tulip

Peony-flowered Tulip

T. Mariette. A deep rose flower with a satin sheen.
T. Maytime. The blossom is purplish violet broadly edged white; the base is yellow.
T. Red Shine. It is, indeed, a shiny red, the bloom large.
T. White Triumphator. Flowers are pure white, extra large, and long lasting. Stems are strong.

Peony-Flowered Tulips. This is a race of double Tulips that look like double Peonies, hence the name. They are May-flowering and bloom on stems considerably shorter than most Cottage or Darwin Tulips. They are useful, but little used. All varieties noted are about 2 feet high.

T. Brilliant Fire. Vermilion-red flowers.
T. Clara Carder. A large rosy pink with snowy-white center.
T. Lilac Perfection. A new color in this group, a deep lilac blue.
T. Grand National. Its creamy-yellow flowers are effective.
T. Mount Tacoma. A giant white.

Parrot Tulips. These flamboyant flowers should be planted in groups by themselves for the best effect. They have an orchid-like form. The varieties below are the best of the race. They are all good cut flowers.

T. Black Parrot. A very black Parrot Tulip. If massing them, plant with *T. Texas Gold* or *T. White Parrot;* 27 inches high.
T. Blue Parrot. Bright violet over-shaded by steel blue. Strong 28-inch stem.
T. Fantasy. This is a soft rose pink; the shadings of the cup are of velvet textured rose. It is 26 inches high.
T. Firebird. This sport of Fantasy is vermilion scarlet on 26-inch stems.
T. Orange Favorite. Fragrant. A very bright orange with green markings and a yellow base. About 23 inches high.
T. Texas Flame. This gaudy thing is a bright buttercup yellow, flamed carmine red, the base green. It is a sport of Texas Gold. Blossoms show at 20 inches.
T. Texas Gold. This sensational Parrot is clear yellow. The petals are deeply lacerated and the 20-inch stem is straight and strong.
T. White Parrot. Pure white and truly lovely. About 23 inches high.

TUNIC FLOWER—*see* Tunica

*Tunica
Tew'nik-a

Tunic Flower. An Eurasian genus of some 20 species, some of them annuals, that are low-growing, tufted, and have a spreading habit of growth. Tunica is from the Latin word for tunic, and refers to the close-fitting calyx of the flowers. Plant spring only.

T. Saxifraga rosea. A neat, tufted perennial covered from July until frost with masses of dainty pink flowers very similar to those of Baby's Breath, to which the plant is closely related. Use this creeper anywhere—in the rockery, between cracks in walks or on walls, or in the front of the perennial garden.

Tunica Saxifraga rosea

turkestanica (*tur-kish-tan'i-ka*) *of Turkistan*

umbel (*um-bell*) *an inflorescence with stalked flowers arising from a single point*

UMBRELLA PINE—*see* Sciadopitys Verticillata

Valeriana
Va-leer-ee-ay'na

Valeriana. The many species of this excellent genus are literally spread all over the world, but only a few are hardy in cold northern climates. One, *V. officinalis,* is a great border plant. It is widely used in England, but not known well in the United States. Plant spring only.

V. officinalis alba. The white form of Garden Heliotrope. Flowers are set in clusters on 12- to 18-inch stems, foliage is dense and a rich green, and it blooms from June to October. It is very sweet-scented, hence its common name. It is also an excellent cut flower.
V. o. rosea. A gem in old rose. It has all of *V. o. alba's* fine qualities.

variegata (*vary-gay'ta*) *irregularly colored*

VARIETY—*see* Plant Family

vegetus (veg'i-tus) of vigorous growth

Verbascum phoeniceum

Verbascum

Ver-bass'kum

Mullein. A huge family of mostly biennial species originating in the Mediterranean; man has spread it all over the Northern Hemisphere. There are a few hardy species. English hybridists have done wonders with both biennial and perennial forms. The woolly foliage makes them interesting border plants; flowers appear on well-branched spikes. Verbascum likes well-drained soil and grows best in full sun. All the following varieties are perennial. Plant spring only.

V. Cotswold Gem. Soft amber petals with purple centers make this a striking variety. Height: 36 inches. Blooms June to September.

V. nigrum. Because this perennial reaches only 30 inches in height, it's considered a dwarf in this genus. The flowers are big for Verbascum—about ½- to ¾-inch across—and borne in clusters on strong slender stems. Put it in a hot, dry location.

V. phoeniceum. Colors are mixed—white, pink, salmon and violet. All are nice. It blooms from June to October. Height is 3 to 6 feet, depending on culture.

V. Pink Domino. Pink flowers with maroon eye. It grows to 4 feet.

verna (ver'na) of spring

Veronica

Ver-ron'i-ka

Speedwell. Another very large genus of useful plants. The shrub species, however, are all from New Zealand and are hardy only in the warmest United States climate zones. They are widely used in Southern California. The perennial species are rather broadly distributed in the North Temperate Zone. They are varied in form, and many of them are excellent garden plants. Faded flowers should be cut back to promote new bloom and growth, and once established the perennial border forms should not be moved. Plant spring or fall.

***V. alpina alba.** This species, white, of course, blooms all summer. It's only 6 inches high and excellent for the rockery or front of the border.

***V. Barcarole.** A vigorous and compact grower producing spikes of rose-pink flowers 10 inches high from June to the end of August. It is a new hybrid from England.

V. Blue Peter. A profusion of navy blue flowers on 18-inch spikes in early summer.

V. Crater Lake Blue. It has intense blue flowers and produces dozens of 18-inch spikes in early summer. Excellent cut flower.

V. Icicle. Pure white form of Blue Peter. It blooms heavily in the early fall, and is one of the longest-lasting cut flowers we have found.

V. incana. Silvery white foliage and vivid blue spikes are the mark of this species. It is about 12 inches high and blooms in July and August.

***V. rupestris Heavenly Blue.** This spreading plant forms a solid mat. It is one of the best spreaders for use between stones on walks or terraces. Sapphire-blue flowers smother the mat in May and June. Requirements are minimal—it does as well in semi-shade as full sun, and is drought-resistant. In time the thing will take over from the weeds.

verticillata (vur-tis-il-lay'ta) arranged in a whorl

Viburnum

Vie-burr'num

Viburnum. This is an important and broad genus of about 120 species, native to the North Temperate Zone, which are grown for decorative effect. A few might be classified as small trees; the majority are shrubs, some of them low-growing and quite usable in small gardens. The flowers (mostly white or changing from pink to white) of the principal ones are generally intensely scented. They show in May and June. The fruit provides color and food for birds;

Veronica Blue Peter

the leaves of many turn to various degrees of russet in the fall. The following varieties are hardy in zone 4. Lovely *V. tomentosum Mariesii* grows to 9 feet, and its horizontal branches carry its lacey flowers and red berries like Dogwood. *V. Carlesii* rarely grows to more than 6 feet, and it is covered with clusters of pinkish or white flowers so fragrant that on a still night the fragrance carries 50 to 60 feet; its fruit is black and ripens before fall. *V. Burkwoodii,* originated in England in the 1920's, is similar to *Carlesii.* Some authorities think it is an improvement. If it has proved out in your climate, use it, but it is a touch less hardy than *Carlesii. V. Carlcephalum,* patented, has been heavily promoted here, and, if you like big snowballs more than the dainty clusters of, say, *Carlesii,* it's your dish; it's not mine. *V. Opulus compacta* is floriferous, its red berries effective, and the fall color of the leaves is a good, clear red. It stops growing at about 5 feet. *V. Opulus nanum,* a 2- to 3-foot dwarf, is a good rock garden or hedging plant. There are many others. *V. Tinus,* hardy in zones 7 and 8, is a variety few southern gardeners would be without. The better nurseries usually have a wide selection; mail order houses also offer some.

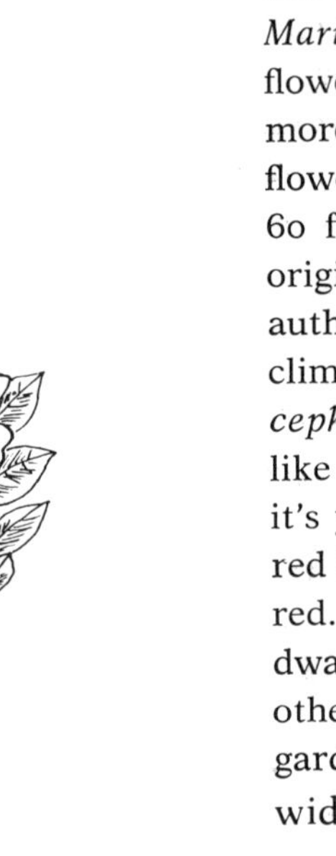

Vinca

Vinca

Vin'ka

Periwinkle. Only 2 of the many species of this genus are commonly cultivated in the North, one of them by florists. It is hardy and an excellent ground cover for shady banks and under trees. Propagate by division in the spring. Plant spring or fall.

***V. minor* Bowles' Variety.** Foliage is broad, strong, and glossy evergreen; flowers are a rich blue; bloom is profuse. The white form, *V. minor alba,* is a very satisfactory plant, but hard to find.

Viola

Vie-owe'la

Violet. An extremely valuable group of perennials widely distributed in the world's temperate regions. The species listed below, *Viola odorata,* the Sweet Violet, is a lovely plant for any garden. They like well-rotted stable manure, leaf mold, or a mixture of 2 parts peat and 1 part dried cow manure dug deeply into the soil. They do best with a reasonable amount of moisture in semi-shade. Bloom comes in early spring and again in the fall; they spread quickly in locations they like. Plant spring or fall.

*V. **odorata Rosina.** The rosy-pink form of the sweet-scented Russian violet.
***V. o. Royal Robe.** Deep violet-blue blooms produced on strong 6-inch stems are delightfully fragrant. This variety grows equally well in full sun or partial shade. Use it in the rockery, for edging, or for ground cover. Plant on 1-foot centers.
***V. o. White Czar.** A beautiful, large, white, sweet-scented violet carried on strong 4- to 6-inch stems.

violetta (vie-owe-let'ta) violet

virens (vie'renz) green

virginale (vur-gin-ay'lee) white

VIRGINIA BLUEBELL—*see* Mertensia

VIRGINIA CREEPER—*see* Parthenocissus

virginianum (ver-gin-ee-ay'num) of Virginia

VIRGIN'S BOWER—*see* Clematis paniculata

viscaria (vis-kay'ree-a) with sticky stems; similar to the genus Viscaria

VOLUNTEER. In horticulture a "volunteer" is always a seedling that has appeared without being planted. It can be a tree, a perennial, or an annual. Actually, some of the best varieties in horticulture have been volunteers, natural hybrids, in other words, which have suddenly popped up and have been recognized as unusual by gardeners or nurserymen.

vulgaris (*vul-gare'is*) *common*

WEED KILLERS—*see* Herbicides

WEEDING AND MULCHING. Weeding is an onerous chore in gardening only when it is put off. Then weeds must be pulled by hand, which is tedious work. Actually, regular cultivation every 10 days is not tiresome. Merely scuffle the surface. One shouldn't cultivate deeply around plants, for this destroys the fine feeder roots which lie close to the surface. Cultivating lightly also provides a light earth mulch, and kills germinating weed seeds before they can be seen. If one cultivates before a hard rain, the ground may have to be cultivated again, for such a rain will reset weed seedlings, which will start growing again. But only a few of them, so don't put off weeding because rain is predicted. The best way to hold down weeds is by planting a perennial garden thickly—then the spreading branches and leaves of the perennials will shade the ground so heavily that few weed seedlings grow, and those that do, starved of light, will be spindly and weak.

The best stand-up weeding tool we know about is made of stainless steel and called a *Swoe;* one pushes it. It is never necessary, as it is with a hoe, to step on the ground just cultivated—tramp on cultivated ground and weed seeds will grow quickly in the foot marks. To work the *Swoe,* step back—away from the ground being cultivated. It is made by the Wilkinson Sword Company. A *Swoe* is probably as expensive as a sword—and it lasts as long.

Mulching is generally recognized as the business of putting enough organic material on the surface of a planting to make weeding unnecessary and to hold a steady soil moisture content. Because of the skyrocketing cost of boy-weeders, who generally hate to weed and are both slow and don't know weeds anyway, there is a large demand for mulches which is being met by various industries with surplus products unusuable otherwise. We have tried several kinds and have had no success in mulching herbaceous perennials to control weeds either in the gardens or the nursery blocks. The following remarks are addressed to weed and moisture control in shrubs, evergreens, and Rose borders.

Buckwheat hulls. These are very expensive and hard to obtain. They do, however, inhibit weeds—until a strong wind blows them away or a summer downpour floats them out on top of an astonished lawn. Many gardeners we know have tried them, once.

Grass clippings. An excellent mulch if applied thick enough—2 inches or more. But clippings shouldn't be used on Azaleas or Rhododendrum, because when fresh they generate considerable heat, which is not good for the shallow-feeding roots of those plants. While rotting they form a thick crust which holds together even though it floats during a heavy rain. When fresh and green clippings are pretty, but they soon turn a rather unpleasant brown. However, grass clippings are an immediately available material and gardeners who don't chose to follow regular weeding schedules should use them.

Evergreen bark. More and more the cedar, pine, and redwood bark mulches are coming to market. If put on at twice the thickness recommended by their makers, they make a handsome and efficient

Narcissus

summer and winter mulch. The principal negative is expensive. Weeds, of course, still appear, but they are few and easily removed.

Peat Moss. This is used a lot but it shouldn't be. It soon forms dry crust that sheds rain water like a duck. It is also the most expensive of all mulches.

Wood Chips. Usually available from local tree men. Chips should, however, be a year old because they heat when fresh. They were put on 3 large borders here and were successful—air gets to the surface of the soil, water enters easily, and the few weeds are quickly removed. They are not cheap. Unfortunately, a wood chip mulch is unsightly.

Cocoa and tobacco stems. Efficient and costly. But the constant smell of chocolate or tobacco indicates that such materials have no place in a garden.

Weigela

Wy-gee'la

Weigela. This genus of 10 species is Asiatic in origin. It also has far too many named varieties, which, it is argued, are improvements, but they generally do not perform as well as some of the species in cold climates. About all they have to recommend them is color not found in the species. *W. Bristol Ruby,* an improvement of *Old Eva Rathke* (it's a true red) is said to be hardy in zone 4. However, there are years when bloom does not appear above the snowline, and its branches, like those of all Weigela, including the species, get clipped by the cold, which makes rather extensive pruning necessary. When in flower, these shrubs' clusters of funnel-shaped flowers are effective, but none set berries and only a very few have leaves that distinguish them. It probably doesn't make sense to grow any of them north of zone 5. The only reason we have any success with them is because they are planted in protected locations. One of the 2 species that are outstanding, but not readily available in commerce, is *W. florida variegata.* Its leaves are edged yellow and the flowers are white to dark pink at random in the clusters. It is hard to think of a more outstanding variegated shrub. The other is *W. florida foliis purpuriis.* It rarely grows over 4 feet and is very dense. It is covered with bloom in early June, but the color of the blossoms, except for light shadings, is so close to the almost purple leaves that they don't show well. One plant in a windswept spot has had practically no branch damage, but blooms sometimes appear only on wood below the snowline. *W. Middendorfiana,* which we imported from Europe 16 years ago, is intensely yellow with just a suggestion of red dust on the lower lip of its trumpet-like flower. It is very floriferous. It burst into heavy bloom for the first time in the spring of 1970. The plant itself is a runt hardly 30 inches high, the result, obviously, of its fight with the 15 cold winters it never expected to experience. Extremely deep snow which stayed until late spring undoubtedly protected its flower buds in 1970. It is probably a zone 6 variety.

WILD GINGER—*see* Asarum

WINDFLOWER—*see* Anemone

WINTER ACONITE—*see* Eranthis

WINTER PROTECTION. Perennials, most of which are shallow-rooted, should be covered in winter. They are covered, not to keep them warm, but to keep them frozen in the ground. The reason—winter thaws are inevitably followed by freezing weather, and if plants freeze and then thaw, roots are broken off from the crowns by the heaving action. Evergreen boughs, which provide shade and trap snow, keep the ground frozen. Also, evergreens do not mat on the crowns of the plants, which can kill them. That's why leaves should always be raked up before winter; otherwise they mat and suffocate plants under them. If evergreen boughs are hard to find (unsold Christmas trees are free), use salt hay or oat straw (no weed seeds), but be sure these materials are tucked *around* the crowns, *never* on them, and hold them in place against wind drift with branches. Snow fence put over plantings, but held off the ground on blocks, is a good cover that provides the necessary shade and also traps snow. Protecting Hybrid Tea or Floribunda Roses requires the mounding of soil over the crown. The top of the soil pyramid should be about 12 inches high. Protection should not be provided until winter has really come; the work is done in the gardens here immediately after Christmas.

WINTER SAVORY—*see* Herbs

Wisteria arborea

Wisteria Arborea

Wis-tair'ee-a Are-bore-e-uh

Tree Wisteria. Zone 4, southward. This is the hard-to-find tree form of Wisteria, one of the most beautiful of all shrubs. It grows as wide as it is tall, which is rarely over 6 to 8 feet, and when established makes a breath-taking spring display. Gardeners fail with tree Wisteria, as well as with newly planted vine varieties, because they don't pamper them during the only critical period—its first few months. Pampering means keeping the plant damp when first planted—hose the top every day and keep the roots wet until growth starts. When the plant gets 2 to 3 years old, prop the branches during winter to keep them from being broken by ice or snow.

This is necessary because the wood is brittle and tends to split under weight. Tree and vine Wisteria come in white, pink, or lavender varieties. The tree forms are somewhat expensive to buy; the vines are not. If either form fails to bloom after a decent period, root-prune them; cold can kill the flower buds, but if protected from wind Wisteria can stand temperature down to –20° F. Plant spring only.

WOOD HYACINTH—*see Scilla hispanica*

WOUNDWART—*see* Stachys

YARROW—*see* Achillea

yunnanensis (*yun-nan-en'sis*) *of Yunnan, west China*

Wisteria arborea

Zantedeschia

Zan-tea-desh'-ee-uh

Cally Lily. This genus of about 6 tropical non-hardy species is widely used by florists and is commonly grown outdoors in climates free of frost. Our species, *Z. pentlandii,* is extremely rare. Plant spring only.

Z. pentlandii. The bloom of this golden-yellow Calla is the same size as the common yellow Calla and even more beautifully shaped. It is one of the longest-lasting cut flowers—2 to 4 weeks, depending on room temperature, is not uncommon.

Mass Plantings Are Effective And Increasingly Popular With Gardeners

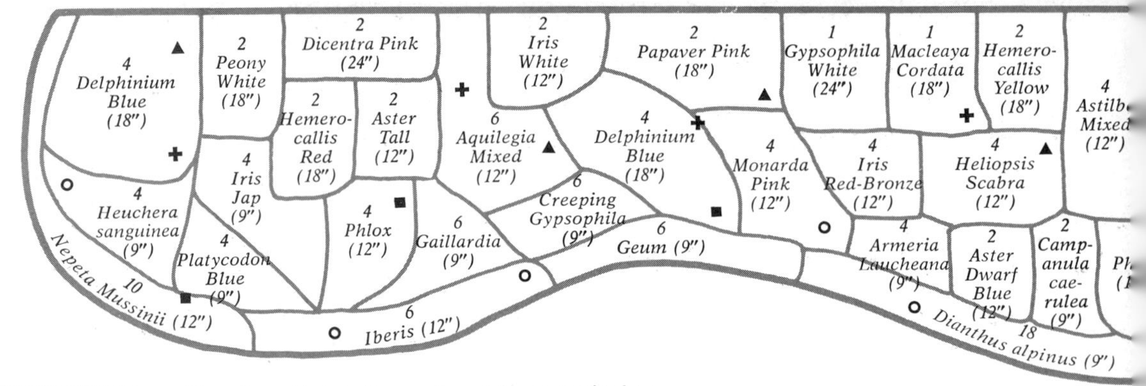

Perennial Garden Without a Background

Cost of plants: about $250

Size: 14-foot square

Top row: 3 Artemisia Silver Mound | 6 Fraises des Bois | 3 Gypsophilia repens | 3 Artemisia Silver Mound

- 6 Fraises des Bois; 6 Dianthus alpinus
- 3 Armeria; 3 Veronica; 3 Oenothera; 3 Lavender
- 3 Platycodon Blue; 3 Pole-monium; 3 Lysimachia; 3 Campanula Tall; 3 Anthemis
- 3 Gaillardia; 3 Phlox Red; 3 Iris Kaempferi Blue; 3 Hemero-callis Red; 3 Del-phinium Blue; 3 Heuchera
- 3 Asters Dwarf; 3 Aquilegia Mixed; 3 Iris Blue; 1 Macleaya Cordata; 3 Iris White; 3 Astilbe Mixed; 3 Asters Dwarf
- 3 Achillea Pale Yellow; 3 Del-phinium White; 3 Hemero-callis Yellow; 3 Rudbeckia Gold Drop; 3 Phlox Pink; 3 Anchusa Myosotidi-flora
- 3 Physostegia; 3 Campanula Tall; 3 Liatris Cobalt; 3 Lythrum Dwarf; 3 Platycodon White
- 3 Catananche; 3 Iberis; 3 Linum; 3 Alyssum
- 6 Dianthus alpinus; 6 Fraises des Bois

Bottom row: 3 Artemisia Silver Mound | 3 Gypsophilia repens | 6 Fraises des Bois | 3 Artemisia Silver Mound

There is no limit to the number of forms a mixed perennial garden can take, nor a limit to the arrangement of the plants in them. Basically, one seeks the longest possible period of bloom, from earliest spring to Chrysanthemums in the late fall. This leads to the immediate question: Why are no Mums shown here? Because Chrysanthemums are more easily grown in the cutting garden and moved into bare locations when they bloom. Also, as the perennials recede it is good practice to fill in with annuals, which will bloom vigorously until cut down by frost. The English border (above) requires a staunch green background, a hedge or a wall, about 8 feet high. Shelter from prevailing winds is vital, for without it blooming plants blow down and winter losses mount. Be sure to leave a small path between the background and the border so plants in back can be worked easily.

"Sensational" is the only word that describes a planting containing only Lilies. The bulbs like a solid planting of low-growing white annuals over them—it keeps them cool.

—Nineteen Great Varieties of Lilium, Mid-Centuries and Trumpets, in a Triangle

Cost of plants: about $110

Size: Bottom and right side: 8 feet

						3 Enchantment
					3 Prosperity	3 Destiny
				1 Imperial Silver	3 Fireflame	1 Sentinal
			3 Paprika	1 Auratum Platyphyllum	3 Harmony	3 Golden Chalice
		3 Harlequin	3 Golden Chalice	3 Fireflame	3 Joan Evans	1 Moonlight Strain
	3 Croesus	3 Harmony	3 Cinnabar	3 Valencia	1 Olympic Hybrids	3 Cinnabar
3 Enchantment	3 Joan Evans	1 Black Dragon	3 Destiny	1 Golden Splendor	3 Destiny	3 Enchantment

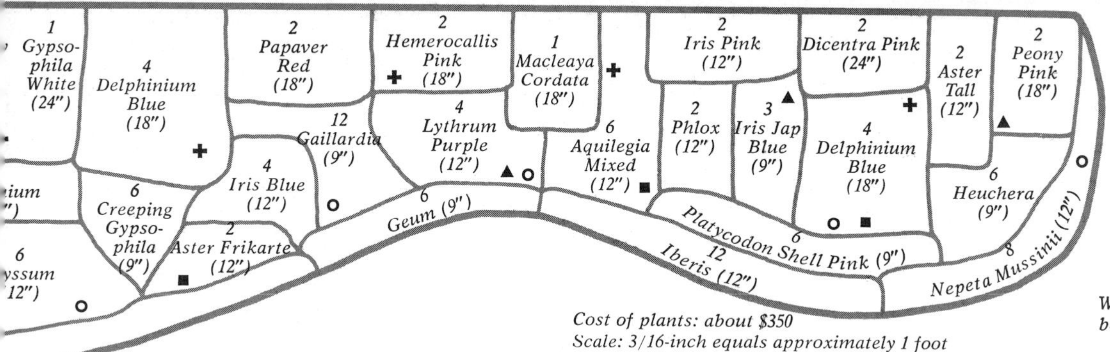

Symbols For Under-planting

▲ *Trumpet Lilies*

■ *Mid-Centuries Lilies*

○ *Narcissi*

✚ *Tulips*

Wherever these symbols appear, 1 Trumpet Lily should be planted, 3 Mid-Centuries, 3 Narcissi, 6 to 12 Tulips.

Sweeping Classical English Perennial Border

Note: Number before plant name (above) equals quantity of variety required; numeral in parenthesis indicates planting distance.

Mass planting of varieties from a single genus are more popular than ever, for they are easily cared for and when in bloom are spectacular. They are also relatively inexpensive, and many bloom for years before needing thinning. Iris in mass (below) put on a good show the year after they are planted, then they bloom magnificently for 4 to 5 years, when it is best to dig and separate them. Phlox lend themselves particularly well to this kind of growing, for varieties can be chosen that extend the blooming period amazingly. Peonies, which have an extremely long life (we have seen plantings 100 years old; some here have been in place for 30 years) are great in specialized mass plantings—as hedges bordering a sunny path, for example, where they stand strongly as greenery after the gorgeous blossoms fall, and then disappear neatly when cut back before winter.

Day Lilies In Mass

Cost of plants: about $80

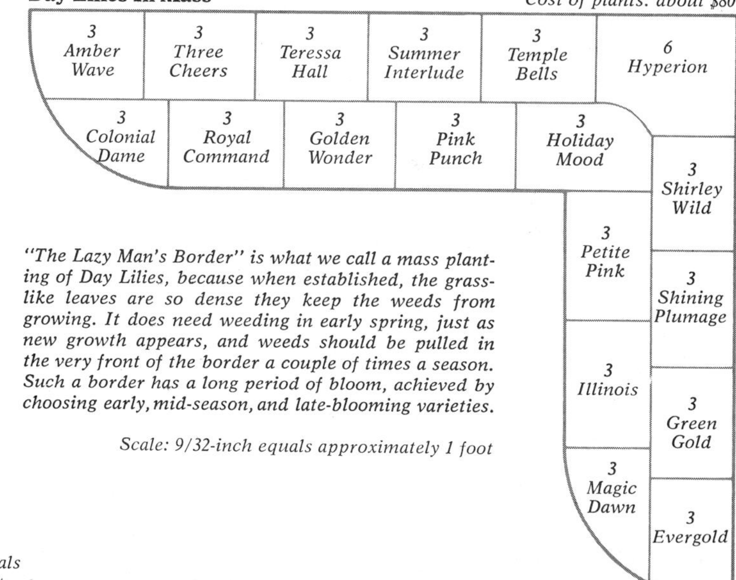

"The Lazy Man's Border" is what we call a mass planting of Day Lilies, because when established, the grass-like leaves are so dense they keep the weeds from growing. It does need weeding in early spring, just as new growth appears, and weeds should be pulled in the very front of the border a couple of times a season. Such a border has a long period of bloom, achieved by choosing early, mid-season, and late-blooming varieties.

Scale: 9/32-inch equals approximately 1 foot

Bearded Iris In Mass

Cost of plants: about $75

3 Rococo	3 Happy Birthday	3 Brasilia	3 Trophy	3 South Pacific	3 Bronze Bell	3 Lynn Hall	3 Amethyst Flame
3 Accent	3 High Above	3 Green Quest	3 Solid Gold	3 Whole Cloth	3 Top Flight	3 Crinkled Ivory	

Scale: 9/32-inch equals approximately 1 foot

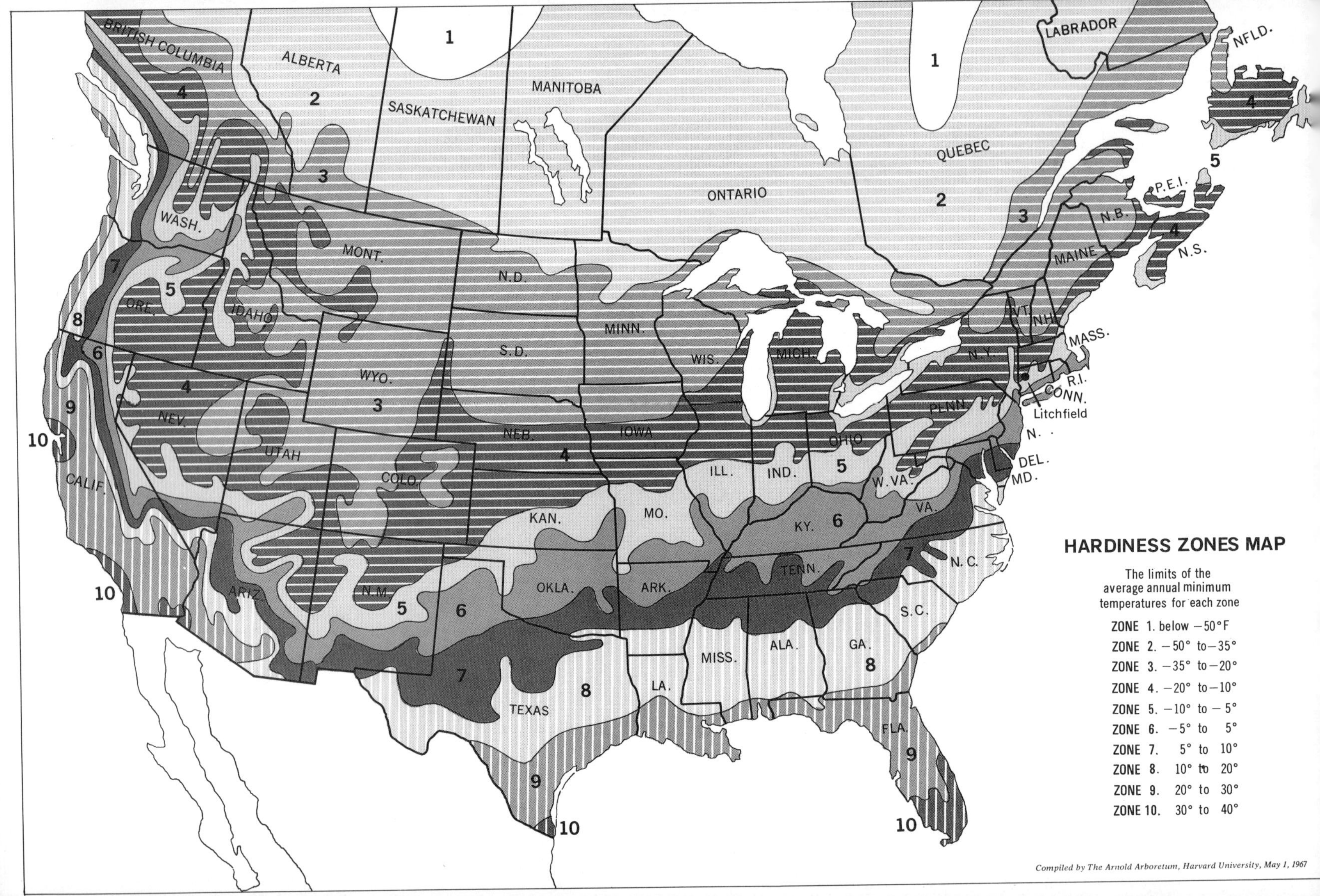
HARDINESS ZONES MAP
The limits of the average annual minimum temperatures for each zone
ZONE 1. below −50°F
ZONE 2. −50° to −35°
ZONE 3. −35° to −20°
ZONE 4. −20° to −10°
ZONE 5. −10° to − 5°
ZONE 6. −5° to 5°
ZONE 7. 5° to 10°
ZONE 8. 10° to 20°
ZONE 9. 20° to 30°
ZONE 10. 30° to 40°
BRITISH COLUMBIA
ALBERTA
SASKATCHEWAN
MANITOBA
ONTARIO
QUEBEC
LABRADOR
NFLD.
P.E.I.
N.B.
N.S.
WASH.
ORE.
CALIF.
NEV.
IDAHO
MONT.
WYO.
UTAH
ARIZ.
COLO.
N.M.
N.D.
S.D.
NEB.
KAN.
OKLA.
TEXAS
MINN.
IOWA
MO.
ARK.
LA.
WIS.
ILL.
MICH.
IND.
OHIO
KY.
TENN.
MISS.
ALA.
GA.
FLA.
S.C.
N.C.
VA.
W.VA.
PENN.
N.Y.
VT.
N.H.
MAINE
MASS.
R.I.
CONN.
Litchfield
N.
DEL.
MD.
Compiled by The Arnold Arboretum, Harvard University, May 1, 1967

Supplementary Index

A Note About the Author

Amos Pettingill is William B. Harris, who with his wife, Jane Grant, has gardened since the late 1930's in Litchfield, Connecticut, where they founded a unique nursery, White Flower Farm, in 1940. But gardening has not always been Harris's principal occupation.

His college education ended abruptly after two years at the University of Colorado—"I was thrown out by the Student Council, because the student paper, of which I was an editor, decided to rate professors... that was 1921." A stint as a reporter for the Denver Post *followed a year or so of farming near Boulder, and in 1924 Harris became merchandising and power sales manager for various operating properties of National Power and Light Company, where he recalls "winning a $2500 first prize for selling an unreasonable number of G.E. lamp bulbs." In 1928 he came to New York to work for highly successful Wall Streeters. He joined the staff of* Fortune *in 1937, "became a writer (of sorts)," and "discovered the electronics industry" for the magazine. The purchase of a country house brought on the inevitable involvement with lawns and gardens and led eventually to the purchase of additional acreage and greenhouses and the development of White Flower Farm. Harris continued, however, to keep one foot firmly in New York (in 1960 he left* Fortune *to return to Wall Street as a general partner in an old-line house, Laidlaw & Co.) until in 1968 White Flower Farm preempted his total energies. Except for hunting around for growth stocks like IBM or Xerox, both of which he missed, he is now "actively retired" to the world of gardening.*

A Note on the Type

The text of this book was set on the Linotype in Aster, a typeface designed by Francesco Simoncini (born 1912 in Bologna, Italy) for Ludwig and Mayer, the German type foundry. Starting out with the basic old-face letterforms that can be traced back to Francesco Griffo in 1495, Simoncini emphasized the diagonal stress by the simple device of extending diagonals to the full height of the letterforms and squaring off. By modifying the weights of the individual letters to combat this stress, he has produced a type of rare balance and vigor. Introduced in 1958, Aster has steadily grown in popularity wherever type is used.